Clouds above the Hill

Clouds above the Hill, a longtime best-selling novel in Japan, is now translated into English for the first time. An epic portrait of Japan in crisis, it combines graphic military history and highly readable fiction to depict an aspiring nation modernizing at breakneck speed. Acclaimed author Shiba Ryōtarō devoted an entire decade of his life to this extraordinary blockbuster, which features Japan's emergence onto the world stage by the early years of the twentieth century.

Volume III finds Admiral Tōgō continuing his blockade of Port Arthur. Meanwhile, a Japanese land offensive gains control of the high ground overlooking the bay as the Russians at last call for a ceasefire. However, on the banks of the Shaho River, the Japanese lines are stretched, but the Russian General Kuropatkin makes a decision to flank the troops to the left and in doing so encounters Akiyama Yoshifuru's cavalry.

Anyone curious as to how the "tiny, rising nation of Japan" was able to fight so fiercely for its survival should look no further. *Clouds above the Hill* is an exciting, human portrait of a modernizing nation that goes to war and thereby stakes its very existence on a desperate bid for glory in East Asia.

Shiba Ryōtarō (1923–1996) is one of Japan's best-known writers, acclaimed for his direct tone and insightful portrayals of historic personalities and events. He was drafted into the Japanese Army, served in the Second World War, and subsequently worked for the newspaper *Sankei Shimbun*. He is most famous for his numerous works of historical fiction.

Translated by Juliet Winters Carpenter, Andrew Cobbing, and Paul McCarthy
Edited by Phyllis Birnbaum

Shiba Ryōtarō is Japan's best-loved author, and *Clouds above the Hill* is his most popular and influential work. In it he celebrates the transformative spirit of Meiji Japan and examines Japan's unexpected victory in the Russo-Japanese War, providing a thoughtful and thought-provoking perspective on those dramatic times and the people at their center. This distinguished translation of a modern classic is a landmark event.

Donald Keene, University Professor Emeritus,
Columbia University, USA

Shiba Ryōtarō wrote that from the Meiji Restoration of 1868 through the Russo-Japanese War of 1904–1905, Japan transformed its premodern "brown sugar" society into a modern "white sugar" one, eagerly scooping up crystals of the new substance in the drive to create society anew. During the Pacific War, by contrast, the nation's leaders merely went through empty motions, and Japan collapsed. This book looks back on that earlier era through the lens of the later tragedy, depicting the struggles and growth to maturity of Japan's young men.

Tanaka Naoki, President of the Center for International
Public Policy Studies, Japan

When the siege of Port Arthur was over and Japan had won, the commanding generals from both sides came together face to face at Shuishiying. They paid honor to each other's bravery and expressed mutual condolences, and before parting they shook hands. I have visited that very place, which seems to me less the site of a Japanese victory than a monument to the souls of fallen soldiers on both sides. I have no doubt that *Clouds above the Hill* was also written to honor those souls.

Anno Mitsumasa, author and illustrator of
children's books in Japan

Clouds above the Hill

A historical novel of the Russo-Japanese War,
Volume III

Shiba Ryōtarō

Translated by Juliet Winters Carpenter

Edited by Phyllis Birnbaum

Routledge
Taylor & Francis Group
LONDON AND NEW YORK

THE JAPAN DOCUMENTS
381 KAMIYAKIRI MATSUDO CHIBA-KEN JAPAN 271-0094
TEL: +81-(0)47-312-2201 FAX:+81-(0)47-312-2202

First published in hardback 2014
First published in paperback 2015
by Routledge
2 Park Square, Milton Park, Abingdon, Oxon OX14 4RN

and by Routledge
711 Third Avenue, New York, NY 10017

Routledge is an imprint of the Taylor & Francis Group, an informa business

British Library Cataloguing in Publication Data
A catalogue record for this book is available from the British Library

Library of Congress Cataloging in Publication Data
Shiba, Ryōtarō, 1923–1996.
    [*Saka no ue no kumo*. English]
    Clouds above the hill: a historical novel of the Russo-Japanese War/
    Shiba Ryōtarō; translated by Juliet Winters Carpenter, Andrew Cobbing and
    Paul McCarthy; edited by Phyllis Birnbaum.
    p. cm.
    Saka no ue no kumo, Shiba Ryōtarō." 1. Shiba, Ryōtarō, 1923–1996.—Translations into
English. 2. Japan—Politics and government—1868–1912. I. Carpenter, Juliet Winters
II. Cobbing, Andrew. III. McCarthy, Paul. IV. Birnbaum, Phyllis. V. Title.
    PL861.H68S2513 2012
    895.6'35—dc23
    2012033404

ISBN: 978-0-415-50887-2 (hbk)
ISBN: 978-1-138-85892-3 (pbk)
ISBN: 978-1-315-88350-2 (ebk)

Typeset in Scala Sans and Times New Roman
by Florence Production Ltd, Stoodleigh, Devon

Cover image: Kobayashi Kiyochika, Japanese, 1847–1915
Great Battle for the Occupation of 203-Meter Hill (Dai gekisen Nihyakusan Kōchi senryō)
Japanese, Meiji era, 1905 (Meiji 38)
Woodblock print (*nishiki-e*); ink and color on paper
Vertical ōban triptych; 35.4 x 71 cm (13 15/16 x 27 15/16 in.)
Museum of Fine Arts, Boston
Jean S. and Frederic A. Sharf Collection
2000.77a-c

CONTENTS

PRINCIPAL CHARACTERS—VOLUMES III AND IV

Abo Kiyokazu (1870–1948): lieutenant commander, chief of artillery for the entire Japanese fleet.

Akashi Motojirō (1864–1919): colonel and agent provocateur who helped foment revolution in Russia.

Akiyama Saneyuki (1868–1918): Yoshifuru's younger brother; staff officer of Japan's Combined Fleet at the time of the Russo-Japanese War.

Akiyama Yoshifuru (1859–1930): Saneyuki's older brother; father of the modern Japanese cavalry; defeated Russian Cossacks in the Russo-Japanese War.

Alexeyev, Yevgeny Ivanovich (1843–1918): Russian tsar's viceroy in the Far East.

Clapier de Colongue, Konstantin Konstantinovich (1859–1944): chief of staff to Rozhestvensky in the Russian fleet.

Felkerzam, Dmitri Gustavovich von (1846–1905): commander of the Russian fleet's Second Division; died from illness just before the battle of Tsushima.

Fok, Aleksandr Viktorovich (1843–1926): the highest-ranking officer in Russia's Port Arthur army after Stoessel.

Fujii Shigeta (1858–1945): chief of staff of General Kuroki's First Army.

Gapon, Georgi Appollonovich (1870–1906): Russian Orthodox priest who organized the march that led to "Bloody Sunday" in St. Petersburg on January 22, 1905.

Grippenberg, Oskar-Ferdinand Kazimirovich (1838–1916): commander of the Russian Second Army in Manchuria; very critical of Kuropatkin's tactics of drawing the Japanese Army deep into Manchuria.

Hayashi Tadasu (1850–1912): Japan's ambassador to Britain at the time of the Russo-Japanese War.

Iguchi Shōgo (1855–1925): staff officer of Japan's Manchurian Army during the Russo-Japanese War.

Ijichi Kōsuke (1854–1917): chief of staff of General Nogi's Third Army.

Itō Hirobumi (1841–1909): head of the Privy Council; prime minister at the time of the First Sino-Japanese War.

Itō Sukeyuki (1843–1914): fleet commander during the First Sino-Japanese War; chief of the Navy General Staff during the Russo-Japanese War.

Kamimura Hikonojō (1849–1916): commander in chief of the Second Squadron of the Japanese Combined Fleet during the Russo-Japanese War.

Kataoka Shichirō (1854–1920): commander of the Third Squadron of the Japanese fleet.

Katō Tomosaburō (1861–1923): chief of staff of Admiral Kamimura's Second Squadron.

Katsura Tarō (1847–1913): prime minister at the time of the Russo-Japanese War.

Kaulbars, Aleksandr Vasilyevich (1844–1925): commander of Russia's Second Manchurian Army, the main force behind the Russian offensive in the battle of Mukden.

Kodama Gentarō (1852–1906): chief of staff at General Headquarters of Japan's Manchurian Army during the Russo-Japanese War.

Komura Jutarō (1855–1911): foreign minister at the time of the Russo-Japanese War.

Kondratenko, Roman Isidorovich (1857–1904): Russian general revered by officers and men at Port Arthur; known for his strong defense of the port.

Kuroki Tamemoto (1844–1923): commander of the Japanese First Army in the Russo-Japanese War.

Kuropatkin, Alexei Nikolayevich (1848–1925): Russian war minister and the commander in chief of the Russian Manchurian Army during the Russo-Japanese War.

Linevich, Nikolai Petrovich (1838–1908): commander in chief of the Russian Manchurian Army; after the battle of Mukden, succeeded Kuropatkin as commander in chief of the Russian armies in the Far East.

Makarov, Stepan Osipovich (1848–1904): commander in chief of the Russian fleet at Port Arthur and author.

Matsukawa Toshitane (1860–1928): staff officer of Japan's Manchurian Army noted for his abilities in offensive strategies.

Meckel, Klemens Wilhelm Jacob (1842–1906): German military officer and advisor to the Japanese Army.

Mishchenko, Pavel Ivanovich (1853–1918): commander of the Cossack cavalry brigade involved in many battles of the Russo-Japanese War.

Nagaoka Gaishi (1858–1933): vice chief of the Army General Staff during the Russo-Japanese War; proud of his mustache, which was said to be the world's second longest.

Nebogatov, Nikolai Ivanovich (1849–1922): commander of the Russian fleet's Third Division during the battle of Tsushima.

Nicholas II (1868–1918): Russian tsar at the time of the Russo-Japanese War.

Nogi Maresuke (1849–1912): commander of the Japanese Third Army during the Russo-Japanese War.

Novikov-Priboy, Alexei Silich (1877–1944): writer on board the battleship *Oryol* who participated in the battle of Tsushima.

Nozu Michitsura (1841–1908): commander of the Japanese Fourth Army during the Russo-Japanese War.

Ochiai Toyosaburō (1861–1934): chief of staff of General Nozu's Fourth Army.

Oku Yasukata (1846–1930): commander of the Japanese Second Army during the Russo-Japanese War.

Ōyama Iwao (1842–1916): army minister at the time of the Russo-Japanese War.

Politovsky, Evgeny Sigismondovich (1874–1905): chief engineer of the Russian fleet who was killed during the battle of Tsushima; his letters to his wife were published as a book.

Rennenkampf, Pavel Karlovich (1854–1918): commander of the Russian left flank during the battle of Mukden.

Rozhestvensky, Zinovy Petrovich (1848–1909): favorite of Tsar Nicholas II and commander of the Russian Baltic Fleet, which traveled via the Cape of Good Hope all the way to the Sea of Japan.

Sakharov, Vladimir Viktorovich (1853–1920): chief of staff to Kuropatkin in the Russian Manchurian Army.

Saneyuki (see Akiyama Saneyuki).

Semenov, Vladimir Ivanovich (1867–1910): staff officer of the Russian fleet and author.

Shimamura Hayao (1858–1923): chief of staff of the Japanese Combined Fleet at the time of the Russo-Japanese War.

Smirnov, Konstantin Nikolayevich (1854–1919): commander of the Port Arthur fortress.

Stakelberg, Georgi Karlovich (1851–1913): commander of the First Siberian Army Corps.

Stoessel, Anatoly Mikhailovich (1848–1915): commander of the Russian forces at Port Arthur.

Tatsumi Naobumi (1845–1907): a seasoned veteran who assisted Akiyama Yoshifuru's cavalry detachment at Heigoutai; commander of "Tatsumi's provisional army."

Terauchi Masatake (1852–1919): army minister at the time of the Russo-Japanese War.

Tōgō Heihachirō (1847–1934): commander in chief of the Japanese Combined Fleet in the Russo-Japanese War.

Tsunoda Koreshige (1873–1930): Nogi's staff officer who later, at Nogi's suggestion, campaigned to have Stoessel's life spared.

Uehara Yūsaku (1856–1933): chief of staff of General Nozu's Fourth Army.

Uesugi Kenshin (1530–1578) A prominent sixteenth-century daimyo known for a series of battles with his rival diamyo Takeda Shingen at Kawanakajima.

Uryū Sotokichi (1857–1937): commander of the Fourth Division of the Japanese Combined Fleet in the Russo-Japanese War.

Utsunomiya Tarō (1861–1922): Japanese military attaché in London.

Vitgeft, Vilgelm Karlovich (1847–1904): acted as commander in chief of the Russian fleet at Port Arthur after Makarov's death.

Wilhelm II (1859–1941): German kaiser.

Witte, Sergei Yulyevich (1849–1915): Russian finance minister 1892–1903; strong opponent of the Russo-Japanese War.

Yamagata Aritomo (1838–1922): architect of the modern Japanese Army and chief of the Army General Staff during the Russo-Japanese War.

Yamamoto Gombei (1852–1933): Satsuma-born officer responsible for modernization of the Japanese Navy; navy minister at the time of the Russo-Japanese War.

Yoshida Shōin (1830–1859) A scholar and ideologue; he educated young samurai who would later become leaders of the Meiji government. He was executed by the shogunate.

Yoshifuru (see Akiyama Yoshifuru).

Yuan Shikai (1859–1916): Chinese army leader; first president of the Republic of China.

CHRONOLOGY OF MAJOR EVENTS

1603	Establishment of the Tokugawa shogunate
1825	Shogunate issues order to repel foreign ships
1853	U.S. Commodore Perry's warships appear in Edo Bay (now Tokyo Bay)
1854	Perry reopens Japan to the Western world, ending the period of national seclusion that began in 1639 and lasted more than two hundred years
1868	Collapse of the Tokugawa shogunate Meiji Restoration
1868–1869	Boshin War
1877	Satsuma Rebellion
1889	Promulgation of the Meiji Constitution
1894	Outbreak of the First Sino-Japanese War (August) Yalu River naval battle (September)
1895	Destruction of the Chinese fleet at Weihaiwei (February) Peace treaty signed at Shimonoseki (April) Triple Intervention (April–May)—Japan forced by Russia, France, and Germany to relinquish the Liaodong Peninsula
1898	Spanish–American War
1900	Boxer Rebellion in China
1902	Anglo-Japanese Alliance signed in London (January)
1904	Outbreak of the Russo-Japanese War (February) Battle over the crossing of the Yalu (April) Siege of Port Arthur (August–January 1905) Battle of the Yellow Sea (August) Battle of Ulsan (August)

Battle of Liaoyang (August–September)
Battle of Shaho (October)
Russian Baltic Fleet departs the Baltic Sea (October)
1905   Battle of Heigoutai (January)
Battle of Mukden (March)
Tōgō's Combined Fleet defeats the Baltic Fleet at Tsushima off the coast of Kyushu (May)
Peace treaty signed in Portsmouth (September)

A NOTE FROM THE EDITOR

This translation project has benefited from the expertise and assistance of a number of people, most importantly, Takechi Manabu, of the Center for Intercultural Communication, who has checked the translations, researched background information, and created most of the introductory materials. He is a devoted fan of *Clouds above the Hill*; Shiba Ryōtarō and our project are fortunate indeed to have his invaluable help. Noda Makito checked the translations in Volume IV.

Lynne Riggs, also of the Center for Intercultural Communication, has been our indefatigable behind-the-scenes advisor and liaison with various business concerns. Assisted by Imoto Chikako, she obtained appropriate images for the covers and the required permissions. Anne Bergasse and Kiwaki Tetsuji of Abinitio Design are the cover designers.

We are grateful for the cooperation of the Shiba Ryōtarō Memorial Foundation, with special thanks to Uemura Motoko, who helped answer our various questions.

Tamara Agvanian has toiled as our official Russian expert, going to great lengths to track down the English equivalents for the Russian names and terms in our text; Miguel Romá joined the search for other non-Japanese names. Komiyama Emiko of Komiyama Printing Company created the map graphics. HyunSook Yun was a great help with Korean names and terms. Bruce Carpenter looked up Chinese sources, interpreted Chinese poems, and provided vital advice.

Robert Patrick Largess was our military consultant, finding the appropriate English for the many guns, ships, and other military terms in the text; he compiled our explanatory "Japanese and Russian fleets in 1904" and "Japanese and Russian fleets at Tsushima." In addition, his vast knowledge in other fields has served to improve these translations in many ways.

My personal thanks to Teruko Craig and Stuart Kiang for their helpful, speedy advice.

Above all, everyone who has contributed to this translation of *Clouds above the Hill* thanks Saitō Sumio of Japan Documents, whose enthusiasm and determination have brought this project to fruition. He did not only decide to have this immense novel translated and succeed in organizing a translation team, but he has also been a tremendously loyal supporter of our efforts. His patience, generosity, and, most importantly, his calm in the face of assorted difficulties have made this work a great pleasure for all.

*   *   *

Clouds above the Hill was originally published as a serial in the newspaper *Sankei Shimbun* from April 22, 1968 to August 4, 1972. Traces of the serialization remained when the entire novel was published in book form; those traces can be seen in this translation as well. The section breaks are often indications of the end of a day's installment, although there are times when we've merged sections or moved the breaks around. At the start of a new section, Shiba frequently summarized what had gone on just before to help readers who had missed the previous installment. We've tried to eliminate some of these repetitions, but they are too numerous to eliminate entirely.

In the main, we have used pinyin to transcribe Chinese place and personal names; exceptions are well-known places and names like Port Arthur, Mukden, and Genghis Khan. Some of the famous sites around Port Arthur are in English.

Shiba alternates between the metric and imperial systems in his measurements, but we've made certain measures consistent: we've used the imperial system for naval guns; metric for land guns.

Japanese names are in Japanese order, the family name followed by the given name. Ages are cited in the traditional Japanese method of calculating ages—a child is one on the date of birth and two the following New Year's Day.

We have not corrected any errors Shiba may have made regarding historical fact or translations from other languages. "General Staff" refers to the Army General Staff unless otherwise noted.

Phyllis Birnbaum

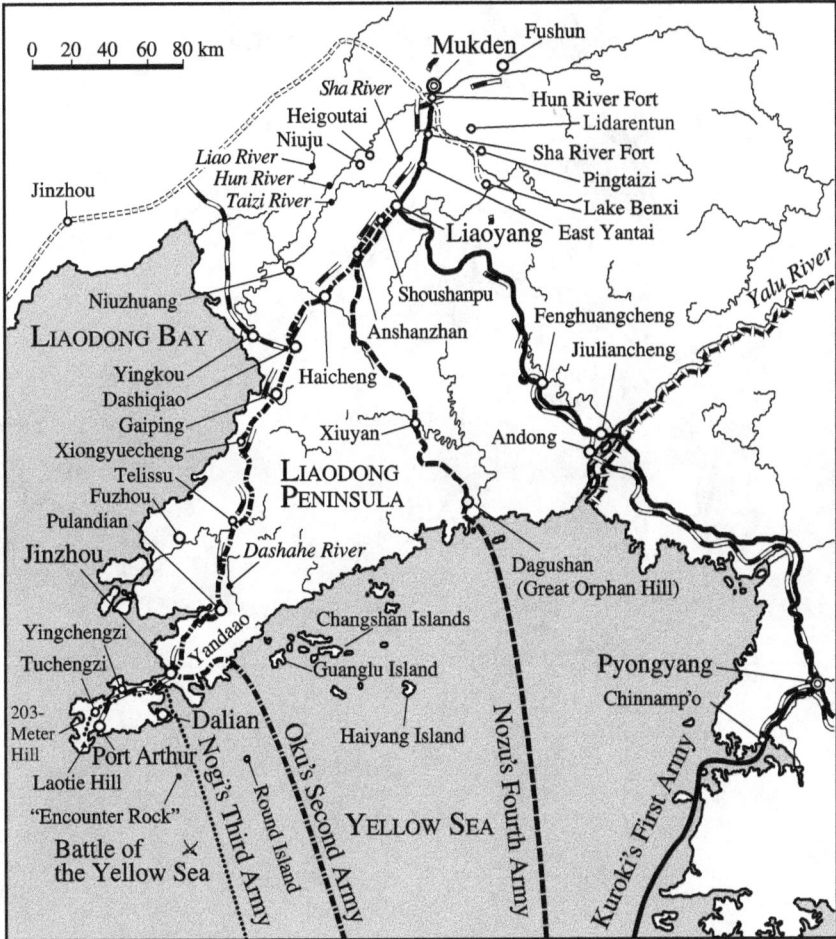

Russo-Japanese War

Map labels:

0 20 40 60 80 km

Mukden · Fushun
Sha River · Hun River Fort · Lidarentun
Heigoutai · Sha River Fort
Niuju · Pingtaizi
Liao River · Lake Benxi
Hun River · East Yantai
Taizi River · Liaoyang
Jinzhou

Niuzhuang · Shoushanpu · Fenghuangcheng
LIAODONG BAY · Anshanzhan · Jiuliancheng
Yingkou · Haicheng
Dashiqiao
Gaiping · Xiuyan · Andong
Xiongyuecheng
Telissu · **LIAODONG**
Fuzhou · **PENINSULA**
Pulandian

Jinzhou · *Dashahe River* · Dagushan
(Great Orphan Hill)

Yingchengzi
Tuchengzi · Yandaao · Changshan Islands · **Pyongyang**
203- · Guanglu Island · Chinnamp'o
Meter
Hill · Dalian
"Encounter Rock" · Port Arthur · Haiyang Island
Laotie Hill

Battle of · **YELLOW SEA**
the Yellow Sea

Yalu River

Nogi's Third Army · Oku's Second Army · Round Island · Nozu's Fourth Army · Kuroki's First Army

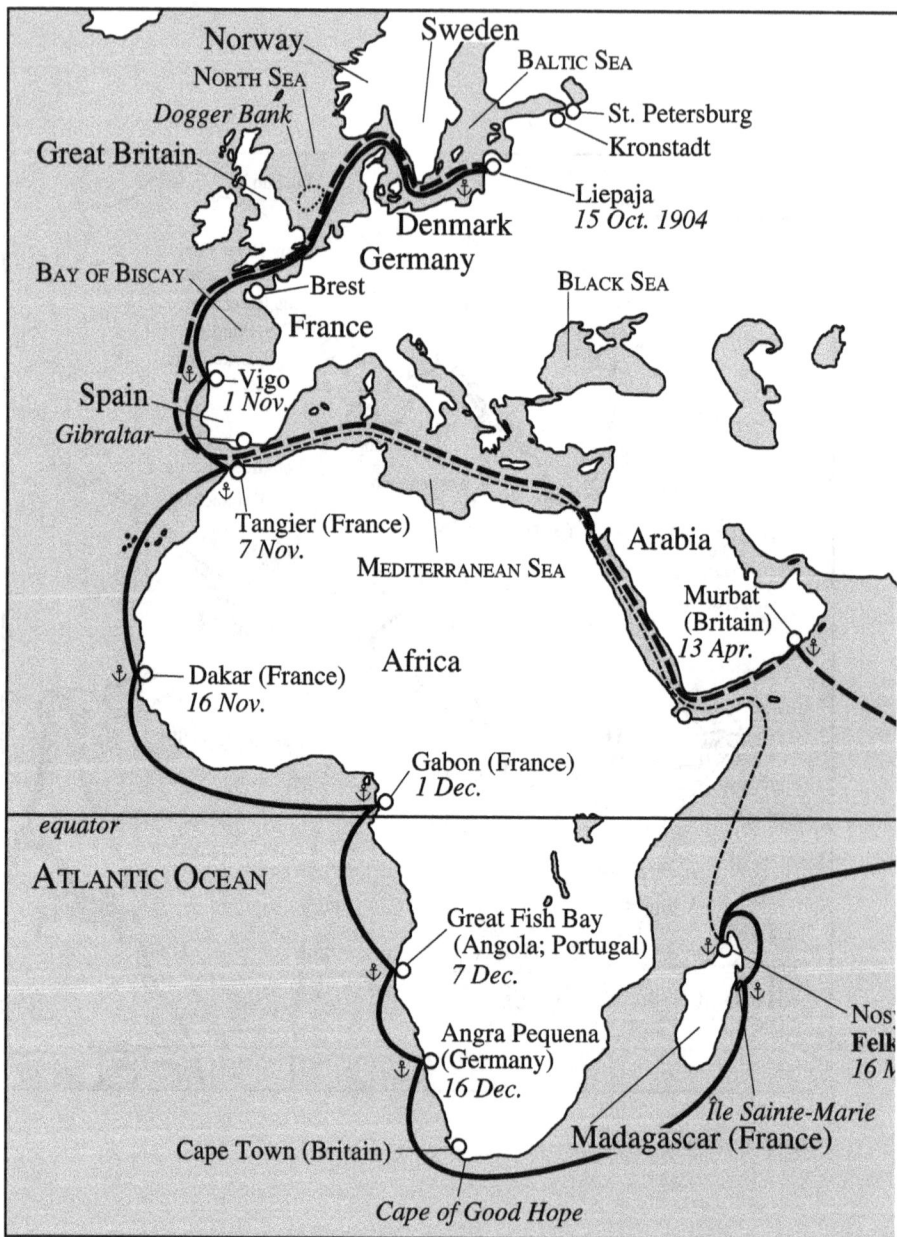

Route of the Baltic Fleet from European Russia to the Sea of Japan

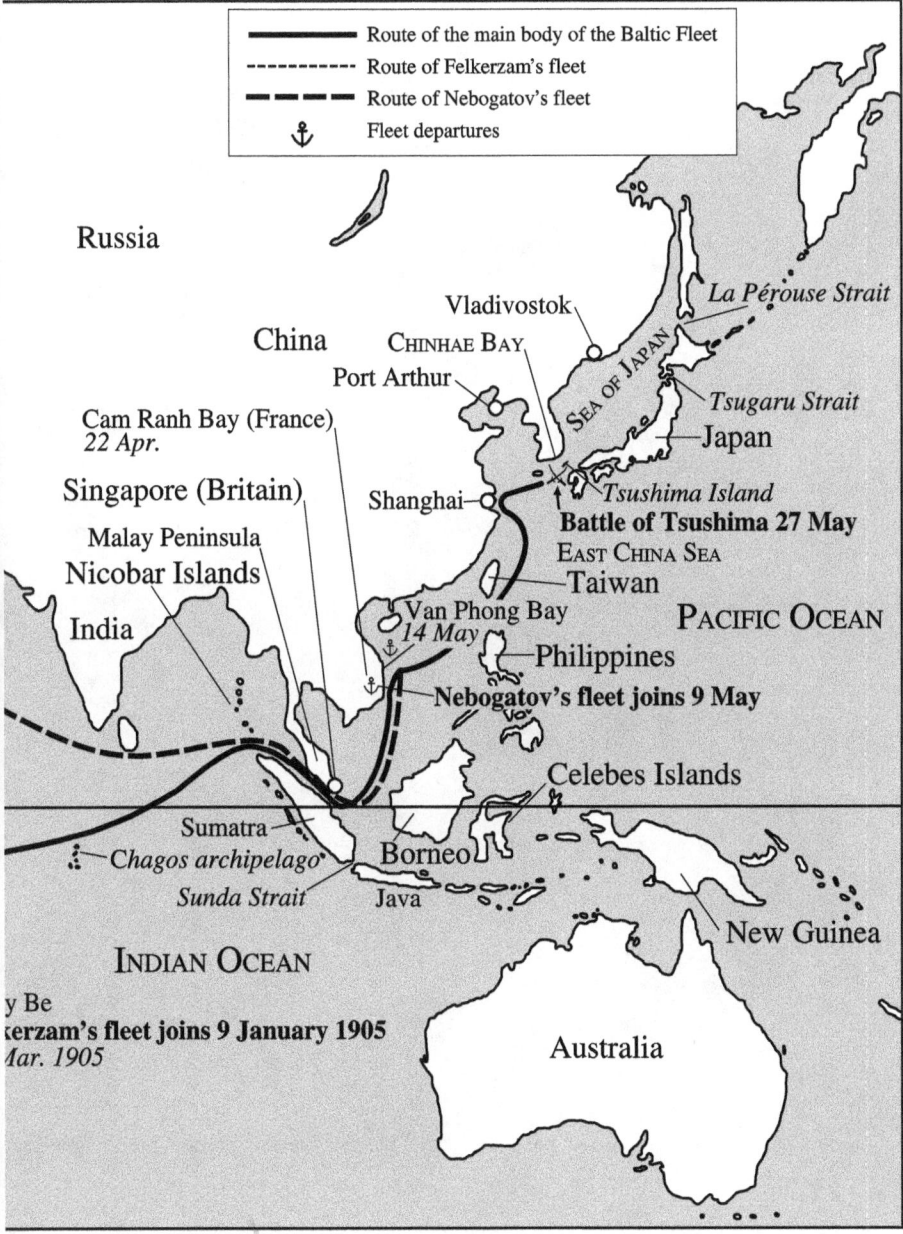

Russia

China

Vladivostok

CHINHAE BAY

Port Arthur

Cam Ranh Bay (France)
22 Apr.

Singapore (Britain)

Shanghai

Malay Peninsula

Nicobar Islands

India

Van Phong Bay
14 May

Philippines

Nebogatov's fleet joins 9 May

Celebes Islands

Sumatra

Chagos archipelago

Sunda Strait Java

Borneo

New Guinea

INDIAN OCEAN

y Be

kerzam's fleet joins 9 January 1905

Mar. 1905

Australia

La Pérouse Strait

SEA OF JAPAN

Tsugaru Strait

Japan

Tsushima Island

Battle of Tsushima 27 May

EAST CHINA SEA

Taiwan

PACIFIC OCEAN

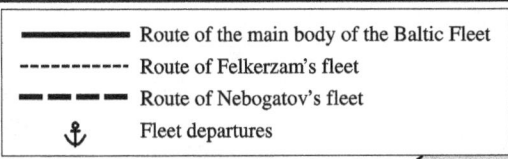

——————— Route of the main body of the Baltic Fleet

- - - - - - - - Route of Felkerzam's fleet

━ ━ ━ ━ ━ Route of Nebogatov's fleet

⚓ Fleet departures

Part 5

Translated by Juliet Winters Carpenter

1

203-METER HILL

Yet prospects were dim.

The reports that Kodama received from Nogi's headquarters at Port Arthur invariably brought news of defeat. Of course, Nogi never wrote, "We lost." Instead, his writing was bureaucratic and embellished, along these lines: "Despite a vigorous assault, the enemy proved stubborn. Our army's morale is soaring." Nogi was a first-rate poet, and his prose style wasn't bad either, but his reports lack the grim reality of battle accounts. Embellishment is unnecessary in reports of fighting and can lead to errors of judgment by the superior command.

After the Russo-Japanese War, the habit of embellishing reports became entrenched in the Japanese Army, although whether that was Nogi's influence is debatable. Battle reports, like descriptions of ongoing science experiments, require absolute objectivity, but in the wake of this war Japanese military leaders took to sprinkling their reports with the kind of effusive adjectives usually used by poets. Granted, most reports filed by the various army headquarters during the Russo-Japanese War were not on a par with Nogi's. Kodama scolded Nogi for sending in reports that made objective appraisal of battle conditions difficult.

The absence of phrases like "We captured Fort Such-and-such" gave away that the Third Army was being pummeled by the Russians. Reading between the lines, Kodama's staff had no trouble deducing that Nogi was losing. Judging by the extent of the damage, moreover, this was no mere setback, but a disastrous drubbing that could lead to the collapse of the entire Japanese Army. The initial assault alone took so many lives that a follow-up assault was difficult, great numbers of men perishing in what Nagaoka Gaishi called "useless slaughter."

Kodama suddenly stood up. An aide asked in surprise where he was going. "I'm going to take a piss."

Kodama set off wearing his cap, but he didn't go toward the latrine. He went outside—not for any particular reason, but just because on his way he got turned around and ended up out of doors. His behavior was decidedly strange.

The outdoor world was already frozen. Scarcely aware of what he was doing, Kodama unbuttoned his fly and began to relieve himself. The harshest period of winter hadn't yet set in, so the stream did not immediately freeze. Still, the cold was of a dimension far beyond traditional seasonal sensibilities of the Japanese people.

Far in the distance, several soldiers who had just come off guard duty saw Kodama and gave him an "eyes-left" salute, maintaining their grip on their weapons. He was urinating straight in their direction—an unthinkable breach of military etiquette under any circumstances, and certainly an action ill befitting an army general. The soldiers at General Headquarters in Manchuria, however, were well aware of Kodama's lack of concern for such matters. "There he goes again," they probably thought. Yet as he relieved himself, his face streamed with tears. The real reason he went outside was undoubtedly his deep, unconscious desire to weep. What drove him from the room was his profound anguish over the soldiers being uselessly slaughtered at Port Arthur.

*　*　*

Back inside, instead of returning to the conference room, Kodama went to his own room and issued the order: "Send for Matsukawa." Soon Colonel Matsukawa Toshitane hauled his skinny frame into the room and stood before Kodama's desk.

"I have two Manjusri on my team." Privately Kodama often praised Matsukawa and Major General Iguchi Shōgo by likening them to the bodhisattva of transcendent wisdom. Though both staff members were indeed outstanding strategists, their approaches differed. Iguchi was cautious and rather inclined to wait things out, Matsukawa active and eager to take the offensive. Kodama relied on these two models, but the two officers found him rather frustrating. Though they presented their views, many times Kodama followed his own line of thinking in the end. Gifted as Iguchi and Matsukawa were, Kodama had a touch of genius and may at times have leaped beyond their plane of thought onto a higher one.

At other times, perhaps because Kodama's thinking was conversely on a lower plane or because he tacked on various conditions, he reshaped their proposals into a different form. Perhaps "low" is the wrong word, but

Kodama blithely ignored the principle that political strategy has no place in military strategy. Military strategy and tactics should be worked out purely for their own sake, the commander's attention zeroing in on the task at hand. That wasn't Kodama's style.

Let me expand a bit. At the time, revolution was in the air inside Russia. Japan's General Staff Office gave a million yen to Colonel Akashi Motojirō, then in Europe, to fan the flames of revolution. That is an example of political strategy. If a field commander banking on political strategy fails to make strategic decisions or attack when he should, his strategic thinking has become adulterated.

For example, at this point, Matsukawa Toshitane made a forceful argument to Kodama about the need for a second field operation. "Sir, there is no point in sitting around doing nothing like this. Now is the time to renew the attack."

Kodama refused to take the bait. "I'll think about it" was as far as he would go. The battle of Shaho was over, but the enemy's main force in front of them was strong as ever. Matsukawa could not fathom what the general was thinking.

Kodama, meanwhile, knew from a secret wire sent by Yamagata Aritomo that peace talks were in the air (although this was actually Yamagata's wishful thinking), but he never let on about it to Matsukawa. Kodama wanted to enter on peace talks with the Japanese Army intact, and, if peace talks, the ultimate aim of the war, were on the horizon, then he didn't want to carry out a needless campaign that would only cost lives.

Kodama could not be purely a military strategist as he was burdened with political concerns of a different dimension, that is, the fate of the nation. He was burdened with Japan itself, a country so small and poor that one individual had no choice but to take on more than one role.

* * *

"Matsukawa, you're not going to like this." Kodama's expression was completely lacking its usual cheery vigor. He rubbed the tip of his nose with the back of his hand, rubbing so hard that it turned red. This was the gesture of a boy planning mischief.

"Like what, sir?" Matsukawa spoke cautiously.

Kodama became irritated. "You know exactly what! I'm leaving soon for Port Arthur. Things there are in such a sorry state, the whole Manchurian Army could collapse at any time."

Everybody knows that—Matsukawa did not go so far as to say this, but his expression gave him away as he nodded. He was opposed to Kodama's proposed visit. The last time Kodama had left the front to visit Port Arthur as an observer was just before the battle of Shaho. Initial strategy in that battle did not get communicated smoothly, precisely because Kodama, just back from Port Arthur, was distracted. Matsukawa had pointed this out to Kodama directly at the time. For the chief of staff to vacate headquarters was risky, whatever the reason. Then, too, Kuropatkin's vast army was poised in front of them. For Kodama to turn his back on the northern front and go to the southern front in Port Arthur to observe the assault there was an unpardonable breach of fundamental principles of military command. That's what Matsukawa thought, and that's what he said. Where strategy was concerned, he didn't have the slightest regard for the sensibilities of his superiors.

"Do you intend to repeat the same mistake you made before?"

"What?" Kodama growled.

"If you intend going off as an observer the way you did before," an undaunted Matsukawa went on, "it's utterly pointless. If you have a bone to pick with Nogi's headquarters, why not just issue a summons to his vice chief of staff, Ōba Jirō?"

"There's no time to waste. If things go on this way, all the troops Nogi holds in his hands will die."

"That's still no reason for you to leave your post."

"The time before, I went as an observer. This time will be different."

"How so?"

"I'm going there to take command of the Third Army in Nogi's place."

Matsukawa was briefly stunned by the momentousness of this revelation. If Kodama meant it, his action would sabotage the chain of command that was the lifeblood of the army.

*   *   *

In any case, Matsukawa Toshitane didn't want to see Kodama leave. He argued against his going, on the principle of upholding military discipline.

"Matsukawa, you're wrong!" Kodama yelled, cutting him short. "I don't need you to lecture me on the importance of maintaining the chain of command. But would you have me protect military discipline at the cost of letting our country collapse? The way Nogi is going"—he broke off in mid-sentence—"he will destroy Japan!" Kodama wanted to yell the words, but friendship with Nogi made him desist. That Nogi's fecklessness would be his country's undoing was Kodama's greatest fear.

Matsukawa made a good point. Although Kodama held the rank of general and was chief of staff of the Manchurian Army, he was merely a member of Commander in Chief Ōyama Iwao's staff. Nogi Maresuke, on the other hand, had been granted command of the Third Army by the emperor, the ultimate and supreme authority. What if Kodama were to cancel or limit Nogi's authority and then do with the Third Army as he pleased? Military order would collapse. It would be as if Nagaoka Gaishi from Imperial Headquarters in Tokyo came along and told Ōyama, "Move over, I'm taking charge." Yet out of his near-certain conviction that allowing Nogi to carry on in Port Arthur would spell Japan's defeat, Kodama took the position that this extreme measure was unavoidable.

It was a difficult situation. Subverting the chain of command is in a sense the greatest offense possible in the military. Kodama was prepared to face the consequences, including a court-martial if need be. Let them do their worst. Matsukawa suggested sending someone else, but Kodama was adamant. He and only he could go.

Political considerations were involved. If Kodama had been from Satsuma, or anywhere else but Chōshū, the plan would have been impracticable. Nogi would not have cooperated, and Kodama's aggressiveness would have had grave repercussions on the two men's relationship. But Nogi and he were members of the same powerful Chōshū clique. They had maintained close ties ever since the Restoration and knew one another inside and out. Nogi would not be devastated if replaced by Kodama, of that much Kodama was certain.

"No, there's no one but me who can go. If you went, Matsukawa, he'd rip you to pieces."

"Very well, sir." Matsukawa spoke earnestly. "But as long as you do go, I recommend you take along a handwritten letter from the commander in chief." That way, Kodama's action would be within the boundaries of the law—barely.

* * *

Kodama decided to call at Ōyama's quarters.

When discussions were underway to choose a commander in chief before the troops left for Manchuria, Kodama had argued strongly for Ōyama: "Toad is someone I can work under." The nickname "Toad" was presumably based on Ōyama's appearance.

At the time, Yamagata Aritomo had wanted the job of commander in chief. However, as we have seen, even though Kodama was on familiar terms with Yamagata, the head of the Chōshū clique (they called each other "old man Yamagata" and "old man Kodama"), he had rejected his candidacy, declaring Yamagata impossibly hard to work under. In the end, Kodama's plan won out. He came to Manchuria with Ōyama Iwao of Satsuma as commander in chief.

From the late years of the Tokugawa period through the first decade of Meiji, Ōyama was regarded as a fount of wisdom, but as he took charge of others he gradually acquired the habits of self-effacement and thoroughgoing detachment. Admiral Tōgō Heihachirō also shared these traits, which suggests that men of Satsuma shared a traditional view of the proper way for a supreme commander to conduct himself.

Just recently at the battle of Shaho, when there had been one bout after another of fierce fighting with no prospect of victory and the headquarters staff was in a state of bedlam, Ōyama woke up after an afternoon nap, poked his head into the room, and addressed Kodama. "More fighting going on somewhere today?" Those present were dumbstruck. This brief query had an immediate calming effect, raising spirits and quieting hysteria.

I would like to touch further on this aspect of Ōyama's personality. Back when he was still army minister, serving under him were Kodama Gentarō, Kawakami Sōroku, and Katsura Tarō. Each of them loved to argue, and meetings would be filled with long altercations that had no hope of resolution. Ōyama would sit calmly observing, saying nothing, until eventually he seized his chance. Leaning forward, he would without further ado pass judgment on the spot. "You do this. You do that," he would order, looking at each person and giving appropriate instructions. His pronouncements were so on the mark that those who would happily have gone on arguing all day, given half a chance, were silenced.

Just a few months earlier, after the battle of Liaoyang, the Qing general Yuan Shikai had sent his subordinate Duan Zhigui to General Headquarters of the Japanese Manchurian Army with items like blankets, milk, and champagne. Ōyama invited Duan—who was at the time something like Yuan's executive secretary—to lunch.

"You know, Duan, it's best when people know nothing at all." As Ōyama suddenly made this remark over lunch, Duan shot him a suspicious look, but Ōyama was perfectly serious. "Take me. I'm a complete ignoramus. It's exactly because I don't know anything about anything that I got to be chief of the General Staff, and army minister, and superintendent of police, and, even more shamelessly, minister of education. Not knowing anything makes me equally suited for all posts. I am truly a valuable sort of man."

For the rest of his life, Duan Zhigui ardently admired Ōyama Iwao.

* * *

Kodama was on his way to Ōyama's quarters. This was at the juncture of the war known in military histories as "the standoff on the Shaho." While there were no major infantry skirmishes, every day gunners on both sides were kept busy, and the sound of gunfire rang out from dawn till dusk. During this time, Duan Zhigui paid another courtesy call on Ōyama. "How do you spend your days?" he inquired.

Ōyama replied with his usual polite bow. "A commander in chief has relatively little to do, so I go for walks in the countryside." By "countryside," he probably meant the outskirts of the town. It was true, he did roam frequently. What did he do when bullets came whizzing by? Duan wondered. Ōyama went on nonchalantly.

"Mostly I'm making a study of Chinese cabbage. That's a fine vegetable you have there, lots of nutrition and lots of ways to prepare it. Makes particularly fine pickles, but the technique is hard to master. . . ."

He was always like that. Whether the topic was the dire situation at Port Arthur or the need for vigilance against Kuropatkin's troops, he spoke smilingly with an expression of airy unconcern.

"I wonder if Toad is in?" Kodama thought as he walked across the dirt floor to the office of the commander in chief. Despite the affectionate nickname, he held Ōyama in the highest regard. His absolute respect for him as commander in chief was also beyond question.

He knocked on the door and found Ōyama in. Though Kodama himself was a high-ranking general, and though after serving under Ōyama for years he had grown closer to him than a brother, when he entered the commander in chief's quarters, he straightened up like a young, fresh-faced officer and gave a snappy salute.

"Ah, Kodama. Is Kurobato on the move?" Ōyama used his usual nickname for Kuropatkin, Kurobato, meaning "black dove," motioning his guest to a chair as he spoke. At the suggestion, Kodama smiled wryly. If the Russian general were on the move, then, instead of departing for Port Arthur, he, Kodama, would have to stay and lead another fierce and bloody battle.

"No, sir, I think for the next ten days or so we're in the clear."

"And so you're leaving for Port Arthur?"

The question took Kodama by surprise. With keen intuition, the brilliant commander in chief had guessed his plan. Ordinarily, Ōyama would never have preempted his visitor and spoken in a know-it-all manner. The difference today showed what a serious view he, too, took of Nogi and his Third Army.

"Yes, sir. I am going to Port Arthur. I leave things here in your hands."

*　*　*

What if Nogi turned him away? Apprehension filled Kodama. After all, by requesting temporary command over the Third Army, he would be committing an affront without precedent in military history. For this reason, he needed a secret order from Ōyama to Nogi, instructing Nogi to yield authority to Kodama. Even so, unless he was careful, he feared that shame might drive Nogi to take his own life.

Ōyama understood. For the first and only time in the entire Russo-Japanese War, he issued a secret order. As he faced the piece of paper, his expression was downcast. After a moment, he picked up his brush and wrote a few lines that said in gist: "I send General Kodama in my stead. Take whatever he says as coming from me." In other words, Kodama was going to Port Arthur not as chief of staff but as proxy for the commander in chief. This piece of paper meant that he could avoid subverting military order. Moreover, it had the force of a Tokugawa period *osumitsuki*, a paper bearing the signature of the shogun, leaving Nogi no choice but to yield.

"But will you use this, Kodama?"

"Don't worry. Nine chances out of ten, I won't have to." Kodama understood that waving this piece of paper would disgrace Nogi irreparably. He wanted to have a frank discussion and, if at all possible, get Nogi to request that he take charge for a few days until the situation settled down. This would eliminate any risk of legal or personal repercussions.

"Do I have it right—you intend to tackle 203-Meter Hill?"

"It will mean a drastic change in each division's battle allotments and artillery positions, a huge undertaking, but I want to pull it off at one stroke."

Kodama went back to his room, summoned Matsukawa Toshitane, and dictated an order that Matsukawa transcribed using a stubby 3-inch pencil. Kodama took the order with him back to Ōyama and sought his approval. It was a directive to Nogi's Third Army, issued in Ōyama's name. Ōyama ran his eyes over it and signed. The first section opened with a savage censuring of Nogi. "Lack of clarity regarding battle conditions at 203-Meter Hill is due primarily to the failure to achieve unity of command." There were two other sections as well, but, in any case, given that the incompetence of a single commanding officer had jeopardized the nation, the directive represented not so much a censure as a scream of desperation. It was issued after Kodama left.

* * *

At eight o'clock in the evening on November 29, Kodama boarded a train at Yantai Station. The South Manchurian Railway, laid and subsequently abandoned by the Russians, was at that point in the control of the Japanese Army. The train used for Kodama's journey south consisted of a locomotive engine and a single boxcar containing tables and chairs, with woven mats on the floor. Boxcar, locomotive, and rails were all of Russian make.

One other thing was made in Russia—the stove, taken from Yantai Station. Soldiers from General Headquarters burned enough coal in that stove to turn its pot belly bright red. Should the fire go out, they might all perish of cold.

Whenever Kodama looked out the small window, the scenery flying into the distance was always the same. Rolling hills stretched far to the horizon, their frozen hillsides white with frost that built up every night. Here and there the white was chipped away by patches of brown withered grass that vividly suggested the ghastly hue of death.

Now and then, the locomotive came to a stop. Every time this happened, Kodama's lower lip jutted out. "Wheels spinning again, eh?" The rails would freeze, causing the train wheels to skid.

Kodama was accompanied only by Major Tanaka Kunishige as adjutant.

In fact, November 27, two days earlier, had been a red-letter day in the history of the assault on Port Arthur. At three in the morning, as the failure of the latest all-out attack became evident, Nogi had personally revised his longstanding policy and resolved to make 203-Meter Hill the focus, if not the center, of attack. In short, he gave in.

To be sure, in the latest attack, 203-Meter Hill had been a secondary target. But the proper way to attack fortifications is to concentrate all one's strength on the enemy's weak point. By rights, the idea of secondary targets has no place in warfare. No taking of life could be more useless than a secondary attack carried out piecemeal.

"I wanted to beg Nogi to stop it." Nagaoka wrote words to this effect in a letter to Iguchi. But Nogi's order to attack 203-Meter Hill, issued at three in the morning on November 27, was no secondary afterthought. "When I came across the cable indicating that he was heading toward 203-Meter Hill," Nagaoka's letter continued, "even though I had a visitor I couldn't help leaping up and shouting out in joy. Had the idea come to him sooner, he need not have incurred ten thousand deaths, and there would have been no need for an imperial rescript."

In any case, while Kodama was on the southbound train, Nogi was attacking 203-Meter Hill.

* * *

One way or another, Nogi Maresuke finally made 203-Meter Hill the focus of attack. He made the call on his own judgment, not at the initiative of his chief of staff Ijichi Kōsuke.

When the decision was reached, Ijichi remained silent. Even at this stage, he remained convinced that capturing that high ground would accomplish nothing. To those who argued that a hilltop observation post could be used to fire land guns at the Russian squadron harbored at Port Arthur, he countered that even if the peak could be captured, it would take an inordinately long time to set artillery in place. He dismissed the idea as empty "desktop" theorizing. Afterward, of course, the task was accomplished, showing that it was Ijichi's own theorizing that was empty.

Be that as it may, now, for the first time in the war, Nogi had ignored the opinion of his chief of staff. That 203-Meter Hill was the key to the deadlock had been drummed into Nogi's ears by Imperial Headquarters, by Ōyama's General Headquarters, and by the Japanese Navy. Now for the first time he was going to turn the key. What if that plan had been incorporated into his program from the first?

On September 19, when the hill was still only partially fortified, the Japanese First Division had stormed it. They were repelled, but had they been reinforced they could definitely have taken the hill. General Nogi passed up a golden chance. After that, he ignored the hill, while in the interim Stoessel erected his strongest fortifications there.

203-Meter Hill rose from the ground at a point some 2 kilometers northwest of the town of Port Arthur. Nearby, across a valley, were the hills of Anzishan and Chair Hill. And adjacent to 203-Meter Hill were Flat Hill and Long Hill (known to the Japanese as Akasaka Yama and Namako Yama respectively). All of these were well fortified, the undulating hills bound together in a tightly interlocking defense system. Not even a rat could have run through without being hit by a cascade of gunfire.

The killing potential of those hills went far beyond the Japanese concept of fortification. A strong fort was built on the southwest part of 203-Meter Hill. The depth of the inner trenches at the fort was more than 2 meters. There were a number of covered ways connecting them, and the fortress headquarters was securely covered over. On the northeast part of the hill was another fort with 6-inch guns. Each gorge was fortified with light gun batteries, and interconnecting underground passages served as a traffic route. Abatis were laid running up the hill, and before them were trenches for deployed troopers. In the firing line were covered embrasures fitted with machine guns, and all around the perimeter were wire entanglements.

Besides the First Division, Nogi decided to send in the Seventh Division, freshly arrived from Asahikawa in Hokkaido. If need be, he could reinforce them with troops from the Ninth and Eleventh Divisions, he thought.

On November 27, the First Division led the charge. The order went out: "Tonight at 1800 hours, mount a concerted attack on 203-Meter Hill." Ninety minutes later, the first shock troops from Lieutenant Colonel Katsuki Saburō's regiment rushed in with bayonets glinting and were cut down almost instantaneously at the foot of the hill. By midnight, the regiment had withdrawn, virtually annihilated.

*   *   *

One of the biggest taboos in military strategy is to dole out troop strength piecemeal, but Nogi's military headquarters was indifferent to this elementary bit of strategic common sense. Particularly in regard to the First Division's attack on 203-Meter Hill, this was the sole reason for failure. Instead of having the First Division attack in full force, Nogi's headquarters sent out a succession of small units, each one to be destroyed by Russian artillery before the next went out.

Finally, Nogi decided to have the Seventh Division attack 203-Meter Hill in full force. At long last, common sense prevailed. The First Division, which had led the attack on 203-Meter Hill and suffered severe losses, continued to remain in charge. The main force was the new and powerful Seventh Division. The two divisions were combined, with Lieutenant General Ōsako Naotoshi, commanding officer of the Seventh Division, given united command over them both.

The new plan was to attack in full force, not allowing the enemy a moment's respite. The Seventh Division moved to implement the plan. Ōsako arrived on the scene early in the morning on the twenty-ninth. At seven, he climbed 164-Meter Hill—better known as Takasaki Yama—to get a distant view of 203-Meter Hill and heard a report from the head of the First Division. The attack plan and the timing of its execution were discussed.

"Our siege cannons are powerful enough," said a staff member of the First Division. "But however fiercely we attack and rain destruction on them, the enemy is so quick to recover that by the time we launch the next attack, their batteries are as good as new. They just never lose strength."

This caught Ōsako's attention, and he raised a question. "Tell me, how many shells would our siege cannons have to fire in order to damage the enemy batteries to any real extent? That is, how strong an attack would force them to spend an entire day recovering?" This point became the focus of his on-site fact-finding. In the end, it was concluded that four hours of steady pummeling ought to significantly reduce enemy strength the following day.

Finally, an efficient attack plan was in place. The siege cannons would roar continuously for four hours, and afterward the infantry would charge. That should do it. Ōsako decreed that the attack would resume on the thirtieth. The day before would be devoted to digging trenches.

In line with this plan, on the morning of the twenty-ninth, Japanese siege mortars began a thunderous volley, and the field and mountain guns also began firing ceaselessly. The infantry and engineers of both divisions, meanwhile, used every available means to draw closer to the enemy in order to shorten the distance for their final attack. In an attempt to stave them off, the Russian side returned fire with such ferocity that the entire hill seemed to erupt with fire. Sky and earth turned dark with the gunpowder smoke of friend and foe.

*   *   *

Nogi's change of plan met with some success. Battle conditions at 203-Meter Hill on those two days, the twenty-ninth and thirtieth, can probably never be accurately conveyed in words. Lives were consumed at a rate so fierce that it took not fifteen minutes for a thousand men to become ten. And yet, among the heaped-up corpses of Japanese soldiers on a southwest corner of the hill, there were survivors. Surrounded by exploding shells, those survivors clung to their weapons, operated levers, pulled their gun hammers, and kept firing bullets at the enemy's concrete.

"The southwest corner has been occupied." This report that reached Nogi's headquarters meant simply that a tiny band of men had, under conditions that must be considered miraculous, *survived*. On the thirtieth, Ōsako dispatched the Twenty-seventh Infantry Regiment (Asahikawa) as reinforcements.

The Russian commander on 203-Meter Hill was Colonel Nikolai Tretyakov. He served under Major General Kondratenko, the commander so revered by Russian officers and men at Port Arthur. Kondratenko held him in great trust and said of him with characteristic brevity, "Tretyakov will get it done." Not only was Tretyakov intrepid, but he issued commands of remarkable appropriateness and precision. Having heard from General Headquarters that "Nogi likes the twenty-sixth of the month. He's bound to launch a major attack on that date," he was perfectly prepared. Astoundingly, he even foresaw that this time Nogi would show interest in 203-Meter Hill and, accordingly, petitioned headquarters for reinforcements, borrowing a naval landing party from the squadron at Port Arthur.

There were two peaks on 203-Meter Hill. On the night of the twenty-eighth, Japanese forces heading toward these had been repelled by an infantry attack, and forces that had dug in midway up the hill in preparation for attack were virtually wiped out in a series of raids. Tretyakov relied on the tactic of using hand grenades in great quantity. After two hours of infantry combat, nearly every soldier in the Japanese second skirmish trench on the southwest part of the hill had also been killed.

"Think of Japanese soldiers as dolls." Tretyakov said this constantly in an attempt to rid his officers and men of fear. He had only three thousand men. The enemy numbered over twenty thousand, and they were led by two lieutenant generals, whereas Tretyakov was a mere colonel. He feared the terror that his men might feel, knowing themselves outnumbered. "As proof that they are mechanical dolls, they keep on repeating the same actions over and over again, getting themselves killed."

At four in the afternoon on the twenty-ninth, Tretyakov saw a large Japanese detachment advancing on the established course toward the summit.

They swarmed up the hill like ants. Immediately, he sounded an alarm at the nearby batteries and ordered firing to begin. At the same time, he had Captain Belozerov prepare for infantry combat. Then, seeing that Japanese forces had appeared near the southwest peak from another angle, he swiftly dispatched an explosives unit in response and also sent the Fifth Company of the Fifth East Siberian Rifle Regiment, which had been positioned farther back, rushing to the scene. After dark, the surviving Japanese soldiers were driven off. That night, Tretyakov ordered rush repairs on all the damaged batteries. Of all the officers in the Russian Army, none had such a chaotic command as he.

* * *

While Japanese losses increased by a factor of ten at thirty-minute intervals, the Russians did not get by unscathed. Tretyakov repeatedly sent his infantry unit into dangerous defensive and offensive combat, losing many soldiers along the way.

Stoessel, whose headquarters were in Port Arthur, saw 203-Meter Hill as the key to the struggle and so sent in reinforcements unstintingly. The reinforcements were, of course, taken from the total reserves, over which he had full control. As their numbers dwindled, he took a drastic step: he decided to put rifles in the hands of medics, railway workers, and other noncombat personnel. There was a surprising number of such men, easily enough to form a battalion (four companies). Stoessel expressed confidence in them: "Even a medic is capable of throwing a hand grenade." After the medics left for the front, he saw that officers' wives and daughters were given intensive training and took up duty in the hospital. Further, he demanded in no uncertain terms that the squadron sitting idle in the harbor supply more men. Finally, of the wounded soldiers hospitalized at Port Arthur, he forcibly discharged all who were capable of holding a weapon and restored them to their original units.

The stubborn resistance of the fortress at Port Arthur, a source of such mounting frustration to Japan's General Headquarters in Manchuria as well as to Imperial Headquarters in Tokyo, was not achieved without cost on the defending side.

What heartened Stoessel was that all Russian fortifications remained intact and strong. What troubled him was that the Japanese Army had begun to focus intense interest on 203-Meter Hill. From the point of view of tactical defense, having the vast strength of the Japanese Army focused on a single point posed a tremendous challenge. Taking men away from other positions to defend 203-Meter Hill was not an option. There was little choice but to defend the hill with partial, limited strength. In that sense, putting rifles in the hands of medics and sending them off to 203-Meter Hill was not a sign of defeatism.

"Nogi seems to have had a change of heart." Some of Stoessel's staff were of this opinion, but others thought it might be a diversionary tactic. As proof, they pointed out that other fortifications were also under attack from the Japanese. In any case, while the attacking side enjoyed the freedom of choosing where to concentrate its efforts, the defending side was hampered by the need to spread itself out evenly in all directions.

*   *   *

A phrase like "fierce fight" is insufficient to describe the bloody action that then unfolded.

The newly beefed-up Fifteenth Infantry Standby Reserve Regiment (consisting mainly of soldiers from Gumma), led by Lieutenant Colonel Katsuki, was put in charge not of 203-Meter Hill but of Flat Hill. The Russian camps on 203-Meter Hill were connected with camps on the adjacent heights of Flat Hill and Long Hill. Katsuki's regiment headed for Flat Hill along with other friendly troops. The night before, Katsuki had sent off a handpicked special operations unit of thirty men. Their mission was to open an attack route. They cut through the barbed-wire entanglements laid around the foot of the hill, bent them back, and created a road so that the attack planned for the next night might go smoothly.

The difficulty of that mission bears consideration. During the early stages of the attack on Port Arthur, these wire entanglements were double-layered, but as the Japanese forces took to following the same paths each time, those areas alone were triple-layered. Moreover, the ground beyond was planted with sharp, impenetrable abatis, behind which lay the Russian trenches. Behind all that was the fortification itself, a gigantic killing device. Searchlights swept the base of the hill constantly. Should a passing breeze so much as ruffle the uniform on a dead Japanese soldier, cannon and machine gun fire exploded. When a burst of gunfire set all the corpses in the area dancing, the intensity of the shelling only multiplied.

The special operations unit crawled forward like bugs, playing dead whenever a searchlight came by. Or rather, they worked themselves in among the corpses to begin with and inched forward the moment the beam of light moved on. In that fashion, they approached the wire entanglements and set to work.

The Russians knew perfectly well what the Japanese were up to. "Let them do it." This was Major General Kondratenko's verdict when he received a report by telephone that night. "The Japonskis are building their own road to hell."

Roman Isidorovich Kondratenko, commanding officer of the Seventh East Siberian Rifle Division, played a central role in designing the elaborate plan for the defense of fortifications at Port Arthur and was a dynamic force in its instigation. Eighty percent of what Stoessel accomplished was owing to Kondratenko, people said, and it was true. Known as the finest soldier in Russia, at Port Arthur he may well have been the finest soldier on either side. Not only were his abilities as a strategist outstanding, but his courage and personal charm won him the respect of every soldier at the Port Arthur garrison. It was Nogi's misfortune to face an enemy of such caliber.

"The Japanese Army will come pouring through the breach they make. All your men have to do is aim the sights on their machine guns and keep on pulling the trigger." This was Kondratenko's remark to Colonel Tretyakov.

* * *

In any case, the Japanese First and Seventh Divisions stormed 203-Meter Hill with artillery support. Japanese projectiles literally changed the shape of the mountain. Amid that heavy gunpowder smoke, the assault forces crept forward immediately following the last shot in each round of firing and were wiped out, or suffered greater than fifty percent losses and retreated.

"Next to Gibraltar, Port Arthur was the most impregnable fortress of all time." So wrote Stanley Washburn, an American war correspondent attached to the staff of Nogi's Third Army at this time, in his book *Nogi: A Man against the Background of a Great War*. Washburn greatly admired Nogi's stoic military character, even referring to him as "my father." His admiration was lifelong. In his book, he praised Nogi as a superlative human being but deliberately avoided commenting on his idol's tactical abilities, repeatedly writing in effect, "It is not my intention to discuss matters of strategy." Still, he does include a small amount of such commentary, not always accurate. For example, he wrote that Nogi was nothing but an "instrument" to execute a plan conceived by the General Staff Office. That was half true. Nogi had complete freedom to take action, while those in Tokyo's high command could only tear their hair in frustration. "Nogi watched his divisions, brigades, and regiments dissolving before Russian fire like mist before sunshine. . ." Washburn continued. "The plan was not his, but he bore the responsibility of executing it." The implication is that Nogi's chief of staff Ijichi was to blame. Washburn must have gone to some pains over this description.

The above quotations are taken from Meguro Masumi's Japanese translation of *Nogi*. In his afterword, the translator tells of a question he asked General Ichinohe concerning Washburn's character, and the response he received. "Washburn was a jolly young man of around twenty-seven or twenty-eight. He was a great admirer of Nogi, calling him 'Father Nogi' and apparently looking on him as a father figure."

A brigade commander at the time of this attack, Ichinohe Hyoe harbored secret criticisms concerning Nogi's strategy, although later, as his contact with Nogi deepened, he became captivated by the general's personal charm. But for the Japanese privates forced to participate in the Port Arthur attacks as a duty to their country, serving under that officer so bursting with poetic charm was a colossal misfortune.

The persistence and unbelievable courage of the Japanese sowed greater and greater consternation in the Russian defenders of 203-Meter Hill. One unit, for example, was nearly wiped out, but the surviving few never faltered in their mad dash up the hillside. They carried oilcans on their backs. The last surviving soldier reached the enemy's covering, scattered oil on it, and perished in the ensuing fire. According to the report, "Even as the covering burned, he stayed his ground and fought stubbornly."

* * *

As a result of the heroic fights to the death carried out repeatedly by Japanese troops under heavy Russian artillery fire, at ten o'clock on the night of November 30, a miracle took place. 203-Meter Hill fell into Japanese hands. Unfortunately, this success was only temporary.

On the previous morning, commanding officer Ōsako Naotoshi had climbed Takasaki Yama to look at 203-Meter Hill and observe battle conditions. The sergeant major at his side murmured, "This is a true hell." Every inch of the mountain was piled with the corpses of Japanese soldiers. Lying flat on Ōsako's left, his binoculars trained on the enemy camp, was Lieutenant General Matsumura Kanemoto, head of the First Division. Matsumura described the course of the fighting from November 27, bringing Ōsako up to date concerning conditions among friend and foe alike. His sunburned face was rust-colored from the dust and smoke of battle. A longtime advocate of a full-scale attack on 203-Meter Hill, Matsumura had time and again urged Nogi's headquarters to adopt that plan, only to be ignored each time.

"If we could just get to the top of 203-Meter Hill, we could look down on the harbor." This was Matsumura's pet saying. Ōsako Naotoshi had just come from Tokyo where he met with Nagaoka Gaishi and so was well aware of the fundamental error in Nogi's strategy. He also understood that 203-Meter Hill held the key to capturing the fortress at Port Arthur.

"Matsumura, if we all die, we can somehow capture it." Ōsako made this comment after the deliberations on strategy ended, sitting cross-legged in a hollow in the ground, his prematurely white beard yellow with sand. He had a younger brother named Naomichi who was a major general; his son Sanji, a first lieutenant, had already fallen in battle.

"We will reopen the attack before dawn on the thirtieth." Ōsako and Matsumura came to this agreement on November 29 as they deliberated on Takasaki Yama. New troop allotments were decided.

From a tactical standpoint, the newly assigned Seventh Division from Asahikawa would have to be called unlucky. Like a shopkeeper with no talent for laying in supplies, Nogi kept dribbling away his troops. Had he diverted another two divisions to 203-Meter Hill for a quick and total assault, the grisly losses incurred on the thirtieth would have been considerably eased, the victory perhaps not temporary.

Before dawn on November 30, Japanese heavy artillery pounded enemy camps on 203-Meter Hill and Flat Hill with an unprecedented amount of ammunition. But no sooner did Japanese gunfire die down than the Russian forces roared back to life, returning fire with vigor.

Japanese infantry advanced by every means possible. Five companies of the Twenty-eighth Infantry Regiment from Hokkaido, commanded by Colonel Murakami Seiji, crawled on their bellies one by one to advance from one point to another. Russian gunfire raked them mercilessly, and of a thousand men barely 150 or 160 made it safely to their destination. Those soldiers who died never engaged in battle. They were killed in transit without ever firing a bullet.

* * *

Concerning the various commanding officers of the Japanese troops heading for 203-Meter Hill and Flat Hill, the foreign press reported that they had "iron determination." Stanley Washburn uses similar language about Nogi Maresuke: "He looked on himself as a mere machine." And as for the companies who fell in a hail of bullets, he writes that Nogi "was utterly impersonal with respect to the lives of his men."

Such demeanor reveals something characteristic about the Meiji period. Until that time, unlike in other countries, never once did the authority of the state weigh too heavily on the common people in Japan. There is a tendency for some latter-day historians to write the history of the common people with a certain fantasy, as the history of indignities suffered at the hands of power. But to take one example, there is no evidence that the politics of the Tokugawa shogunate in its own domain was any more sadistic than that of other civilized nations. Overall, it can be said rather that the attitude was one of enlightened rule.

Japanese people first participated in the state after the founding of the Meiji government. It was through the draft that Japan's emergence as a modern nation most directly affected the lives of its people. Universal conscription was enacted through the constitution, and ordinary people, who, until Meiji times, had never been impressed into war, were made soldiers. The illusion of "modernity" brought about by the modern state did not necessarily contribute to the people's welfare but could compel them to die on the battlefield.

By comparison, during Japan's endemic civil wars in the fifteenth and sixteenth centuries, all military men down to the lowly ashigaru made a career of their profession. They were free to leave that profession if they so chose, and they had the even greater freedom of being able to leave the service of an incompetent leader. Incompetent generals of that era generally self-destructed before ever losing to the enemy, their men abandoning them and scattering far and wide.

But in the modern nation brought into being by the Meiji Restoration, things were different. The constitution made the people into soldiers with no right of escape. On the battlefield, however rash the order an incompetent commander might give, compliance was the only choice. Disobeying an order was punishable under the military penal code by death. Never before in Japan's history did the state bring such a crushing weight to bear on the populace.

And yet people felt no particular distress on that account. Often, that heavy weight was even welcomed with delight. For the Japanese people, Meiji was a time of collective excitement over their ability to participate in the nation for the first time. That mentality and those historical circumstances underlay the impressive bravery of Japanese soldiers on 203-Meter Hill.

*　　*　　*

One more example.

That day, Lieutenant Colonel Katsuki's regiment made repeated attacks on the Russian battery on the southwest corner of 203-Meter Hill, finally driving the enemy out in hand-to-hand combat. Japanese soldiers far excelled the Russians in techniques of hand-to-hand fighting. Japan had an ancient tradition of drilling with spears, and with that as a foundation the military had already perfected the techniques of bayonet practice.

Katsuki's men took the battery, but their orders did not allow them to rest on their laurels. Their orders were to "proceed from the southwest corner through the saddle point and on to the top of the hill." But Russian gunfire was concentrated heavily on the battery they had occupied. They were unable to poke their faces out. The Katsuki regiment had orders to act in liaison with Colonel Murakami's Twenty-eighth Infantry Regiment, which was aiming for the northeast corner. But every move Murakami's men made attracted a burst of concentrated gunfire resulting in many deaths. The main force was thus pinned down at the Second Infantry tunnel, from which the charge was to be launched. Since Murakami's regiment, the left flank, was unable to move, Katsuki's regiment, the right flank, was also stuck. For an hour, both units were blasted by continuous enemy gunfire. One of Katsuki's men stuck his head out in an attempt to leave the battery and promptly had his face shot off. The situation was the same with Murakami's men.

Naval commander Eguchi Rinroku, captain of the *Akagi*, watched from the sea through binoculars and left a record of his observations. "The friendly troops look like a swarm of ticks midway up 203-Meter Hill." But the "swarm of ticks" was held immobile by fierce enemy gunfire.

Major General Tomoyasu Harunobu, brigade commander, also had his eye on the ticks, and he issued Murakami's men a stark order: "Leave camp and advance." Leaving camp meant annihilation. But that was the order.

At that point, headquarters was blown up by a cannon shell fired from a fort on Laotie Hill. Headquarters was underground, heavily protected, yet the explosion ripped through, so the power of the weapon may be imagined. The heavy shell came flying through the air with all the noise of a locomotive. Twenty-four-year-old Nogi Yasusuke, the brigadier's aide-de-camp (and Nogi's second son), wrote a letter to a boy in Tokyo, a relative, describing the sound. "The Russian bastards fire huge cannons at us. The sound is really loud, louder than when you're at a railroad crossing and a train goes by." The blast instantly killed or wounded almost everyone. The only ones unscathed in headquarters were Tomoyasu and his aide-de-camp Nogi Yasusuke.

Tomoyasu had to order Murakami to advance, but because the phone was dead he told his aide-de-camp, Second Lieutenant Nogi Yasusuke, to deliver the message.

Yasusuke grabbed the hilt of his sword and dashed out of the underground trench. By nature cheerful and brisk, he had a greater aptitude for soldiering than his older brother Katsusuke, who had been killed at the battle of Nanshan.

Yasusuke dodged bullets, arriving miraculously unharmed at the Second Infantry camp where Murakami's regiment was huddled. He dove for cover and gave Colonel Murakami the order to advance. He had one other order to convey. Headquarters had been decimated, and so Murakami's regiment was to provide replacements.

Murakami had no choice but to comply with these orders. He did not say, "How am I supposed to advance under these conditions?" Probably never in the history of Japanese warfare did an order carry as much weight as during the Russo-Japanese War. "Report back that I will advance immediately."

Yasusuke repeated the words and tore out of Murakami's camp, but he never got the message to Tomoyasu. On his way back, a bullet struck him in the forehead and killed him. Since he was running alone, the exact circumstances of his death are unknown. The time was around four o'clock in the afternoon. On the battlefields of Nanshan and Port Arthur, Nogi Maresuke mourned the deaths of his two sons.

Though the messenger died, the message he had delivered succeeded in prying Colonel Murakami and his unit from their position.

The charge took place in a shower of blood. One entire company was annihilated in front of the enemy's second barbed-wire obstacle. There were just over a hundred survivors. At six o'clock in the evening, Murakami led the hundred forward. When word that the Twenty-eighth Infantry Regiment (Murakami's unit) was in motion reached Lieutenant Colonel Katsuki, hunkered on the southwest corner, he swung into action. It is fair to say he rushed forward recklessly. There was no other choice. By running the men till their legs gave out, he could hold losses to a minimum. Murakami's troops did the same. Murakami and his hundred were not ruled by reason. It was sheer madness.

The two regiments rushed the Russian infantry camp in concert from north and south. The camp held a thousand Russian infantry, while the Japanese forces numbered about five hundred. Swords flashing, the five hundred and the thousand began their hellish fighting.

The key to victory in hand-to-hand fighting is selfless valor—but Russian soldiers facing hand-to-hand combat were by and large cowards, soon turning and running. The fight lasted half an hour before the Russians fled. Though the Japanese side also suffered huge losses, Murakami's men persisted, driving forward until at around nine o'clock they reached the peak. By then, there were barely fifty survivors.

Tomoyasu ordered Murakami and his fifty to "push on without fear of annihilation till you take 203-Meter Hill." Surely no starker military command has ever been issued, anywhere. His reserves down to a mere two companies, Tomoyasu gave Katsuki the same command. Katsuki's and Murakami's men rushed forward like demons and finally took possession of 203-Meter Hill. It was then ten o'clock on the night of November 30.

*   *   *

That day, Lieutenant General Kondratenko (he had been promoted) maintained a command post on the front, where bullets flew thick and fast. "I am in the headquarters of the Fifth East Siberian Rifle Regiment at North Taiyanggou." His fortitude must have been of inestimable value in lifting the morale of the Russian troops.

At that point, the defense of the entire Russian Army centered on the defense of 203-Meter Hill. This was because Kondratenko had advised Stoessel that "the fate of all Russia hangs on 203-Meter Hill." As we have seen, Stoessel, in his headquarters in the town of Port Arthur, at first laid no significance on the nameless hill. But under Kondratenko's lead he gradually revised his estimation and began responding to Kondratenko's requests for reinforcements virtually without limit.

"More men died on 203-Meter Hill at this time than at any other," wrote an officer in Stoessel's headquarters. "There weren't enough soldiers to replace them, so we borrowed sailors from the navy. With the squadron squatting motionless in the harbor, the sailors had time on their hands. Every day a crowd of them went through town and climbed 203-Meter Hill. They marched with jaunty spirits, yet there was something melancholy and heavy in their gait."

The heaviness of their gait was not owing solely to their having traded in the low shoes of the navy for heavy army boots. None of their comrades who set off before them ever returned. No one who went up that hill came down alive, as they well knew. But they did not resist going. Some were kids of seventeen or eighteen, others were veterans in their forties. One older noncommissioned officer said with a cheerful laugh, "I've been a sailor since the days of sail, and now instead of dying at sea I'm going to die on that gray hill? Who would've believed it?"

The purpose of their march toward death was to bring glory to their fatherland. But as happens in armies everywhere, marching toward certain death brought on a kind of frenzied cheerfulness.

The sailors were also well versed in the enemy's traits: "Japanese are lousy rifle shots. They get too excited. But in a bayonet attack they come at you like thunder."

Naturally, Kondratenko did not rely only on sailors for reinforcements. He nimbly shuffled units in every battery and fort, sending them to defend 203-Meter Hill. Still, on the evening of November 30, the Russians were no longer able to keep the enemy at bay.

*　*　*

The fierceness of the fighting on 203-Meter Hill was so great that in the words of Russian major general Kostenko, "The violence of the assault guns and their never-ending fire was sheer hell." He went on to give this description of a charge by Japanese infantry: "They come at you in columns, quick marching in strict formation all the way."

There were some three hundred soldiers in a column. One time, three columns fought their way up the hill, one on the heels of the other. The first succumbed to a minefield. Pillars of fire flared up with a roar, and, when the smoke cleared, corpses littered the ground. Japanese military tactics were characterized by repetition. Landmines blew the second column to bits also, then the third. It all happened in the space of less than an hour.

Command was unbelievably dimwitted. By rights, when landmines destroyed the first column, headquarters should have withdrawn the other two and sent in an artillery squad to fire on any areas where mines were likely to be, like filling in squares on graph paper. The Japanese artillery of that time was fully capable of carrying out such a mission. Why on earth would headquarters not do that and instead make the same mistake three times running, causing a thousand—by the Russian estimate, three or four thousand—soldiers to die for naught? Sole responsibility does not rest with Nogi's army or Ōsako's division headquarters. This was a chronic disease of the Japanese Army overall. Once a strategic or tactical pattern was laid out, it was adhered to absolutely, like a religious precept, and repeated ad infinitum. That disease ended up destroying the Japanese Army in the Pacific War. But perhaps it should not be seen as a disease of the army, but a sign of something deep in the Japanese psyche.

The problem was certainly not lack of artillery. At that stage of the attack, Nogi's army lobbed more shells than ever before at the little hill. Moreover, the Japanese made liberal use of heavy siege guns and the 28-centimeter howitzers.

"The shelling was so fierce," wrote Kostenko, "that people in the town of Port Arthur could not carry on a conversation."

Japanese attacks were all too straightforward, with none of the deceptiveness needed in combat. For example, around five o'clock in the afternoon on the twenty-seventh, a Japanese battalion occupied part of the Russian trenches on 203-Meter Hill—but the Russians had vacated the trenches on purpose, following Kondratenko's plan. They proceeded to counterattack, surrounding the Japanese and virtually wiping them out. In short, the Third Army's attack on the Port Arthur fortress was carried out with an excessively rigid mentality, from overall tactics to the leadership of even small skirmishes.

* * *

In any case, it was around ten o'clock at night on November 30 when a surviving unit of Japanese soldiers largely took possession of the top of 203-Meter Hill. The news reached Lieutenant General Kondratenko at his command post in North Taiyanggou. "War is like breathing," he said. "Sometimes you inhale, sometimes you exhale." With no change of expression, he added, "In three hours, we will take it back."

Soldiers in the Port Arthur garrison cared less for aristocratic, high-strung Stoessel than for Kondratenko, who had the face of a peasant as well as courage and ability that roused their heartfelt admiration.

Kondratenko telephoned Colonel Viktor Reis, Stoessel's chief of staff, and asked for reinforcements. After considering, Reis said, "We too are short of reserves, sir. What do you advise?"

Kondratenko was familiar not only with his own situation but with that of the front as a whole. "How about vacating some of our less important positions and moving their garrisons to 203-Meter Hill? I can think of three." He suggested the fort at Da-anzi Hill, the infantry camp near Sanli Bridge, and the fort at Huatougou. Reis quickly concurred. The garrison at Huatougou in particular was said to be the finest in the whole army.

The general then took a series of actions aimed at recapturing the lost ground. First, he summoned his regimental commanders, officers of the rank of colonel and lieutenant colonel. "The men fear an attack by Japanese troops. The way to rid them of fear is to always take the initiative, attacking before the Japanese do and with greater daring. You officers need to lead the way with your swords held high." He further counseled, "The way to victory is set. You need only to act with valor. Do not allow the men to sit idle to no purpose. Action is the only remedy for fear."

He then obtained extra grenades and explosives from Stoessel. Hand grenades were effective, hand bombs still more so. The hand bombs were big weapons weighing as much as 18 pounds each. Lobbed from on high at Japanese soldiers climbing up the slope, they had greater effect than shelling with field guns. Those hand bombs were not an official part of the Russian Army arsenal but were invented by a naval lieutenant named Podgorsky specifically for the defense of 203-Meter Hill. One time, a single bomb felled a hundred Japanese soldiers.

* * *

The last item that Kondratenko saw to in preparation for the recapture of 203-Meter Hill was medals. Only army commander Stoessel had discretion to bestow medals for heroism. Kondratenko sent a rider to Stoessel requesting permission to give out medals just this once. He wanted to reward bravery on the spot and so raise morale.

Stoessel did not respond immediately. He was a man who liked to do things strictly by the book. That, he believed, was the only way to maintain military order and prestige. But he was won over by Kondratenko's repeated insistence that the fall of 203-Meter Hill would lead to the fall of Port Arthur. Under those exceptional circumstances, he decided, there was no choice but to comply with division commander Kondratenko's request and grant him the necessary authority. He summoned his aide-de-camp, had him bring out a selection of every kind of medal, and handed them to Kondratenko's orderly. "Remember," he cautioned, "these go only to soldiers and non-commissioned officers." The orderly of course understood. Bestowing medals on officers was the sole prerogative of the tsar.

This sort of business would normally have been conducted over the telephone, but the line had been disrupted by Japanese shelling. The communications team was busy trying to restore service, but in the meantime Kondratenko was forced to use mounted orderlies to convey his wishes, and commands to the rear and the front.

When the orderly returned to Kondratenko's headquarters, a massive counteroffensive was underway. The time was just around midnight.

Colonel Tretyakov was leading reinforcements from Kondratenko alongside exhausted survivors of the last few days' battle. He positioned his men in a hilltop battery and along the line of fortifications to the southeast and began a fierce battle with Japanese forces occupying part of the hilltop. The ground between the two sides could have been covered in a ten-minute dash. Stationed on either side of the peak, they exchanged fire at close range. Numbers tell the grim intensity of the fighting: after thirty minutes, the number of surviving troops on both sides was halved.

Tretyakov had an advantage in that he was backed by Kondratenko, a shrewd judge of battle conditions who kept sending in reinforcements as needed.

On the Japanese side, the surviving units of Katsuki's and Murakami's regiments were, unbelievably, left entirely on their own. No reinforcements came from anywhere. Troop strength of brigades and divisions had dried up, the last few days of fighting having cost the Japanese over five thousand casualties. Here was another sign of miscalculation in Nogi's headquarters. Troop strength is not something to use sparingly, but to apply in full strength as necessary. Had another division of fresh soldiers waited in ambush at the foot of 203-Meter Hill, the outcome might have been quite different.

* * *

Late that night near the top of 203-Meter Hill, Japanese and Russian forces engaged in a literal battle to the death. It was Colonel Tretyakov's good fortune that just as he seemed on the point of retiring in defeat, he was bolstered by a fresh unit from Huatougou Hill and a naval landing force from the city of Port Arthur. The reinforcements numbered approximately three hundred, but they were well fed and well rested, so given the condition of the exhausted Japanese soldiers fighting on in total isolation, this represented a dramatic increase.

During the fighting, Colonel Tretyakov's saber was struck twice by shells, so that he was unable to unsheathe it. He managed to draw it out by having a soldier step on the end of the scabbard while he pulled with all his might. After that, he led his troops with a naked sword. Brave an officer as he was, the bravery of the Japanese troops left him speechless with admiration.

The Japanese had to be on the edge of exhaustion, but at half past midnight they all opened fire at once as if to resume attack. Before that, Tretyakov tried to surround them. First, he sent a troop of light infantry from the Fifth East Siberian Rifle Regiment to the southwest peak and had half of the Seventh Company of that same regiment charge the northeast peak, while he himself led a company of the naval landing force toward the sharp ridge between. He rushed madly forward, brandishing his sword. Every soldier held a rifle in the left hand and a bomb in the right. The hilltop was instantly ablaze with hundreds of points of light. For a while, the Japanese troops withstood this onslaught, but in the end they could not hold the enemy at bay and withdrew, abandoning the northeast peak. But this retreat was only temporary, soon shifting to an encirclement operation. They came at Tretyakov in waves.

Strictly speaking, the Japanese forces in this battle hardly deserve to be called an army. Colonel Murakami's regiment was down to a single warrant officer and forty soldiers, while in the Katsuki regiment nearly a hundred survivors remained in action. The two regiments each were reinforced by two companies from the brigade, but these too were virtually wiped out by Tretyakov's resolute attacks. By dawn, Murakami's camp on the northeast peak had been whittled back to forty men.

Nor was there any replenishment of ammunition or rations. As the sky lightened, every soldier's ammunition pouch was empty. The exhausted men didn't even have water to give them the slightest refreshment. Those forty were victors all right—the most miserable victors the world has ever seen. They hung on to the northeast peak without a shell to fire or a drop to drink, or any hope of reinforcements. Moreover, the sun was rising. When the sun came up, the Russian Army was bound to see that there were only forty men on the northeast sector. Those soldiers were in dire straits; the high command was clearly responsible.

At daybreak, half of the forty "victors" descended the hill, followed by the remaining twenty. The northeastern peak of 203-Meter Hill was once again in Russian hands. The remnants of the Katsuki regiment still held the southwestern peak and were still putting up a fight, but their destruction was merely a matter of time.

* * *

The train bearing Kodama Gentarō continued south. Occasionally, the wheels would spin due to ice on the rails, as we've described before.

"He sure can sleep." That's what Kodama's attendant, Major Tanaka Kunishige, thought as he looked over from time to time at the general's bed. The curtains were half open, showing Kodama's small, childish frame lying on the bed. Tanaka was unable to get to sleep that night.

To Tanaka, Kodama was the man with the heaviest burden in the entire Manchurian Army. (In fact, as soon as the Russo-Japanese War ended, Kodama died, as if burned out.) "You'd never know it from the way he sleeps, though!" Tanaka was strangely amused.

Now and again, the train came to a halt. Each time, he picked up the sounds of distant gunfire, a sure sign they were getting closer to the battleground. Tanaka Kunishige was from Satsuma, thirty-six years old. For a Satsuma man, he was generous in his appraisal of men of Chōshū.

Both Nogi and Kodama were men of Chōshū. Both suffered deep personal losses around the time of the Meiji Restoration. Nogi's boyhood mentor Tamaki Bunnoshin, an old-time samurai to the core, was uncle and teacher of the brilliant revolutionary Yoshida Shōin. Following the Restoration, Tamaki was involved in a failed rebellion led by Chōshū samurai Maebara Issei and took his own life. Nogi's younger brother Masayoshi, who was Tamaki's adopted son and bore his surname, participated in the revolt and died in battle.

Kodama was from Tokuyama in Chōshū, where his family had a hereditary stipend of one hundred koku. After his father's early death, his older sister's husband became head of the family. This brother-in-law was killed by supporters of the shogunate in a most gruesome way: masked desperadoes stormed into the house and ran him through with swords before his family's eyes. Kodama, then a boy of thirteen still wearing his hair in the childish *chigomage* style, was out when the killing took place but returned home soon thereafter and calmly disposed of the body, it is said.

"A lot happened in the old days." That was all Kodama would say. He did not care to reminiscence about the past. After his brother-in-law's death, the family endured terrible suffering. Their stipend was revoked, and they were ordered out of their house. Following the success of Takasugi Kensaku's coup d'état, the domain was swept by anti-shogunate sentiment and the Kodama family fortunes changed again. Gentarō was made head of the family with a stipend of twenty-five koku. The amount was small, but family honor had been restored.

Both Nogi and Kodama, in short, suffered great trauma around the time of the Restoration, and their personal difficulties were intimately bound up with the birth of the new nation. At the very time when the new nation was in peril, one became chief of staff of the Manchurian Army and the other commander of the Third Army, leader of the siege of Port Arthur. To Tanaka, whose generation had no personal experience of the Restoration, it was all dramatic and thrilling.

*   *   *

Kodama slept five hours and awoke in the middle of the night. The train continued to speed through the darkness.

"Tanaka, you up?" Kodama jumped down from his berth. He was past fifty, but as nimble as a rabbit springing from its cage. Tanaka, who had been seated, got hastily to his feet. Kodama had gone to bed with his trousers on, and as soon as he got up he threw his jacket around his shoulders. He went over to the table, picked up a plain unfiltered cigarette, and stuck it in his mouth.

Tanaka searched for a match, but Kodama had already lit one himself. "Sorry, sir." Tanaka apologized for his failure.

"Don't apologize over something so stupid." The general snorted as he sat in a chair. "Tanaka, you know why it is that the higher up men go in the military, the more senile they become?"

Taken aback, Tanaka replied, "No, sir."

"It's because their staff does everything for them, including striking their matches. I always said that if I became a general I would take care of myself, by myself." It was true. In daily life, Kodama saw to his own needs as much as any private. "Doesn't give me much dignity, though." He chuckled. If he let his staff see to his personal needs, he would doubtless acquire more of an aura, but that sort of aura was better left to some dolt. No need for that for a staff officer, he maintained.

After finishing his cigarette, Kodama tossed aside his jacket and climbed back into bed. "Tanaka, you go to bed too."

"Can't sleep, sir."

"Just imagine you're a baby again, and you'll get right to sleep." Kodama threw the blanket over his head. Clear your mind of all thought and sleep will come, he apparently meant.

"Easy for him to say," thought Tanaka. After the war, however, he gained some retrospective insight into Kodama's state of mind. Free and easy as he seemed, Kodama had set out for Port Arthur expecting to die. He wrote a will and left it in a briefcase in his office at General Headquarters. His life was on the line. He intended to make sweeping changes in Nogi's offensive strategy, and to do so he meant to get as close to the enemy as he could and do thorough reconnaissance. All along, he had held that the greatest flaw in Nogi's headquarters was the failure to do just that.

In any case, only after the war, following Kodama's death, did Tanaka realize that the general had made the trip to Port Arthur expecting to lay down his life.

*   *   *

Tanaka must have dozed off briefly. When he awoke, he found that at some point the train had come to a stop. He heard the sound of a dozen voices on the platform. He checked his watch in the light of a signal fire. Half past two in the morning. As he started to get out of bed, from beyond the curtain came the shrill voice of the sergeant major traveling with him. "Major Tanaka, 203-Meter Hill has fallen."

"Eh?" Tanaka wondered if it could be true. At the time of their departure, the hill had seemed far from falling. To calm his excitement, he asked where they were as he pulled on his riding boots.

"This is Jinzhou Station, sir."

"And?"

"And there was a telephone call from General Headquarters to this station, sir."

Tanaka went out on the platform. A cherubic young second lieutenant in the transport service saluted.

The report had first gone from Nogi's headquarters to General Headquarters. In order to inform Kodama, who was en route south, General Headquarters had phoned the station. Tanaka longed to know more, but that seemed impossible. The railway, once the property of the Russian Empire, was at that point being run by the Japanese logistical command. The phone line connected only to the supply base at each station, and reaching someone from General Headquarters might prove difficult. Besides, if the hill had *not* fallen, details might be necessary, but if it had been taken, that fact alone said all they needed to know.

Tanaka went back in the train. Kodama was already awake and seated at his desk, all five buttons of his coat buttoned for once.

"I heard." His face was glowing. "They say it fell."

"Yes, sir, apparently so."

"Shall we drink a toast?"

"I'll have the drinks ready immediately." Tanaka gave orders to the sergeant major, who went back to the kitchen area and ordered a Western-style meal to be prepared in a hurry. "Western-style meal" meant pork cutlet, a first-class delicacy of this era. Champagne was brought out, and champagne glasses were set on Kodama's desk. There were only two.

"Drinks all around," Kodama ordered.

The noncommissioned officers and privates traveling with them poured each other drinks in a variety of containers.

Kodama stood up. If this were Tokyo, he would have needed to say a few words, perhaps a toast in honor of the emperor (*"Tennō heika, banzai!"*), but he was clearly too moved. His shining eyes moved from face to face, making a full stop at each one, until at length he downed his drink in silence. Unable to bear the tension, the sergeant called out softly, stifling his voice, "Banzai!" Everyone responded in chorus.

A Western-style meal, as it turned out, was not possible with the cooking facilities available. Kodama was little concerned. "Well, that's hardly surprising." He decided to stop off in Dalian in order to send a congratulatory wire to Nogi's headquarters. Now that the hill had been captured, there was no need to go straight to Nogi, he thought.

They arrived in Dalian early in the morning. Here was the logistical headquarters for the entire Manchurian Army, as well as a hospital and a hotel. Transport ships came and went incessantly, and the town was bustling. Kodama went into the hotel to rest for an hour until breakfast. For barely thirty minutes, he stretched out in a comfortable bed and slept deeply. When the sergeant major came to wake him for breakfast, he pulled the blanket over his head, asked for five minutes more, and was soon snoring again. The sergeant major kept his eyes on his pocket watch. When five minutes to the dot had gone by, he called to the general again.

Kodama jumped out of bed with vigor, put on his uniform and shoes, and sat back down on the bed. He took out a pad of paper from his pocket and began to scribble on it.

"Orders, sir?" asked the sergeant major, drawing himself up.

"No, a poem." Kodama had been composing a poem under the covers. He wanted to write one in honor of Nogi for capturing 203-Meter Hill.

Eventually, he went downstairs and entered the dining room. As soon as he was seated, the waiter brought him a bowl of soup. Major Tanaka was at the same table.

Kodama was in high spirits. He discussed the poem he was working on with Tanaka. Kodama was no great shakes as a poet, a fact he himself cheerfully admitted. "My poems are just lines of square characters." Tanaka, meanwhile, had no knowledge of Chinese-style classical poetry. Higher-ranking generals, being older, were trained to compose Chinese poetry, but no one of the rank of major general could do it. To someone as young as Tanaka, writing poetry in classical Chinese was an alien idea.

Before long, the phone rang. Tanaka set down his knife and fork, got up, and went out of the dining room. When he came back, his expression was transformed, his eyes wide open and unblinking.

"What is it?" Kodama felt a premonition of calamity, but he steeled himself to show no surprise, whatever had happened. Calamity was unavoidable in war.

"The call was from Colonel Ōba of Third Army headquarters. He says that early this morning the enemy recaptured 203-Meter Hill."

"*What*?" Kodama turned bright red with fury. He threw down his knife and fork, which clattered against the plate and flew off. "Tanaka, this is no time to be eating Western-style food!" After venting his anger on Tanaka and Western food, he grabbed his hat and stood up.

* * *

Kodama heard from Tanaka the gist of what had happened. "I never heard anything so goddamned stupid!" He was incensed about the use of the expression "occupied"—*senryō*—in Nogi's headquarters' first report. After piling bodies one on top of the other from the foot of 203-Meter Hill to halfway up the side and spilling rivers of blood, the Third Army had finally managed to capture two strongholds on the summit. One housed a hundred or so survivors, the other around forty. Without replenishing these strongholds with fresh soldiers, ammunition, or rations, Nogi's headquarters had made its report to General Headquarters on the basis of reports heard at several removes from the front. This was proof, as Kodama noted with displeasure, that none of the staff officers at Third Army headquarters had gone in person to 203-Meter Hill.

Rather than reporting that the hill had fallen, they should have filed a more detailed and accurate report: "One hundred survivors of the Katsuki unit and forty survivors of the Murakami unit have captured a pair of strongholds on the summit."

Then General Headquarters could have responded, "What are you planning next? What is the condition of the enemy?"

The word *senryō*, meaning "occupation" or "possession," signifies the end of a war or the conclusion of hostilities. That was why Kodama drank a toast. Under the circumstances, the word should never have been used.

He would have to make the trip after all, as originally planned. The first thing he did was fire off a telegram to Ōyama Iwao requesting that a regiment of infantry for him to command be sent south on the double. Without waiting for a response, he then boarded his private train. The train went north a ways, then got on the tracks to Port Arthur and proceeded south. Aboard the train, he received Ōyama's response: "Done."

Kodama was anxious to get to the battlefield as soon as possible. Given his state of mind, the train's speed was too slow. He let his displeasure be known. The engineer raced as fast as he could, under a full head of steam.

However, he was obliged to stop at every station along the way. There might be a message for Kodama at any one of them.

When the train stopped at Changlingzi, a sunburned field officer came aboard. This was Lieutenant Colonel Ōba Jirō, vice chief of staff, sent by Nogi's' headquarters to welcome Kodama. Unfortunately for him, he became the target of Kodama's ill humor.

Kodama offered Ōba a seat and asked for a status report. Because of the fierce look on Kodama's face, Ōba began somewhat nervously, unable to sit down. Kodama listened intently. Kodama, a veteran who'd been dodging bullets ever since the Boshin War and the Satsuma Rebellion, had a gut feeling that something was off. The information Ōba was giving him was not current, but several hours old.

From Ōba's perspective, this was only natural. Having been ordered by Ijichi to go meet Kodama, he had left Third Army headquarters several hours ago and so had no new information at hand. Probably he should have admitted that fact. However, he was so intimidated by the look on Kodama's face that he had gone ahead and presented the earlier status report.

"You blasted idiot!"

Kodama's angry outburst revealed a character flaw. He was incapable of maintaining the calm and sober demeanor that is deemed a necessary component in the character of a commander. He was rather the type to explode with anger, guffaw, rejoice. Given his innate selflessness, such flare-ups only added to his charm and rarely caused undue pain to anyone. But at this juncture, the psychological pressure he brought to bear on Ōba, one of the army's brightest talents, unfortunately had driven the officer to make an unnecessary report.

"Ōba," he roared, "who files hours-old reports during time of war!"

Ōba, all too aware of the impropriety, saluted and squeaked. "Yes, sir. I'll go and get fresh information right away." He was not happy.

Kodama was even less happy. "Is there a communication post here in the station?" he asked, just to be sure. As a matter of principle, there should have been one in every station, but there wasn't. As it turned out, the nearest one was in a little village 4 kilometers from Changlingzi Station. Galloping there and back again would take considerable time.

"Why the hell isn't there a communication post in the station? This is typical. This is why we do nothing but lose." Kodama was irate, his breath coming in angry huffs. "Never mind, start the train," he ordered. "I'll wait till we reach Third Army headquarters to hear what's going on."

Tanaka stuck his head out the window and gave the signal. The train began to move.

Ōba remained standing, his face pale. The man was spineless, thought Kodama. He had ability, yet with a personality like that he must be under Ijichi's thumb, unable to put his talents to full use. The incident gave Kodama an idea of the mood of Ijichi's staff.

* * *

The train continued south.

Ōba finally sat down.

"Ōba," said Kodama, "at this very moment, the Baltic Fleet is steaming to Japan."

Why belabor the point, thought Ōba.

"Displeased, Ōba? I mention this only because it hasn't sunk in yet at Nogi's headquarters."

From ancient times, an isolated castle has never held out long. The strategy of taking refuge in a castle works only when there is hope that reinforcements are on the way. In the case of the Port Arthur siege, those great reinforcements were the Baltic Fleet. That was why everyone in the Russian Army from Stoessel on down fought so hard in defense.

"If the Baltic Fleet gets here while the fortress at Port Arthur is still alive, Japan is doomed. That's what the navy is screaming about."

"I get it," said Ōba. Wasn't that why the Third Army was launching daily attacks, creating heaps of corpses and rivers of blood? He began to feel the conversation was absurd.

"No, you don't!"

Kodama was deeply concerned about a different impression he had formed. When Imperial Headquarters in Tokyo conveyed the navy's urgent request to Nogi's headquarters, chief of staff Ijichi had replied, "We are in frequent communication with the navy. Admiral Tōgō's request is by no means urgent. He is sympathetic to our plight." This reply was illogical in the extreme. Caught between Tokyo and General Headquarters, Ijichi had clearly become overwrought. Tōgō, in the midst of blockading Port Arthur Harbor, had sent a stream of staff officers to Nogi's headquarters. But with one or two exceptions, the officers had been deferential, in keeping with military protocol. Ijichi's response was based on the impression he had gained from those personal encounters, without due consideration of the overall strategic situation. This attitude was appalling to Kodama. Moreover, if it was any indication of the mood at Nogi's headquarters, Port Arthur wasn't about to fall any time soon. That was what Kodama wanted to say.

During the train journey, Kodama saw something that left him still more exasperated. On either side of the train tracks were numberless markers of plain unvarnished wood, stretching as far as the eye could see. They marked the graves of fallen soldiers.

"Tanaka, look." Kodama pointed out the window. "This railway is the main line for transporting troops. Planting all these grave markers alongside the tracks goes to show you how heedless and thoughtless Nogi's headquarters are. Soldiers on their way to the battlefield as replacements can't help seeing all these graves. Those men will be demoralized before they ever fight."

* * *

As the ear-shattering sound of gunfire came closer, the train arrived in the vicinity of Liushufang. There was no station. Noncommissioned officers put a step up to the train car. The door opened, and people got out.

There was nothing to see all around but yellowish-brown, rolling earth. Here and there the sharp branches of a wintry tree pierced the sky.

"I'll walk." At these words from Kodama, even the officers who had ridden to meet him on horseback were forced to dismount. Soldier though he was, Kodama did not like to ride. Or I should say, he had been born prematurely by several weeks and, for a military man, always had a small physique. His legs were not long enough to allow him to press the belly of a large Western horse.

"Will you walk all the way, sir?" Major Tanaka pressed the point. He intended this remark half teasingly.

"Yes."

Kodama started off. Just at hand he could see the village of Liushufang and a grove of leafless trees. Eventually, the road sloped down, and they came to the bed of a stream. Naturally, there was no water. Just beyond was the building that contained Nogi's headquarters.

The building was the residence of a prosperous local farmer named Chou Yunlai, from whom it had been requisitioned. Just inside the gate was a plot of land used for drying unhulled rice, and to the right was a large pagoda tree. A telephone and telegraph equipment had been installed under the tree. The oblong main house, where the headquarters had been established, was straight ahead. Army commander Nogi Maresuke used the room on the left just inside the central entrance and his chief of staff Ijichi Kōsuke, the one on the right. They each worked and slept in their respective rooms.

Kodama gave his sword a rattle and entered Nogi's room, but the general was not in. He was inspecting the front, Kodama was told.

"Well, Ijichi must be around." He went into the room on the right where Ijichi, who suffered from chronic neuralgia, was stretched out on the bed with his boots on. He didn't notice when Kodama came in.

These were the circumstances of this unhappy encounter.

"Ijichi, what's going on?"

Hearing Kodama shout, Ijichi finally realized that he had company. He got out of bed and saluted. But the pain of his neuralgia was too great for him to remain on his feet and so he quickly sank into a chair—even though his superior officer, Kodama, was still standing. Realizing the impropriety of this, Ijichi asked Kodama to sit down. "Please take that chair, sir."

"What have you got, neuralgia?" Things were not getting off to a good start.

His lower back hurt, said Ijichi, launching into an explanation of his illness. When Kodama shouted, "What's going on?" he had wanted an explanation of the loss of 203-Meter Hill and the unfavorable war situation, but what he got instead was a detailed account of Ijichi's neuralgia.

*　*　*

After that, Kodama delivered a scathing denunciation of the strategy adopted by Nogi's headquarters. The words he let fly at Ijichi were positively scalding.

The message can be summed up in various adjectives—"incompetent," "cowardly," "craven," "stubborn," "obtuse," "shiftless"—any one of which was strong enough to make a soldier take his life in shame. Ijichi went white with anger and for an instant rested his hand on the scabbard of his sword. There can be no doubt that he suppressed the impulse to kill Kodama. In the end, he counterattacked.

"For you to lay blame for the situation at Port Arthur entirely with Third Army headquarters is cowardly on your part, sir. The real fault lies in Imperial Headquarters. At the same time, sir, you yourself also bear responsibility, do you not?"

Kodama was surprised by the childishness of Ijichi's argument. "Ijichi, are you confused? The empire gave responsibility for this aspect of the war to Nogi and you. You are the chief of staff." He felt as if he were lecturing a little child.

"I'm not talking about that, sir. I'm asking, for example, if you ever once gave me all the ammunition I asked for."

He is a child, thought Kodama again.

Ijichi was talking about recent history. He had done his best to get the supply of ammunition increased, writing pleading letters to the General Headquarters of Ōyama and Kodama, sending telegrams, and finally dispatching Lieutenant Colonel Shirai Jirō, chief of operations, to make his case in person. Each time, Kodama had turned down the request.

"How do you expect us to fight with insufficient ammunition?"

"Lack of ammunition is a problem for the entire Japanese Army. Production can't keep up with demand. We are ordering from overseas, but it takes time. We divide what little ammunition we have between field operations and the siege here at Port Arthur, but there isn't half enough. Ijichi, Japan isn't fighting only at Port Arthur. Don't you know that?"

"I hold you responsible."

"What are you, a woman?" Kodama got up. He may have been implying that Ijichi's view of things was narrow and self-centered. "Look, you're the chief of staff. If you're trying to shirk responsibility for your own strategy, you might as well go to Stoessel and hold him responsible! Tell him, 'You're too strong. This is all your fault.'"

"What kind of nonsense is that!" Ijichi snapped. "In any case, if you intend to do something about the situation here, give us ammunition!"

"All the armies want more ammunition. It's the job of the chief of staff to do the best he can in the conditions he faces."

"I am doing the best I can."

Kodama decided that there was nothing to be gained by prolonging the discussion. He would search for Nogi and deal with him.

* * *

There was miscommunication between Nogi and Kodama.

Since Kodama had long expressed the opinion that Third Army headquarters was located too far back from the action, Nogi had wanted to conduct the day's meeting at the front, in a swirl of gunfire smoke and dust. The infantry front was dangerous, to be sure. A siege artillery emplacement would provide a strategic observation post and also pose less risk. For that reason, when he set out that morning, Nogi had left word that he would be carrying out reconnaissance at the front and would meet up with Kodama around Tuchengzi. This message, however, was somewhat unclear. No one knew exactly when Nogi would be there.

Kodama started to scold. "Don't any of you know where your commander is?" He held back the words, though. Nogi was fighting a war. It was only understandable if he couldn't predict exactly when they would be able to meet.

Although Ijichi was at Third Army headquarters, Kodama was surprised not to find Nogi there as well. This was also lucky. As Kodama's mission in Port Arthur would reflect heavily on Nogi's honor, if at all possible he wanted to meet with his friend in private.

Nogi's journal entry for this day reads, "In the morning, waited for Kodama at Tuchengzi. He didn't come." Kodama never made it to the spot because his altercation with Ijichi back at Liushufang went on too long.

"Climbed to Toyoshima." The diary indicates that from Tuchengzi Nogi climbed the hill with the siege artillery emplacement. He waited there, but noon came, and still no Kodama. He lunched at the headquarters of Major General Toyoshima Yōzō, the siege artillery commander. The underground headquarters was protected by thick walls, and of course received no sunlight. Two lamps hung from the ceiling.

"Kodama's not coming." After lunch, Nogi murmured these words.

"Won't he wait back at Liushufang?" suggested Toyoshima.

"Maybe so." Nogi smiled vaguely. In all truth, Kodama's arrival was not a happy event as far as he was concerned. "Guess I'll be getting back." He stood up.

Toyoshima got up first and opened the door. Outside, tiny snowflakes were starting to fall. "I don't like the look of that."

Nogi silently went over to his horse. He was accompanied solely by his aide-de-camp.

* * *

Nogi left the siege artillery emplacement by the Port Arthur Road. He headed north, the fortress to his back. The road was a gentle downward slope. When he reached Tuchengzi, frozen fields stretched out on either side as far as he could see, punctuated by villages and clumps of forest. Each tiny village in turn was surrounded by the bare branches of the trees.

The wind was picking up.

Nogi cut east through Tuchengzi. At the crossroads was a shrine. From there the road branched off. When he turned right, the wind hit him squarely in the face, pelting him with snow. In no time his breath froze his whiskers.

After a kilometer or so, he was near the hamlet of Caojiatun. On the outskirts was an abandoned building. It had a long earthen wall to discourage bandits, and a gun port in one corner. The redoubt was half crumbled.

When he got there, he saw in the distance two officers on horseback riding toward him. They were wearing hooded overcoats, the hoods drawn up snugly over their heads. One of the figures was distinctly unimpressive, perhaps because the rider was seated on a small Chinese horse.

That would be Kodama. Nogi was fairly sure it was, but the thick snow clouded his vision. Just to be safe, he drew his horse up by the earthen wall and waited.

Kodama came closer, spurring his horse on. "That you, Nogi?" he called through the snow. Nogi nodded briefly by the sepia-colored wall and raised his arm in salute. Kodama did not salute back, but his face crumpled into a wide grin as he came closer yet. Finally, he drew adjacent to the general, twisting his hips to maneuver alongside him, saddle to saddle.

"Nogi, your beard is white." He said this leaning over the horse's neck, the words oddly sentimental. He was struck by how emaciated his old friend looked. He had not seen him since they fought side by side in the Satsuma Rebellion. In the old days, he had teased his friend for being a "lousy fighter." When still only twenty-nine (by the old way of reckoning), Kodama had been leader of the Tokyo Garrison Corps Second Infantry Regiment in Sakura, Chiba Prefecture. At that time, Nogi was also part of the Tokyo Garrison Corps, assigned to the First Infantry Regiment. The two regiments once staged war games against each other, and Kodama had defeated his friend easily. Even after losing, Nogi had stayed in the training ground on his horse, oblivious. As Kodama looked Nogi in the face, memories of that earlier time came flooding back.

He, Kodama, was the only one who could save Nogi from this terrible predicament, he realized anew. He would take his unhappy friend and turn him into the triumphant general of Port Arthur. But unless Nogi quietly yielded command of the troops, things would get messy. In that case, Kodama would have to show Nogi the emergency decree Ōyama had written out and forcibly remove him from command.

"Nogi, I'd like to have a little chat, just the two of us. Is there somewhere we can talk?"

* * *

In the end, they decided to go to Takasaki Yama. This was the hill 3 kilometers due north of 203-Meter Hill, where in the past Russia had built an infantry camp. In a hard-fought assault on August 15, however, Takasaki's Fifteenth Infantry Regiment had taken the hill. At the time, it was nameless, but after being captured by the Takasaki regiment, it was crowned with the name of their hometown.

The village where Kodama and Nogi met was far back from the front. It was a 10-kilometer ride to Takasaki Yama, but Kodama said, "Let's go, then," and started urging his Chinese horse to move. Unlike Western horses, Chinese horses move their legs the way dogs do, trotting along with a bobbing motion. The rider, therefore, scarcely looks imposing. Kodama's head bobbled with every move his horse made.

Nogi, in contrast, cut a splendid figure on horseback. He may have read few books on military science, but he was scrupulous about his attire and had all his uniforms made to order by a British tailor in Yokohama. Ordinarily, an officer's uniform sold for fourteen or fifteen yen in the officers' club, but Nogi paid two hundred yen for his. His concept of soldiery had less to do with the study of strategy and tactics than with how a man carried himself, the distinctive spirit, style of dress, and daily demeanor he maintained. His military uniform was in a style of his liking. Unlike other officers, he wore a boxy cap that was already old-fashioned, a ribbed jacket of heavy black wool, and white trousers. Even his army boots were not standard issue, but exceptionally large ones that came up all the way to the knee. Nogi had long legs for his build, and the boots showed them off well.

Moreover, despite the murderous cold, Nogi never wore a coat. By going without a coat, he may have been making a statement about his style and spirit, but Kodama, riding alongside him, found this quirk amazing.

"Nogi, you don't wear a coat?" he asked, incredulous.

"No." Nogi smiled.

"You're a Zen monk going through hard training!" Kodama was curiously impressed, and deep down felt renewed respect and admiration for his old friend. Kodama was extremely sensitive to cold. Under his outsize coat he was wearing a vest of sea otter fur that had been a gift to Ōyama Iwao from the Chinese general Yuan Shikai.

On the occasion of Kodama's departure for Port Arthur, Ōyama had let him have the vest. "I have no gift to give you, but at least wear this when you go."

Sitting astride his horse, Kodama constantly wiped his nose. He was coming down with a cold, and his nose ran. If he wasn't careful, the snivel would freeze on his upper lip and cause a chilblain.

Along the way, they passed one Chinese peasant after another. The peasants all doubtless assumed that Nogi was a great general. Kodama, riding alongside him, they may well have taken for the general's aged attendant.

*   *   *

Takasaki Yama was the first of many rolling hills leading up to the Port Arthur fortress.

Kodama and Nogi entered a small village named Nianpangou, the last place of habitation along the way. As they passed through, Kodama called out to Nogi and asked him the meaning of the first character in the village name.

Nogi, whose knowledge of Chinese characters was profound, replied without hesitation. "It means stone mortar." Indeed, they were in a low, flat area surrounded by high ground, shaped much like a mortar. The last character in the village name meant "narrow stream." A river not much bigger than a ditch flowed off to the northwest, but its water supported life in the village.

From there, the road climbed up and up. As they went higher, they spotted heavy artillery emplacements of the Third Army scattered among various heights. Kodama saw the First Battery, followed in order by a 28-centimeter howitzer emplacement, the Second Battery, a 12-centimeter emplacement, and so on. Headquarters of the First and Seventh Divisions, which were engaged in the attack on 203-Meter Hill, were also located next to the Second Battery. They were firing from there at 203-Meter Hill, lobbing artillery shells across as many as five hills to the south. The Third Army referred to the whole area sweepingly as "Takasaki Yama."

"I wonder. . ." Kodama nudged his horse closer to Nogi's. "Isn't this a bit far away for an artillery emplacement to be firing on 203-Meter Hill?"

It wasn't as if this were a game of chess and they could jump their knights sideways, he thought. As long as they were going to launch a major attack on 203-Meter Hill, there had to be some place where the heavy artillery could demonstrate its power more directly and boldly. But Kodama merely entertained the thought as an amateur. He had no training in gunnery.

"Nogi, what do you say?" he pressed.

Nogi had no answer. He smiled wanly, as if at a loss for words. "Ijichi does a fine job," he said diplomatically, trying to cover for his chief of staff. Since Ijichi was trained in gunnery and he himself was not, Nogi had made up his mind not to interfere in his chief of staff's disposition of artillery. "He's the expert, you know."

Expert my ass, thought Kodama. When you came down to it, heavy artillery was only a mechanical device for firing shells from a muzzle. If he had to operate such a device himself, he'd have been at a loss, but even an amateur was fully capable of making the decision about where to set the artillery so its shells could do the most damage. That was tactics.

The positioning of the heavy artillery was wrong. Kodama had more faith in his own two eyes than he did in Ijichi's supposed expertise.

*   *   *

The sun was already starting to sink in the sky. They had to find shelter for the night. As Kodama rode on through the foothills of Takasaki Yama, he came on a shelter dug into the side of a hill.

"Nogi, let's you and I sleep here tonight."

The suggestion caught Nogi by surprise. He had never slept anywhere but at Liushufang, the headquarters far removed from the fighting. Although they were still far from the front line, it was indeed a battlefront since the vicinity was crowded with gun emplacements.

Kodama had always lambasted Nogi's staff for locating headquarters so far from where bullets flew. How could they possibly know what was happening at the front that way? Now he was tacitly communicating to Nogi the idea that if his military headquarters seriously wanted to wage war, they needed to relocate to a place like this. He summoned Nogi's aide-de-camp and told him to spread woven mats on the ground, and bring in various items including bedding, heaters, a desk, and a lamp.

Soon all was ready. Kodama ducked under the blanket hanging in the entryway and invited Nogi in. The space inside was around 3 meters square.

"Don't anyone come in until I call for you." Kodama did not want even the major on Nogi's staff coming in. Tanaka stood guard at the entryway, putting up a bunk there so that he could rise quickly if summoned by Kodama. Nogi's aide-de-camp followed suit.

Inside this hollow, Kodama intended to tell Nogi the most important information about leadership in the history of the Russo-Japanese War. He would tell him to relinquish command for a time, yielding his place as army commander to himself, Kodama. For Nogi Maresuke, there could be no greater dishonor or humiliation.

As Nogi's friend since childhood, Kodama was pained to be the one forcing him into this position. But for the sake of Japanese troops dying uselessly at the Port Arthur fortress, for the sake of the nation of Japan, he knew he had no other choice. His greatest fear was that Nogi would say no, as he certainly had every right to do. Army commanders, like division commanders, were personally invested by the emperor. Accordingly, no one but the emperor had power to divest them of their authority.

But as we know, in preparing for this unprecedented move Kodama had armed himself with an order from Ōyama Iwao. The secret document lay tucked in his pocket at that moment. As commander in chief of the Manchurian Army, he conceivably did have the legal power to order Nogi to step aside. However, the document did not name Ōyama himself as the one who would take command of the Third Army. Rather, Kodama would do so in Ōyama's stead.

The two men sat down across from each other at the small table.

* * *

Kodama broached the vital subject. He had long agonized over how to bring it up in the way least likely to bring dishonor and humiliation to his friend, but when the time actually came he was matter-of-fact. He put the blame on Ijichi.

"You know, looking at the way Ijichi is handling things, it seems to me he's making some major mistakes."

Unless he blamed Nogi's chief of staff, rather than Nogi himself, Nogi would suffer an intolerable loss of face.

Nogi was silent. Ordinarily, as a general should, he spoke favorably of his chief of staff—"Ijichi does a fine job"—but perhaps this time he sensed unusual determination behind Kodama's smile, for the usual phrase was not forthcoming. Indeed, the battle situation had worsened to the point where it could not be glossed over by any such perfunctory comment.

"Speaking as your friend. . ." (Kodama deliberately chose the informal word "friend") ". . .I want to tell Ijichi what I think, without reserve."

Nogi nodded.

"But if I do that, depending on how things go, he might get his back up and take offense. I wouldn't want that. If he took offense and none of my opinions got listened to, I wouldn't know why I came to Port Arthur in the first place."

Nogi nodded again. This struck him as reasonable. If Kodama spoke to Ijichi merely as Nogi's friend, with no other qualification, then as chief of staff Ijichi would be under no obligation to listen. Ijichi's direct superior was Nogi, and he would have no reason to take orders from Kodama.

"And so," continued Kodama, "I am asking you to let me have temporary power of command over the Third Army."

He had handled it perfectly. Nogi himself, listening, probably missed the momentousness of the request.

"Of course, without your written permission it can't happen. Would you write out a statement to the effect that I am acting on your behalf?" He said it with the smoothness of a con artist.

Nogi fell for the con. "All right," he agreed.

As he spoke, Kodama kept his hand in his pocket and fingered the order from Ōyama countless times, on the verge of pulling it out. But if he did that, Nogi would never live down the dishonor. To keep that from happening, Kodama took a lateral approach and managed to sweet-talk Nogi into voluntarily yielding command. By letting himself be sweet-talked, Nogi had the good fortune to avert personal catastrophe.

Nogi promptly wrote out the requested statement.

Kodama took the piece of paper in hand and held it up reverently for a moment. He next filed it in his pocket and called for a staff meeting of the Third Army.

* * *

Kodama had intended to lead a staff meeting there at Takasaki Yama, until he realized that there were too many people on hand. Not only Nogi's staff was present but also Major General Fukushima Yasumasa, sent from General Headquarters early on to be Nogi's "advisor," and Captain Kunishi Goshichi, there in the same capacity. Two representatives from Imperial Headquarters in Tokyo were present as well: Lieutenant General Samejima Shigeo and Lieutenant Colonel Tsukushi Kumashichi. All shared the same mission— to do something about Nogi's and Ijichi's stubborn refusal to take seriously the strategic importance of 203-Meter Hill. Once on the scene, however, to a man, they were so dazed by the ferocity of the fighting and so intimidated by Ijichi's diehard obstinacy that rather than delivering any stern message, all they had done was wander around and get in the way. In any case, too many people needed to attend the staff meeting. No buildings in Takasaki Yama had a room large enough to accommodate such a crowd.

"Then we'll return to headquarters at Liushufang." Kodama made the decision with alacrity, and they set off at once, getting back after nine o'clock in the evening. He was by then exhausted.

"Why not put off the meeting until tomorrow?" Major Tanaka urged, out of concern for the general's well-being, but Kodama took no notice of the suggestion. The meeting could not be postponed. At that very moment, men at the front line were dying. The knowledge weighed heavily on Kodama's mind. This was the "useless slaughter" of which Nagaoka Gaishi, vice chief of the General Staff, so often spoke. The only way to end it was for him to overhaul strategy at Port Arthur.

While Kodama was riding back to Liushufang, Lieutenant General Ōsako Naotoshi, commander of the Seventh Division, caught up with him. He was on his way to join in the meeting, riding with a lantern hanging from his saddle.

"That you, Ōsako?" Kodama called out.

"Yes, sir. So here you are." Ōsako slowed his horse.

"The Hokkaido troops are strong fighters, I hear."

Ōsako concurred, but suggested that the description might better be put in past tense: the Hokkaido troops *had been* strong fighters. When the Seventh Division from Asahikawa arrived in Port Arthur, it was composed of fifteen thousand troops. In days, their number had shrunk to a thousand.

"A thousand!" For a while, Kodama rode in silence in the dark. He had already been briefed on losses, but hearing it directly from the commander of the division brought home the monstrousness of the loss. One thousand men was roughly the size of a battalion headed by a major. It was scarcely enough men for a grizzled lieutenant general to be leading.

When they reached headquarters at Liushufang, Kodama ordered that preparations for the meeting be made and then went to Nogi's room to rest. He was worn out.

"Nogi, have you got any brandy?"

"I certainly do." Nogi smiled and produced a bottle from the floor beside his trunk. There were no glasses, so instead he got out the cap of his canteen, but by then Kodama had already raised the bottle to his mouth.

*　*　*

The staff meeting opened. For the first thirty minutes, Kodama listened to reports. He did not look at the speaker but sat off to one side, for some reason as red in the face as if he had just stepped out of a hot tub. He had just drunk brandy, but he was not a man to become inebriated on a small amount of alcohol.

What was needed wasn't meetings or reports, he thought, but orders. The orders he was about to issue signified a 180-degree change in Third Army strategy. At that stage, nothing else was required.

Finally, he cut short the reports and got to his feet. "I am issuing orders," he began, and those present showed signs of confusion. This was only natural. Kodama Gentarō might be an army general and Manchuria chief of staff, but he had no authority to issue them orders. For a mere staff officer to do so was a violation of the chain of command, an act of sabotage against military order.

All he needed to do was say, "I am here as proxy for Commander in Chief Ōyama. Here is the paper that proves it. Furthermore, I have temporarily removed General Nogi from his command. I will take his place. I have in my possession written orders to do so, as well as a written agreement from General Nogi." Everyone would have then fallen behind him, more or less. But even if Kodama's orders had some legal standing, the situation was so unusual as to constitute a virtual coup d'état. That would be the overriding impression. Better to avoid giving any such impression, he thought. Besides, if he showed them the papers his own position might be clarified, but Nogi's honor would be irreparably destroyed. Affection for Nogi made him want to avoid that outcome at all cost.

And so he said only this: "By order of Commander in Chief Ōyama, I am here to confer with General Nogi." The term he used was garden variety, nothing that carried weight in military society with its stress on law and order. But that was all Kodama said. Then he added, "I am requesting that the attack plan be revised."

That line should have been spoken by Nogi. All eyes turned to him, seated at Kodama's side. Nogi erased all expression from his face and sat as silently as if he were made of stone.

Kodama's orders were earthshaking, in that they contravened basic ideas on military strategy in the Third Army.

"First," he went on, speaking quickly, "in order to secure the occupation of 203-Meter Hill, a heavy artillery unit—the one near Huoshiling—will be relocated swiftly to Takasaki Yama, where the emplacement will be set up and Chair Hill brought under our control to prevent recovery attack by the enemy.

"Second, once 203-Meter Hill has been occupied, 28-centimeter howitzers will fire at fifteen-minute intervals for twenty-four hours to guard against enemy counterattack."

Basic artillery common sense said the above orders were quite impossible.

* * *

"That's crazy talk," thought artillery lieutenant colonel Satō Kōjirō. He wondered if Kodama had gotten heavy siege guns mixed up with the mountain guns and field guns that horses carted around.

The 28-centimeter Krupp howitzers were monster cannons. Even for the heavy artillery emplacement in rearmost Huoshiling, laying foundations had required enough concrete to make an entire building. Yet here was Kodama talking about "swiftly relocating" the heavy artillery unit, as if the howitzers were toys.

Everyone sat in silence, looking dazed.

To Kodama, this strategy was the only choice. The thing to do was gather near 203-Meter Hill all the large-caliber heavy artillery capable of blowing up the fortifications and lambast the enemy with heavy shells. The logic was so simple a child could have thought it up. To him, the real question was: why had Nogi's headquarters failed to discover this simple logic for themselves? His interpretation was that Nogi was "drowning in experts."

When Imperial Headquarters had assembled Third Army headquarters, they surrounded Nogi with authorities on artillery. Even his chief of staff, Major General Ijichi Kōsuke, had received his training in artillery. Moreover, to systematize operations, the siege guns had all been put under the command of one man: Major General Toyoshima Yōzō. One of Toyoshima's top assistants was the above-mentioned Satō Kōjirō. There were many other young authorities on artillery as well. In short, Nogi was surrounded by minds full of the latest information on the handling of large land weapons.

Nogi was content to let those minds do the work. He himself had made little or no study of modern military science, let alone of gunnery. He had no choice but to respect the opinions of his experts.

But to Kodama, letting experts dictate strategy was a recipe for trouble. At that point, Japan's experts were little more than translators of information from foreign countries. Sadly, as mere followers, they lacked the breadth of knowledge and spirit to come up with unexpected approaches. In Kodama's experience, when you asked the advice of experts, nine times out of ten they said, "It can't be done." He was painfully aware of just how narrow their vision was. Once, at headquarters he had shouted in frustration, "You people may be yesterday's experts, but you are not the experts of tomorrow!" Expert knowledge was by its nature conservative, as Kodama well knew.

The exigencies of the war demanded swift removal and concentration of the heavy artillery. Conditions never matched the experts' expectations. But if they could not relocate and concentrate the heavy artillery, the war was lost. That's what Kodama thought. Tension over the issue had become his driving force.

* * *

The silence continued.

Amid the general silence, Kodama lifted his chin and looked out the window. He too was silent. He knew very well the meaning of everyone's silence. First, they were thinking, "Kodama is violating Nogi's authority." Second, "He doesn't know the first thing about heavy artillery." Furthermore, the staff of Nogi's army headquarters was resentful of Kodama's unreasonable intrusion, sensing with the typical group mentality of bureaucrats that this constituted an invasion of their territory. Kodama's nerves were acutely sensitive to the screams that lay beneath the silence. But he was determined to prevail, knowing that there was no other way to save the Japanese nation than to take on this crowd.

Remember, before leaving headquarters at Yantai, Kodama had written his will and secreted it in the bottom of his trunk. He knew that getting hit by one of Stoessel's bullets was not the only foreseeable event that might cause his death. Depending on the circumstances, there might be an unplanned incident of some kind within military headquarters. People in military headquarters during wartime were often subject to violent emotions that could not be understood in the context of ordinary life.

"Are there any questions?"

If there were none, he intended to go into particulars of the orders. But some men did voice objections. Kodama had anticipated resistance from Ijichi or Toyoshima, but officers of their rank, major general, did not speak out rashly at such a meeting.

Artillery Major Nara Takeji and Satō, a lieutenant colonel also in the artillery, each rose and launched a fierce counterattack.

"Moving the emplacement swiftly can't be done." This was Nara's opinion.

Kodama did not believe it. In the past, when Imperial Headquarters had first proposed that the 28-centimeter howitzers then serving as fortification guns in Tokyo Bay be sent to Port Arthur, chief of staff Ijichi had replied, "With fortification guns, it takes one or two months just for the concrete in the gun platforms to dry. If you send us white elephants like that, they won't be of the slightest use. Don't bother."

Yet Tokyo had overridden those protests and sent them. Under the direction of artillery captain Yokota, installment of the gun platforms had taken a mere nine days. The howitzers that Ijichi and all the other artillery experts at Port Arthur had deemed unnecessary were presently, more than anything else, causing Stoessel to shake in his boots. Nogi's headquarters had eighteen of the monsters roaring at the enemy. Nagaoka Gaishi would later write, "Those guns must long be remembered for the great service they rendered in contributing to the fall of Port Arthur."

"This is an order!" Kodama turned to Nara and shouted. "Finish relocating the heavy artillery emplacement in twenty-four hours."

The result was that, just as Kodama ordered, within twenty-four hours the heavy artillery was redeployed by 203-Meter Hill.

* * *

Next, concerning the second part of Kodama's order, Lieutenant Colonel Satō Kōjirō raised an objection. "Sir, you said that after the infantry occupies 203-Meter Hill, the 28-centimeter howitzers are to provide covering fire at fifteen-minute intervals over a twenty-four-hour period in order to cement the occupation."

"Correct." Kodama looked directly at Satō.

"Then our forces will be at risk of friendly fire. There's a high probability that we'll kill our own troops."

This was the argument of a professional. Providing covering fire is difficult because it involves shooting just over the heads of friendly troops and pulverizing only the enemy. But in a narrow space like the top of 203-Meter Hill, where the line between friend and foe crisscrosses, providing covering fire is impossible. The risk of blowing up friend and foe indiscriminately is too great. Satō wanted to make the basic point that in such a case, covering fire is not an option.

"Take care of it somehow," Kodama said mildly.

Satō was not satisfied. "I cannot use His Majesty's weapons to fire on His Majesty's subjects."

Tears sprang to Kodama's eyes. Tanaka Kunishige never forgot the sight as long as he lived. Emotions that Kodama had been holding tightly in check finally spilled over.

"Whose slipshod strategy has caused His Majesty's subjects to die in vain until now? The reason I want a change of strategy is to prevent any more soldiers from dying useless deaths. It's true that covering fire kills friend and foe indiscriminately. But compared to the hell that would unfold without this change in strategy, the loss of life will be far less. Already the infantry has charged the hill and taken it a number of times. Each time, they were

CLOUDS ABOVE THE HILL 49

counterattacked and killed. We have to prevent counterattack. The only way to do that is to provide covering fire with mammoth guns. The hidebound thinking that says covering fire is dangerous so we shouldn't do it has already cost the lives of countless soldiers."

General Nogi said nothing.

"According to what we just heard," Kodama went on, "fewer than a hundred soldiers on the southwest flank of 203-Meter Hill have been sticking it out since last night. They have no reinforcements, no covering fire, but up there in the cold winds they are fighting to the last man. Has anyone here seen this?"

Kodama looked around the room. Amazingly, no one from headquarters, neither the army commander nor any of his aides, had gone to witness the spectacle.

"These heroic fighters face imminent death. Why make no attempt to save them or to widen the occupied territory on the hill?"

Kodama's anger started to boil over again. He had heard before that the commanders at the front line did not trust military headquarters.

"How is it that the staff officers have never once been to the front?"

For Nogi, this was a headache. Yet his expression was unwavering as he sat beside Kodama.

"From what I hear," said Kodama, "this headquarters is under the impression that it would be disadvantageous to leave Liushufang."

From the beginning of the siege, Ijichi had adopted that policy. Some of the young staff officers expressed a desire to do reconnaissance at the front lines of battle, but Ijichi forbade it on the curious grounds that "staff headquarters has its own work to do. Seeing the wretched fighting at the front would only disrupt strategy." Nogi was dragged along by this and had never yet been to the front line where the infantry's attack trenches were. This was a main reason for the constant gap with reality that arose between the strategy and orders issued by Nogi's headquarters.

Kodama scathingly pointed this out and declared with finality, "A staff headquarters that doesn't know what's going on at the front is of no use." Next he called out the name, "Ōba," summoning the lieutenant colonel.

Ōba kicked over his chair as he got to his feet.

"Take two or three men with you and go to the front now. Find out exactly what is going on. Tomorrow I will go and hear your report." A pause. "What are you waiting for? Get on your way."

They left the room and soon returned in full uniform. There were three of them. Ōba saluted and said, "Leaving to inspect conditions at the front, sir."

Nogi got up, went over to the men and shook hands with each of them. They were putting their lives at extreme risk. "Be very careful," he told them kindly.

According to Tanaka's observation, Kodama remained seated and never even looked at the party. What need was there to show concern for staff officers going to the front since until then they had stayed away, only sending untold soldiers there to die? That must have been what he thought.

After they left, Kodama was tired. He had a bed made up in Nogi's room and crawled under a blanket without undressing. A stove was lit in the room, but it was strangely cold.

Nogi suffered from insomnia during this time. Kodama went right to sleep.

*   *   *

When Kodama woke the next morning around six, Nogi's bed alongside his was already empty. Wondering where the general had gone, Kodama called out to someone in the hallway and asked where Nogi was. He found that Nogi had already set out for Takasaki Yama an hour before, apparently to encourage the work of relocating the heavy artillery command.

"So he has finally gone into action." Kodama was amused.

Kodama knew very well what a difficult job it was to redeploy heavy artillery. Besides the gunners, the engineer corps would also have to turn out in full force. The standby reserve infantry would also be called on, probably to do the bulk of the towing. With ten thousand men pulling on tow ropes, there was nothing, however heavy, that couldn't be moved. Nogi had doubtless gone to cheer on the troops doing the towing. Kodama was optimistic about the redeployment.

After a quick breakfast, Kodama called for Tanaka, who hurried to the doorway.

"Let's be off."

"Yes, sir. The horses are ready."

When Kodama went outside, he found Major General Fukushima Yasumasa, the General Headquarters emissary, waiting there for him. They left Liushufang together.

"Fukushima, tell me something. Wouldn't Shuishiying be a better place for army headquarters than this?" The village of Shuishiying was far closer to enemy territory.

"That suggestion had better not come from you, sir. I will present it to General Nogi as my own opinion, first chance I have." Fukushima was concerned that if Kodama kept interfering in details, Nogi's headquarters might get agitated. Kodama understood this point very well.

Fukushima was from Matsumoto in Shinano. At the beginning of Meiji, he had left home for Tokyo, going virtually without food and drink to study. He received assistance from Minister of Justice Etō Shimpei and wished primarily to be a scholar. Chance landed him in the Army Ministry, but he never received any military training. He used his linguistic ability in the Army Ministry and was made an officer as an exceptional case. Thereafter, he was promoted in the normal way and reached the rank of major general.

Fukushima had a phenomenal memory. He was familiar with ten languages and fluent in seven. When he was a major, he served as military attaché to the Japanese embassy in Germany, and after his tour of duty left Berlin on horseback, riding through the Russian capital and crossing the Urals and all of Siberia, then entering Mongolia, passing through Manchuria and finally arriving in Vladivostok, a feat that won him world fame.

When the Russo-Japanese War began, he joined the staff of General Headquarters. His job was battlefield espionage. Under him, military spies, Japanese "China adventurers," local secret agents, and bandits worked together at everything from intelligence gathering to fomenting disturbances behind the front lines in a spy network of unparalleled size in Japanese history. Due to his success in this area, Fukushima was later made an army general. He was a singular general, one who never, apart for a brief interval during the Boxer Rebellion, led any troops.

* * *

Kodama set off for the front. It was December 3. Every fortification on 203-Meter Hill was silent. Every Japanese soldier had put away his weapon, and the guns were no longer spitting fire.

A ceasefire was in effect. The purpose of the ceasefire was the recovery of the dead. During the siege, fighting was often called off for this purpose. The practice had become customary. For the Japanese Army, which suffered overwhelmingly greater losses than the Russian Army, the ceasefire was indeed used to recover the dead, but for the Russians it also meant a chance to repair their fortifications. They were always happy when Japan proposed a truce.

The benefit for the Japanese Army was different. Japanese offensive trenches crisscrossed halfway up the slope of 203-Meter Hill, but they were always lined with bodies of fallen soldiers. More and more bodies would pile up until the trenches lost their function. Live soldiers gamely trampled the corpses of their fallen comrades, but the piled-up corpses often bulged over the top, forcing the living to expose themselves to the enemy. During a ceasefire, the trenches could be cleared and so recover their function. This was the use that Nogi's army always made of the ceasefires. In contrast, the

Russians, having repaired their fortifications in the interim, always returned from the ceasefire with fresh force. The difference in use of ceasefires between the two sides scarcely bears discussion.

"What an idiotic waste of time." Kodama had been angry about the practice since he came to General Headquarters in Yantai. But when he arrived at the battleground on December 1, Nogi's army had proposed a ceasefire to the Russians. The Russians approved, and from that day the two sides had embarked on a four-day truce.

For once Kodama was glad. This was just the breathing space he needed to come up with a change of plan. Concerning the new heavy artillery emplacement, he gave orders that it be ready in twenty-four hours. This left the artillery commander in Nogi's headquarters speechless. Kodama reasoned that the camp had to be set up during this lull in the fighting, since under a hail of bullets the operation would be impossible.

That was why 203-Meter Hill was still when Kodama arrived at Seventh Division headquarters on Takasaki Yama. And yet Port Arthur itself was never perfectly still. The fortifications on the north and east sides of the great fortress were still active, pounding out thunder without rest.

Division commander Ōsako, huddled in a trench, seemed to look up at Kodama in supplication. "Sir, please let my men attack once more." He seemed exhausted, unable to control his emotion. The old officer's voice filled with tears. His division was down to barely a thousand men.

Kodama gave his consent. He had already planned to include the decimated Seventh Division in his new attack plan. Otherwise, the Seventh Division would go down in history as having come to Port Arthur only to be massacred.

*   *   *

At Seventh Division headquarters, Kodama set about learning in as much detail as he could about the ongoing battle. The night before, he had ordered his aide to have the staff office of the Seventh Division draw him a map of the attack front. That map was ready.

Kodama took out his magnifying glass and studied the map. The sheet of paper was inscribed with innumerable military symbols, crammed in higgledy-piggledy. Various units must have been mingled on the field due to the severity of the fighting. Kodama stared intently at the map, absorbing the meaning of each symbol, and then he saw that the same company was on the eastern flank and the western flank simultaneously.

What could it mean? He was stumped. Finally, he realized that the division staff officer had made a mistake. Or rather, the map proved that the staff lacked any personal knowledge of the front. Clearly, all they did was assemble various reports from the front and work out strategy based only on that information. At both military headquarters and division headquarters, this was the principal cause of the string of defeats they were suffering. Kodama had made the point time and again.

These people were murderers. The thought made him do something bizarre. He sprang at the major standing on the other side of the map, reached for his shiny gold military sash, and tore it from the man's chest with all his might.

"Where are your eyes?" he bellowed. The next words he spoke were long remembered. "Your country sent you to university to learn. You weren't sent there to learn for your own glory."

The major stood transfixed, his face pale. He had no idea why Kodama was enraged.

"Look here!" Kodama tapped a point on the map. The major peered at it and then looked up with dawning understanding. Yet he showed no sign of contrition at the poor quality of the map. He controlled his own facial expression, the better to gauge the extent of Kodama's wrath. This bureaucratic psychology of self-defense was ingrained in Japanese staff officers.

"But that's what the reports said." Humiliation at having had his sash ripped off made the major slightly defiant.

"Didn't you go to see for yourself?" Kodama yelled, so the other officers would hear too. None of them found the treatment being meted out amusing in the least. What need was there for any of them to go to the advance line of attack? Kodama quickly sensed the unspoken question and responded. "To get a handle on conditions, you go straight into the enemy stronghold if you have to. Give a thought to the people who die needless deaths because of an empty battle plan conceived at a desk."

Kodama grabbed his hat and left the room. He intended to go to the front.

* * *

It was December 5. The newly redeployed siege guns began firing at daybreak. Simultaneously, the fortifications on 203-Meter Hill crackled with gunfire, and behind, to the east, the batteries on Chair Hill sent shells over the top of 203-Meter Hill, raining down on Japanese infantry trenches and blasting dirt and sand, weapons, human beings, and sometimes old corpses sky-high. Japan's mammoth siege guns at the new camp were no longer silent when this happened. In retaliation, they replied with a storm of shells aimed at the concrete fortifications on Chair Hill.

Shells from the enemy's distant fortifications rumbled like far-off thunder as they came. Those on the ground could count the seconds before they fell.

The Japanese heavy artillery was closer to its targets, and so each time one of the big guns fired, a short, angry report was followed by an immediate explosion in enemy territory, the two sounds almost overlapping. The sounds produced a striking surge in morale among Japanese infantry charging up the hillside.

Just then, Kodama was climbing a hill near 203-Meter Hill. Shells from Chair Hill fell all around. He charged up the slope like an infantry private first class. Following behind him was a crowd of staff officers in decorated uniforms, some from Third Army headquarters, others from division headquarters. The commanders of the First and Seventh Divisions were both there along with their aides-de-camp. Never before had so many top strategists from Nogi's headquarters come out together under a hail of gunfire.

Major Tanaka Kunishige walked protectively alongside Kodama over the dun soil. Behind them shell fragments littered the ground. Major General Fukushima Yasumasa walked with his arm around the diminutive Kodama. Fukushima, the one who had ridden horseback clear across Siberia, had a saying: "I am like the air." The meaning isn't quite clear. If he himself became like the air, then he could cross Siberia or walk calmly through a storm of bullets. That might be what he meant.

When Kodama reached the top of the hill, he threw himself flat, trained his binoculars on the ridge line, and took a close look at the top of 203-Meter Hill. He could see both the dead and those who were living and moving. The sight of the soldiers grimly defending the peak, less than a hundred of them, moved him deeply. Though abandoned by their senior command, they fought on without complaint in a life-or-death contest.

"Anybody who could look at that and not have his heart stirred isn't human," Kodama commented to Fukushima beside him. A staff officer whose heart was stirred should have his brain stirred too. Some way to cope with the situation ought to spring naturally to mind. It wasn't a matter of intelligence, Kodama thought, but of heart.

These thoughts lay behind his famous outburst, which took place the next moment. The division commanders and staff officers who had followed him up were idle, as if they had been forced to make the climb out of duty.

"Nobody feels any responsibility!" thought Kodama. If they did, there ought to be some action they could take on the spot. They showed as little sense of responsibility as a party of sightseers.

* * *

"Tanaka, what in God's name are you waiting for!" Kodama looked back at Major Tanaka and yelled. Shells whizzed overhead. "Are you a fool?"

Tanaka was surprised to find himself the new target of Kodama's wrath.

"You're slated to be division commander and army commander someday! When you see friendly troops engaged in bitter combat like this, you've got to get a move on, issue an appropriate command. What are you doing just watching? Are you a foreign observer?"

Tanaka raised his chest off the ground. "No, sir." But as he was in point of fact neither a division commander nor an army commander, he lacked authority to give orders, and to do so would have been inappropriate. He hesitated before realizing that in scolding him, Kodama was indirectly scolding Nogi and the two division commanders, who were also there observing the fighting. He turned and looked at Nogi, but quickly looked away again in pity. The two division commanders at Nogi's side were in a daze.

It was hopeless, Tanaka thought. Kodama insisted they do something, issue a command, but what *could* they do from there, looking at the scene through binoculars? A general and a lieutenant general couldn't just leap into the fray, take over an infantry platoon or squad, and lead a charge against the enemy.

A second later, Kodama, his outburst apparently forgotten, called to the siege artillery commander. "Toyoshima! Are the 28-centimeter howitzer guns all ready?"

"In another twenty minutes they will be, sir."

"Use the howitzers to fire across the top of 203-Meter Hill at the fleet in Port Arthur Harbor."

The recklessness of this command left Toyoshima flabbergasted and indignant. From his perspective as an artillery officer, the idea of doing such a thing was impossibly rash. He did not reply.

Kodama trained his binoculars on the peak of 203-Meter Hill, where the redeployed heavy artillery was having a tremendous effect.

All along, Japanese soldiers attempting to take 203-Meter Hill had suffered repeated annihilation less from enemy gunfire on the hill itself than from artillery fired from batteries on the surrounding hills. The Japanese Army had learned to respect the Russian's well-constructed ring of fire by throwing into it the lives of countless soldiers. The point of Kodama's artillery strategy had been to silence the deadly batteries circling 203-Meter Hill.

At last, the batteries at Yashizui that had rained such mayhem on Japanese infantry were silent. Only those on North Taiyanggou were still viable. They too, however, were steadily weakening under the nonstop onslaught from Japanese heavy artillery.

*   *   *

The infantry's charge up 203-Meter Hill had begun earlier that day, at nine o'clock in the morning. It was carried out by two columns, one on the right and one on the left. The column under the direction of Major General Saitō Tarō headed for the southwest flank of the hill, the one commanded by Major General Yoshida Seiichi for the northeast.

Kodama's use of the artillery to support this charge was substantial and appropriate. The infantry was able to advance under cover of friendly fire. The 28-inch howitzer guns alone fired 2,300 heavy rounds, each round weighing in at 218 kilograms.

Saitō sent thirty-man death squads charging up the hill, one after another. Survivors who managed to reach the southwest corner built defensive works while engaging desperately with the enemy. At short intervals, thirty new men climbed up and did the same thing, over and over again.

Nogi's diary entry for that day reads, "Bombarded 203 since early morning. Saitō's division advanced starting at nine. Goal achieved."

The terse phrase "goal achieved" is an apt description for a mission that was briskly carried out. The attack began at nine o'clock in the morning, and at twenty past ten the southwest corner of 203-Meter Hill was completely occupied by Japanese forces. It took only eighty minutes.

Around that same time, the Russian Army located northeast was still putting up a spirited defense. Yoshida's column went on the attack at half past one in the afternoon. The first unit to succeed there at a climbing attack was the First Company of the Twenty-eighth Infantry Regiment. They charged with bayonets aloft and succeeded in taking the corner. From start to end, the fighting lasted a mere half hour. The success was so extraordinary that it seemed magical, unbelievable.

Kodama kept a steady watch on the progress of the fighting. At two o'clock in the afternoon, when possession of 203-Meter Hill was a virtual certainty, he spoke by phone to an officer on top of the hill.

"Can you see Port Arthur Harbor from there?"

This was the point that had long been debated.

Early on, Admiral Tōgō's blockading fleet had looked on the lay of the land from the ocean and insisted that it would be possible to see the harbor from 203-Meter Hill. By capturing the hill and establishing a hilltop observation post, the army could fire heavy artillery at the Port Arthur Squadron from land and so sink it. Nogi's headquarters had always refused to give ear to this plan. Kodama paid attention. By redeploying the heavy artillery, he made infantry attacks much easier, and in amazingly short order 203-Meter Hill fell.

The voice from the hilltop sounded in his ear. "I see it. I have a bird's-eye view that takes in every ship in the squadron."

Kodama hung up the phone. His strategy had succeeded. All that remained was to fire over the hills at the Russian ships.

* * *

When Kodama ordered that the 28-centimeter howitzers be used to fire on the Russian ships in Port Arthur Harbor, by going over 203-Meter Hill, Toyoshima told himself that he had to protest in every way he could. This was the last bit of resistance shown to Kodama from Nogi's headquarters.

Major General Toyoshima had been led around by Kodama like a bull with a ring in its nose. This had happened again at ten that morning. When one of Major General Saitō's death squads charged the southwest flank of 203-Meter Hill, Kodama had ordered Toyoshima to have an observation team climb up that side at once. At the time, Russian troops were still putting up strong resistance on the northeast flank.

The idea of a battle in which an artillery observer went along after an infantry charge, climbing the hill with a telephone wire in tow, defied common sense. It was risky, and Toyoshima was concerned about sending the artillery observer to his death. But Kodama wouldn't listen.

The observation post was set up.

"Can you see Port Arthur Harbor from there?" That famous line of Kodama's was spoken over the telephone to the observer at the top of the southwest flank.

Once Kodama heard that the Russian ships could be seen clearly from the top of the hill, he resolved to start firing on the Russian ships. The artillery team could adjust its sights appropriately as directed by observers on high.

That was the order he gave Major General Toyoshima, commander of siege artillery in the Third Army. Long aware of Kodama's intention to do just this, Toyoshima promptly voiced his objection. "That is impossible, sir."

"Reason!" Kodama barked. State your reason, he meant.

The reasons were apparent to any student of artillery. First, a 28-centimeter howitzer, however gigantic, fired not armor-piercing shells but high-explosive shells, which were incapable of penetrating a battleship.

Second, once a battleship was hit, it would return fire. The observation post on 203-Meter Hill would quickly be blown to bits. Then the hilltop emplacement would be destroyed and undoubtedly the infantry advancing toward the foot of the hill would also come under attack. Between small-caliber army guns and large-caliber navy guns, it was clear which would come out on top.

These were the problems Toyoshima described.

"The fellow's a bit thick"—thinking this, Kodama stared at Toyoshima's mustache in fascination, watching it jerk as he spoke.

As far as Kodama was concerned, Port Arthur had come under siege basically because the navy had requested it. Unable to lure the Russian Port Arthur Squadron from the harbor out onto open sea, the navy had turned to the army and asked that the fortress be captured by land. That was why Nogi's Third Army was having to fight this long-drawn-out battle. The purpose of the siege, however, remained clear-cut. All they had to do was sink the ships in the harbor. Once that was done, Tōgō's fleet would be freed from blockading the harbor and could return to Sasebo Harbor for repairs in advance of the Baltic Fleet's arrival.

"This severe battle has gone on too long. It's turned Toyoshima's brain to mush." As this thought went through Kodama's mind, his expression remained dour.

*   *   *

Kodama listened with an unchanging expression as Major General Toyoshima stated his reasons for opposition. Then he countered, "So what do you propose?"

Toyoshima, a gunnery expert, had a ready answer. His answer was superb.

"To lower the risk of damage from return fire, we need to gradually put steel plates around all the heavy artillery, beginning with the 28-centimeter howitzers, and construct protective covers."

"What do you mean, 'gradually'?"

"Sir, I must have three days' leeway to prepare the steel plates and construct the covers."

"Toyoshima." Kodama was trying to placate him. "You're tired. Do that after the war is over. Right now we're in the middle of a war." Kodama said this in a low voice, but the impulse to jump up and yell proved overpowering. "I gave you an order!"

Kodama had no authority to give orders. Only Nogi, the commander of the Third Army, had that authority. The words were on the tip of Toyoshima's tongue, but he did not have courage to say them.

"An order!" Kodama yelled again, cutting him off. Reluctantly, Toyoshima straightened up. "Siege artillery commanders are to use the 28-centimeter howitzers to fire on the fleet in the harbor at once and sink every last ship."

Still doubtful that such a thing was possible, Toyoshima went to the telephone installed in the covered trench and gave the order to all posts. Ten minutes later, the booming sound of 28-centimeter howitzers began to reverberate. The din was so great that it seemed cracks would form in the earth.

The accuracy rate of the howitzers was, it can fairly be said, one hundred percent. Of the ships sitting in the harbor, first the battleship *Poltava* (10,960 tons) was hit, the shell penetrating its deck and blowing up its magazine, causing a fire that led to its sinking. Next the *Retvizan* (12,902 tons), a battleship of the Port Arthur Squadron, took eight direct hits, one after another. Admiral Viren, who was aboard, was seriously wounded.

The bombardment continued methodically for several days. Eventually, apart from the battleship *Sevastopol* and a few smaller ships, every ship in the squadron—four battleships, two cruisers, and a dozen more—was sunk or severely damaged. The harbor shipyard was also blown up so the ships could never be repaired. The town was destroyed.

*   *   *

Kodama had succeeded.

By drastically repositioning the artillery emplacement, he had facilitated the infantry charge so that the southwest corner of 203-Meter Hill, which had claimed the lives of 6,200 Japanese soldiers, was captured in one hour and twenty minutes, and the northeast corner in barely thirty minutes. The date was December 5, 1904.

Nogi's journal entry for the following day reads, "Fair weather. In the afternoon climbed 203. Shook hands with Watanabe and Murakami, the two regiment commanders, also the observation officer and the rest. On the way back, called on Major General Saitō. The enemy has withdrawn from Flat Hill and points east."

Just as the entry indicates, on the afternoon of December 6, Nogi stepped for the first time on the soil at the foot of 203-Meter Hill and climbed its slope. He did it to express his appreciation to the officers and men of the Third Army. He was accompanied by a large retinue of staff.

But at that time Kodama was in Seventh Division headquarters on Takasaki Yama. Absurdly, he never climbed the hill that he had taken. He told Nogi he had a stomachache. From Kodama's point of view, inspection of newly occupied land was the equivalent of a victory parade. It should be done by the army commander. If he and his staff accompanied Nogi on his climb up 203-Meter Hill, Nogi would lose prestige.

Only Nogi and his staff knew that Kodama had temporarily taken command away from Nogi by order of Ōyama Iwao. In Tokyo, only Yamagata Aritomo, chief of the General Staff, and Nagaoka Gaishi, his vice chief, knew. The fact must not be leaked. All credit for the victory must go to Baron Nogi Maresuke, commander of the Third Army. Otherwise, Kodama's action would remain as a fearsome precedent to threaten the army chain of command thereafter. Kodama understood this perfectly.

That was why Kodama excused himself from the inspection tour of 203-Meter Hill that day. Basically, once the hill had fallen, he had no further use for it.

Besides the stomachache, Kodama told Nogi, he had a toothache. That much was indeed true. Because Kodama feigned illness to remain on Takasaki Yama that day, military physician Ochiai Taizō was duty-bound to stay with him and keep him company. Kodama quizzed Ochiai at length on why the medical service of the Japanese Army included no dentists. "Most of the high command are old men, and as fighting in the field goes on for extended periods, their false teeth wear out. Everybody has a hard time. Stomachaches I can stand, but this toothache is unbearable. Can you do something?" He was half serious.

Flustered, Ochiai told him that not even the German Army had dentists. Kodama was strangely impressed by this bit of information. Didn't Germans get toothaches? he wondered.

* * *

The fall of 203-Meter Hill had a great impact on the Russian defense system. Strongholds from which the Russians had inflicted massive death and injury on Japanese troops lost topographical importance—I'm referring to places like the fort at Flat Hill, formerly a strategic point in direct liaison with 203-Meter Hill. On the sixth, the garrison there withdrew without a fight. Naturally, Japanese troops took over.

At the same time, a cluster of Russian batteries in the hills north of Siergou were abandoned. The Japanese sent spies to check them out and found no trace of the Russian military. At two o'clock in the afternoon of the sixth, Japanese troops entered the area and took possession.

Hence, Nogi's journal entry for December 6: "The enemy has withdrawn from Flat Hill and points east."

On the evening of the sixth, Kodama left Takasaki Yama and climbed 203-Meter Hill, accompanied as always by Major Tanaka Kunishige. When they reached the summit and looked east, they could see just how amazing the hill's position was. A panoramic view of the harbor spread at their feet.

The hills and streets below were white with snow. Slightly to their left rose Baiyushan, and straight ahead was the highest mountain in sight, Golden Hill, with a long skirt like that of a volcano. Framed between those hills was the bright blue of the harbor, and huddled in the eastern corner of the harbor were the ships of the Port Arthur Squadron. From every ship rose black smoke caused by the howitzer shells flying over Kodama's head without cease. Not one ship had returned fire. Under the unremitting onslaught of shells from every type of heavy artillery in the Japanese arsenal, retaliation was out of the question.

"Strange how afraid Toyoshima was of return fire from naval guns," Kodama murmured to Tanaka as they watched. "He knows too much. That's why. I don't know anything. I just figured if we kept firing so hard the enemy had no time to shoot, that ought to do it."

"So we won by a fluke, sir?" Tanaka asked teasingly.

Kodama snorted in amusement. He denied having won by a fluke. "More like sheer determination. War is the business of capturing subtleties that change by the second, shaping events your way. You don't do that by knowledge but by spirit."

Kodama was not a good climber and fell twice on the way down. Once, he tumbled into a huge shell crater. The smell of smoke lingered inside it. Tanaka grabbed him by the arm and pulled him up.

When Kodama mounted his horse at the foot of the hill, he gave Tanaka an order. "Telephone Yantai tomorrow and ask about the enemy's situation up north." He was desperately concerned about increased enemy activity in the north. With Japan's future at stake, where he really belonged was not there in Port Arthur but on the northern front.

* * *

The fall of 203-Meter Hill proved fatal to the Port Arthur fortress, which had been such a torment to the Japanese Army. Soon after the hill was taken, heavy artillery began to rain shells from on high across the harbor and town.

Kodama had succeeded. Numerous forts remained in the Port Arthur fortress, but with Japanese gunners freely training their sights on the inner nerve center, the fortress as a whole was bound to weaken quickly.

Kodama judged that what was left was basically a mop-up operation. This was a job that Nogi's Third Army could be safely trusted with, and actually it was their duty. Looking back, it seemed clear that once the navy had discovered from the sea that 203-Meter Hill was the weak point in the Russian harbor defense, Nogi's headquarters should have meekly acquiesced and carried out the navy's plan—a plan supported by the Army General Staff Office in Tokyo. If Nogi's headquarters had done this, the staggering total of over sixty thousand dead and wounded Japanese soldiers could have been prevented. But if Kodama hadn't taken the emergency measure of taking over Nogi's post when he did, that number would certainly have been inflated even more.

"My job is done." Kodama made this remark to Major Tanaka on December 5, when the first shell from a 28-centimeter howitzer gun was fired from the summit and scored a direct hit on a battleship in the harbor. Over the next two days, Kodama continued to direct the operation. After breakfast on the seventh, Nogi left the front at Takasaki Yama, but Kodama stayed on.

Nogi's journal entry for that day reports, "Dec. 7, fog." The morning mist was so heavy that the surrounding hills were obliterated. Only the report of gunfire echoed near and far. Sometimes the ground shook, as giant shells from surviving Russian strongholds flew through the air and burst on impact.

"After breakfast," General Nogi's journal continues, "returned from Takasaki Yama to Liushufang. Pound cake, tea, and tilefish arrived from Lieutenant General Ōshima. Sent back apples."

Nogi was back in his headquarters at Liushufang, beyond the reach of enemy fire. Though exhausted from continuous days at the front, he made no attempt to rest but went straight to his work desk.

In the evening, Kodama returned to Liushufang. Nogi recognized him by his voice at the gate. He seemed to be calling loudly to the telegraphist, who had climbed a tree. Nogi got up and went outside to greet Kodama, whose face and beard were yellow with sand. As Nogi was searching for the words to express his gratitude, Kodama spoke first. "I'm really hungry." He tapped Nogi's right arm as if to say, feed me.

Nogi's journal notes, "In the evening, General Kodama returned."

*　*　*

Continuing with Nogi's journal entry for the seventh, the notation "Called p.m." means that in the evening, Nogi visited Kodama's room. (A room for Kodama had been set aside in the rear of Nogi's military headquarters at Liushufang.) When Kodama had returned from the front, he had suggested to Nogi that they get together for a poetry gathering that night. Impressed by Kodama's high level of energy, Nogi agreed and went to visit him that evening.

Although the crackle of gunfire may have been ongoing, for Kodama, the battle had passed its turning point. The task of the strategists had ended. Once general policy instructions had been given out, matters could be left in the hands of the various commanders for the rest of it. Kodama had to return to his post in Yantai, but on the occasion of his parting from Nogi he wanted to take time to enjoy an evening of poetry together with his friend.

At the same time, he pitied Nogi. He felt bad about the effect on his friend of what he had done. By causing Nogi to lose face, he had prevented the slaughter of many Japanese troops and changed the course of the fighting. After suffering repeated defeats, the Third Army was at last on track to win the victory. All that remained was the question of Nogi's honor.

Kodama planned to spread the word in Japan and abroad that Nogi had captured Port Arthur. That he, Kodama, was actually responsible for the fall of Port Arthur would remain secret forever. To that end, he had never divulged the real purpose of his mission in Port Arthur to the foreign or domestic reporters, calling it a simple courtesy call. Moreover, he pressed the point to the Third Army staff office. "My interference in this case is a bit of a problem in terms of the high command. This must not become a precedent, so even after the war I would like it kept quiet."

All credit for the successful attack on Port Arthur was to go to Nogi, a point that Kodama intended to make directly to Field Marshal Yamagata Aritomo.

Kodama was demonstrating meticulous concern for Nogi, his friend since his youth. However, he was unable to imagine that after the war Nogi, like the navy's Tōgō, would be hailed as a hero and the savior of his country. Nor did he ever see Nogi emerge as a heroic figure. That's because he passed away the year after this battle. Of course, given Kodama's character, there is no reason to suppose that he would have particularly minded even if he had seen how Nogi was idealized by the public.

That evening, his suggestion to Nogi that the two of them get together for a poetry party had a dual purpose. Besides Kodama's own enjoyment, he had in mind Nogi's welfare as well. Nogi had suffered a strategic defeat. But as a poet, he was vastly superior to Kodama. It is possible that Kodama chose to hold a poetry party in order to encourage Nogi the poet. The bonds of friendship between these two men of Chōshū were stronger than anyone in later ages can imagine.

*   *   *

Nogi's journal for the seventh continues, "Shiga was there." He notes laconically, "Discussed poetry." By "Shiga was there" he meant that when he opened the door to Kodama's room, Shiga was inside. He was referring to Shiga Shigetaka, about whom some explanation is in order.

The Japanese Army in Meiji times started off by imitating Western armies. Western armies (and navies as well) would often take along a noted man of letters when heading into a major battle. That was one reason why Shiga Shigetaka was sent to Nogi's headquarters as an observer accorded the special treatment of a *chokunin*, an imperial appointee. The system is difficult to explain, but *chokunin* officials included ministry vice ministers and prefectural governors. Those receiving comparable treatment included teachers at universities, colleges, and high schools.

But whatever Western countries might do, it was not the style of the Meiji government to make novelists and the like into *chokunin* officials and send them off to observe the conduct of the war. Instead, candidates were selected from the ranks of those who wrote, in the parlance of the day, "hard" literature, that is, nonfiction. Moreover, no one could be chosen who lacked an appropriate title. Though a journalist, Shiga had served for a time as head of the Bureau of Forestry in the Ministry of Agriculture and Commerce and as chokunin counselor in the Foreign Ministry. His impressive experience won approval, and so he was chosen as one of the observers of the war. Still, both as a writer and as a man of keen insight, he was undoubtedly one of the most exceptional Japanese of those times.

Shiga Shigetaka was born in 1863 in Okazaki in Mikawa Province and graduated from Sapporo Agricultural College, the precursor of Hokkaido University. He was particularly interested in geography. In 1886, he went along on the graduation cruise of the Imperial Japanese Naval Academy, visiting South Pacific islands in the training ship *Tsukuba*. His observations of the Western powers' colonial management of the islands formed the basis of his later study of geography from the perspective of statecraft. In the book he wrote at this time, *Conditions in the South Seas*, he argued that the state needed to strengthen production, thereby shocking the political world and the press, which were then absorbed in frivolous political squabbles. He never altered his opinion from then through his late years, when he became an honorary member of Britain's Royal Geographical Society. His journalism was published in *Nihonjin—The Japanese*—the journal he founded, as well as in the newspapers *Nippon* (where Kuga Katsunan and Masaoka Shiki worked), *Tokyo Asahi Shimbun*, and others. He was an iconic figure of the rising nation in Meiji times.

Shiga was assigned to Nogi's headquarters also because of his ability to write English. He could write a call to surrender vis-à-vis the Russian Army or serve as interpreter should Stoessel capitulate. Moreover, as the Japanese Army was extremely concerned about following wartime international law to the letter, they intended to forestall any errors in that department by assigning the knowledgeable Shiga to Nogi.

Shiga was at that point forty-two years old. He wore an old frock coat he had had made in London. Kodama invited him to Nogi's poetry gathering so that he could serve as commentator. Shiga also had a certain reputation as a composer of poetry in classical Chinese.

A long string hung down from the ceiling, with a light at the end. Kodama sat beneath that light, writing in a small notebook.

"What's this, your draft?" Nogi smiled, making as if to peer into the notebook.

"Don't look!" Kodama acted strangely shy, pushing the notebook out of the light. Shiga laughed out loud, and even Major Tanaka, seated behind Kodama, chuckled.

"What's so funny, Tanaka?" Kodama twisted his mouth into a frown, as was his habit. There came the crackle of distant gunfire. "My poem isn't finished yet." "You first, Nogi."

"Mine's just a rough draft too." Nogi took a notebook out of his pocket.

Tanaka brought over an inkstone and paper, and in a beautiful hand Nogi wrote out his composition.

> Just death and no life, but why be sad?
> Who will see them in a thousand years, war memorials?
> Among the emperor's hundred thousand who is bravest?
> Impress the age and gain a name—now is the time.

This poem Nogi composed on horseback while returning to Liushufang from Takasaki Yama.

Kodama was sincerely impressed. "This is great! Your poem that starts out 'Hills, rivers, grasses, trees' is full of pathos, but this one is spirited and stirring, as befits an army commander!" He studied the rows of Chinese characters, working out their meaning in Japanese.

To paraphrase, the poem means, "Here on the battlefield there is only death, no life. But that is nothing to feel sad about. Life is short anyway. Intangible monuments to war alone withstand the passage of a thousand years. The emperor's hundred thousand are heroes one and all, and now is the time for them to do great deeds to amaze the world."

"And yet. . ." Kodama cocked his head, considering. "This line 'Who will see them in a thousand years, war memorials' seems a little too melancholy. Why not change it to 'A thousand years incorruptible—stone memorials'?"

At this bold suggestion, Nogi said meekly, "Hmm, you may be right," erased two characters, and rewrote the line as Kodama had suggested. Then he signed his name as "Sekishō," meaning "stonecutter." This was Nogi's pen name. He also used the name "Sekirinshi"—"stone forest child."

* * *

After this, Ochiai Taizō, the army surgeon attached to Nogi's army, came into the room, making a crowd. Kodama had just picked up a brush to write out his poem.

"Ah, Telissu," commented Ochiai, peering over his shoulder. En route to Port Arthur, Kodama had looked out the train window at the site of the hard-fought battle of Telissu and inscribed the poem in his notebook while he gazed at the far-off grave markers for the fallen soldiers.

> The wind blows sorrowfully around Telissu.
> Crows flying home return to mourn the fresh graves.
> Ten years of bitterness are as the morning dew.
> Hearts of the brave are great.

"I can't get the final line to come out right," Kodama said, head tilted to one side. In fact, when it came to Chinese poetry, Kodama was no match for Nogi.

"'The wind blows sorrowfully' isn't so good," commented Shiga Shigetaka, taking a look. The trope of wind blowing sorrowfully over a blood-soaked battlefield was hackneyed. Shiga was not impressed with the line about the crows flying home either, seeing it as conventional. The image of crows flying over fresh graves was like something from an old tale, he said disparagingly. Only the third line needed no alteration.

The "ten years of bitterness" was a reference to the Triple Intervention led by Russia after the First Sino-Japanese War, when Japan gave in to pressure from the Great Powers and returned the Liaodong Peninsula to China. Afterward, Russia itself forcibly leased that very peninsula from China, built a military harbor at Port Arthur, and established a government-general in Dalian. Thus, the "ten years of bitterness" alluded to the very origins of the Russo-Japanese War. Now that that bitterness had been consumed in the gunfire at Telissu, and the smoke of that fire was dissipated, the ten years were as fleeting as the morning dew. That was the sense of the line.

"No good, is it?" Kodama started to write again, commenting as he wrote, "The worse the poet, the more he writes." This time he began, "Triumphantly taking the castle." Even Major Tanaka, in the background, saw the line and thought to himself that it sounded like a line from a primary school song.

Tanaka, by the way, was in charge of collecting wastepaper. He intended to make such scraps family treasures and hung onto them on the sly—but he only kept Kodama's drafts and threw away Nogi's. After the war, unfortunately, Kodama's fame dwindled while Nogi was touted as the great general of Port Arthur.

"I should have set aside Nogi's too." Tanaka would always say this when he spoke of Port Arthur. Whether he meant it ironically or not, who knows?

*   *   *

Nogi was the archetypal man of Chōshū. He studied under Tamaki Bunnoshin, as did Yoshida Shōin, although Nogi and he became known in different eras. Tamaki was Shōin's uncle and disciplined his young nephew with a whip, intending to raise him in conformity with his idea of the perfect samurai. The boy's mother, overcome by the harshness of Tamaki's tutoring, is said to have silently cried out to her son more than once, "Torajiro"—that was Shōin's childhood name—"die!" But Shōin was remarkably docile by temperament. He bore the harsh training and brilliantly internalized Tamaki's concept of the ideal samurai, which meant finding value in one's life and existence only in public service. In the cultivation of that spirit, Tamaki tolerated no corrupting impurities.

For example, once when Shōin was reading a book, a fly landed on his cheek and instinctively he scratched the spot. "Reading a book written by a sage belongs to the public realm," Tamaki declared. "Scratching yourself while reading because you itch is in the realm of personal feelings. If you allow yourself that small expression of personal feelings, there is no telling what personal interest or desire you may indulge when you grow up." And he proceeded to strike the boy cruelly.

Nogi received the same sort of treatment as a boy. He must have been beaten even more than Shōin since he was a live-in disciple. Nogi too was remarkably docile by temperament and bore this discipline without a murmur. Tamaki Bunnoshin ended up taking his own life for his involvement in the 1876 Hagi Rebellion. His greatest accomplishment was producing for history two samurai, Yoshida Shōin and Nogi Maresuke, cast in the ideal mold he himself had envisaged.

But Tamaki never conceived of the ideal samurai as a practical man. Once during Shōin's sojourn in Edo in his student days, friends from other domains started a debate at a drinking party: "If this were the era of Warring States, who would we be?" So-and-so could do work valued at a million koku, so-and-so would be a brave warrior commander, spearheading attacks. The discussion warmed until it was Shōin's turn, but he happened to be absent. "He'd be worth several thousand koku at most," someone said. "Not as a fierce general in charge of open battles or sieges—his strength would be in defending a castle to the end." Someone else spoke up and said, "No, he'd be best at tending to the sick wife of the castle lord." Extremely straitlaced where women were concerned, in his lifetime, Shōin had as little to do with the opposite sex as if he were a celibate monk. Afterward, when he heard about the conversation, he felt no rancor. In later years, he himself wrote, "I do not have the makings of a hero." The wiliness and shrewdness of a hero were alien to his nature.

A giant in the history of Japanese thought, Shōin was also a writer without peer in his times. Nogi Maresuke in turn was the finest writer of Chinese verse in the Meiji period. In that respect, the general may have borne some resemblance to his fellow student.

* * *

203-Meter Hill was already taken.

Nogi's journal for December 11 reads, "Wind, bitter cold, -10 degrees." That morning, he had to make the rounds of camps on Toyoshima Yama. When Nogi left headquarters at Liushufang, Shiga Shigetaka saw him to the door. Outside blasted a cold wind mixed with snow. After stepping into the garden, Nogi suddenly turned back to Shiga and said with a self-conscious smile, "Here, Shiga, take a look at this afterward if you will." He laid a scrap of paper on Shiga's palm.

After returning to his room, Shiga spread out the paper and saw that it was a Chinese poem written in pencil. This was Nogi's famous poem "203 Hill."

> 203 Hill, though steep, is not impossible to climb.
> Men know that to obtain glory they must overcome obstacles.
> Covered in blood and iron, the hill scarcely retains its shape.
> All look up with deep emotion at the hill where thy spirits lie.

Shiga read the poem aloud in a low voice. He was struck with admiration. "I could never compose anything like this. Nor could Kodama," he thought, remembering Kodama's efforts at the poetry gathering of a few days before.

The rendering of the hill's name was brilliant. In this, Nogi displayed a poetic gift that is truly sublime. The figure 203, which marks the height of the hill, can be read in Japanese as *ni-rei-san*. Using Chinese characters with the same pronunciations but different meanings, he recast the hill's name as "hill of thy spirits." This is no mere play on words but a fitting tribute in only three characters to the souls of the uncountable numbers who perished on the hill, including Nogi's own son Yasusuke. The poem ends by intoning again, "hill of thy spirits."

In fact, the day after 203-Meter Hill fell, a hilltop discussion was held to decide what the place's official Japanese name should be. Matsumura Kanemoto, head of the First Division, suggested "Hill of Iron and Blood" to reflect the carnage with which it had been taken. Shiga Shigetaka came up with "Port Arthur Fuji," but on later reflection realized that was a poor idea. "What about Kodama Yama?" someone suggested, and that name was nearly agreed on, but opinion did not quite gel, and the matter was left unresolved. It had been left to Shiga to come up with a final proposal. As he read Nogi's poem, he could think of no more fitting name than *Nireisan*, "203," written "Hill of Thy Spirits."

* * *

The poem "203 Hill" was not composed on December 6, the day after the hill's capture, when Nogi climbed to the top. On that day, the hillside was deep in the remains of friend and foe, so mangled they were barely distinguishable. Rocks had been pulverized to ash by gunfire, as if put through a blender. With every step, his boots sank in. The horror of the reeking battlefield was not conducive to thoughts of poetry.

The idea for the poem apparently came to Nogi on the night of December 10, during a raging snowstorm. He polished the rhyme and tonalities of the poem, which was written in classical Chinese, and handed it to Shiga Shigetaka on the morning of December 11. That same afternoon, the ashes and personal effects of his second son Yasusuke were delivered to headquarters.

Nogi composed the poem keeping in mind the spirits of all Japanese who perished on the hill. At the same time, his heart must have been full of thoughts of his son Yasusuke, a young man of cheerful disposition compared to his older brother Katsusuke, who had fallen in combat earlier. Nogi's journal entry for December 11 reads simply, "Yasusuke's ashes and effects arrived."

On the fourteenth he wrote, "At night, 6 inches of snow. . . .Called on Hirasa at Twin Dragons (and on Ichinohe along the way) and arrived at Songshugou." The Ichinohe he refers to is Major General Ichinohe Hyōe, brigade commander, an able leader throughout the Port Arthur siege, and one whose dauntless courage inspired the troops. Subsequently, he became chief of staff of the Third Army, and Nogi showed him the poem.

"It seems to me," Ichinohe later wrote, probably referring to this occasion, "that the idea for that poem came to him when he visited my camp." Ichinohe's journal entry for the day in question began with the weather: "At night there was snowfall, piling up over 6 inches." The entry continues with a description that is, naturally enough, consistent with Nogi's journal account: "Weather clear, wind moderate, not to say bracing." It was a fine morning after a snowfall, the weather clear and calm.

"General Nogi came to camp," Ichinohe continued. "On entering my tent, he abruptly called for a brush, wrote out a poem on 203 Hill, and showed it to me. I served sweets."

The sweets came as a surprise to Nogi, who commented on the unusual refreshments. Ichinohe explained how he had come by them. A few days earlier, during a lull in the fighting, he had personally led his brigade in picking up the dead below the eastern fort. A unit of Russian soldiers was also out collecting their dead at the same time. When Ichinohe smiled and saluted, the officer in their midst smiled and saluted in return, and sent over a gift of sweets.

Nogi was delighted by the story and requested several sweets to take with him. In Ichinohe's words, "He left, taking with him a few sweets as mementos."

2

ON THE HIGH SEAS

We take up our story after 203-Meter Hill had fallen to the Japanese, a hilltop observation post had been set up, and under the guidance of an observation officer, shells began catapulting over the hill and landing on Russian battleships in the harbor. When Tōgō realized this, he gave a terse nod of satisfaction. "Good." He did not go so far as to break into a smile. His thoughts remained stubbornly fixated on the Russian Port Arthur Squadron holed up in the harbor. In that matter, he was a perfectionist. Remember, letting even a single ship get away was unacceptable. Should even one battleship remain seaworthy and get out on the open sea, Japanese transport in neighboring waters would be greatly endangered. To prevent that, he would be forced to leave at least two battleships behind to stand guard. Never before had war on land or on sea demanded such perfectionism.

As soon as the observation post was ready on 203-Meter Hill, the navy dispatched an officer. Identifying ships by kind and by name was no job for an army gunnery officer to tackle.

Seen from the top of 203-Meter Hill, the Russian squadron in the harbor proved to be much larger than anticipated. In all, they counted twenty-one ships: five battleships, five cruisers, five destroyers, two gunboats, two torpedo gunboats, one minelayer, and a three-masted transport ship named the *Yermak*. Not only in numbers but in composition as well, the Russian squadron was formidable.

But from December 6 to 8, following directions from the observation post atop 203-Meter Hill, all but one of those ships were sunk or destroyed, reduced to scrap. The results of the bombardment were phenomenal.

Only one lucky ship managed to avoid a fatal blow from the shelling. That was the battleship *Sevastopol*. (One insignificant gunboat stuck close by the lucky battleship.) At dawn on December 9, the *Sevastopol* began to move quietly, left the harbor, moved along Laohuwei Peninsula, and slipped behind Chengtou Hill on the peninsula, out of sight of the Japanese observation post.

* * *

With the *Sevastopol* missing, the big guns of Nogi's Third Army joined in a massive hunt on the morning of December 9, firing in and out of the harbor. The only way to hit a target outside the range of vision was to rely on instinct. If even a single shell hit home, a telltale plume of black smoke would rise in the air and draw concentrated fire.

Meanwhile, Tōgō's fleet did its best to hunt down the missing battleship on the sea. One destroyer ventured close to the minefields, going as far as Longwangtang, and spotted the *Sevastopol*. Getting any closer was too risky, so the destroyer raced back.

The commanding officer of the *Sevastopol* was Captain von Essen, said to be the bravest man in the entire Port Arthur Squadron. A Russian of German descent, he started out as commanding officer of the small protected cruiser *Novik*, taking advantage of its lightness and speed to challenge Tōgō's fleet from the first. The ship became famous among Tōgō's crew. "Here comes the *Novik* again," they would shout. While immobilized during the harbor blockade, von Essen was promoted from commander to captain and put in command of the *Sevastopol*.

Although his battleship had lost the greater part of its fighting capacity, to von Essen the prospect of being sunk by army guns fired from shore was so humiliating that he preferred rather to leave the harbor and be sunk by Japanese naval guns. A brilliant ship handler, he had made arrangements to evacuate his crew to shore at Chengtou Hill on Laohuwei Peninsula if necessary. In short, he prepared to go down with his ship on the spot, ending its life and his in a shared watery grave.

But to the Japanese, the enemy ship was, however weakened, still a battleship. A staff meeting was held aboard the *Mikasa* to decide what to do.

"We can't have friendly ships suffering damage because of that ship. The only thing to do is send torpedo boats on a night raid to take care of it." This was from Akiyama Saneyuki, who by then had been promoted to the rank of commander.

In the end, they decided on a torpedo attack. The fleet mustered all its torpedo boats, and one by one they went out. The attack continued for a full week, December 9–16, without ever producing any report that the *Sevastopol* had definitely been sunk.

It was night, and visibility was poor. Waves were high too. Sometimes a little torpedo boat would be so tossed around by the waves that its screw was exposed, high in midair. Then there was the possibility that the *Sevastopol* was laying mines. Worse, the enemy vessel was a battleship, considered a Goliath in those days. No torpedo boat commander had the guts to take this ship on in a suicide attack. They fired their torpedoes from a safe distance and got the hell away. Dying at sea in a major naval engagement was one thing, but the prospect of dying over such a trivial incident held little appeal. That attitude was what kept the torpedo boat commanders from taking down this lone stationary battleship for such a long time.

* * *

While the *Mikasa* staff was dining on the evening of December 16, conversation focused on the one topic that had them all concerned. Had the *Sevastopol* been sunk or not?

According to the reports of torpedo boat commanders who had been firing at the *Sevastopol* in turns for eight nights in a row, the battleship was down. But the *Mikasa* staff doubted their reports, and with good reason.

First off, the torpedo boats had low attack capability. The previous February 8, a group of destroyers had made a night attack on the Russian squadron outside the harbor with pathetic results, even taking into account that it was a first effort. Twenty torpedoes had caused light damage to a mere three ships. It seemed likely that the firing had been cowardly, from too far away. And, since perpetrators of night attacks must cut out quickly after firing, results were unverifiable. At best, the reports could only claim, "Almost certainly scored a direct hit. Target very likely demolished." The same was true with the *Sevastopol*. Although the attack force claimed that the battleship had already been sunk, the *Mikasa* prudently kept sending out torpedo boats. The staff all shared the opinion that it would be a serious mistake to alter policy on the basis of the attackers' reports.

The second reason was purely psychological. Tōgō and his staff were unsettled by the pressure of knowing that if the *Sevastopol* had somehow survived the bombardment unscathed, then the Japanese fleet could not leave the harbor after all. Should the *Sevastopol* turn out to have been playing dead and later stir up trouble in Far Eastern waters, all the effort of the past ten months' blockade would come to nothing and the unprecedented loss of over sixty percent of General Nogi's officers and men would be in vain.

Lieutenant Commander Iida Hisatsune, from the cruiser *Iwate* in the Second Squadron, happened to be present. "I have good long-distance vision," he said. "In the morning I'll go check it out."

Everyone approved. A speedy transport ship was brought out for Iida's use. The mission was extremely risky. Overhead, enemy guns might still be functioning, and below decks there might well be mines. Even if he died in the attempt, Iida's death would have meaning—that's how important it was to go and see what was happening. "The matter was virtually settled at mess," he commented later.

But something interfered. Commander in Chief Tōgō Heihachirō took it into his head that he himself would go. He was present that evening and heard Iida volunteer. At the time, he remained absorbed in characteristic silence, wordlessly plying his knife and fork. After dinner, he returned to his private room and summoned Akiyama Saneyuki. When Saneyuki came into the room, Tōgō spoke with all the casualness of a remark about the weather. "Tomorrow morning I'll go check on the Sevastopol, so handle the arrangements."

Saneyuki was not surprised. His mind always worked quickly, to a fault in fact, and so instead of being struck by the weightiness of Tōgō's decision he assumed that the words of Iida, who had been sitting at the far end of the table, had not carried. In other words, Saneyuki decided that Tōgō never heard what Iida had said.

"That won't be necessary, sir. Lieutenant Commander Iida has excellent eyesight, and he will be going." He spoke in a matter-of-fact way.

That attitude of Saneyuki's grated at times on Tōgō's nerves. He frowned, seemingly annoyed. "I shall go. I have no objection if Iida comes along." Implicit in his words was the sentiment that even if a hundred men with Iida's superior eyesight went along, he would find their reports hard to believe. Into those few words he packed his belief that for once he needed to verify facts with his own eyes, as clearly as if he had expounded on the idea for an hour.

Had Saneyuki given any thought to the matter, he would have understood the admiral's feelings. At issue was the survival of a remnant of that Port Arthur Squadron, which from the harbor recesses had indirectly caused the deaths of so many Japanese in the siege of Port Arthur since the past summer. All the ships in the squadron had gone down except for the Sevastopol. The nation's time of peril seemed finally to be at an end, but was it? Had the Sevastopol truly been sunk? The tension of the last ten months had been so great that Tōgō needed to know with obsessive precision. Only after verifying with his own eyes that the ship had indeed gone down could he lead his fleet back to Sasebo and begin preparations to do battle with the Baltic Fleet.

"Very good, sir." Saneyuki left Tōgō's room, slightly pale. For Tōgō to go in person meant that he might very well be killed. The loss of the commander in chief of the Combined Fleet would deal morale a devastating blow.

Saneyuki reported to Rear Admiral Shimamura Hayao, the chief of staff. When Shimamura heard the news, his big face stiffened in shock. "I'll talk him out of it." He rushed into Tōgō's room, but soon came back out. He walked past Saneyuki over to Iida in the corner and told him about the change in plans.

"I can't do anything about it. The chief insists on going in person."

* * *

"Terrible, terrible." Shimamura kept on repeating this, but in the end he had no choice but to comply with Tōgō's wishes.

"The *Tatsuta* would be good to carry the chief."

At this suggestion from Saneyuki, Shimamura nodded. "Let's quietly send a couple of destroyers along as escort."

The *Tatsuta* (866 tons) was a dispatch vessel. Saneyuki wrote down various orders, and after Shimamura looked them over they went out.

On the morning of the eighteenth, Tōgō transferred to the *Tatsuta* and set out from the Combined Fleet's base at the Changshan Islands at a speed of 20 knots. Along the way, the ship put in at Dalian, setting out again on the morning of the nineteenth.

The sea was a little rough, the sky clear.

At Tōgō's side stood Iida Hisatsune. Neither Shimamura nor Saneyuki was with them. Tōgō forbade it, lest the *Tatsuta* be hit by a floating mine and the Combined Fleet lose all its top command at once.

Soon after the *Tatsuta* started out, two destroyers came up quickly from behind and followed closely astern. Tōgō must have found this strange, for he held up his binoculars and studied them.

"Tōgō looked aft the whole time," Iida later wrote. He and Commander Kamaya Tadamichi, the *Tatsuta*'s commanding officer, kept their eyes focused frantically on the sea ahead. They had to keep watch for any floating mines that might pop up between the waves. The more pairs of eyes on the lookout, the better. The commander in chief might well have shown a little more concern, but all he seemed interested in was the pair of destroyers astern.

Before setting out, the commanders of the two destroyers had been given strict orders by Shimamura. "If worse comes to worst, draw up on either side and carry out your duty." The worst-case scenario he referred to was, of course, the possibility of the *Tatsuta* striking a floating mine. In that event, the two destroyers were to immediately veer off to port and starboard respectively, drawing alongside the *Tatsuta* to rescue Tōgō.

Just as ordered, the commanders handled the destroyers in such a way that they could swing into action on a moment's notice. Sometimes they even practiced doing so, leaving their position at the stern to draw close alongside the *Tatsuta*'s gunwales and staying there cheek by jowl for a time before slipping back astern.

At the beginning of the war, none of the destroyers had been capable of such fine handling, but constant drilling during the ten-month blockade had made this virtuoso performance possible. That was doubtless what attracted Tōgō's attention. A more talkative man would have surely praised the demonstration. "Good work." But Tōgō, taciturn as always, never even asked if the destroyers were present as escorts.

The *Tatsuta* was headed for the small promontory of Longwangtang—which wasn't really big enough to dignify with the name "promontory." The navy had put up a watchtower there, which gave a good view of the mouth of the harbor, off to the west-southwest. Apparently, the Russians carelessly missed the fact that the Japanese Navy had stealthily erected an observation post similar to a fire lookout tower. The site was vulnerable to gunfire from the battery at East Cockscomb Hill in the Port Arthur fortress. The Japanese had camouflaged it with trees, however, to hide it. Tōgō was headed there.

Eventually, the *Tatsuta* pulled quietly up on the eastern side of the promontory and dropped anchor without being discovered by anyone in the fortress. The sea there was peculiarly blue. A boat was quickly lowered into the water, and Tōgō and Iida sped off to the watchtower.

Up in the tower, Iida held up 2-magnification binoculars and looked off to the west-southwest. Tōgō used his own big binoculars, which, as we know, he alone of all the officers in the Combined Fleet possessed—brand-new 8-magnification Zeiss binoculars. He looked at Laohuwei Peninsula, which blocked the harbor entrance. On the peninsula were several hills. The one on the far southwest, at the very base of the peninsula, was Chengtou. Crouched in the sea just at its base was a large battleship: the *Sevastopol*.

Iida checked with his binoculars and again with his naked eye. Either way, the condition of the enemy battleship was unmistakable. The gunwales that should have been riding high out of the water were extremely low. Moreover, the ship was listing, clearly scraping bottom in shallow waters. In other words, the battleship had been sunk.

Doesn't the boss get it? Iida wondered to himself as Tōgō stared unremittingly at the spot, hardly breathing. But at last Tōgō gave his verdict.

"It's been sunk."

For the rest of his life, Iida Hisatsune would repeat those few words from the taciturn commander in chief. In that moment, the ten-month blockade came to an end. Tōgō was finally released from tension in the waters of the Far East. All he had to do now was await the coming of the Baltic Fleet.

Tōgō went back to the *Tatsuta*. "I'll spend the night at the port authority in Dalian," he informed Iida. "Wire Commander Akiyama to join me there tomorrow."

Those were Tōgō's plans. He intended to leave Dalian the next day and visit Third Army headquarters to express his thanks and appreciation to Nogi.

* * *

That winter's day, the Liaodong Peninsula was enjoying the finest weather it had seen since the Japanese military first arrived. Even when evening set in, there was scarcely a cloud to be seen in the sky.

That evening, Tōgō went ashore in Dalian and entered the port authority. He was accompanied only by Lieutenant Commander Iida Hisatsune, with no formal escort. The wharf was crowded with coolies. Nobody guessed that of the two Japanese naval officers, one was commander in chief of the Combined Fleet.

The red brick building where Tōgō stayed had formerly been used by Russia as its port authority, and the Japanese took it over for the same purpose. The Dalian defense unit headquarters was also located there.

Tōgō took a room on the second floor with a window overlooking the bay. Straight ahead was a Russian-built breakwater, and jutting out to its left was a small promontory, seemingly protective of the harbor.

The Russian Empire forcibly took possession of Liaodong Peninsula and built that port in 1898. Until then, there was nothing along the coast but a scattering of sleepy fishing villages. The Russians built a city, intending to make it the axis of their domination of the Far East. They replaced the original Chinese name of Qingniwa, rechristening the area Dalny—"far away"—instead. Around the time when Tōgō stayed the night there, the Japanese also called the town "Darunii." The name "Dairen" existed, but was not yet official. Not until 1905 did "Dairen" become the official Japanese name for the city.

The following morning, Akiyama Saneyuki arrived as ordered. Tōgō went downstairs, and Akiyama saluted him in the entrance. Other than that, neither man spoke. There was no need for words. Together with Iida, they left the building. Train arrangements had already been made.

They were going to Nogi's headquarters in Liushufang. The train that would take them there was waiting just outside, exclusively theirs. An officer from the Third Army was present to greet them. Everyone boarded the train. As soon as they were on board, the train pulled out with scarcely a tremor—probably because of the broad gauge.

On the way to Liushufang, the officer who had come to meet Tōgō explained the progress of the war since the fall of 203-Meter Hill. Despite that victory, the second and third defense lines behind the hill remained stubbornly intact. The forts on Twin Dragons Hill and Pine Tree Hill, where ever since the previous August so much Japanese blood had been spilled, were as strong as ever. But the fall of 203-Meter Hill had considerably simplified the army's attack strategy. They had reverted to the former method of wearing down enemy strength primarily by artillery while digging tunnels to various forts so that they could be blown up with powerful explosives. Two days earlier, on the eighteenth, the troops had tunneled as far as East Cockscomb Fort where so many Japanese soldiers had been killed and wounded, and destroyed it.

"The forts on Twin Dragons Hill and Pine Tree Hill will both be blown up in the next ten days." This confident prediction was made by Lieutenant Colonel Ōba Jirō, vice chief of staff of the Third Army, the same officer who had previously gone to meet Kodama.

* * *

Tōgō's purpose in going to see Nogi was first to thank him for capturing 203-Meter Hill, second to express condolences for the loss of his two sons in battle. Concerning the second purpose, for a fleet commander in wartime to carry out such a social ritual may seem incongruous, but by the standards of the day it was normal. Both Tōgō and Nogi maintained themselves as old-school samurai warriors. One of the most important charges of the samurai was to live by duty and humanity.

His third purpose was to inform Nogi that the mission at Port Arthur Harbor had ended and he, Tōgō, would be returning to the Japanese mainland. He surely wanted to extend his old war comrade the courtesy of sharing this information. Tōgō did not let on about these things to anyone. He said nothing even to Saneyuki. Iida and Saneyuki simply made the inference, and they were generally right.

Saneyuki was fond of saying that he was "born in the new era." His birth year was indeed 1868, the first year of Meiji, but by emphasizing that he did not necessarily mean that his thinking was fresh and bold. Rather he was being self-deprecatory. Having been born at a time when samurai were disappearing, he never acquired many samurai attributes, he meant to say. Not only he but most men of his generation looked down on old-fashioned people, while at the same time harboring enormous admiration and respect for the iconic figure of the samurai warrior. One reason for Saneyuki's lifelong affection for Hirose Takeo was surely that Hirose, a member of his same generation, had the cultivation of a samurai and strove to be a true samurai in every sense.

Saneyuki looked on Tōgō as a man of that caliber, and Nogi even more so. Amid the struggle for 203-Meter Hill, Saneyuki had frequent occasion to write to visiting naval staff stationed in Nogi's headquarters and state his opinions on army strategy. In those letters, he often couched his respect for Nogi in his usual well-crafted language.

In any case, this literary-minded youth, with a natural inclination to feel a surge of emotion over dramatic events, had already built up Tōgō's visit to Nogi at Liushufang into a moment of high drama. "Pen and paper can never convey the full story of the meeting between the two leaders," he wrote later to a colleague at Imperial Headquarters. He was well positioned to appreciate as few others could have done just how much the drama of Tōgō's liberation from Port Arthur heightened the drama of this encounter.

* * *

As already noted, there was no train station at Liushufang, so trains simply halted in the middle of a grassy field. The assistant engine driver would quickly jump out and set out a coal box for the use of alighting passengers.

The train drew closer.

Nogi waited by the rails with his staff to greet Tōgō on his visit from the sea. For once there was no wind. The afternoon winter sun warmed the frozen snow, but if the officers stayed on horseback there was risk of their feet freezing inside their boots, so they all dismounted. Noncommissioned officers and soldiers from headquarters took the reins of each horse and held them together. Only Nogi remained mounted. As the train pulled in, he quickly dismounted.

The train stopped, and the coal box was set out.

When the admiral's small frame emerged in the doorway of the train, Nogi ran over and grasped him by the hand. "The general and the admiral said only 'Oh!' and then for a time spoke no words." So wrote Iida Hisatsune.

Saneyuki detached himself from the admiral and mingled with Nogi's staff. Nogi and Tōgō led the way. It was a distance of some 500 meters to headquarters. Along the way, not a word of conversation passed between the two men.

"Neither of them had anything to say," recalled Iida. "They just walked briskly along."

Behind Tōgō walked Saneyuki and Iida, who both must have been all ears to hear what momentous conversation might take place. But Nogi was taciturn by nature, Tōgō even more so. They walked in silence.

Finally, they arrived at headquarters. As already described, this was a farmhouse, by no means small given the size of local houses, but to Iida it looked like a "tiny Chinese shack."

"The two men entered that shack," he wrote. Only the general and the admiral went inside. All the staff waited outside. What words were spoken inside the "shack" no one knows. In the West, it is customary at such times to include a scribe to take notes. But Nogi and Tōgō were both men of Meiji, and they did not think along those lines. Nor was there any tradition of writing memoirs, so the contents of their conversation remain a mystery.

Saneyuki and Iida, however, imagined that Tōgō expressed appreciation and thanks for the siege of Port Arthur that had climaxed with the taking of 203-Meter Hill. He surely expressed condolences over Nogi's loss of his two sons. And finally, he must have broached the main topic of this visit, his report that he was ending the blockade and returning to Japan. Throughout the visit, the rattle of gunfire between Russian and Japanese troops continued like distant thunder.

*　*　*

This much is certain—after Tōgō had said everything else he had come to say, he expressed a desire to "go to Kuroi" to express appreciation for services rendered. Equally certainly, Nogi picked up his cap from the table and offered to lead the way.

Here a word of explanation is in order. "Kuroi" was a reference to naval commander Kuroi Teijirō, whose name was used as shorthand for an artillery installation. To cooperate with Nogi, the navy had brought naval guns ashore and built batteries for them, with Kuroi in command.

Once, when an aide of Tōgō's expressed a desire to contribute to the siege of Port Arthur by donating naval guns, Nogi's chief of staff Ijichi Kōsuke had rejected the offer: "That won't be necessary." The army could take care of itself. Back in the First Sino-Japanese War, Ijichi had had a similar dispute. Apparently, the man was pathologically opposed to cooperating with the navy.

But this time the navy persisted. To the navy way of thinking, breaking down a concrete fortress with small-caliber army guns was simply not going to work. Why not put ashore ships' guns capable of destroying an armored battleship, and use them instead?

"The army will take care of the army's concerns." This was Ijichi's response. He tended to pride himself on his expertise and scoff at amateurs. What did they know? The most ridiculous thing about Ijichi was his firm belief that among military personnel some were experts, the rest mere amateurs. "I am an artillery specialist," he was always saying. In short, he dismissed the navy's suggestion out of hand as "amateur."

When it comes to the technical aspects of operating guns, there may be a difference between the amateur and the expert, but let us emphasize that when it comes to military strategy, no such difference exists. This fact gets to the heart of what the military is all about. In the 1575 battle of Nagashino, for example, generals under Takeda Katsuyori were clearly far more "expert" than their enemy, the hegemon Oda Nobunaga, but thanks to the enemy's innovations of wooden stockades and rotating volleys of fire they suffered a devastating loss. Instead of incorporating the winning strategies of Nobunaga and Hideyoshi into Edo-period military science, however, the military establishment continued to practice the outmoded tactics of Takeda Shingen, Katsuyori's famous father, for the next three hundred years. There you have the lineage of the Japanese mentality that eventually produced an Ijichi Kōsuke at Port Arthur.

In any case, Nogi's headquarters ultimately approved the navy's suggestion. Along with the 28-centimeter howitzer guns, naval heavy artillery under the direction of Commander Kuroi became a powerful, steady force that shook the fortress of Port Arthur. It was a force never fully acknowledged in the annals of the army.

Tōgō set off for the emplacement of Kuroi Teijirō to express his appreciation.

* * *

Officially, they were the "naval land artillery corps." They had left Tōgō's command to join Nogi's headquarters, where they served under siege artillery commanding officer Toyoshima Yōzō.

The number of naval guns gradually increased as needed, but in the beginning, around June, the guns aboard the old ironclad battleship *Fusō* (3,783 tons), which was moored in Dalian Bay, were dismantled and taken ashore. Quick-firing guns that the navy had already prepared for land battles were also included.

The *Fusō* was equipped with auxiliary 12-pounder guns, twelve of which were taken ashore. After that, large 12- and 15-centimeter guns were shipped to Dalian Bay from the Japanese mainland and taken ashore as well.

The naval guns made their way uphill. They were only gun barrels, without mounting or chassis. How they would be set up and used on land was left entirely in the hands of Commander Kuroi. A man of considerable ingenuity, he hauled shipbuilding materials, iron, and iron plates up the hill, and built his own unique mountings and chassis based on a special design. He constructed three batteries based on Huoshiling, fortified with forty-three guns of various calibers and staffed by over thirteen hundred men.

The batteries first opened fire on August 7. Deployment of the army artillery was not yet complete, so initially it was the naval guns, hated by Ijichi, that did all the roaring.

On November 3, Kuroi conducted an interesting experiment. That day was the emperor's birthday, so they had to fire a salute. In the navy 21-gun salutes were standard, but in the army it was 101 guns. "We are assigned temporarily to the army, so let's fire a 101-gun salute, army-style." This was Kuroi's idea. He further proposed using live shells instead of blanks. The live shells would, of course, be fired into enemy territory, specifically the harbor. This was prior to the capture of 203-Meter Hill, so there was no vantage point overlooking the harbor, and they had nothing to aim at when they fired.

Kuroi created a grid map of the harbor and decided to fire into each square of the grid. Each battery would fire 101 guns for a total of 303. Once this was done, they saw huge pillars of fire erupt in the harbor in the middle of the bombardment, followed by billowing clouds of black smoke. It was a prodigious sight.

The number of shells used by the naval land artillery corps in the attack on Port Arthur totaled five thousand 15-centimeter shells, seventeen thousand 12-centimeter shells, and twenty-three thousand 12-pounder shells. This comprised the greatest activity of any long-range heavy artillery.

Tōgō was set to return to Japan with his fleet, but of the men under his command, Kuroi and the rest of the land artillery corps would have to stay behind until the fall of Port Arthur.

That was the background of Tōgō's visit of appreciation.

* * *

Saneyuki later gave an account of the meeting between Tōgō and Nogi to Ogasawara Naganari of Imperial Headquarters, which Ogasawara wrote up. "Never before did I ever participate in any event that affected me so strongly. The moment when Tōgō and Nogi shook hands in utmost sincerity left an indelible impression on me." Henceforth, the siege of Port Arthur with its dreadful toll of national suffering would be transformed into a national lyrical ode.

As they made their way to the emplacements of Commander Kuroi, the gunfire kept up its fearsome roar. The ground along the way was full of wavelike undulations. To conceal themselves from enemy eyes, the men threaded their way along the low ground, as if they were walking below an embankment. The moment they became visible, the still-operational forts at Pine Tree Hill and Chair Hill would open fire.

As they walked along, twice Nogi said the same thing to Tōgō. Iida, who had an excellent memory, was able to recall his exact words. "You are an admiral of the sea, and we can't have you getting injured on land, so keep your head down. If they see it, they'll fire at it."

On the left was the enemy fortress. Nogi walked on the left, protecting Tōgō with his own body. He walked stooped over. The ground was always higher on the left. Nogi kept Tōgō continually on the lower side as they proceeded, and Tōgō offered no resistance, but walked as directed. When the ground rose slightly, Nogi would say, "Go more that way," pointing out the low ground.

Finally, they came to the land emplacement set up by the navy. Commander Kuroi was waiting to greet them. He led Tōgō and Nogi into the command post, which was surrounded by sandbags.

"Thank you for all you've done," Tōgō told him. He broke off, then grinned. "Not done yet either, are you?" Kuroi's assignment was to remain until the fall of the Port Arthur fortress, which Tōgō referred to in his own way. He went on to tell Kuroi the same thing he had told Nogi, that he would be leaving a portion of the fleet behind and returning home to Japan. He stayed for thirty minutes before going back to Liushufang for dinner.

At the table, there was very little conversation of any substance. Tōgō was a man of extremely few words, and Nogi wasn't much of a talker either. Only Ijichi brought up various topics. He talked mostly about his neuralgia.

As soon as dinner was over, Tōgō left. In the train, Saneyuki asked, "Will you be staying in Dalian tonight, sir?"

"No, I'm going back to the *Mikasa*."

That was as it should be. Tōgō needed to get the Combined Fleet out of the waters of Port Arthur as quickly as possible, to ready them for a new foe.

* * *

As soon as Tōgō got back to the flagship *Mikasa*, he sat down and sent off a lengthy telegram to Imperial Headquarters. As usual, Saneyuki wrote the draft. He picked up his pencil and finished writing in thirty minutes. The wire confirmed that the blockade of the harbor at Port Arthur was now officially ended.

A reply came from chief of the Navy General Staff Itō Sukeyuki, with instructions to depart leaving the Third Squadron behind. The Third Squadron was commanded by Vice Admiral Kataoka Shichirō and consisted mainly of four protected cruisers (over 4,000 tons)—the *Itsukushima*, *Hashidate*, *Matsushima*, and *Chin'en*. Only the *Chin'en* (over 7,000 tons), which had been captured during the First Sino-Japanese War, differed from the rest in make, size, and speed. There were also four small protected cruisers; ten armored gunboats, and the like; and three torpedo boat divisions. The Third Squadron was to remain behind to cut off supply routes to the enemy fortress and to offer assistance to Nogi's army.

"Commander of the Combined Fleet Tōgō and Commander of the Second Squadron Kamimura shall report to Imperial Headquarters at their earliest convenience." Itō added this at the very end.

Tōgō's fleet, from the *Mikasa* on down, left its base at the Changshan Islands. The First Squadron went to Kure, the Second Squadron to Sasebo. Every ship was in woeful shape. They had been afloat at sea for a long time, and their guns and other equipment were considerably damaged from attacks in the battle of the Yellow Sea as well as other engagements, large and small. Several of the *Mikasa*'s guns needed replacing.

The *Itsukushima* and other ships that had sustained particularly significant damage had gone back before the rest and were already in dock at Kure. The *Itsukushima* needed to have all of its main guns and some of its auxiliary guns replaced, and damage to its machinery was extensive. The technician who assessed the damage estimated that repairs would take two and a half months.

But the movements of the Baltic Fleet were hard to ascertain, and, fearful that the enemy might enter Far Eastern waters at any time, Captain Teragaki Izō, commander of the *Itsukushima*, protested. "By then the enemy will be here! Can't you make it any faster?"

The technician was well aware of the situation. Even so, he had to reply that there was just no way to speed things up. Yet once repairs got underway, the fired-up workmen got things done at a breakneck pace, beyond anything he had ever expected. The workmen took no breaks and ate their meals standing. The ship's company took pity on them, and made them tea and snacks. In the end, Captain Teragaki went around pleading with the workmen to take it easy. "You can't keep working like this without damaging your health. The *Mikasa* is coming and another hundred ships besides. You've got to husband your strength."

To give some idea of the force of the workmen's exertions, normally it takes ten to twenty hammer blows to shatter the head of a rivet, but every man used all his strength and smashed the head in only five or six tries. And so it was that instead of the predicted two and a half months needed to repair the *Itsukushima*, the job was finished in about a month and twenty days.

*   *   *

Tōgō and Kamimura went back to Tokyo on December 30. When they got off the train at Shimbashi Station, a crowd of tens of thousands surged forward to meet them.

The two men rode to Imperial Headquarters in a carriage sent round for them by the Imperial Household Ministry. Staff members, Saneyuki among them, went straight to the Naval Ministry.

In the evening, Saneyuki headed first to the home of his absent brother Yoshifuru in Shinanomachi, Yotsuya to pay his respects to his aged mother and his sister-in-law Tami. Sada was by then seventy-eight. Compared to the old days before he went to war, she seemed shrunken. He found it so hard to meet her eyes that finally she complained. "Jun, what's wrong with you!" His eyes must have betrayed his uneasiness.

That was typical. When his father Hisataka died in Matsuyama in 1890, his brother Yoshifuru had been off studying in France, and he himself had been in Constantinople aboard the battleship *Hiei*, studying to be a sublieutenant second class. When Yoshifuru went home to Matsuyama afterward, he had addressed his mother without any change of expression, as if chatting about the most ordinary things: "So, Mother, I hear Father died." Yoshifuru was a person who worked to keep emotion from his face at all times, but Saneyuki was different. After he'd been home for a while, he was overwhelmed as he looked at his mother's face and burst into tears. He wept so violently that Sada was concerned.

Now also, overwhelmed by fear that his mother might die, Saneyuki was unable to get a handle on his emotions. Sada, who had always lavished particular affection on this youngest child of hers, understood his feelings perfectly well and so made an effort to appear lively. In fact, her legs had weakened to the point that it was all she could do to get up and go to the toilet. She lived the life of an invalid.

That day, Sada did something a bit unusual. Until then, she had never commented when Saneyuki received a promotion, but now she expressed delight that he had been made a naval commander.

His brother Yoshifuru, who was stationed on the far left flank of Oku's army, had also sent a letter of congratulations. Saneyuki had the letter in his pocket, intending to show it to his sister-in-law, but he was so afraid that his mother might see it that in the end he never brought it out. After congratulating his brother on his promotion, Yoshifuru had written these words: "The destruction of the family is not worth worrying about. If both you and I are able to die for our country in its unprecedented time of trouble, that is a matter for rejoicing. I look forward with great pleasure to the next theater of war."

After dark, Saneyuki went back to his new home in Takagi-chō, Aoyama. His bride Sueko, whom he had married the previous July, was waiting for him with dinner on the table. When she came to meet him at the front door, he must have been quite bashful. Apparently, he said not a word and just stood there awhile looking sullen.

*　*　*

In any case, the ships were now in dock. For the crews it was a time of rest. Saneyuki went to the Navy General Staff Office every day but left early. When he came home, he would give Sueko a one-word request—"Pillow"— and then lie down on the floor still in his uniform. He spent all his time staring up at the ceiling.

Sueko was at a loss every day over what she could do for him. When she brought over a cup of hot tea, he kept his eyes on the ceiling and never gave the tea a glance. She took to setting the cup by his pillow, but invariably he let it grow cold, untouched.

Sometimes he would say, "Beans." When he was in Europe or at sea, Saneyuki had always had a pocketful of roasted beans, and now that he was back in Tokyo he set off for the Navy General Staff Office with his pocket bulging with them and munched as he walked.

He had ended a recent letter to his mother, written aboard the *Mikasa*, with a request. "I would like you to send me a bushel or two of peas and beans, roasted." Apparently, only his mother could roast them just right. Sueko took special lessons from her in an effort to learn the technique.

In any case, while Saneyuki was at home, if he wasn't eating he was staring up at the ceiling. To Sueko the ceiling he stared at so much was just an ordinary ceiling, but to Saneyuki it was a peerlessly accurate map of the Japanese archipelago. The inland seas and outer seas were all represented— the East China Sea, the Sea of Japan, the Pacific Ocean, the Sea of Okhotsk.

Which way would the Baltic Fleet come? The survival of Japan hung on that question. Would it swing up around the Pacific Ocean side of the islands and down from the north to Vladivostok? Or cut through the Sea of Japan? The answer was known only to God and Rozhestvensky, the commander in chief of the Baltic Fleet. But Japan had only a single fleet with which to blast the enemy when it arrived. Setting an ambush in two places at once, the Pacific Ocean and the Sea of Japan, was impossible.

They would have to pick one and gamble on it. The research and the gamble were not Saneyuki's sole responsibility, but the responsibility of the Navy General Staff Office as a whole. However, working out strategy once the Baltic Fleet had arrived was his sole prerogative. The task demanded of him, his supreme order, was nothing so simple as securing a victory. To repeat, the Combined Fleet was bound by the unheard-of need to sink every last ship in the enemy fleet. If three or four ships remained afloat and escaped to Vladivostok, they would represent a huge threat to Japanese sea transport and the survival of the Manchurian Army.

This was the problem that Saneyuki mulled over daily, driving himself almost to distraction. He had already formulated a plan known as the "seven-stage strategy," one inspired by ancient Japanese naval tactics he had found in the book borrowed from his friend Ogasawara Naganari. Would it work? As he stared up at the ceiling where he could see the waters of Japan mapped out as plain as day, moving friendly and enemy fleets around at will in his head, that was the question he pondered long and hard.

*   *   *

The Baltic Fleet continued its epic voyage. For a fleet of such size to set out from the North Sea in Europe and sail across the world's oceans to the Far East was a heroic undertaking in and of itself. Meanwhile, the Japanese architect of the plan to repulse that enemy fleet spent his time lying flat on his back in a rental house in Tokyo munching roasted beans and staring hard at the ceiling. This contrast is a bit of hilarity worthy of Japanese Zen paintings, which delight in unconventional humor.

While most Russian officers were aristocrats, strategist Saneyuki's rental home didn't even have a bath. Fortunately, Sueko had relatives living in the neighborhood whose facilities they could use.

Sada wanted to live with Saneyuki at least for the duration of his stay in Tokyo, she said, and two days after he came back, she moved in with the young couple. She had always had a soft spot for her younger son. When she went to take a bath at the neighbors' house, he would hoist her easily onto his back and carry her over. He always carried her piggyback, even if in uniform. Sada did not like him to carry her and invariably objected. "It's mortifying! Stop it." But her son's strong point was that everything he did was efficient and practical. He was strong, so for him to carry her only made sense. If they got someone else to do it, they would always have to be expressing thanks, which was troublesome. That was all there was to it. So he would quickly lift her on his back and set out for the relatives' house nearby.

When they got there, someone would inevitably ask, "What's happening with the Baltic Fleet?" Saneyuki would shake his head and answer, "I only wish I knew." He never breathed a word on the subject. But newspapers and gossip were all focused on the coming of the Baltic Fleet, and, on days when foreign wires reported which harbor the fleet had shown up in, all Japan talked of little else. The people whose bath Saneyuki used must have thought it was only natural to sound him out.

"Will we win the war?" Sometimes they asked him this too.

That sort of question he could answer with an easy conscience. "Yes, we will." That was all he had to say. As a military man, he certainly wasn't going to predict defeat, and, in fact, he did believe that the war was Japan's to win.

But saddled as he was with absolute orders to sink every last enemy ship, coming up with a victory plan was far from easy. He knew the speed of every ship in the Baltic Fleet, and naturally the maneuvering speed of every squadron in Tōgō's fleet was fresh in his memory. As Saneyuki peered at the ceiling, all those different ships traveling at their various speeds ceaselessly came and went in the emptiness overhead, jumbled up together. Now and again he would think, "That formation's no good," and wipe the slate clean. Then Tōgō's fleet would reappear in some fresh formation and set out anew on the ceiling's billowing waves.

* * *

"Military strategy is something to be acquired on your own, not something to be learned from elders and bygone generations through books and lectures." Saneyuki later stated this opinion in a lecture at the Naval Staff College.

He carefully explained the way to acquire such knowledge: pore over all sorts of history books, read every book on military science available, and extract principles from them yourself. The only way to master the subject was to study it on one's own. In short, textbooks were things each student had to make for himself.

Saneyuki's strategy against the Baltic Fleet was his own creation, one not to be found in the strategy textbooks of any country in the world. As we've said, the attack plan he worked out came to be known as the "seven-stage strategy." They had to sink every last enemy ship—this, he believed, was the only way. Basically, he divided the sea from around Cheju Island to Vladivostok into seven sectors, each representing a stage in the strategy.

In stage one, as soon as the Baltic Fleet appeared in the waters around Japan, rather than engaging it in a major battle right away, the navy would start by sending out speedy small craft—torpedo boats, destroyers, and the like—to attack the enemy's main force and sow confusion. This plan bore a strong resemblance to the tactics of Takeda Shingen, the brilliant sixteenth-century general; Saneyuki read about him avidly.

In stage two, the Japanese fleet would attack the enemy fleet the following day in full force. This would be the most important phase of the battle. In stages three and five, after sundown following the full attack, small craft would again be sent on an all-out torpedo attack. This was to be more of a surprise raid than a frontal attack.

The following day, the curtain would rise on stages four and six. The greater part of the fleet, not all of it, would pursue the remnants of the enemy from around Ulleung Island to Vladivostok Harbor. The harbor itself represented stage seven and would be lined with mines ahead of time.

Enemy ships would be shepherded into the harbor minefield and every last one sunk.

It was a bold plan. The seven stages were interconnected, the various phases smoothly interlocking, without gaps. No naval battle plan before or since could rival this one in precision and thoroughness. Before Saneyuki, naval battles were largely rough-and-tumble affairs, hit or miss. Saneyuki's painstaking approach was something he learned rather from his study of land battles.

Saneyuki thought of nothing but this seven-stage strategy. He pondered it while carrying his mother piggyback to and from her borrowed bath, not to mention all the time he lay flat on his back with his eyes on the ceiling.

"A repeat of the August 10 battle of the Yellow Sea would be Japan's undoing." That thought lay always in the back of his mind. In that earlier battle, as we've seen, Japan had barely managed to squeak out a victory when a shell happened to land squarely on the enemy flagship, thus sowing wild disorder in the enemy's leadership and formation. Without that happy coincidence, "There's no way we could possibly have won." Saneyuki would always say this in later years when the conversation turned to the battle of the Yellow Sea.

Indeed, that earlier battle had turned on a fluke. In preparing to do battle with the fast-approaching Baltic Fleet, Saneyuki sought to rule out the element of chance. That was his "seven-stage strategy."

*　*　*

The Baltic Fleet, having set out on the trouble-plagued voyage now known as "Rozhestvensky's crossing," was just entering waters off the coast of Africa. Its commander in chief was aiming at the record-setting goal of leading more than forty ships of various sizes and functions some 18,000 nautical miles around the globe, all the way from Russia to an archipelago in the Far East. The mere thought of all that the task involved boggles the mind.

"If we can sink Tōgō and his fleet to the bottom of the sea, all these hardships will be converted to memories that sparkle like jewels." That was how people felt about it.

Yet among the crew of twelve thousand, no one was confident of victory. That level of anxiety is perhaps only natural in the military. Even in Tōgō's fleet, not everyone was sure of winning by any means. Total confidence was probably a sign of either ignorance or mental instability.

But with absolute authority the Russian state, that largely medieval icon, commanded everyone from Rozhestvensky to the cooks and paymasters to join in the voyage of 18,000 nautical miles. That was all there was to it. To a man, they had no choice but to yield. Anyone who did not was subject by law to death or imprisonment.

The source of difficulties lay in the failure to guarantee the conditions necessary for the success of the epic voyage. Most harbors along the route were controlled by Britain or under British influence. Great Britain was Japan's representative on the seas of the world. To the extent possible under international law, Great Britain intended to interfere with the voyage of the Baltic Fleet and wear out its crew.

"They are rascals of the sea and rulers of the sea. They are Russia's eternal enemy. How many impediments have they put on our voyage? But we swallow our bitterness and endure it." So wrote ship's engineer Politovsky in a letter to his wife dated November 2.

By then, the Baltic Fleet had already passed by the shores of nine countries: Germany, Sweden, Norway, Denmark, Holland, Belgium, Great Britain, France, and Spain. All that remained was Portugal before they entered on the shore of Africa.

After Politovsky wrote that letter, the fleet experienced heavy rain. Even though it was November, the ships were unbearably hot and stuffy. As they steamed on, those same pesky followers—the British cruisers—stayed hot behind them. As a result, the crews slept fully dressed next to their guns, as they had done ever since first setting out. They were exhausted. Wearing out the Russian sailors was the primary goal of the British fleet. Exhausting sailors was no violation of international law.

In all other respects, the voyage was going smoothly at that time. On November 3, at Tangier in the French colony of Morocco, even the officers turned pitch black from coal dust as they loaded coal before setting sail again on the fifth. Every ship was so weighted down that although Russian ships normally rode high in the water, they were quite low. One of the battleships carried over 3,000 tons of coal. Had the fleet been able to purchase coal freely in any harbor along the way, things would have been different, but the limits imposed by British interference impelled them to load coal in this immoderate fashion when they could.

* * *

Their view of the west coast of Africa afforded no tropical good cheer. Especially to the Russians, who were from a northern climate, it was full of dark and ominous shadows. The farther south they went, the more brutal the heat became. Even if they could have borne the heat, the humidity was unbearable. Laundry would not dry. Everyone longed for the snowbound Russian winter.

The fleet entered Dakar Harbor at eight o'clock in the morning on November 12. The harbor enfolded a small island called Gorée, and the city of Dakar, built by the French, lay along the coast. Part of the town, however, was also on the island. France had control of the harbor, which was a command center for their operations in West Africa and served also as a military harbor.

"This is the military harbor of our ally, so here we can load all the coal we want." Rozhestvensky's mind was at ease on that score. Ship after ship entered the harbor and dropped anchor. Humidity apart, this was a fine harbor for the fleet.

In any case, the need to coal was urgent. Rozhestvensky's concern was less how to fight with Tōgō's fleet in the Far East than how to get enough coal. Without coal, they would never even make it to the final battleground.

Though any above-par harbor in the world should have had an ample supply of coal, the Baltic Fleet experienced extreme difficulty in obtaining sufficient coal. That's because Great Britain interfered. In Tangier, British merchants caused enormous inconvenience by deliberately buying up all the barges and coal baskets. Such things happened over and over again. Great Britain was a staunch ally to Japan, but to Russia a devil. At harbors where coaling was possible, therefore, the Baltic Fleet had to load far more coal than they had any immediate use for.

"We just took on all that coal at Tangier! The admiral has a screw loose." Grumbling like this was heard among the noncommissioned officers and sailors, but the situation was not nearly as rosy as those little malcontents assumed. For one thing, while some of the ships had taken on a full load of coal at Tangier, others had not.

"Shore leave will be granted after all the coal is loaded. Until then, no one leaves ship, including officers." Those were Rozhestvensky's orders.

"The success of the voyage hinges on coal," the staff reminded every ship's commander. "Our destiny depends on how much coal we can load." Decks were piled high with dense mounds of coal. Sometimes the stuff was even piled around the turrets.

Nothing was so arduous as shoveling coal. Moreover, the job had to be done speedily, which is why Rozhestvensky ordered prizes handed out. Whichever crew coaled the quickest would receive a prize.

The coalers had to toil in thick clouds of coal dust. Every door and porthole had to be tightly closed or the fleet would turn coal black. Inside the ships, temperature and humidity levels soared to murderous heights.

* * *

The main impressions crew members of the Baltic Fleet took from their experiences on the voyage were of coaling, coal dust, and dreadful stuffiness. Everyone worked in the buff. Their hair grew as hard as wire, their faces turned soot-black, even their lungs seemed to blacken.

One of those who experienced the ordeal, Novikov-Priboy, called it "torture." Night duty was not so bad, but during the daytime at Dakar Harbor it felt as if your body was on fire. Men began to succumb in ever-increasing numbers.

"Faster!" Rozhestvensky was constantly shouting at his men like a nagging sergeant. He himself was on the edge of exhaustion.

The windows of the captain's cabin were tightly shut to keep coal dust from penetrating. The temperature in his room was above body temperature. At times, it went over 50 degrees Celsius. Not only that, the humidity swelled the drawers of his desk so they wouldn't open. His room was like a steam bath. If he went on deck to escape, the sun beat down strongly enough to cause sunstroke.

Black Africans rowed around the ships in small boats, begging to have coins thrown at them. Every ship was surrounded by a swarm of such boats. Sometimes a beggar would come up on deck, or, worse, get into the captain's cabin. One of them sitting in his boat held up both palms for Rozhestvensky to see. They were the color of dried leaves. Rozhestvensky did not have the energy to yell at him.

He had to hurry and get the coaling done. That was that.

As mentioned, Dakar Harbor belonged to France. Though an ally, France did not seem to be as faithful a friend to Russia as Great Britain was to Japan. Around the start of hostilities, it had been friendly, but as time went on, the French attitude had grown chillier. Clearly, Russia's string of losses on the Manchurian plains was having a dampening effect.

Yet neither was France favorably disposed toward Japan. In French diplomacy, Japan was scarcely worth bothering about. As Japanese victories began to pile up, France began to defer to Japan's ally, Great Britain.

When Rozhestvensky requested permission to anchor in the harbor in order to coal, the West African governor replied with surprising acerbity that he must check with France. The fleet had entered the harbor at eight o'clock in the morning, and it was five in the evening when the governor came to the flagship and told Rozhestvensky, "Unfortunately, I cannot permit you to load coal here." The admiral inquired if that was on orders from Paris and was told that the governor was awaiting instructions from the home government, but none had yet arrived. The admiral said forcefully that, in that case, the fleet would go right on loading coal until the reply came. The governor fled, apparently overcome by the heat in the cabin, but in any case the loading of the coal had to be finished before the arrival of the telegram from the Foreign Ministry in Paris. That was why Rozhestvensky was pushing his men so hard.

*   *   *

The Baltic Fleet remained anchored in that sweltering harbor. Fortunately, after the governor sent off a wire to the French Foreign Ministry inquiring about whether it was all right to allow the Russian fleet to anchor there, the ministry had responded with deliberate silence. To order an ally to leave would have been harsh, but at the same time, to give them permission to stay would certainly have offended Great Britain. France was in a delicate position.

Basically, they must have decided to leave it at this: The Russian fleet had barged into the harbor. Told to refrain from coaling, the commander in chief had deliberately and illegally flouted the prohibition. In other words, France was turning away from Russia and casting its lot with Great Britain.

"It's all because our army is losing," fretted some of the weaker-minded staff. "As long as battle outcomes determine diplomacy, France will go right on acting cold and high-handed." Or, in Novikov-Priboy's apt turn of phrase, "France treated us like poor relations." France was still related to Russia but had no desire to continue the relationship.

At bottom, the French Foreign Ministry was displeased that its ally, Russia, would head off for the Far East with a military force so excessively strong that it left a vacuum in Europe. "Then what's the point of the Franco-Russian Alliance anyway?" the minister wanted to shout. France was under pressure from Great Britain concerning French interests in Africa, where the Baltic Fleet was heading. French-African territory and interests were subject to constant pressure from Great Britain. A few years back, when a French explorer planted the tricolor flag in a certain wild region and proclaimed it a new French territory, Great Britain had objected so strenuously that France had no choice but to back off in the face of the threat. At the time, the French government was resolved on war with Great Britain and sounded Russia out about whether it would commit troops or not, but because at the time Russia was ill prepared to fight Great Britain, the business was dropped. Such strained relations still continued between Great Britain and France, mainly concerning Africa as rich prey.

France doubted its ability to prevail in a contest with Great Britain. There was no choice but to turn to Russia for aid, yet where was Russia? Off in the Far East, its entire army locked in a grim battle to the death with Japan. However France looked at the situation, it saw nothing to like. Moreover, the Russian Army was sustaining defeat in Manchuria. From the French point of view, France's prestige in the international scene was plummeting because its ally Russia had exposed great weakness to the world. Great Britain knew this. To Great Britain, impeding the Baltic Fleet was, beyond being a sign of friendship with Japan, a way to intimidate France. France, meanwhile, was obliged to tremble at this intimidation. Why? To repeat, France had barely managed to stand up to Great Britain by maintaining, "We are not isolated. Don't forget we've got the backing of Russia, the world's greatest military power." With the military power of its vaunted ally now in steep decline in international estimation, naturally France would bend over backwards to avoid antagonizing Great Britain.

These were the diplomatic waters over which the Baltic Fleet continued to make its way south.

* * *

With France turning cold toward the Baltic Fleet, what would happen if they were denied harbor, fuel, and water on the voyage ahead? Would they even be able to make it to the Far East?

Why were no diplomatic overtures made before sailing from Liepaja? This was Novikov-Priboy's question, and he came to understand the problem. The fleet's difficulties were, he wrote scathingly, "largely the fault of Rozhestvensky, who saw no point in taking preemptive diplomatic measures and so did nothing to facilitate our voyage. As a result there was not a single port on our route where we could expect to coal unmolested." However, this assessment of Rozhestvensky is harsh. Even granting that he was the tsar's favorite court official, diplomatic negotiation was not part of his job. That responsibility should have been borne by the foreign minister or the navy minister. Rozhestvensky had only the honor and the duty of fighting Tōgō's fleet in the Far Eastern theater. Resolving the fleet's problems at its various ports of call on the way was not up to him.

But it was true that he did say such efforts were "unnecessary." He was a military man who believed in the prestige of the Russian Empire and assumed with pride that wherever the Baltic Fleet might go, no country along the way would dare hinder Russian military power. Those in the military profession always have that narrowness of spirit and vision, which is of course fine as long as fighting is their only duty. They have no need for schooling in the arts of politics and diplomacy.

But the issue in this case was the Russian Empire, an autocratic regime without parallel in the world. Theodore Roosevelt once said that autocratic nations were in the end frail, predicting that Japan, which was not an autocratic nation, would come out victorious against Russia. The frailty of the autocratic regime was also laid bare in the problem of finding ports on the long journey. When Rozhestvensky declared diplomatic overtures unnecessary, the emperor went along with that policy. There was no room for the foreign minister to venture an opinion. Therein lay the frailty of the autocratic regime Roosevelt talked about.

And yet in Rozhestvensky's further defense, let it be said that the great Russian Empire, backed by its military prestige, did not conduct diplomacy piecemeal. Rather, other countries consulted Russia's wishes and followed Russia's suit. "Russian prestige depends solely on the greatness of its military power. There is no other Russia. If its military power ceases to be great, Russia itself will disappear." Even the enlightened Witte clearly said words to that effect. That way of thinking continued to define Russian diplomacy, and Rozhestvensky was simply following along the same lines. Unfortunately for him and for Russia, out on the Manchurian plains Russian prestige was rapidly becoming a thing of the past.

* * *

The Russian fleet, normally domiciled in the North Sea, was for the first time in history proceeding down the hot African shoreline. Between the heat and the rigors of coaling, morale was plunging. Military organizations rely on orders and discipline to function, but in the torpor brought on by extreme heat, discipline started to break down.

During the day, the steel warships became fiery hot—too hot to touch. The upper decks were wooden, and even the planks became so hot that a man could feel the heat through the soles of his boots. Sleeping in one's cabin at night was impossible, and so everyone slept out under the stars. Not even the officers could maintain their dignity but slept on deck like common sailors. Military protocol began to crumble from just such small lapses.

The undermining of morale even affected the orderly operation of shipboard machinery. After the fleet left Dakar, ship after ship reported mechanical trouble. Rozhestvensky's nerves, already stretched to the limit, snapped. He roamed around the *Suvorov* and, when he found anything not to his liking, beat sailors with his fists. Sometimes he would hit them with his telescope, causing blood to gush from the victim's head and even wrecking the instrument.

The transport *Malaya* developed engine trouble, so the whole fleet had to halt. But on closer inspection the problem turned out to be not a defective engine but a mishap. The commander had carelessly allowed the ship's bottom to scrape in shallow waters, causing sand to get in the Kingston valves. Such accidents normally do not occur in a well-run navy.

When the repairs were finally made, the fleet could move on. Not long after they were at sea, the battleship *Borodino* signaled that it too had mechanical trouble. The engines weren't working. Once again the entire fleet had to stop. Finally, one of *Borodino*'s two engines started up, and at least the fleet could sail on. They were barely making 5 knots.

"Call this a navy?" Rozhestvensky swore bitterly at his own fleet. Captain Konstantin Clapier de Colongue, his genial chief of staff, was proud of his French ancestry but timid by nature, and he avoided knocking on the admiral's door as much as possible.

The following night, the *Borodino* broke down again. The entire fleet had to stop for the third time. By morning, the trouble was finally fixed, and they moved on.

For the next few days, they navigated the seas of the tropics. On the night of November 21, the *Malaya* signaled trouble. Due to the above-mentioned malfunction of its Kingston valves, the *Malaya* had been taking in seawater and sand. Now it seemed that the pumps to get rid of the water were not working. No longer capable of sailing under its own steam, the *Malaya* would have to be towed by ropes to the next port.

*　*　*

Around the time when the *Malaya* trouble was settled, it was the *Kamchatka*'s turn to break line all of a sudden.

"Serious damage, not operational" came the signal. Rozhestvensky, aboard the *Suvorov*, cursed the commander of the *Kamchatka* with such fury that had he been present, the hapless fellow might have been beaten to death. But, in fact, there was no engine breakdown. Instead, some of the stokers had staged a small rebellion. They quarreled violently with the engineers, who were accorded officer status, and attacked them with their fists. Taken aback by the report, the commander sent up the signal for "damage," thereby attracting the attention of the admiral and the entire fleet so that he could seek their aid if need arose. What kept the outburst from being merely ridiculous was that Russia already seethed with revolutionary fervor. Officers feared that dangerous elements were mixed in among the conscripted sailors, repair crew, and stokers.

The *Kamchatka*'s little rebellion was soon suppressed. The ship took down its distress flags and began to steam along with vigor.

Several similar incidents took place around the same time, though not on any of the battleships. They took place among the conscripted sailors on the transport ships. The firemen banded together and declared themselves too exhausted to man the furnaces anymore. This meant that they didn't want to do the physical labor necessary to keep the needed amount of steam in the boilers. Every such incident was reported by signal flags to Rozhestvensky, who yelled like a sergeant in the military police as he doled out punishments.

Another time, the entire fleet halted at sea. This time, the problem was neither a mechanical breakdown nor a rebellion. Rozhestvensky himself did not know where to find Gabon, the next port of call. The fleet drifted at sea, lost. Such a thing might have happened in the age of explorer-adventurers like Columbus and Magellan, but it was unprecedented in the age of modern navies. Russia had an ancient seagoing tradition, but quite apart from that, Rozhestvensky should have mastered naval technology before setting out on such a long expedition. For the leader of a sea crossing that would determine the fate of the tsar and the fatherland, he was exceedingly deficient in ability, as the men and officers in his fleet seemed to realize. Morale cannot rise when troops lose faith in their commander.

Hopelessness took hold of many sailors. "Rozhestvensky isn't leading us to victory. He's going to get us all killed."

Rozhestvensky yelled at the navigator aboard the *Suvorov* and had him signal the swift tug *Rus* (1,202 tons): "Where is Gabon?" The tug went off to look, leaving at eight o'clock in the morning and returning before sundown.

That was how they found Gabon Harbor, which turned out to be another 20 nautical miles to the south. As soon as word came in, the fleet went into motion and anchored offshore from the harbor in neutral waters just after sundown.

Gabon was in French Equatorial Africa. The Ogooué River emptied into the sea there, and the coastal waters were shallow, making it a less than ideal anchorage. When dawn broke, they found a dark emerald forest, the very emblem of a hot and humid climate, pressing up to the edge of the shore.

*   *   *

Gabon had only a single wharf, and no facilities to justify dignifying it with the name "harbor." Seven hundred white Europeans lived there. The sudden appearance of the fleet raised a huge stir.

"With a harbor that small, there's no reason for us to force our way in and cause trouble." Rozhestvensky had each ship in the fleet lower anchor outside the harbor. Since they were outside French territorial waters, there was no need to obtain formal permission. "What most gets under my skin," the admiral also said, "is the French spirit. Have they ever once acted like our friends?"

They spent the night anchored offshore, swaying all night in the unquiet waters.

The next day before noon, a steam launch came along from shore with a lieutenant of the French Navy on board. He came up to the stern of the *Suvorov*, intending to bring his launch alongside the flagship, but ran into trouble. The sheer size of the battleship interfered with the motion of the waves, causing eddies in the wake. His boat nearly capsized, but finally he drew it alongside and came aboard. Though he was only a lieutenant, he represented the French nation, and so Rozhestvensky and his elegant chief of staff greeted him with great courtesy and invited him to lunch.

"Have you any fresh news of the war?" Clapier de Colongue, whose name was French, asked the question in French.

Smiling, the French officer shook his head. "*Non.*" In that part of the world, newspapers were sometimes two weeks late, he explained. He seemed to know nothing. Hard as it is to believe, Rozhestvensky was not updated routinely on events in Manchuria and Port Arthur.

"And, by the way, I presume it is all right if we lie at anchor here?" Rozhestvensky asked with dignity. In reply to this all-important question, the French officer said no orders had been received from his home country.

"That's fine, of course," said Rozhestvensky. "After all, your country and ours are bound by an alliance." To himself, he thought, "Poor devil. The tropical climate has gone to his head."

After the French officer left, a steamship flying the German flag appeared and provided coal for the fleet. Of the two allies, Germany proved the more reliable. Once again, the men started up the arduous task of coaling ship.

But soon a messenger arrived from France's local governor. "We must insist you refrain from coaling here."

Why were the French so hardhearted?

"These are neutral waters!" Rozhestvensky deflected the interference with an angry roar. Yes, said the governor's messenger, they knew. They weren't trying to engage him in a debate over international maritime law, they were making a request. Could he not pick some other, more remote harbor and do his coaling there?

Rozhestvensky let this go without comment. The hot-tempered admiral came dangerously close to yelling, "Damn you Frenchmen, currying favor with the British!" Apparently, he thought better of provoking another international incident there in the wilds of Africa and contained himself. Studiously ignoring the request, he had his men carry on with the coaling.

What upset Rozhestvensky even more was the arrival of a telegram from St. Petersburg concerning the fleet's anchoring outside the harbor of Gabon. "Unwise to offend the French. Even though you are in neutral waters, avoid stopping around Gabon. Go elsewhere." The psychology of Russian diplomacy was on full display. Although allied to the two powerful nations of France and Germany, Russia was at war with Japan, a nation with no European connections, and the theater of war was way off in the Far East. Russia's allies had grown distant and worse—France in particular was downright chilly.

"What's the Russian Foreign Ministry up to?" The staff of the fleet were severely critical of their country's diplomacy, and clearly St. Petersburg did deserve their criticism. But Rozhestvensky merely cursed French hard-heartedness. When it came to the ineptitude of Russian diplomacy, he did not have the passion to leap on the sailors and knock them around.

There is a real question about whether the Russian Empire had any foreign policy at all. Notorious in Europe for brazenly ignoring obligations to its allies whenever doing so suited its purposes, Russia was in no position to rail at other countries for turning a cold shoulder. Rozhestvensky, moreover, was decidedly Russian in his makeup, insensitive to diplomatic niceties and convinced that foreign policy was decided by military prestige alone. He, like other Russian politicians and military men, had little fear of diplomatic isolation.

Forsaken by the world's diplomats, the ships of the Baltic Fleet were, in Novikov-Priboy's memorable description, "vagabonds"—though Rozhestvensky was quite oblivious to this fact. Or, to put it another way, he was brazenly audacious.

He ignored the telegram from home and finished the coaling.

* * *

The Baltic Fleet lingered for some time in the waters off Gabon. Securing coal was not the only reason. A storm warning had been issued for Cape of Good Hope—though no one knew how much faith to put in the weather report.

Some of the officers were allowed to go ashore. None of them did so with great glee. As a matter of fact, the town of Gabon was abuzz with talk of four Frenchmen who had been captured and eaten in the jungle a few days earlier.

The Russian officers who went ashore included some who had grown friendly with a French officer and under his guidance, paid a visit to the king. To their amazement, he appeared wearing a British naval uniform and a cocked hat.

The Russians had some pleasant memories of Gabon. They all bought souvenirs, including lances tipped with a wild animal's fang, musical instruments made of bone, parrots, and other brightly colored birds, and the like. All of them visualized what it would be like to return home with those souvenirs in hand.

But concerning the progress of the war in the Far East, they remained pretty much in the dark. A certain transport ship had received a private telegram from Hamburg with the news that "Kuropatkin has routed the Japanese Army from the Manchurian plains and is driving it to the sea."

Word spread like wildfire through the fleet, filling everyone with delight even though they remained somewhat skeptical.

On December 1 at five o'clock in the evening, the fleet weighed anchor and left Gabon. Where they would go next, not even the officers of the fleet had any clear idea.

The next day, December 2, each ship celebrated the crossing of the equator with a festival. On the *Suvorov*, from nine o'clock in the morning, men dressed up as Africans, their bodies painted black, appeared dragging a gun carriage used in land battles. On top of it were people dressed up as Neptune, Venus, the sea god Triton, and so on. Members of the military band gathered around them and marched gaily in a parade from stem to stern. Rozhestvensky watched too from his place on the bridge.

As he watched the parade, not even Rozhestvensky had yet made up his mind concerning that all-important question of where the fleet should head next. His chief of staff suggested someplace held by Portugal, a small country unlikely to show much inclination to impede their progress. But the navigator opposed this on the grounds that he could not find any likely place. There was also the possibility of entering German territory. Germany seemed more amiably disposed to the fleet than France.

Rozhestvensky's approach to ports of call was much more high-handed than that of his staff. "No need to worry about diplomacy." But in the end he would create diplomatic incidents everywhere he went.

*   *   *

Around this time, there was a flurry of communication with the German colliers who were supplying the fleet with coal. They agreed to meet again in Great Fish Bay, a Portuguese territory where, as the name suggests, fish were plentiful. The German ships set off in that direction and arrived a day ahead of the Baltic Fleet.

Probably no scenery is as bleak as that along Great Fish Bay. The jagged, rocky shore had no vegetation and was unrelievedly brown. With no river or spring on hand, there was no town to speak of either. There was a scattering of perhaps a dozen houses lacking any urban amenities. A single Portuguese gunboat kept continual watch over the bay.

The orders were a sign of British interference. Calculating that the next port of call for the Baltic Fleet would have to be somewhere in that area, Britain filed the request with the Portuguese government in advance. For a small, weak country like Portugal, getting on Britain's wrong side would make maintaining its colonies that much more difficult. A decision was made. When the Russian fleet came, they would chase it off.

But how could a lone gunboat that resembled a mangy old dog chase away one of the world's most massive fleets? The old dog was serene in the confidence of knowing itself backed by the might of the British Navy. First, it went up to the German colliers and ordered them to leave. The German ships held firm—but then the gunboat raised its guns and let fly a thunderous volley. They were blanks, but the noise ricocheted around the bay ferociously. Taken by surprise, the German ships weighed anchor, fled out of the bay onto neutral water, and spent the night drifting there, waiting for the arrival of the Baltic Fleet.

At ten minutes to two in the afternoon, when the warships of the Baltic Fleet popped up on the horizon, the Germans were so happy that they went to meet them—and inadvertently got so close that they were rocked violently in the beam sea. The German ships then reentered the bay along with the Baltic Fleet.

The Portuguese gunboat lurking deep inside the bay sprang out like a faithful watchdog. It acted with bravery, passing alongside the flagship *Suvorov* and rounding the fleet to get a sense of its scale. After that, it returned to the *Suvorov* and cast anchor.

"Withdraw to neutral waters," the gunboat captain warned Rozhestvensky, who ignored the order. His fleet set to work coaling, finished in twenty-four hours, then left the bay. As things were, Rozhestvensky had no choice but to go on barging into the barrier stations of every country along the way.

*   *   *

The fleet headed next for a harbor in German possession. This would be the first German-owned harbor the fleet had entered during its long and arduous voyage. "Now we'll be treated right for once." Relief flooded the crew. Germany and the German people were not merely formal allies, but sympathetic backers of Russia in its war against Japan.

Germany was something of a latecomer to the struggle for colonies in the Far East. For that reason, it had matched its stride to that of Russia, seeking a toehold on the Liaodong Peninsula and luckily succeeding in leasing Jiaozhou Bay. Still, Germany was a Johnny-come-lately to imperialism, always struggling with a sense of frustration and well aware that Russia was its true comrade on the diplomatic scene.

On July 24 two years earlier, the Russian tsar and the German kaiser met in state at sea by Reval (present-day Tallinn). It was a most impressive sight, which promoted the development of closer ties between the two countries. The two leaders each arrived at the head of a great armada and in what seemed to the British sensibility an exceedingly childish gesture, dressed as one other—Tsar Nicholas II wearing the uniform of a German admiral,

Kaiser Wilhelm II the uniform of a Russian admiral. Two days later when they parted, Wilhelm tacked high on the mast of his ship the following signal: "The admiral of the Atlantic sends greetings to the admiral of the Pacific." It was his witty and roundabout way of saying, "Go ahead and dominate the Far East with my blessing."

Since then two years had passed.

When Russia went to war against Japan, Germany's diplomatic position was not as simple as that former signal would indicate, but out of a sense of racial superiority the Germans naturally supported Russia. Wilhelm II wrote to Nicholas II, "You may be at ease about your western border. Germany will take no action." In other words, Germany would not behave like a looter at a fire, taking advantage of its neighbor's distraction to attack the Russian border with Europe. Go ahead and use your whole army in the Far East, he meant.

But when Russian fortunes in the Far East later slipped, Wilhelm II rejoiced that this was "extremely fortunate for Germany." Russia was the giant of the north, and any weakening of its power was good news for Germany. At the same time, the power of Germany's rival, France, was also sure to weaken commensurately. That is because France and Russia were allies, and France's voice in Europe relied in large part on the size of the Russian Army. If the army weakened, that was definitely good news for Germany.

Yet through a treaty of amity and commerce, Germany continued to extend diplomatic goodwill to Russia. The next port of call selected for the Baltic Fleet was the German-owned harbor of Angra Pequena. Here the fleet would not be ordered off brusquely.

*   *   *

Entering Angra Pequena was definitely a lucky break for the Baltic Fleet. The commander of German troops stationed there took the position that he was no diplomat, and so he said nothing about the fleet's anchorage. "I haven't been officially informed of the arrival of the Russian ships, so I have no obligation to take any steps. The ships are anchored behind a bend anyway and are not visible from my windows." In other words, he was willing to turn a blind eye.

"A kind man." Rozhestvensky was pleased. As long as he himself was "invisible," there could be no official visits between the two men, but he dispatched a goodwill messenger nevertheless.

Newspapers were available. There was an English-language newspaper printed in Cape Town, 900 kilometers south, and the articles weren't very old. When the bundle of newspapers was delivered to the fleet, the seafaring

Russians learned for the first time of the fall of 203-Meter Hill. The hill was not yet named in the reports. The gist of the article was that a strategic site with command of the harbor had passed into the hands of the Japanese.

"Then what about the Port Arthur Squadron? What's become of it?" Chief of Staff Clapier de Colongue, his black hair hanging down on his forehead, was on edge all day. By uniting with the squadron at Port Arthur, the Baltic Fleet was to bring enormous power to bear on Tōgō's fleet. But what if the ships already planted in the Far East had been destroyed? What would that do to their battle strategy?

"They're a bunch of lousy cowards, relying on the army for their survival. I never expected anything from them to begin with." Rozhestvensky spat the words out with all the harshness of someone smashing crockery. But he was fooling himself. The grand strategic plan for his fleet's voyage depended on the health of the Port Arthur Squadron.

Of course, whether the newspaper account was accurate or not was impossible to say. The fleet could only continue eastward as commanded by the tsar.

While the ships lay at anchor, an officer aboard the battleship *Oryol* and a sailor aboard the transport *Koreya* each went mad and was hospitalized. Their madness may have been unconnected to the war news, but the news was certainly grim enough to make the officers and men uneasy about what lay ahead.

Though there was no diplomatic tension at the German harbor, its small size meant that only battleships could anchor there while the rest of the fleet, cruisers on down, remained at sea. Gale force winds had been blowing from the first—hardly ideal conditions for the crew to get rest.

"It's always like this here," said a German resident. To the Russians headed to do battle in the distant Far East, there seemed to be precious little in the way of divine protection.

*　*　*

The fleet continued south with the gloomy African coast on its port side, offering nothing to look at but dun-colored undulations. Eventually, they got farther from shore, until land was no longer visible. "Where are we headed?" The sailors took to asking each other this needless question. Whoever was asked would answer, "South."

As if pulled relentlessly by the South Pole, the fleet steamed farther and farther in that direction. The Russians, as might be expected, strongly felt the lure of the south. Their national aggression might have been the direct expression of an instinctive desire to push southward. But the image conjured in the Russian mind by the word "south" was, in Europe, the Black

Sea coast, and in Asia, China, at best. As far as the Russians were concerned, Manchuria and its southern point of Port Arthur definitely felt like "the south." That was all the more reason why they were so determined to fight Japan with blood and iron, to hang onto the "south" they had wrested for themselves.

But now the fleet had gone too far south. With the equator far behind them they had entered upon waters that the Russian geographic sense did not embrace—and still they kept heading south.

The southernmost point was, they all knew, the Cape of Good Hope. There they would swing left and for the first time begin to sail eastward. In any case, the very name "Cape of Good Hope" had a dark and chilling ring. It sounded like a transparent trick meant to calm a worried child—but the men were not taken in by it. They had the typical northerners' impression of the sea beyond the cape as tumbling toward the bowels of the earth in a great cataract. Moreover, the impression was bolstered by their knowledge of reality. The difficulty of rounding the Cape of Good Hope was well known. The sea at the southern tip of Africa was notorious for hellishly fierce winds and angry billows that had sent many a brave seaman to the bottom of the ocean across the centuries.

"Cape of Storms" would have been a more appropriate name, and that, in fact, was how the cape was first christened. It had been discovered well over four hundred years before, by the first explorer from the civilized world ever to sail those seas. That had been a significant era in Russian history as well, back when Ivan III defeated the khanate of Qipchaq (the Golden Horde) and so freed the Russians from Mongol rule for the first time. In Japan, it corresponded to a period of decline in the Muromachi shogunate, a time when shogun Ashikaga Yoshimasa was building the Silver Pavilion in Kyoto's Higashiyama district and laying the foundations for the flowering of Higashiyama culture, which became, with its emphasis on refined simplicity, a template for Japanese culture as a whole.

The discoverer of the cape was the Portuguese explorer Bartolomeu Dias, who ran into a fierce tempest there, was shipwrecked and cast ashore. He dubbed the place "Cape of Storms." But the opening of a route from the European world to India boded well for European prosperity, and so the king of Portugal later changed the name to "Cape of Good Hope." Still later, Vasco da Gama set out by order of the king and became the first to make safe passage through, opening a route to the Indian Ocean and so connecting Europe with the Orient. From that time forward, the Orient had gone on serving to increase Europeans' wealth. Now, however, four centuries after da Gama, the Russian people's armada was rounding the cape bent on delivering a crushing blow to a "rebellion" by the people of the Orient.

* * *

There was something strange about the sea.

Around the time they left the harbor of Angra Pequena, the weather worsened. The wind was calm, yet the swell of the waves was high.

"How come the waves are so high when there's no wind?" The staff puzzled over it among themselves. The waves were so huge it was as if the sea itself were rising, and, when they entered a trough between waves, the crests rose higher than the ship's deck. The ship would ride high on the next giant wave, then gently be let back down again. All with no wind.

"There's the proof." Lieutenant Vladimir Zotov, navigator on the *Suvorov* and an eloquent speaker, pointed to a vast number of fresh tree leaves and branches floating on the surface of the sea. "That proves a storm went through here a few days ago. The storm is over but the sea hasn't yet quieted down. It's still in turmoil."

The commander of the ship, Captain Vasily Ignatzius, listening alongside him, erupted with his characteristic peals of laughter. "That's a new one on me! I've been riding the waves since the days of sailing ship fleets, and I never heard an explanation like that before."

Ignatzius, though by no means incompetent, was prone to sentimental laments over the coming of the modern age of steel battleships with mechanical devices.

"I am sorry to disagree with you, sir, but I stand by my theory."

"You know very well that waves are caused by wind."

Was Ignatzius serious? At that very moment, they were experiencing great waves without any wind, a physical phenomenon causing the ship's bow to point to the heavens one minute, the bottom of the sea the next.

"There is no wind now, and yet we have these waves. High waves in fine weather. How do you explain it, sir?"

"That is the province of God." Slamming his fleshy palm on the table, the commander said this with evident enjoyment. He had introduced God into the conversation perhaps to chaff the scientific bent of the navigator, who was so well versed in the art of handling a steam battleship, or perhaps because his obsession with the fate of his armada after it reached the Far East put him in constant mind of the Almighty. Captain Ignatzius had a far clearer vision of the navy than did Rozhestvensky. In particular, he rated the quality of men and ships in Tōgō's fleet many times higher than the admiral. To be blunt, he was pessimistic about the coming naval battle in the Far East.

"The affairs of seas and navies belong largely to God in the first place." Whether or not he meant it, he said it.

Rather than sympathizing with the commander's state of mind, the eloquent navigator was caught by his words and spoke up proudly. "Science exists for the purpose of saving God time and effort."

"Correct. And war, instead of taking up God's time and effort, needs to rely on scientific thinking. Building a first-class navy is not God's job. To fail to do that and turn to Him for help in time of war may be blasphemy."

The commander had changed the topic. Like other capable leaders, he was savagely critical of the officers in the court at St. Petersburg.

*   *   *

Everyone in the fleet feared the geographical position of the Cape of Good Hope, not so much for any symbolic reason but for a very down-to-earth one: the weather. Would there be a storm there? Uneasily, the men talked of little else.

But although the waves remained high, the weather stayed fair.

At some point, a strange formation appeared along the port side of the fleet—an elevation with a flat, table-like summit. This was Table Mountain, which meant that they were near the British settlement of Cape Town. Beneath that mountain were the finest harbor and city in South Africa, but they remained invisible to the fleet as it steamed on by. The city there boasted better amenities than smaller cities in Europe, and the white population alone was said to number one hundred thousand. But because it was British territory, the Baltic Fleet would have nothing to do with it and steamed by at a speed of 10 knots.

Cape Town was situated with Table Mountain to its south, and from there rocky formations spread south to form a promontory that became the Cape of Good Hope. When they arrived, everyone gathered on the port side to stare. So this was the Cape of Good Hope.

The cliffs were dark and treeless. They resembled the bones of the earth in the shadow of death. The name of the place notwithstanding, there was nothing in the scene to inspire hope of future happiness.

And yet, to a man, the Baltic Fleet officers and crew were thankful for their present situation. The seas by the cape, although said to be wild, had remained surprisingly calm. They steamed serenely around the tail of Africa, cutting a broad swath. From ahead came a four-masted schooner, brushing close by the ships as it passed before disappearing in their wake. The historic sight of the huge armada steaming by the Cape of Good Hope must have been a shock. In any case, for the Baltic Fleet, the Atlantic Ocean was now a thing of the past.

That night, they cut through the beam from the lighthouse at Cape Agulhas. Strictly speaking, that, and not the Cape of Good Hope, was the southernmost point of the African continent. Once past it, they entered the Indian Ocean.

"In terms of direction, up to now we have been going away from Japan." Engineer Politovsky addressed the fat man seated beside him in the staff officers' room.

This was Commander Vladimir Semenov. Just as Politovsky said, on this roundabout voyage, they had been going farther and farther from Japan. Once they had rounded the Cape of Good Hope and Cape Agulhas, however, every meter they traveled as they cut through the waves brought them another meter closer to Japan. Although the way ahead was longer than the distance they had traveled so far, as they went forward they inched steadily closer to the battlefield.

"This is your first crossing, right?" Semenov smiled at him with a red, ripe face. "The first time you do anything, it's poetic. What you just said is pure poetry." Reputed to have the greatest literary bent of any of the fleet officers, Semenov seemed quite taken with the young engineer's turn of expression.

But Politovsky had merely expressed his fear of the battlefield in those terms. He felt not the least inclination to say anything poetic.

* * *

The fleet had indeed gone safely past Cape of Good Hope and was steaming on toward its next goal, the island of Madagascar.

During that interim, prayer services were held a number of times, and the fleet asked God for a safe crossing. What ultimately threatened their safety, however, were the gale force winds and high waves for which the seas at the southern tip of Africa were well known. The crew had been dreading them, and now they attacked from behind.

The first night of the storm was a wonder. Not a drop of rain fell. The sky was perfectly clear, and the moon lit up the waves brightly, and yet the sea rose and fell incessantly, the mast creaked in the wind, and the ship danced on the waves. Not only that, a huge silver shape loomed on the sea in the moonlight—an iceberg. To understand why an iceberg would appear in the tropical sea requires a bit of geographical knowledge. It sometimes happens that a chunk of ice will break free at the South Pole and drift that far north. Some of the sailors, looking out from the portholes of their stuffy cabins at the mysterious object, hastily made the sign of the cross. All the while, the ships rolled and pitched, and their decks were continually washed by huge waves.

Dawn came, but instead of letting up, the storm grew fiercer. The wind still attacked from behind. Looking aft was not for the faint of heart. At the stern, giant waves higher than the ship's mast roiled up and assaulted the ship with ferocious speed. The next moment, the sea poured onto the deck with such force that it seemed as if the entire ship must be underwater. When that ended, the ship would be thrust up, rising to the heavens, only to begin its slide back down into the trough between waves.

Seen from the portholes, the awfulness of the sea was a wonder. The auxiliary ships were at the mercy of wind and waves, their masts snapping to and fro. "She'll be laid on her beam ends!" There were moments when this cry was on the tip of everyone's tongue. Undoubtedly those on the consort ships looked back at the flagship with the same alarm. Sometimes a consort ship would ride the crest of a wave with its stern in midair, the racing screw exposed.

Through it all—amazingly enough—the fleet did not break line and actually maintained its regulation speed of 10 knots. Call the crew persistent or pitiful, there is no doubt that together they brought to bear the greatest energy that any human group could muster. The numerous acts of patience and bravery that led to this result, which individuals acting on their own free will could never have achieved, were being carried out simply because it was their country's order. In all the time since the Russian people had acquired a country whose leader possessed greater dictatorial powers than God himself, perhaps nothing shows more clearly the sweeping extent of their domination than this voyage.

* * *

Many of the crew and officers became seasick in the storm, but Rozhestvensky did not flinch. His appetite stayed robust. "I've been a seaman since the days of the sailing ships," he liked to say when bragging that he never got seasick, but surely it was more a matter of constitution than experience. His own record of hours at sea was thin.

That morning, he seated himself at the admiral's table at the prescribed time. His staff was there ahead of him, but some of them looked greenish. Never before had the ship's swaying been as violent as it was during that meal. A large wave rolled on to the upper deck, and a cascade of water poured in through the open door. The floor was quickly swamped. All present raised their legs and held them in the air while below them the seawater roiled.

"Do something, damn you!" Legs in the air, Rozhestvensky raised his fork in his left hand and shouted at the sailors waiting table. They sprang up and dashed around, brought out canvas buckets, and began bailing out the brine. "Get more men!" Rozhestvensky yelled again.

The admiral yelled habitually, whether addressing a ship's commander or a sailor. The Russian Navy had created that Rozhestvensky, and so much of the blame for his behavior lay with the navy itself.

In the Russian Navy, officers struck seamen routinely. In the Japanese Navy, unless an officer had severe psychological problems, he would never grab a sailor and pummel him or yell at him. Disciplining sailors was held to be the province of veteran sailors or noncommissioned officers. But in the Russian Navy, ensigns and lieutenants junior grade knocked sailors around on the slightest provocation. The likely roots of the practice lay in the Russian social system. Most Russian officers were from the aristocracy or the landed classes, while sailors were conscripted from among the serfs. Landowners in Russian farming villages were frequently seen to strike their serfs, and when the same relationship was incorporated into the navy structure, the practice continued.

Rozhestvensky was no mere officer but the commander in chief of the entire naval force. Never in Japanese history had there been a high-ranking commander who allowed his natural disposition to show through by yelling directly at his men. From the days of the Genji and the Heike through the era of Warring States, the commander in chief was a symbolic figure, someone who appeared to those in his command as a demigod. Even in the modern Japanese Army, which was based on the German model, and the Japanese Navy, based on the British model, this aspect of traditional military leadership did not change one bit. The idea of Tōgō Heihachirō, commander of the Combined Fleet, collaring noncommissioned officers and sailors on the *Mikasa* and yelling at them or beating them up was simply unthinkable.

But Rozhestvensky laid into his men with no qualms, even for the way they bailed out water.

* * *

The next day, the wind and waves were calm.

The fleet was headed for Madagascar. The days of stormy weather had provided a tailwind, so they were ahead of schedule and seemed likely to arrive at this island in the western Indian Ocean in another week.

The sun went down, the sun came up, and the fleet continued its voyage. It became habitual among the sailors to avoid thinking about what might happen at the voyage's end. Good military personnel are accustomed to blunting their imaginations along those lines anyway, and the busyness and discipline of shipboard life and duties rob the mind of its ability to dwell on things. Only noncombat personnel, those who had not acquired the habit of suppressing their imaginations, were always tormented by the terrifying thought that this was a voyage of the damned.

The flagship *Suvorov*, for example, since it carried Rozhestvensky, had hired a staff of French stewards and cooks—all of whom were long gone, having fled when the fleet entered the port of Vigo. The Russians cursed the vanished Frenchmen, calling them "rats." Before a shipboard fire breaks out, rats instinctively smell danger and frequently desert the ship en masse. The Russians were referring to that phenomenon.

One of the ships in the fleet was constantly causing trouble, and that was the repair ship *Kamchatka*. Even the ugly incident in the North Sea—when the fleet mistook a band of British fishing boats for Japanese torpedo boats and fired on them—arose, to be precise, from the *Kamchatka*'s panic. Apart from the commander, there were few military men aboard *Kamchatka*. Most of the crew were conscripted repairmen who, lacking the sense of mission and the discipline of the military man, were at the mercy of their richly active imaginations.

"We're just going to be killed by Tōgō anyway."

"They say the Japanese Navy is better than the British Navy."

They traded such imaginings back and forth among themselves, creating a shared fantasy of terror.

On the voyage to Madagascar, the *Kamchatka* caused trouble. It began to lag behind the rest of the fleet. Rozhestvensky sent frequent signals berating this misconduct. There was some justification, however. The ship's coal was of poor quality and did not produce enough steam to maintain speed. The *Kamchatka* was laden with 150 tons of particularly bad coal. "This isn't coal, it's mud." The sailors cursed the stuff and began to sabotage the ship's operations as a result. Under pressure from below, the commanding officer signaled Rozhestvensky his desire to throw overboard all 150 tons.

Rozhestvensky saw red.

*   *   *

The *Kamchatka*'s behavior looked to Rozhestvensky like nothing so much as a quiet mutiny.

"Why are you lagging behind?" When he put this question directly to the repair ship's commander, the only reply he got was "Our coal generates no heat." The commander was worn out by the resistance of his mechanics, who sulked and complained that the stupid coal they'd been given didn't produce the steam required to maintain speed. But the coal was the same on all the ships. The problem wasn't by any means confined to the *Kamchatka* alone.

At the time, the world's finest coal was held to be British coal, which the Japanese called *eitan*. The strong thermal power of British coal was a basic condition for the fighting power of contemporary fleets. Yamamoto Gombei, Japan's navy minister, had his vice minister Saitō Makoto purchase British coal in vast quantities. Yamamoto's almost mathematically perfect strategy took coal's importance into full account, and so a plentiful supply was available.

But here the owners of the Russian Navy had fallen down. The fleet on its way to battle ended up bearing the burden of St. Petersburg's indolence. This problem was one of the festering sores afflicting the Baltic Fleet, a sore that burst on the *Kamchatka*.Whether Rozhestvensky felt a sense of crisis over coal is debatable. His knowledge of the subject was so limited that he may well have felt "coal is coal, what's the problem?" Not only he but all of the older officers, those who served as ship's captains or held the rank of commander or above, were woefully uninformed when it came to shipboard machinery. As discussed above, this had much to do with Russia's overlong naval tradition that started from the era of sailing ships. Of course, back when Rozhestvensky entered the Russian Naval Academy, the world's navies had already converted to the steam warship. But the military being an extremely conservative institution, the tradition of passing on sailing ship techniques survived. In the Baltic Fleet, only officers in their thirties, those of the rank of lieutenant and below, had received an education from the age of mechanical warships.

The Japanese Navy had no tradition of sailing vessels, having been formed in the era of mechanical battleships. Navy Minister Yamamoto was certainly a product of the new era, as was Tōgō. They were both well aware how vital coal's calories were to warships, and they incorporated that awareness into their war strategy as a matter of course.

When the *Kamchatka* commander signaled a request for permission to throw overboard 150 tons of bad coal, instead of considering the matter scientifically, Rozhestvensky saw mutiny. He immediately signaled back, "Throw the mutineers overboard."

*　*　*

The woes of the repair ship *Kamchatka* went on. Even after Rozhestvensky's reprimand, its speed remained too slow. Puffing clouds of black smoke that filled the sky, it wheezed and gasped as it lumbered after the fleet. The huge amount of smoke might have meant that its coal was low grade compared to the other ships, a point that *Suvorov* staff found hard to judge. Some said, "That could be it." Others took a different view. "They're doing it on purpose." By deliberately selecting bad coal, the crew was trying to go slower than the rest of the fleet. The main advocate of this view was Rozhestvensky.

The day after its scolding, *Kamchatka* again used signals to complain to the *Suvorov* about its bad coal and the problem of speed. Unfortunately, by then, it was nighttime. Unable to send flag signals in the dark, the *Kamchatka* instead sent light signals, an unwise choice. Filing a complaint about the coal was scarcely urgent. All they had to do was wait till it was light out and use the signal flags as usual. There was no reason to do anything so foolish as to send out light signals in the middle of the night.

When the *Kamchatka*'s searchlight began to wink in the darkness, the signalman aboard the flagship *Suvorov* naturally tensed up. In fact, he lost all reason. *Something must have gone wrong in the dark.* That was the conclusion he reached, and that was why he misread the signal.

"Did you see the torpedo boats?"

Whatever got into him, somehow the signalman turned "coal" into "torpedo boats" and twisted the entire message around. Normally, in the navy of any country, the signalman of the flagship is carefully selected, but one of the weaknesses of the Russian Navy—a reflection of a weakness in Russian society generally—was the sailors' lack of education. The signalman that night was no different.

Hastily, he informed the officer of the watch, who panicked, woke up all the officers, and announced that a Japanese torpedo attack was imminent. Buglers sounded a general warning accompanied by the roll of drums.

Rozhestvensky too leaped from his bed and yelled at the commanding officer, whose actions were entirely appropriate. He swept the surface of the sea with searchlights and saw to it that every gunner was in position.

The fuss lasted about an hour before the truth emerged. An officer beat up the signalman, and Rozhestvensky threatened to punish the commander of the *Kamchatka*.

3

SHUISHIYING

Even after the fall of 203-Meter Hill, the battle at Port Arthur went on. However, the tide of battle had turned. From then on, the Japanese forces had the advantage in artillery.

Since Japan was fighting a Western country for the first time, analogies from Western military history began to appear in print. On December 3, the *Tokyo Asahi Shimbun* opined as follows: "203-Meter Hill is like Malakhov Hill in the fighting at Sevastopol. After British forces took Malakhov, the fort of Sevastopol fell in a single day."

The battle of Sevastopol was the climax of the Crimean War (1853–1856), and its savagery amply foreshadowed the savagery of modern warfare. Leo Tolstoy, still a youth of twenty-seven, went along as a subordinate officer and wrote *Sevastopol Sketches* during the siege. Though overflowing with patriotism and admiration for heroic exploits, the work also calls down imprecations on humanity for its overwhelming impulse to value the butchery of war. Tolstoy's wartime experiences led him to a vision of humanity that transcended any state policy. The besieging army produced Florence Nightingale, the first person ever to set up a battlefield hospital.

In Japan, 1853 was the year United States Commodore Matthew Perry's fleet of "Black Ships" came to Japan to force open Japanese ports, causing the greatest shock in all of Japanese history. Shortly afterward, in that same year, the Russian Yevfimy Putyatin showed up in Nagasaki and made similar demands of the shogunate government. Those back-to-back events dramatized a hard geographical fact: Japan lay at a friction point, caught between the expanding might of Russia on the one hand and the United States on the other. Fortunately for Japan, the Crimean War broke out that year, and Putyatin went home to aid his fatherland in its hour of crisis.

Russia's continual drive to expand its borders southward was aimed in part at the Far East, but also at Turkey. The Crimean War broke out when Russian aggression against Turkey aroused the ire of Western powers. Thus, in its essence, the Crimean War greatly resembles the Russo-Japanese War, which also grew out of Russia's southern expansionism, with a caveat: the Ottoman Empire was on its last legs and offered no resistance to Russia's advance. In another similarity between the two wars, Britain sided with Turkey to protect its colonial strategy. Unlike the Russo-Japanese War, however, Britain joined directly in the fighting in the Crimea, along with France and other countries.

In the Crimean War, the Turkish Army was pathetically weak. It's fair to say that the glory of the Russian Empire was built on the enfeebled body of the Ottoman Empire. War makes heroes, and the great hero of that war was Admiral Pavel Nakhimov of Russia's Black Sea Fleet. In later years, his name would be synonymous with Russian naval glory. After receiving training at the naval barracks in Petersburg, Nakhimov spent his life on the sea and was literally, as the saying goes, "an admiral raised by billows."

Nakhimov's Black Sea Fleet was formed in the 1780s (corresponding to the reign of the tenth Tokugawa shogun, Ieharu, in Japan), a time when Catherine the Great, the tireless promoter of Russian imperial expansion, sought to build up strength along the Black Sea coast. Facilities to house the fleet—a military harbor and fort—were constructed in Sevastopol, a city on the tip of the Crimean Peninsula along the northern seacoast.

Soon after the war began, Nakhimov led the famed naval battle against the Ottoman fleet at Sinop, on the southern seacoast. He made his name in history by annihilating the enemy fleet and seizing control of the Black Sea.

Half a century later, everyone in the Russian Army hoped that Admiral Makarov, commander of the Port Arthur Squadron after the Russo-Japanese War began, would develop into "Nakhimov's second coming." Unfortunately, as we have seen, his ship struck a mine and he was killed. In his novel *Port Arthur*, Stepanov has Makarov urging the troops soon after his arrival in Port Arthur to "take the lessons of Nakhimov to heart." The passage continues as follows:

"What does Nakhimov teach us? As soon as you find the enemy, don't stop to consider which side has the advantage in numbers, just attack! We must make the battle of Sinop our example."

"But sir," objected Baron Korf, "this is no longer the age of sailing ships, and the Japanese are not Turks. Mere bravery, I fear, is not enough."

"Of course mere bravery isn't enough. We must also be thoroughly versed in the arts of war. But the point is this—we have nothing to fear from the Japanese! They are by no means the giants they are made out to be."

In the Crimean War, Britain, France, and Sardinia formed a coalition in support of the Ottomans, against Russia. The coalition force's political moves and scheming were convoluted, making it difficult for the politicians to gain firm control over events. As a result, the war dragged on with no clear outcome while exacting massive casualties on both sides. War is the politicians' greatest sin, and it is also the fault of politics when that sin spirals into full-blown decadence. The Russo-Japanese War proceeded satisfactorily for the Japanese side mainly because Japan had more clear-cut goals and better leadership than Russia did.

*　*　*

Did the fighting at Sevastopol resemble the fighting at Port Arthur?

In the Crimea, British, French, Turkish, and other coalition forces lacked any clear idea of how to handle the long, fluid, and slippery front line so as to bring the war to a decisive end. Eventually, by trial and error, they reached this conclusion: "If we take over the Crimean Peninsula, we take control of the war. To control the peninsula, we need to control the fort at Sevastopol. To take the fort, we need to attack Malakhov Hill." The realization that they needed to take Sevastopol came only after a terrible eighteen-month-long expenditure of blood and iron. Realizing that Malakhov Hill was the key to attacking the fort took another year. Four times during that year, coalition troops staged all-out attacks, and each time they were beaten back. The fifth time, they directed their main force to Malakhov Hill.

Just as would happen decades later at the siege of Port Arthur, Russia defended Sevastopol with an amazing show of tenacity. The fort had a defending garrison of only thirty-five thousand. Townspeople, men and women alike, joined in to help strengthen the defense. During that time, the Black Sea Fleet took refuge in the harbor. That move was similar to the situation at Port Arthur, but different in that Nakhimov's successor Vice Admiral Vladimir Kornilov blocked enemy invasion of the harbor by sinking his own ships at its mouth. As at Port Arthur, ship guns were carried ashore in order to strengthen the fortifications with many times greater firepower, and naval officers and men were pressed into service on land.

Toward the end of the fighting, Russian strength was seventy thousand men, while allied forces had increased to two hundred thousand. The fall of Malakhov Hill brought about the collapse of Russian defenses as surely as the removal of a major prop dooms a house to fall. Even so, the Russians endured the siege for an astounding 349 days. The allied forces suffered momentous losses, climaxing at the battle of Sevastopol. Britain lost thirty-three thousand men, France eighty-two thousand.

After Malakhov fell, the Russian troops went north, taking vast pride in the heroic battle they had waged. To repeat, for a grand total of 349 days, they withstood the siege while inflicting massive casualties on the enemy. The fortifications completely fulfilled their tactical purpose.

At Port Arthur, the besieged Russians exacted a similarly costly toll on the Japanese. But General Stoessel hung on for a far briefer time—only 155 days.

*   *   *

Asians were insensible to numbers and records, but Europeans loved to take a quantitative approach and find numerical records in history, and Russians, as Westerners, were no strangers to the custom. Though Stoessel had to defend not the bronze cannonry and brick construction of the Sevastopol fortress but a massive concrete fortress bristling with modern weapons, he held out for less than half the amount of time. This fact would later bring him misfortune.

Russian military leaders in the war against Japan all retained high status afterward except for Stoessel, who was treated harshly by the Russian Empire. He was tried before a military court in St. Petersburg and sentenced to prison. The major reason for the sentence was his failure to live up to the standard set at Sevastopol, but there was another reason as well. In the Russian strategic vision for the Crimean War, the defense of Sevastopol had been largely a matter of pride for the Russian Empire and the Russian people. The defense of Port Arthur, which Stoessel had been entrusted with, also involved Russian pride but had far greater strategic importance.

Above all, Port Arthur needed to hold out until the Baltic Fleet arrived. The Port Arthur Squadron in the harbor had to be safely preserved. It would be disastrous if the Baltic Fleet arrived to find that its only home port was Vladivostok, which offered little protection. Port Arthur had to be defended at all costs, even if that meant throwing stones and eating grass. Premature surrender would be nothing less than a betrayal of the fatherland.

Defending Port Arthur was also important because it gave the Russians a decisive edge in their struggle with Japanese forces on the Manchurian plains. Short of manpower to begin with, the Japanese Army was forced to keep one hundred thousand troops tied down at Port Arthur, a fact whose importance can hardly be overstated. Once the fortress surrendered, Nogi's army would be free to rush north and join the main battle in Manchuria, giving the Japanese a huge advantage. Were Stoessel to yield, the advantage to the enemy would be so great, and Russia's loss so significant, that once again the act of surrender would be nothing short of treason.

In that sense, the battle over the fortress at Port Arthur became the key to victory for both sides.

* * *

Perhaps Stoessel ought not to have surrendered.

At the time of his capitulation, the fortress had enough manpower and matériel to hold out for at least another month or two. There were eight hundred officers and twenty-seven thousand noncommissioned officers and soldiers, not counting another fifteen thousand wounded and sick in the hospital. Stoessel had eighty-three thousand rounds of ammunition, two million three hundred thousand rifle cartridges, and enough rations so that even if he had held out another hundred days, not half his men would have died of starvation.

True, with the loss of 203-Meter Hill the battle had turned a corner. Russian positions that had from the first displayed awesome power, among them East Cockscomb Hill, Pine Tree Hill, and Twin Dragons Hill, had lost potency or even been captured, thanks to shelling by Japanese artillery, blasting by Japanese sappers, and repeat attacks by Japanese infantry. Nevertheless, had Stoessel felt like it, he could have fortified Cockscomb and other surviving positions, or even as a last resort ordered the troops to dig in somewhere on Laotie Hill and carry on a literal fight to the death. Either strategy was plausible.

Russian tenacity in the defense of Port Arthur had a deep psychological impact on Japanese troops, moving them to admiration and occasional despair. They believed General Stoessel to be a man of extraordinary bravery and fortitude, and saw the strength of the fortress as the strength of his spirit. Though the massive fortress was an iron wall with the Russian character, ability, and ideology behind it, in the attackers' minds, it quite naturally became identified with Stoessel himself. But as to whether Stoessel was any such iron man, there are a number of doubts.

After Stoessel capitulated and Port Arthur fell, the Japanese Army treated the general and the nearly forty thousand troops under his command with exemplary decorum, in full accordance with international law and custom.

Besides the natural outcome of getting shipped to Japan as prisoners of war, Russian officers were also given the option of repatriation. Those who placed a premium on military honor chose unhesitatingly to be taken prisoner. Repatriation meant giving their parole not to engage in any hostile act for the duration of the war, a restriction that any soldier worth the name would find anathema—and yet that was the path Stoessel chose. He made the pledge with the full intention of going home, turning his back on men who'd fought under him for 155 days, and go home he did. Seven of his officers refused to take the oath, choosing to be taken prisoner instead. All but one of them are known to have fought valiantly in action at the front.

* * *

Nothing indicates that Stoessel had the hearts of his officers and men during the siege. In terms of military psychology, gaining the trust of a combat unit is easy. All you have to do is be a leader who fights well, demonstrating bravery and cool judgment, with emotional displays confined to the task at hand. Those qualities are essential.

Soldiers are a pitiable bunch of men who only follow orders. The very passivity of their role gives them a keen ability to sniff out the character of the leader who puts them in harm's way. They have practically an animal instinct. They want a leader who is valiant and inspires faith that following orders will lead to victory. Under such a man, the fighting, however savage, is bearable. Otherwise, no matter how their leader may cajole, flatter, and urge them on, far from being inspired, they will feel only a deepening scorn.

Most of the soldiers at Port Arthur, including junior officers, felt that way about Stoessel, in whose hands their fate rested. With him in charge, they figured the war wasn't likely to go their way. They knew about his bureaucratic streak and also that he was concerned more with promoting his own glory than serving the interests of his country. That view was widespread. Stoessel was, in short, no leader. Military society is full of examples of inept officers who cover up their own ineptness by becoming sticklers for military rules and protocol, as if they alone were responsible for discipline. Stoessel was one of those. He insisted on proper etiquette as if he were a leader of the honor guard and yelled if he found so much as a speck of dust. He cherished the solemn beauty of the military, a trait he shared with Admiral Rozhestvensky of the Baltic Fleet.

Rozhestvensky, because of his constant harping on such matters, functioned alone. He had the strength not to fear solitude. He felt no love for anyone on his staff, and the lack of affection did not concern him.

By contrast, Stoessel could be called effeminate. A central figure in Port Arthur's social world before the war, he craved friends he could socialize with. He was partial to yes-men on his staff and unfailingly adopted their proposals, which led to a heavy atmosphere of flattery in his vicinity. It may be an overstatement to say that he presided over a salon of fools, but he certainly did nothing to create an environment where opinions of the wise and the brave could easily prevail.

* * *

Then was Stoessel merely a general for peacetime salons? Apparently not. He had a pathologically strong sense of territory. It often happens that lovers of order are afflicted with an animalistic sense of territory. At Port Arthur, Stoessel wrangled with the navy. In the early days of the battle, he saw the Japanese Army as less of an enemy than he did the Port Arthur Squadron. At every opportunity, public and private, he insisted to the point of monomania that the squadron should pack up and leave.

Before his death, Admiral Makarov, then the commander of the Port Arthur Squadron, noticed the strategic significance of Laotie Hill. The squadron was inside the harbor and the Japanese fleet was outside, with the hill between. One of the Japanese ships frequently lobbed missiles at them over the mountaintop. Of course, with the mountain blocking the way the firing was blind, but the attacks caused a degree of agitation among the squadron's personnel.

The ship would fire off a thunderous volley and then beat a swift retreat. Since the ship fled with speed, the Russians could tell it must be a cruiser. Ever since the First Sino-Japanese War, the Japanese Navy had been refining its technology for shipbuilding and engine construction. Generally speaking, its capital ships were of foreign make, its auxiliary ships domestic. The Russians were surprised to find that Japan had built such an extraordinary warship. It was extraordinary not only for the speed of its withdrawals, but also for its ability to fire from beyond the range of guns on top of Laotie Hill that were pointed at the sea. That Japanese cruiser could fire from a distance of roughly 20,000 meters.

In fact, this was the armored cruiser *Kasuga* and, needless to say, this ship hadn't been made in Japan, but in Italy. Its main guns were unusual in their ability to fire at an extremely high angle. Gunners would point the muzzles heavenward and then fire over the mountain into the harbor. After that, the ship would quickly flee well beyond the range of guns in the mountaintop fort.

Makarov figured two could play at that game. He decided to have his squadron in the harbor fire over Laotie Hill on the Japanese fleet beyond. To do that, he needed an observation post on the summit and proposed to Stoessel that one be set up. The general flatly rejected the idea, for one reason: the hill was army territory.

"If I let the navy put an observation post on Laotie Hill, they'll get ideas and start wanting observation posts on White Wolf Bay and Laohuwei Peninsula. Next thing I know, they'll have occupied the entire fortress." Some attribute this frankly appalling statement to Stoessel.

In the end, a naval observation post was set up on Laotie Hill, but it proved useless. Even the brilliant Makarov could miscalculate. Ships in the Port

Arthur Squadron were able to fire over the hill at the waters outside the harbor, but just barely. They lacked the range of Japan's *Kasuga*.

Leaving Makarov's miscalculation as an aside, my main point is that Stoessel was consumed by his sense of territoriality vis-à-vis the navy.

*   *   *

One extremely good thing that Stoessel did at Port Arthur was to make Major General Kondratenko his right-hand man. Early on, he gave him an order: "I want you always at my side." And yet Kondratenko was not Stoessel's chief of staff. The chief of staff was an amiable officer named Viktor Raznatovsky. And in Lieutenant Colonel Dmitriyevsky he had a staff officer who was intelligent and highly efficient, if lacking slightly in imagination.

Major General Roman Isidorovich Kondratenko, regarded as the hero of Port Arthur even by leaders of the Japanese offense, was stationed at the front as head of the Seventh East Siberian Rifle Division. Stoessel had confidence in him and made him an advisor even though he was not an official member of his staff. After the outbreak of fighting, he gave Kondratenko carte blanche to strengthen the Port Arthur fortress. Although Kondratenko may not have drafted the original plans for the fortress, it was he who brought them to completion midstream.

Kondratenko had been in the engineer corps. He had graduated from engineering college, and so he was experienced in the construction of forts. Besides his engineering expertise, he was also knowledgeable about infantry and artillery. Above all, he was a master tactician.

Those credited as being tacticians are often incapable of being fierce front-line generals. Kondratenko was heart and soul a military leader who could muster his men under fire and lead them into the jaws of death. For that reason, he never strayed from the front.

When Stoessel ran up against a major problem, he would dispatch his chief of staff to the front to ask Kondratenko's opinion. Stoessel was by no means a headstrong general when it came to his reliance on Kondratenko.

Kondratenko's personality was one factor. A reticent and taciturn presence in Stoessel's salon, he smiled when spoken to and deferred to others if the topic was nonmilitary, as much as to say, "As you please." That side of him appealed to Stoessel and, more importantly, it appealed to Stoessel's wife, Vera Alekseyevna, the acknowledged social queen of Port Arthur and a woman whom even Stoessel himself held in some awe. Vera even checked up on her husband's battle orders now and then, it was said. Her displeasure could easily hinder military operations.

The highest-ranking officer in Russia's Port Arthur army after Stoessel was Major General Fok. Not a staff officer, Fok, like Kondratenko, was a division commander. He led the Fourth East Siberian Rifle Division.

That tall, thin army officer suffered from jealousy, a disease that was rampant among Russian troops. He despised his colleague Kondratenko and was far more passionate about running him down than he was about leading his division. He spoke ill of Kondratenko to General and Madame Stoessel every chance he got. In the narrow compass of the fighting at the fortress, his Fourth Division and Kondratenko's Seventh should have worked together, but Fok rejected cooperation. He was passive by nature and perpetually on edge, afraid that the more energetic Kondratenko would invade his turf.

At the start of the battle, Kondratenko said that the Port Arthur fortress was "not even half finished." He even went so far as to declare that "for all practical purposes, there is no fortress." That's how sketchy the fortress seemed in the beginning to a valorous officer who knew something about military engineering.

Fortress-building was a job not for a combatant officer like Kondratenko but for a technical officer, a specialist in fortress technology. Colonel Apollon Grigorenko was put in charge. "Grigorenko is feathering his own nest." That was the talk at Port Arthur. Officials of the Russian Empire were in that respect somewhat Asiatic, inclined to be rather too tolerant of those who lined their own pockets or misappropriated official funds.

Grigorenko worked on the fortress for four years before the outbreak of war, but all he finished was a cluster of forts along the coast designed to fight an enemy fleet. In the event of an enemy land offense, the fortress may well have been, as Kondratenko put it, "not even half finished." Some artillery batteries were still having their foundations laid when the fighting broke out, and intermediate batteries and forts, as well as small-caliber artillery mounts, weren't ready either.

According to one theory, Grigorenko's habit of pocketing funds he should have been paying Chinese workmen made it hard for him to assemble a work crew, and that caused the delay. It was the engineer and officer Kondratenko who stepped in, somehow rushed the construction through, and got the fortress ready by the time Nogi's army came. Stoessel's decision to give Kondratenko the needed authority to get the job done dramatically increased defense capability at Port Arthur.

But Kondratenko failed to see the vulnerable spot of the massive fortress, which was 203-Meter Hill. In the beginning, the elevation had no fortifications of any kind apart from a trench halfway up. The Japanese forces awakened Kondratenko to the hill's importance. On September 19, during the second all-out attack, the First Division asked for and received permission from Nogi's headquarters to charge the hill, but the attack was piecemeal, with no follow-through. Headquarters showed no further interest in the hill.

Those events demonstrated to Kondratenko the hill's vulnerability. He constructed a sturdy fort on the southwest peak and another one on the northeast peak, removed auxiliary guns from warships and installed them on the summit, also constructing breastworks, inner trenches, communication trenches, abatis, light batteries, and so forth. It was Kondratenko who forced Nogi's army to pay a terrible blood price for 203-Meter Hill.

* * *

Kondratenko directed the fighting virtually without sleep or rest. The strength of Port Arthur lay not in its concrete, people said, but in Kondratenko himself.

While Nogi continued his policy of storming the permanent fortifications, Kondratenko went around to each fort by connecting trenches and vigorously encouraged his men. When any position seemed in danger of succumbing, he lost no time throwing in reserves and so driving the enemy back. As Nogi's army prepared to assault 203-Meter Hill, not one fort under Kondratenko's command had been lost.

Throughout the campaign, Kondratenko commanded from North Taiyanggou, near the front. He had a firm grasp of the situation, and whenever a rift appeared in the thick of the fighting he swiftly threw in reserves. When army reserves were depleted, and he ran out of men, he obtained support from naval squads, sending them to the front with much encouragement. He even deployed soldiers assigned to hospital duty. In the final stages of the fighting, he was left with only his aide-de-camp and no one else.

After the December 5 loss of 203-Meter Hill, Russian defenses collapsed and morale plummeted, but Kondratenko alone remained staunchly undeterred. This became an encumbrance for Fok, who had little stomach for fighting.

Two days later, Stoessel held a strategic council in the Port Arthur fortress headquarters. The main item on the agenda was the question: What do we do now?

"Our defense has just begun!" Kondratenko declared with force enough to shatter the subdued atmosphere. He argued vigorously that even though 203-Meter Hill had fallen and Japanese shells were bombarding the city and harbor, most of the forts remained viable, and they needed only to regroup. "Now that 203-Meter Hill has been taken," he concluded, "there's no more need to station men around Pigeon Bay. The garrison there should withdraw to Laotie Hill, strengthen its defenses, and base the left flank of our main defense there."

Fok was amazed. Laotie Hill was located at the extremity of the fortress, and beyond it lay the sea. To say that they would put up their last defense there meant fighting to the last man. Before the fighting ever reached that far, they would surely lose two-thirds of their present strength. Whether Stoessel and Fok himself could survive was questionable.

With that in mind, Fok replied, "A fine plan, but where are the soldiers? Most of the men who should be fighting are laid up in the hospital."

He exaggerated. Port Arthur hospital wards were overflowing with the wounded and sick, but even so there were exactly 6,276 patients. Kondratenko pointed this out and went on: "We will improve their nutrition and speed their recovery, returning them to the front one by one. Also, at the rate our ships are sinking they will soon all be gone, and when that happens, we can mobilize the crews for shore defense."

* * *

Throughout the war council, Japanese shells continued raining down on the city. Stoessel and Fok were dejected, and Fok continually mocked Kondratenko's confidence. Though Stoessel was the top commander, he made no attempt to silence Fok, even appearing to join in with him. He seems to have already been leaning toward capitulation by then.

The one person who unreservedly supported Kondratenko's plan for all-out defense was the normally taciturn Major General Vladimir Gorbatovsky, the eastern front commander. "We have lost our navy, but the value of the Port Arthur fortress remains high. We should continue to fight as long as we have ammunition and rations, and create a diversion for the sake of the North Manchurian Army."

Fok's reply injected nothing new into the discussion. "Yes, but we haven't had any news about how that northern army is faring." The lack of communication from the other theater of operations, while psychologically painful for those under siege, had continued all that autumn and scarcely deserved mention at that point.

The new plan decided on at that December 7 council was based entirely on Kondratenko's suggestion and so was extremely aggressive. But when it came time for implementation, Stoessel dragged his feet. For Kondratenko's vantage point at the front, such temporizing appeared to be nothing short of deliberate sabotage. At one point, amid the desperate fighting and confusion, he told Gorbatovsky, "Your understanding is requested. Please be advised that I may resort to emergency measures." He had an idea of arresting Stoessel and Fok, and sending them back to St. Petersburg.

To Gorbatovsky, who knew that Kondratenko was normally affable and avoided friction, this outburst came as a surprise. He could not condone the idea. For a junior officer to arrest his superiors would have a demoralizing impact on the Russian military and create a highly undesirable precedent. Moreover, such a radical measure was unsuited to siege warfare. It was the same as the talk of revolution then emanating from the capital, he warned. "You would be impeached later by functionaries of the court."

Despite this remonstration, Kondratenko seemed poised to act. Should Stoessel decide on surrender, there was little doubt that Kondratenko would go with the men under his direct command and place the general under arrest.

Somehow, by an unknown route, this momentous declaration of Kondratenko's seems to have reached Stoessel's ears. This is mere conjecture since there is no way to tell for sure.

*   *   *

On December 15, Kondratenko was killed while inspecting a fort. His death was significant for the Japanese side as well as for his own army. From that day on, the quality of the defense at Port Arthur began a noticeable decline. Many a Japanese war memoir remarks on the sense of decline, with generous tributes to the fallen enemy general.

It took four days for the Japanese to learn of Kondratenko's demise. On December 18, at a quarter past two in the afternoon, Japanese sappers blew up the breastworks at the north fort on East Cockscomb Hill. Simultaneously, there was an infantry charge, and after nine hours of bitter fighting the Japanese took the position. One of the surrendering soldiers conveyed the news of the general's death, shaking his head sadly. "With him gone, putting up this kind of resistance will come harder." Clearly, Kondratenko had occupied a special place in the hearts of his men.

On December 22, a Russian soldier who surrendered on Chair Hill also mentioned the general's loss. Nogi's headquarters took this as confirmation, and on the evening of December 23 wired the news to Imperial General Headquarters in Tokyo. On December 25, the news ran in Japanese newspapers. The papers knew little about the Russian general, and mostly ran the item without commentary, merely noting the death of the enemy leader in an advance by the besieging Japanese forces at Port Arthur.

Some in the Russian Army suspected that perhaps Stoessel or Fok had led Kondratenko to his death. It was true that Kondratenko stood in the way of capitulation and that had he lived, the surrender would almost certainly not have gone as smoothly as it did. But in the end, there was no way to prove this suspicion.

On the day before Kondratenko died, December 14, Stoessel ordered him to the front for an inspection. Japanese tunnels had been laid within 30 meters of the north fort on East Cockscomb Hill, making the breastworks vulnerable to a blasting operation. Under the circumstances, Fok declared, asking the men to defend the fort with their lives was pointless. He held that it would be far more advantageous to reduce the garrison and transfer it to another position. Kondratenko disagreed, and so Stoessel ordered him to carry out an inspection and assess the feasibility of changing tactics.

The underlying assumption was that at that point no amount of defensive tunneling by the Russians could possibly prevent Japanese troops from blowing up the breastworks. That they would be blasted was taken for granted. The only question was whether the second line of resistance would remain viable afterward. If so, then there was no point in following Fok's advice to abandon the site. That was the crux of the matter.

Kondratenko braved shellfire to go to the north fort on East Cockscomb Hill. He examined the area with care and reported that the second line of resistance was safe and should carry on.

* * *

On the day of his inspection, December 14, Kondratenko was unharmed. The following day, he was at the combat operations center when he received an urgent telephone message from the north fort at East Cockscomb Hill. "The Japanese threw something funny at us. Poison gas came out, and the men are in excruciating pain."

The first combat use of poison gas was by the Germans in World War I. During the Russo-Japanese War, such a weapon was unknown and undreamed of. But Kondratenko was determined to be on the alert about even the smallest events affecting combat. Ordinarily, a general wouldn't go in person to check out such a report but would send a member of his staff or a young officer on the errand instead. No one was as thorough as Kondratenko in his attention to battle conditions.

"Be right there." He hung up and prepared to leave. In order to analyze this new Japanese weapon, whatever it might be, he took along Lieutenant Colonel Sergey Rashevsky, an engineer. It was already growing dark when they left, and after eight at night when they got to East Cockscomb.

"What happened?" Kondratenko asked First Lieutenant Frolov, the fort leader, when he came out to welcome them. The lieutenant explained. The incident had taken place outside, near the Japanese forces, where Russians were tunneling in an attempt to obstruct the Japanese progress. The soldiers who'd been in the tunnels were in agony from poison gas. The Japanese had hurled in some sort of gas-forming agent. To this day, no one knows for certain what the poison gas may have been.

During the course of the fighting, the Japanese tunneled ever closer, and the Russians dug tunnels to try to stop them. Occasionally, the tunnels became the scene of grisly fighting. One of the Japanese soldiers must have said something like, "Back where I'm from, when a hunter wants to smoke out a badger, here's how he does it." He wrapped pine resin, sulfur, or the like in an oily rag, thus creating a gas-forming agent, and tossed the rag into a Russian tunnel. Something on that order probably gave Russian soldiers that shock and sent Kondratenko running to their side.

In any case, Kondratenko needed to take a look around. Just after he went into the neck of the underground shelter, the Japanese 28-centimeter howitzers thundered. Great shells came tearing across the sky, broke through the ceiling, and exploded in the room.

Frolov was sent flying, but he survived, though badly wounded. He recalled later that after the smoke cleared, he looked up and saw stars overhead. In the dark, it was hard to make out what had happened right away, but Kondratenko's body parts lay scattered all about. Every officer in his party was killed, and nearly all the noncommissioned officers present died instantly too.

That night, Stoessel heard the news and appointed Fok to take the dead commander's place.

* * *

Bit by bit, Port Arthur succumbed. After the fall of 203-Meter Hill, the main players on the Japanese side were the sappers and the artillery. The former dug tunnels and blew up forts with mines, while the latter kept up an incessant barrage of shells. On December 28, Japanese sappers blew up one of the most fiercely defended of all the forts in the siege, the one on Twin Dragons Hill. The infantry finished the job off with hand grenades and machine guns in a desperately fought battle, followed by a conspicuous drop in Russian morale.

The following morning, Stoessel assembled his staff officers for a council of war to decide how to carry on the defense. Despite that move, he had already begun to despair. Seated with him around the table were Lieutenant General Konstantin Smirnov, commander of the fortress; Major General Fok, commander of the land-based defenses; Major General Vladimir Nikitin, commander of the army artillery; Major General Vasily Bely, commander of the fortress artillery; Major General Gorbatovsky, commander of the eastern line of defense; Major General Mitrofan Nadeyin, commander of the Seventh East Siberian Rifle Division; Rear Admiral Viren, commander of the Port Arthur Squadron; Rear Admiral Mikhail Loshchinsky, commander of the coastal defense; Colonel Vladimir Semyonov, northern front commander; Colonel Vladimir Irman, western front commander; various unit commanders and chiefs of staff; and Colonel Reis, Stoessel's chief of staff.

There were three possible strategies. The opinions of those present at the council were split as to which was best.

"Defend the first line to the death." This was the first plan. The ferocity of Japanese attacks had left the line in tatters, but the remaining forts still had life in them, and this energy could be mustered to rout the Japanese forces. This plan had the support of Stoessel's bravest officers, including Nikitin, Bely, Nadeyin, Gorbatovsky, Viren, and Loshchinsky. They formed a clear majority.

The second plan was a compromise. "Withdraw slowly while shrinking the line of defense. Concentrate troop strength in a central walled area, and make that the defense strongpoint." This was Colonel Irman's idea.

The third plan was different. "Don't withdraw slowly, but abandon the first line at once. Retire to the third line of defense, concentrate all military power there, and resist with every ounce of strength." The third line referred to the central walled area, an untouched section from Fort Wangjiatun to Jiaochanggou Fort 2.

The pros and cons of each plan were hotly debated, the atmosphere growing occasionally stormy. No surrender plan was ever put forward. All three plans shared the common assumption that the fight was not yet over. Clearly, Stoessel's officers were brimming with fighting spirit. It's strange to think that the council was held just three days before capitulation.

*　*　*

All opinions had been heard. They broke down into the three plans outlined above, and now Colonel Reis, the chief of staff, had to come up with a final assessment. Reis, whose given names were Viktor Aleksandrovich, had flaxen hair, a handsome face, and an excellent understanding of the situation. Brilliant though he was, he lacked the creativity and the will to develop his own strategies and push them forward. He was probably better suited to be aide-de-camp than chief of staff.

Before the council, Reis had shrewdly picked up on Stoessel's growing despair. He was easily influenced by the commander in chief's moods. Or I should say his understanding, though keen, was largely passive, for instead of using his own ideas as the basis for reflection, he tended to absorb his superior's thoughts and moods and translate those into action. The proposal he was about to make by no means reflected his own thinking. It was something the quick-witted chief of staff had devised, thinking, "Stoessel will like this." The proposal was aimed neither at bringing glory to the Russian Empire nor at exterminating the Japanese forces.

Naturally, Reis never said the word "surrender." In a sense, it takes enormous courage to bring up the topic of surrender, a courage that Reis knew Stoessel didn't have. Stoessel's plan was to create the impression back home that they had fought well, while yet ending the war in surrender. For that it would be necessary to create the impression that the course of the fighting had made surrender unavoidable. As Stoessel's trusty aide, Reis came up with a plan reflecting that intent. He never exposed these thoughts while he worked out his plan. He saw before him not the Japanese Army but Stoessel, while Stoessel's own eyes were fixed solely on the Russian government. The abuses of the military in late imperial Russia were exposed even in this crucial encounter.

Reis stood up. First, he spoke glowingly of the Russian troops. The Port Arthur fortress had once been the most important base of the Port Arthur Squadron, but the squadron was now gone and only the fortress survived, having fulfilled its strategic role. Moreover, the fortress had also served the important purpose of tying down one hundred fifty thousand (actually one hundred thousand) Japanese troops in Port Arthur. The battle had gone on for seven months. That mission was fully accomplished as well.

Colonel Reis made the above points, embellishing his words with fine rhetoric.

But before he could say any more, he was interrupted by Lieutenant General Smirnov, the fortress commander.

"Viktor Aleksandrovich," Smirnov began politely, "what in the world are you leading up to? Surely not a call for surrender?" Smirnov had picked up on the surrender talk from the atmosphere among Stoessel and his aides.

Reis was flustered. He hadn't counted on this. The rhetoric he was employing was intended to hint at surrender without actually using the word, and then, by the artful use of vehement language, to get the atmosphere of the council to move in just the direction he wanted. Now he had been interrupted at a critical juncture, and the dreaded word "surrender" had come from Smirnov's mouth. He was forced to show his hand.

"We have just over ten thousand soldiers capable of combat," he said. "Even they are not in adequate condition, weakened by scurvy from lack of vegetables." This was true. There was plenty of food, but the lack of vitamin C, the inevitable result of an extended siege, was causing many soldiers to complain of anemia and painful shins. The worst cases had been hospitalized.

But as long as they still had an abundance of ammunition—eighty-five thousand shells, two million five hundred thousand rifle cartridges—how could they surrender?

Pressed, Reis strove to make his case in a logical fashion. "The fort on Twin Dragons Hill has already fallen. Its collapse will lead in turn to the collapse of the entire area in front of it. And not only that. It's all very well to speak of defending the second line, but in practical terms the terrain consists of independent hills. It's not at all the sort of terrain that is conducive to infantry resistance. And what happens if Japanese troops storm the city? There will be a bloody battle in the streets, and all the wounded in the hospitals could come under the sword."

Stoessel was particularly concerned about that eventuality. At the outbreak of the war, he hadn't evacuated his wife to Russia. Many of the other generals had family in Port Arthur too. Stoessel's concern extended to such nonmilitary factors, and Reis was giving voice to his feelings.

"Instead of letting that happen," persisted Reis, "what if we initiated talks on capitulation even before the second line falls? The talks would be more profitable if we initiated them while we still retained some fighting strength."

"Absurd," said Smirnov. "Granted, the garrison has shrunk to half its size, and the position's guns are reduced by half as well. We may have only enough rations to hold out another month. But those conditions are normal in a siege. There's nothing particularly dire about our situation. Any talk of capitulation at this stage would be the height of folly."

*　*　*

Let me interject that the post "commander of the Port Arthur fortress" had previously belonged to Stoessel. At the outbreak of the war, he received authority over the entire Kwantung Fortified Region, and Smirnov took over as commander of the Port Arthur fortress. So even if Stoessel was Smirnov's superior officer, he could hardly ignore the other man's declaration of opposition to surrendering the fortress.

Many of the officers sided with Smirnov, including Gorbatovsky and Rear Admiral Viren, leaving Stoessel's chief of staff Colonel Reis high and dry.

"We can still fight," said Smirnov. "If we abandon our field positions and shrink the defense front, a handful of men can defend it adequately. Specifically, we should pour all our efforts into defending the old siege wall at the front. Then, while inflicting casualties on the enemy, we can gradually withdraw to the rear line of defense."

That was the standard approach to defense of a fortress. Some of those present pounded their fists on the table in agreement, leaving Reis even more isolated.

By rights, Stoessel ought to have come to the rescue of his trusty chief of staff and revealed his real intention to capitulate. But he judged that the mood was not propitious. At a time when nearly everyone else was calling vigorously for a continuation of battle, for him, the commanding officer, to propose capitulation would not only affect his chances for later promotion but might get him hauled into military court.

The timing was off, Stoessel decided. Reis's remarks had been, in military terms, a probing volley. To find out if the enemy was lurking in a clump of trees, you fired into them. If enemy soldiers were present, they would return fire, and, if not, all would be still. In effect, Stoessel had used Reis to fire a probing volley, and the clump of trees had returned fire. Stoessel learned that his men had far more fighting spirit than he had imagined. To broach the possibility of surrender would lead to his own downfall as military chief.

Stoessel cast Reis to the winds. "I will fight," he concluded. "I agree with General Smirnov. We'll defend the first line to our utmost ability, falling back to the second line if we must, and put up our final resistance there. May God be with us."

The plan was set.

Then General Gorbatovsky stood up. "While we sit here, the war situation continues to develop. Last night Japanese forces took Twin Dragons Hill. My report says they're now rebuilding the fort there in order to train their guns on the city of Port Arthur. I say we need to use our artillery to stop them from doing it."

"That's Bely's job," said Stoessel. He instructed Major General Bely, commander of the fortress artillery, to issue the necessary orders at the front.

*   *   *

The fighting continued.

At the front, Major General Gorbatovsky had one prayer: "May Stoessel's spirit stay strong." He made the following observation to his aide-de-camp: "For the past two hundred days, we've had continuous victories against the Japanese. But ever since we lost 203-Meter Hill, the tide has turned, and the situation is worsening day by day. A military man shows his true mettle not when he's riding the crest of victory but in times like these." By "a military man," he was presumably alluding to Stoessel. He meant that as long as an army was winning, its commander could stay at the rear and drink if he chose, but when the army was losing it was time for him to throw away his bottle, draw his sword, and jump in at the front, encouraging the rank and file and getting them to do their duty as soldiers to the very end.

But as far as Gorbatovsky could see, Stoessel wasn't like that. When the fighting was going well, he made rare rounds of the forts, but after the fall of 203-Meter Hill he stayed in the city of Port Arthur and never went near the front. As a result, he was better informed about the state of the hospitals than he was about conditions at the front.

There were a number of hospital facilities at Port Arthur—eleven army hospitals in all, supplemented by another five treatment centers for army patients. There was one naval hospital and nine treatment centers for navy patients. In addition, there were two Russian Red Cross hospitals. There was also a hospital ship, the *Kazan*, making twenty-nine facilities in all. At first glance, this may seem more than adequate, but there were many patients and not all could be accommodated. There were seventeen thousand wounded and sick to care for, and so every medical facility was stretched several times beyond its capacity. Beds were in such short supply that patients were laid on mat-rush bags in corridors, spilling out all the way to the entryway. Pharmaceutical drugs and other medical supplies were also insufficient. And, as mentioned above, there was an inadequate supply of fresh vegetables, giving rise to disease on that account. Those with external wounds didn't heal easily, and many others went insane. Every burst of gunfire set patients caterwauling. It was a scene of unspeakable misery.

Stoessel's wife Vera Alekseyevna often made the rounds of the hospitals as representative of the volunteer nurses. The dreadful scenes affected her even more than they did the patients. "Why must the fighting go on any longer?" Day and night she badgered her husband. "Surely God and the tsar must approve the efforts that have already been made."

And, day after day, Japanese shells continued to pound the old and new sections of the city of Port Arthur. First, there would be a sound as of distant thunder, and then the shells would fall, shaking windows, floors, and ceilings, and straining Vera's nerves even more.

The horrible plight of wounded soldiers and the terrifying report of guns are part of any war, and those Stoessel was able to bear. What wore him down more than anything else were the desperate screams of his wife.

* * *

On December 30, the Japanese made a ferocious assault on Pine Tree Hill, the eastern mainstay of the fortress. The fort at Pine Tree Hill was not the largest among the cluster of forts at Port Arthur, but it stretched from Battery 1 to Battery 4 and was further reinforced by redoubts, making it a power to be reckoned with. The attack was led by the First Division, from Tokyo.

Around this time, the Japanese forces, formerly sunk in gloom, became filled with the surging spirit of victory. The divisions vied restlessly with one another to push forward. The Eleventh Division (Zentsūji) had already taken the northern fort on East Cockscomb Hill, and the Ninth Division (Kanazawa) had occupied Twin Dragons Hill, but the First Division's assault on Pine Tree Hill was behind schedule.

"If the hill doesn't fall, I personally will lead the charge!" With this bold declaration, the division commander Matsumura Kanemoto led his troops to the foot of the hill. Momentum apparently fills the human heart not just with courage but with a sense of exaltation as well. Before the fall of

203-Meter Hill, no division commander had ever ventured so close to the front.

The method of attack would be the same as usual. First, the sappers would go in and clear the way for an infantry charge by blowing up the earthworks, which served as protection like a turtle shell. The blasting operation would be overseen by Lieutenant Colonel Chikano Kyūzō, head of the First Combat Engineer Battalion. The instant the explosion went off, the infantry corps would then storm the fort while providing cover to the sappers. The infantry was led by Major General Nakamura Masao.

The entire First Division did not participate in the assault. Some three thousand two hundred Japanese troops were involved, including infantry, sappers, and artillery. They were up against two hundred Russian soldiers defending the fort on the summit, led by a Captain Spredov. To draw a naval analogy, the fort was a battleship, the storm troopers' fishing boats swarming around it. But compared with before the fall of 203-Meter Hill, the Japanese artillery was not so hard pressed and could focus on pounding the defenses on Pine Tree Hill and vicinity.

At eight o'clock on the morning of December 31, the Japanese began a fierce bombardment. By nine, each unit had advanced to its assigned position and was ready for battle. At ten, the sappers' demolition squad dashed forward and lit the fuses of the explosives they had laid in the earthwork. The force of the resulting blast literally darkened the face of the earth, followed momentarily by a huge deluge of sand and dirt. After the smoke cleared, the Japanese raised their faces and saw that the shape of the hill above them had been altered. Then the infantry rushed in. After an exchange of machine gun fire and grenades, the two sides grappled with naked swords.

The ferocious assault was too much for Fok, and he ordered the garrison to retreat. Gorbatovsky issued a contrary order for them to carry on, even sending in what reserves he had on hand. The Russian command was in disarray. And on December 31, Pine Tree Hill fell.

* * *

Wang Tai—"Eagle's Nest"—had an elevation of 185 meters and was part of the Russians' second line of defense. The hill was a crucial part of the Port Arthur fortress because, as the name suggests, the summit commanded a view of the old and new city quarters as well as the harbor. The Japanese fully expected Russians defenders to mount a heroic, do-or-die fight.

The charge was led by the Eleventh Division, from Zentsūji. With orders to "celebrate New Year's Day by attacking Wang Tai," they began battle preparations on New Year's Eve. On the last two days of the year, Japanese fortunes fluctuated. Artillery batteries all around Wang Tai remained in action, inflicting heavy losses on Japanese troops with unflagging strength. Although Japanese troops blew up the old siege wall south of East Panlong and occupied the area, the surrounding Russian positions remained tenaciously strong, directing concentrated fire on the occupying troops without letup.

General Gorbatovsky continued to direct such Russian battles. But his superior, Major General Fok, decided that resistance was futile and gave Stoessel an exaggerated report of the difficulty Russian troops were having. "There's no point in defending this area to the last," he said. "The position should be abandoned and soldiers withdrawn to the second line of defense." Over the telephone he begged permission to retreat.

Stoessel gave his immediate consent.

But Stoessel and Fok had committed the grave error of ignoring the chain of command. Fok should have consulted the wishes of Smirnov, the fortress commander, but because Smirnov was a diehard resister, Fok gave him a wide berth, going over his head to seek the judgment of Stoessel, the commander in chief.

Once retreat had been decided on, Fok phoned Smirnov with the news.

"Are you kidding me?" Smirnov growled. "Whether to retreat or not is my responsibility. Whose order is it?"

Fok could not bring himself to mention Stoessel's name. Instead, he lied and said it was the request of General Gorbatovsky. But Gorbatovsky was then enduring a hail of bullets on the eastern front, putting up a brave defense without retreating a step. He had made no such request.

To see whether there was any truth to the matter, Smirnov had Gorbatovsky summoned to the phone. "It's a plot," Gorbatovsky declared. "We will ignore the plot and continue to do our duty as soldiers of the tsar." He kept right on fighting. Stoessel's and Fok's authority were clearly damaged by the episode.

* * *

Fighting heavy odds, the Russian troops hung on gamely. But the Japanese troops kept up a systematic, blistering attack until finally, at thirty-five minutes past three on the afternoon of January 1, they took Wang Tai.

An hour before, Stoessel had made up his mind to surrender, but the officers at the front had no knowledge of the fact. He said nothing even to Smirnov, the commander of the fortress.

Fok, commander of the land-based defenses on the front, was rapidly losing all will to fight, but to Gorbatovsky, commander of the eastern line of the Russian defense, the fighting had just begun. Even as Wang Tai was being occupied by Japanese troops, he sent a messenger to Captain

Galitsinsky, the officer in charge of that area, with orders to "overcome every obstacle and defend your position to the death." The captain accordingly roused himself, cheered on his garrison, and drove back the Japanese repeatedly. Twice Gorbatovsky sent in reserves he had at his disposal, and the captain took them and delivered further blows to the Japanese. But around three in the afternoon, concentrated Japanese fire scored a direct hit on a Russian hand grenade depot, making a huge explosion and wounding Galitsinsky, who finally withdrew and handed over Wang Tai to the Japanese.

Even after losing Wang Tai, Gorbatovsky did not lose hope, but came up with a new plan of defense. Fort 2 on East Cockscomb Hill had survived. They would hook it up with batteries on the hill and also reconstruct the territory stretching from Jiaochanggou Battery 1 to Pine Tree Battery Fort 4, which had also survived. That would become the new defense line.

In fact, Gorbatovsky did not have the authority to implement any such plan. He needed Fok's consent, but when he sent liaison officer Captain Stepanov to consult with him, Fok was silent and issued no reply. It seems likely that he had already detected Stoessel's intent to surrender. Gorbatovsky began giving commands at his own discretion.

The battlefield chain of command was in confusion. Concerning Fort 2 on East Cockscomb Hill, Gorbatovsky gave orders to defend it to the death, just as the fort came under heavy attack from the Japanese. Overwhelmed, the commander went over Gorbatovsky's head to ask fortress commander Smirnov for permission to retreat. Smirnov was of the same opinion as Gorbatovsky and repeated the order to defend the site to the last.

In desperation, the embattled man turned to Fok and appealed with tears in his eyes. "General Gorbatovsky will not permit us to retreat." Fok ordered Gorbatovsky to allow the garrison to retreat. Reluctantly, Gorbatovsky did so, but he gave the men no rest, immediately sending them to the area near the Beidoushan battery with orders to defend that post to the death.

The time was then half past eight in the evening. Six hours earlier, Stoessel had already dispatched an orderly conveying to the Japanese his proposal to surrender.

* * *

Stoessel's decision to surrender did not come about through open debate. It was his own personal decision. Even his execution of the necessary procedures smacked of his self-centered way of thinking. Later, at his court-martial in St. Petersburg, this point would become an issue. Although Stoessel was the tsar's agent in Port Arthur, with power to act on his own authority, it was naturally desirable that he follow standard procedure when he acted, by obtaining the consent of his staff and officers higher than division commander. He was not supposed to cast aside the great fortress as if it were his private possession.

At the front, the officers suffering concentrated fire from the Japanese urged their men on, striving valiantly to hold their ground. Gorbatovsky was at high pitch, ready to take on the enemy with his bare hands if need be. Numbers tell the fierceness of the Russian defense: on January 1, barely two hundred soldiers defended Wang Tai.

The Japanese attacked from below with roughly four thousand troops. Other Russian positions heaped fire on the Japanese infantry, but Japanese siege artillery corps returned their fire by a power of ten, silencing one Russian flank corps after another. Even then, the two hundred on top of the hill fought on with rifles, machine guns, and hand grenades, driving back the Japanese time and again. The battle on Wang Tai had begun sometime after nine in the morning, and it was around one in the afternoon when the Japanese began a systematic attack. At three, their siege artillery directed intense fire on the Russian soldiers atop the hill, causing the Russian defense to falter. Soon they were down to only forty men, too few to continue the fight. The survivors descended the hill and retreated to the valley to the south. Though it was a retreat, they withdrew only to the far side of the elevation.

Even with Japanese forces occupying the summit, Gorbatovsky didn't give up. He ordered all batteries in the area to blast the top of Wang Tai, where the Japanese were, hard enough to lower the hill .

While this desperate struggle was going on, behind the lines Stoessel had resolved on surrender. Later on, people said that the Japanese takeover of Wang Tai was the last straw, but that didn't happen till half past three—an hour or more after Stoessel sent the orderly off with the letter of surrender. In short, he made up his mind while the bloody fighting at the front was at its height.

To execute the crucial mission, Stoessel chose a boyish young officer-in-training named Malchenko. Even though the mission consisted only in bearing Stoessel's letter to the other side, one wonders why the general didn't get a regular officer to do it. Malchenko was little better than a senior waiter in Stoessel's headquarters. Still, there was no need to worry about him protesting to Stoessel, and he could make his way through the embattled Russian troops without arousing suspicion. That may explain in part why he was chosen.

* * *

Stoessel made his decision when the Japanese troops first attacked Wang Tai. In a sense, he was following a preset schedule. Rather than put up a do-or-die battle at the second line of defense, he had apparently made up his mind beforehand that once the second line of defense came under attack, it would be time to surrender. Before drafting the letter that morning, he summoned Rear Admiral Loshchinsky, the coastal defense commander, and ordered him to be prepared to send a destroyer to Yantai at any time, if necessary. Even though Japanese shelling had destroyed the squadron in the harbor, the *Statny* and a few other destroyers had alone escaped with light damage and were capable of going as far as the neutral harbor of Yantai on the northeastern shore of Shandong Peninsula.

Further, in preparation for surrender, he ordered Fok, who was of the same mind, to put the military flag, important documents, and such in one place. Stoessel intended to transport them out of Port Arthur on the destroyer *Statny*.

At around two thirty, Fok rang up. "Unfortunately," he said, "hope is vanishing for Wang Tai. It probably won't last another hour. The Japanese forces have huge momentum, and if we lose Wang Tai they'll probably attack our third line of defense immediately. Putting up a last-ditch resistance there is a desktop plan and nothing more." With those words, he easily overturned the plan they had agreed on at the last council of war.

Stoessel immediately concurred with Fok's statement. Shortly thereafter, he ordered Chief of Staff Reis, standing at his side, to draft a letter to send to the Japanese Army. The letter was in English. For Russians, French was the universal language, but for Japanese it was English, as Stoessel and Reis both knew. When the letter was finished, Stoessel sealed it tightly, called Malchenko, and ordered him to go to the Japanese front and hand it over.

Malchenko set off through the new city quarter, accompanied by several noncommissioned officers and enlisted men from headquarters. He took the road in the northwest quarter, past Fort 1 on West Taiyanggou, and made his way through valleys winding among the complex of forts, heading north. It was windy and cold, and he could feel the hardness of the road through the soles of his boots. The ground must have been frozen solid a good meter down.

"Where are you off to?" a friend called out.

Malchenko had a noncommissioned officer answer. "Red Cross negotiations. Don't want the hospitals getting hit."

Malchenko walked 3 kilometers amid thundering gunfire until finally he had left the Russian vanguard behind. Then he raised the white flag.

*　　*　　*

Malchenko's raising of the white flag was witnessed by soldiers in the Second Infantry Regiment of the Japanese First Division.

Surrender.

No one thought that's what it was. The Japanese troops sensed that the fighting strength of the Port Arthur fortress was as tenacious as ever. It did often happen that the Russians would send over a messenger with a white flag. Generally, it was about gathering up the dead, or a request to please keep Japanese missiles aimed at the city from striking hospitals. That sort of thing.

In any case, the Second Infantry Regiment decided to send an officer to talk with Malchenko. The location was, to use the Japanese Army's geographical nomenclature, "in front of Fort C, south of Shuishiying." Fort C was at this time occupied by Japanese troops.

First Division headquarters on Takasaki Yama quickly phoned Nogi's headquarters. Lieutenant Colonel Shirai Jirō took the call.

"What sort of letter is it?"

"It's addressed to the commander of the Third Army."

When he heard that, Shirai knew instinctively what it meant.

The psychology of a military man under such circumstances is an interesting study. "I'll bet it's a surrender." He started to say the words, but bit them back. The Japanese were battle fatigued, and headquarters was exhorting the men at the front, pushing them to the brink. Fearing that such a hazy observation might be taken as a sign of cowardliness, Shirai said in a carefully controlled voice, "Very well, send it to me." Hastily, he added, "Send it straight here by a mounted orderly."

But the First Division staff officer at the front, attaching little significance to the event, replied carelessly, "Oh, we only heard about the message over the phone from the Second Regiment. We haven't actually seen the letter yet. As soon as it gets here, I'll see that it goes straight to headquarters by mounted orderly."

From Fort C to Takasaki Yama, where division headquarters was located, was a distance of 4 kilometers. The letter, relayed by sentinels, took a full three hours to arrive. From there to Nogi's headquarters in Liushufang was more than 10 kilometers. Because army headquarters was still back in Liushufang even though the entire army had pushed forward, delivery of the letter took a very long time.

The crucial letter reached Nogi's headquarters around eight that evening and was accepted by Lieutenant Colonel Shirai, who personally cut it open with scissors. He was so nervous that his hands shook. Though he was indoors, the fire in the fireplace was languishing, and the temperature had dropped near zero. Shirai threw his coat around his shoulders, took the letter over by the oil lamp, and opened it.

The first thing that struck his eye was the English word "capitulation." Barely able to keep from letting out a whoop, he forced himself to calm down and read the letter through. But he had been a French major in college, and reading English was hard work. More than that, his state of mind made struggling through something written in an unfamiliar foreign language next to impossible. Shirai took the letter and went to knock on the door of chief of staff Ijichi Kōsuke.

"Come in."

Before the words were out of Ijichi's mouth, Shirai was already standing in front of the chief of staff.

"Here." He handed him the letter. Unfortunately, Ijichi had spent years studying in Germany and while he was fluent in German, his eyes were unaccustomed to English.

"What is it, surrender?" Keeping his emotion under control, Ijichi spoke in a low voice, his eyes fastened on Shirai like a sniper's.

Shirai pointed to a word. "How do you pronounce this in English? In French, I know it's *ca-pi-tu-lah-shion*."

"I see."

Ijichi knocked on Nogi's door, then on the door of Ariga Nagao, a staff member. Everyone came out and assembled in Ijichi's room.

Ariga was born in 1860. Though a noted authority on international law, he had studied history in the Faculty of Letters at Tokyo Imperial University. Besides a doctorate in law, he later also obtained a doctorate in literature. He studied law in Vienna and was particularly knowledgeable about international law in wartime.

Ariga Nagao's assignment to join the expeditionary army as a civil officer attached to Nogi's headquarters points up the Japanese government's sense of how to run a war at the time. Ever since early Meiji times, the government had struggled to amend the unequal treaties and on that account had become particular about upholding international law. In the war against Russia, there must not be the slightest deviation from international law, as Imperial Headquarters was careful to impress on its army commanders. That explains the addition of Ariga to Nogi's staff as legal advisor.

After the war, Ariga wrote a book on Japan's active support for upholding international law titled *A Study of International Law in the Russo-Japanese Land War*. He showed the West that Japan, though a developing country, had taken extraordinary pains to be second to none in its observance of international law.

Ariga scanned the letter and announced, "It's an offer of capitulation. There is no doubt about it." He first read the brief letter aloud in English and then translated it into Japanese.

To everyone's credit, not a word was spoken after Ariga finished translating the letter.

*   *   *

Dr. Ariga later commented on that peculiar silence to his students. "It felt as if all the souls of the tens of thousands who died at Port Arthur were gathered in the room. On every staff member's face was not ecstasy, but a kind of crushing anguish."

Had Westerners been witness to the occasion, they might well have found something eerie in the strange Japanese response. Far too many lives had been lost for anyone to rejoice; the emotional toll of the past seven months had been far too great for them to feel like smiling and leaping in the air right away.

"Ijichi, you handle this." When Nogi said this, the mood in the room finally began to shift, as if a spell had been broken.

"Stoessel says he wishes to hold negotiations over the terms of capitulation," Ariga explained, "and seeks Baron Nogi's consent for that purpose. The reply must therefore begin with an expression of consent. He goes on to say that should Your Excellency consent to the above, he wishes you to appoint commissioners for discussing the conditions and procedures regarding capitulation, and also he wants you to appoint a place for commissioners from both sides to meet. The reply should be businesslike in tone."

Headquarters stirred into action. Following Ariga's advice, Ijichi Kōsuke was chosen as the sole commissioner. He would of course be accompanied by Ariga and a host of others, but they could be designated as his entourage. The place chosen was Shuishiying. Concerning time, the sooner the better. Unforeseen contingencies often befell armies in the process of capitulation.

Ijichi finally spoke up with cheer in his voice. "Let's schedule the meeting for tomorrow, January 2, at noon." Nogi agreed, smiling.

Next they had to draft a reply. Ariga, the scholar of international law, was unrivaled in this sphere. He probably had greater expertise in the field of international law than Stoessel's staff did. The commissioner in this case had to be a "plenipotentiary." Ijichi would be invested with full authority to negotiate the surrender. To establish his credentials, he needed a letter of proxy signed by Nogi Maresuke. Ariga wrote asking Stoessel to send someone similarly qualified. When the two sides met, he added, the letters identifying participants as plenipotentiary delegates of their respective commanding officers would have to be exchanged. Without this diplomatic description from Ariga, the capitulation negotiations would probably not have gone as smoothly as the outcome shows they did.

Nogi signed the letter that Ariga drafted, and early the next morning had it delivered to the Russian encampment by Major Yamaoka Kumaji. Stoessel accepted the letter. He appointed Chief of Staff Reis as his proxy in the negotiations with Ijichi.

* * *

Eventually, a ceasefire would come into effect. Naturally, there were procedures that had to be followed. Once the capitulation talks attended by both negotiating parties were completed, sometime after noon on January 2, both armies would issue ceasefire orders to their respective troops. Surprisingly, however, front line soldiers on both sides ceased firing before being ordered to do so.

The ceasefire came into effect in stages. The night that Nogi received Stoessel's letter, he ordered all units of his army to cease attack, without revealing why. Once those at the front learned that Stoessel had sent a letter of surrender, morale would slacken, making it difficult to resume the offensive if for any reason talks should collapse.

Orders to call off the offensive were delivered to all the Japanese troops in Port Arthur that night. However, there was a delay in transmission of the orders to part of the Eleventh Division. With that slight exception, the battlefields fell abruptly quiet.

Surrender talks were set for noon on January 2, and Russian soldiers began to stream out of their army's camp around dawn. "They rejoiced crazily over the capitulation," wrote logistics officer Satō Kiyokatsu, even though it was not yet official. In fact, Russian soldiers stood up in full view, embracing and dancing, and in places along the front Japanese soldiers also came out of their trenches. Men from the two armies beckoned to each other, hugged and danced for joy.

Some Japanese soldiers climbed up on Russian forts and drank sake with their counterparts. And sometimes, when they got drunk enough, soldiers from both sides could be seen going into town with their arms around one another's shoulders, entering what was supposed to be enemy territory for the Japanese and continuing to drink at the local bars. Such a thing naturally violated regulations. But not one officer was capable of restraining this human outburst of sheer delight.

Whether the battle was won or lost, they no longer cared. The carnage was over. The overpowering sense of liberation flowing through men on both sides made them forget that they were soldiers. Though peace was still being negotiated, soldiers of the two armies frolicked together without causing a single incident—surely a sign that human beings are fundamentally not suited to taking up arms and killing one another unless compelled to do so by the state or some such institution.

People on both sides marveled afterward that no quarrels broke out during that unofficial ceasefire. Only the day before, those same men had been locked in a deadly struggle, human bullets hurled against each other.

"Looks like there's going to be a ceasefire and surrender." That a mere supposition could unleash such celebration is a human mystery. You might say it happened because the conduct of war back then was still moral. Or you might say it was because in its length and horrors the war had surpassed the limits of human endurance.

*   *   *

Surrender talks between Ijichi and Reis were completed at half past four on the afternoon of January 2. Nogi promptly sent out an order to all units that acts of war were to cease. Later, at seven o'clock that evening, he gave orders concerning occupation and capitulation. The news flashed around the world.

But those with the greatest right and need to know, those with the greatest stake in the news—Admiral Rozhestvensky and his armada—did not get word of what had happened while they were at sea. The Baltic Fleet was then north of the east coast of Madagascar, which was French territory. Though they may not have known of the fall of Port Arthur, they did have knowledge of something of equally dire consequence. When they had anchored in the straits of Île Sainte-Marie off the eastern shore of Madagascar on December 29, they heard from the sailors on the hospital ship *Oryol*, which had come from Cape Town. The sailors said they had seen an article in the newspaper published at Cape Town reporting that 203-Meter Hill had been taken and the entire Port Arthur Squadron sunk.

Surely not, they thought. How could every last ship of that great squadron end up on the bottom of the sea? The news spread through the fleet like the plague, destroying crew morale. But the report was unconfirmed. The lack of confirmation was their only hope.

Commander in Chief Rozhestvensky was no less cut off from world events than his crew. "Where's my errand boy gone off to now?" he fumed.

His "errand boy" was the steamer *Rus*, which raced ahead of the fleet like a hunting dog. Its primary mission was to find the next anchorage—in other words, the next coaling site. The *Rus* would meet up with a steamer from a German coal company, locate a harbor, and ask French authorities for permission to coal there, scampering around like a transit company's errand boy. As we've seen, France had once been a friendly nation, but out of deference to Britain, it was by then anxious to avoid involvement with the Russian fleet and often meted out blunt refusals—"Do not load coal in any place with French harbor facilities." Picking its way through such diplomatic difficulties, the *Rus* went around searching for likely places to anchor and reporting back to the fleet, always bringing back copies of newspapers from wherever it had been, along with telegrams from home, and passing them to Rozhestvensky. When his "errand boy" came back, he would find out what had happened.

It was January 1 when the *Rus* finally returned. "The Port Arthur Squadron is no more," the captain informed Rozhestvensky. "It's definite."

Rozhestvensky naturally had no way of knowing that not only was the Port Arthur Squadron lost, but that on that very day Stoessel had sent Nogi a letter surrendering the Port Arthur fortress.

*　*　*

Compared to the icy cold of Port Arthur, the heat of Madagascar, where the Baltic Fleet lay anchored, was something else again. The island of Madagascar has roughly twice the area of Honshu, the main island of Japan. Its eastern coast lay on the port side of the fleet, covered with verdure of a green so garish and monotonous that it did nothing to assuage the homesickness or soothe the feelings of the crew from a far-off northern land.

On January 6, Christmas Eve by the Russian calendar, the fleet was still heading north along the east coast of Madagascar. As they proceeded north, the coastline began to show rich indentations, and, just as they started across Antongil Bay, the plucky *Rus* came back. It was there they learned the dreadful news about the capitulation of Port Arthur on January 2.

"Incredible," Rozhestvensky muttered after being informed in his cabin. His eyes darkened, and his expression turned as stony as the rocks on Île Sainte-Marie. But he had to believe it. In front of him was a report laying out the numbers in stark detail: Stoessel had surrendered to Nogi along with a garrison of nearly forty thousand men. Forty thousand men. . . . Then they could have gone on fighting, everyone thought. Was Nogi that brilliant a general, or were Japanese weapons that much more sophisticated than Russian ones, and abundantly available?

As the news raced through the fleet, all the men thought instantly, "It was the weapons." Weapons are a *sine qua non* of any victory at sea. Unable to dig in the ground or run or hide in high grasses like their army counterparts, navy soldiers instinctively understand the importance of weapons. If the Japanese had destroyed the Port Arthur fortress, which cost so many millions of rubles to build, then their weapons must have been superior. And if the Japanese Army had weapons of that caliber, the Japanese Navy must have them too. The sailors whispered such things to each other in fear. Some officers even called out for the fleet to turn around and head home.

Rozhestvensky wrestled with the problem. The double loss of the squadron and fortress at Port Arthur had ripped out the logical underpinnings for the Baltic Fleet's elaborate journey eastward. Now the battle against Tōgō's fleet would be uncomfortably even. The Russian tradition was to outnumber the enemy two to one in any engagement. That advantage had been lost in one fell swoop.

"We'll have to wait for orders," muttered Rozhestvensky in a barely audible voice after conferring with his staff.

* * *

In the meantime, the fleet kept heading north along the east coast of Madagascar, toward Nosy Be. Why did they have to go there of all places, to an impoverished fishing village unknown even to island natives? Their fleet represented the Russian tsar and his empire. The French territory of Madagascar had any number of fine harbors well known since olden times to sailors crossing the Indian Ocean. Diego Suarez Harbor in particular, located at the island's northern tip, was known as an imposing harbor that France had lavishly outfitted.

Why Nosy Be? The answer to that question lay in Russia's clumsy wartime diplomacy. Earlier, the Russian Foreign Ministry had negotiated with France over coaling rights, asking that the fleet be allowed to coal in Diego Suarez Harbor when passing by Madagascar. The Foreign Ministry of France, Russia's ally, had curtly declined with a scowl as big as all of France.

Russia's Foreign Ministry was less competent than those of other strong nations of the day and did not accord great authority to its diplomats. The Russian Empire had no rival among the Great Powers, first in the limitless authority of the tsar, second in the strength of its armed forces, and third in the size and proficiency of its internal secret police. It is fair to say that those three strengths supported the Russian Empire. The Foreign Ministry was in a sense the servant of this structure of absolute power.

As a result, Russian diplomacy had no notable achievements in Europe. Even if there had been a brilliant Russian diplomat who presented the court with thoughtful conclusions and recommendations based on an analysis of international conditions, they would not have been accepted.

"Russia will lose because it is a despotic nation." At such times, we must again remember this prediction by United States President Theodore Roosevelt, made before the Russo-Japanese War ever began, which also bears on this aspect of Russian diplomacy. We have referred several times already to the attitude of France. Alliance with Russia was necessary for France's security within Europe. The Russo-Japanese War had started because of Russia's gallivanting in the Far East, where France had no interests. Though France relied on Russian military might, that might was in the process of shifting to the Far East. The resulting weakening of French national security forced France to play up to Britain, a country France did not particularly like. Britain in effect told France, "Don't lend the Russians any good harbors." The Russo-Japanese War so altered the diplomatic dynamic that France feared offending Britain less than it feared offending its ally, Russia.

"They'll have to make do with Nosy Be then." That was the French attitude.

*   *   *

"Nosy Be" means "the big island." The harbor there was supposed to be a natural anchorage sheltered from the wind by islands. That's what everyone in the fleet had been told. On the way, the metal warships baking in the tropical sun grew unbearably hot. Even with its characteristic triangular waves, the Indian Ocean was calm. Before they arrived at Nosy Be, the fleet observed Christmas (by the Russian calendar). The ships turned their engines off.

Every cruiser and above was equipped with a chapel where prayer services were held. On small destroyers, services were held on deck. Every ship celebrated the birth of Christ and fired thirty-one guns to invoke God's protection on the fleet. The huge, world-renowned armada was instantly enveloped in black smoke from the gunpowder. Without any wind, the smoke hung in the air, completely cutting off the vision of the gun's crew.

"They say Japanese gunpowder doesn't produce terrible smoke like this," whispered many of the sailors. They wondered if it was true. In fact, unlike the old-style powder used in the Russian Navy, Japanese smokeless powder had few such deficiencies. Crew members had little information about the enemy powder, but even so they had a deep and secret fear of it.

Around then, the destroyer *Bodry* signaled that its supply of coal was low. Sharp-eyed Rozhestvensky quickly spotted the signal and shouted, "Damned idiots, look what they're doing!" None of his aides knew why it was idiotic to report that coal was running low. The destroyer was not asking Rozhestvensky for coal either, but merely putting in a fuel request with the collier *Anadyr* (12,000 tons).

"It's a public demonstration of the ship commander's incompetence," Rozhestvensky fumed. But the destroyer was always whipping around on communication and reconnaissance work. If it maintained the same economical speed of 10 knots as the rest of the fleet, it would never catch up with them. The destroyer had to load a great deal of coal and convert it to steam, a physical process that had nothing whatever to do with the competence of the ship commander, except in Rozhestvensky's mind. Above all else, he loved having the fleet make orderly progress as if marching in file, and he hated disruption for whatever reason.

The fleet stopped its engines. The *Anadyr* approached the *Bodry* and began to transfer a load of coal. At length, the job was finished, and the fleet began to steam on again. After the sun had gone down, leaving a dim glow in the night sky, the *Borodino* hoisted a signal: "Four suspicious ships are following us." This communication upset the crew so much they were all on edge. Only the *Borodino*, lagging behind the rest, sent up the signal. None of the other ships saw any trace of the pursuing ships. Was the *Borodino* seeing things?

The sighting was made by a watcher atop the mast. The four suspicious ships were far back in the distance, but steaming in the same direction as the fleet. They were big warships, too, battleships or cruisers by the look of them. After a while, three of them turned and withdrew, disappearing behind the horizon and leaving only one ship in steady pursuit. Eventually, that ship lit its lamps and then changed course, its lights growing dimmer and dimmer, and finally disappearing into the dark.

Fear that Japanese cruisers were going to attack seized everyone in the fleet. Their nerves were on constant edge to begin with from anxiety and rumors of a Japanese ambush. That night, the fleet went on alert.

Were the ships Japanese? "Impossible," Rozhestvensky declared. "That must have been British ships harassing us. Either that or espionage. The whole British Navy is anxious to spy for Japan. They're reporting our position to the Japanese, that's all."

He was probably right. Concerning internal matters Rozhestvensky was temperamental and prone to fly into a rage over any violation of order, but when it came to external phenomena he was an optimist par excellence. He continued to dismiss the Japanese Navy as insignificant. If he could only take the great armada of the glorious Russian Empire to the Far East, he had no doubt the Japanese would shake in their boots. This childish assumption underlay his confidence.

It's a funny thing about career soldiers. As a man gets older, he is promoted higher and higher, and takes on an air of huge importance, but sometimes the higher he climbs the more his mental capacity diminishes. In that sense, Rozhestvensky's childish streak may not be so surprising. Then again, there could be another explanation. Unless he forced himself to take an optimistic view of the situation, his nerves, always on edge to begin with, might snap under pressure from the outside world—pressure that he only imagined. It is possible that he deliberately took an optimistic view of things to keep that very thing from happening. His optimism worked only on himself, however, and took a toll on everyone else.

On that occasion, the gunners slept by their guns, and everyone else who might be needed in battle stayed up all night. The order was a mental palliative for Rozhestvensky, and a necessary way for him to preserve his trademark optimism. For everyone else, it was a massive nervous strain. If the state of tension based on dire imaginings were to continue for the duration of the long voyage, the crew's nerves would be tested beyond endurance.

In fact, the Japanese fleet had been created solely to fight enemy ships in the vicinity of the archipelago, and to patrol and defend the home waters. Never in a million years would the Japanese Navy have pulled armored cruisers from a fleet that was small to begin with and sent them halfway around the world to Madagascar.

* * *

While Rozhestvensky's Baltic Fleet steamed toward Nosy Be on the northern tip of Madagascar, in tropical heat that felt like torture to the crew of northerners, Stoessel and Nogi convened in Port Arthur, the fleet's ultimate destination.

The meeting was held on January 5. The talks on capitulation were over, and the two armies were proceeding with their respective preparations. The generals' meeting was not required by law.

Stoessel had requested the interview. Having surrendered, he had no further obligation to meet with the enemy general or do anything else for that matter. But the military life is full of ceremony, and military men of that time still put a high premium on chivalric courtesy. The Russo-Japanese War marks the end of the era when soldiers set such store by dramatic ceremonies. To repeat, the meeting of Nogi Maresuke and Anatoly Stoessel is the closing of the last time in history when people felt like ending catastrophic war in an aesthetically pleasing way.

Again, Shuishiying was chosen as the place for the interview; more specifically, it took place in the house of a farmer named Liu. During the siege, the Japanese Army had commandeered Liu's farmhouse and used it as a field hospital.

"In the garden stood a jujube tree" go the lyrics of the song "The Meeting at Shuishiying" in *The Common Elementary Reader*, volume 9, and, sure enough, just inside the farmhouse gate, off to the left by the mud wall, there was a jujube tree said to be over a century old. "Full of bullet holes for all to see," the lyrics continue, describing the countless bullets that had penetrated the bark and exposed the wood beneath. "There in the crumbling farmhouse / The two generals met face to face."

The agreed-on hour was eleven o'clock in the morning. Five minutes ahead of time, Stoessel entered the farmhouse gate with his entourage. A Japanese guard respectfully presented arms, and Stoessel saluted smartly in acknowledgement as he walked on by. Nogi had not yet arrived.

Stoessel was ushered inside. The meeting room, which was off to the left, had a dirt floor covered with rush mats. It was furnished with a simple table that was about the length of a man's arm. When the premises had served as a field hospital, that had been the operating table. Bullets used to fly into the room through the window during surgery, leaving the table scarred and pockmarked. To cover the unsightly reminders, a white cloth was spread on the table. Stoessel and his staff seated themselves in chairs around the table and waited for Nogi.

* * *

Nogi and his retinue were arriving from Liushufang. The Swiss watch of Nogi's staff officer Yasuhara, assigned as escort, was half an hour slow. Nogi's retinue consisted of his chief of staff Ijichi, Yasuhara, and various adjutants.

Stoessel was kept waiting for forty minutes. By the time Nogi and his party rode through the gate, it was half past eleven. Nogi dismounted and was saluted by his staff officer Tsunoda, who had arrived before him. Tsunoda and the interpreter, Kawakami Toshihiko, had both been assigned to receive Stoessel.

Lowering his arm from the salute, Tsunoda reported that Stoessel had already arrived. Nogi nodded and quickly strode toward the house. When he entered the room, he went straight to the head of the table and stood there. The place of honor was his not only because he was the victor, but because he was a full general and Stoessel a lieutenant general. Standing, he extended his hand to Stoessel. Stoessel reached out, and the two generals shook hands.

"So this is Nogi!" Stoessel's staff was surprised. There was not a trace of arrogance in Nogi's bearing, and his slightly drooping eyes crinkled in a smile.

Nogi delivered his remarks standing, and Kawakami interpreted what he said into Russian. "We both maintained hostilities for the sake of king and country. But the fighting has now come to an end, and I am delighted that I can meet Your Excellency here today."

Stoessel was no less gracious. "I defended the Port Arthur fortress for the sake of my country. But now that the capitulation has been put into effect, I deem it a great honor to be thus afforded an opportunity of holding an interview with Your Excellency."

Still standing, Nogi proceeded to present the contents of the telegram he had received the previous day from the General Staff Office. It contained a message from Emperor Meiji. "His Majesty is pleased to appreciate the invaluable services rendered by General Stoessel to his fatherland and desires that the general be accorded all military honors."

And so Stoessel and his entourage had been allowed to retain their swords at the meeting. Nogi conveyed this information and added, "I too wish to do everything in my power to accommodate Your Excellency." When he heard that, Stoessel brightened visibly and expressed warm thanks.

When this exchange was over, Nogi gestured for Stoessel to be seated so that they might speak more informally. He too lowered himself into the hard chair.

Stoessel spoke next of the courage of the Japanese sappers in the tunnel battle. "Unrivaled bravery," he called it and went on to praise the superior marksmanship of the Japanese artillery, noting that the 28-centimeter guns in particular were "wonderfully efficient." The valor of Japanese sappers in laying tunnels at the front, the high marksmanship of the artillery, the effectiveness of the 28-centimeter howitzers—these, according to Stoessel, were the three things that made Russian capitulation unavoidable. Those were not empty compliments, but a cool military assessment of the situation. Concerning the bravest men of all, the Japanese infantry, whose mortality rate had been so high, he had no words of praise.

Let us compare the losses of the two armies at Port Arthur. The Russians had 45,000 combatants and suffered over 18,000 casualties, including barely 2,000–3,000 dead. Even granting that the Russian troops were protected by a massive fortress and had a vast quantity of firepower, their losses pale next to those suffered by the attacking Japanese side.

The Japanese forces numbered 100,000, with casualties of 60,212, or fully sixty percent—surely one of the highest rates in history. The dead numbered over 15,400, for a horrific mortality rate of fifteen percent. The highest death rate of all occurred among officers at the front. Barely a dozen Japanese officers made it through the entire siege from beginning to end. Junior officers especially, those who had to unsheathe their own swords and lead the vanguard into the fray, quickly became machine gun fodder.

Stoessel knew all that. The Japanese infantry, the army's main force, had fought with immense bravery—bravery such as the world had rarely seen— yet for the most part the deaths had served no purpose. Especially in the first half of the battle, most of the victims were mowed down by gunfire without making a dent in the fortress defense. As he praised Japanese sappers, artillery, and technology, Stoessel no doubt had a solid conviction that where the infantry was concerned, his side had won.

After that, Stoessel expressed sympathy on the loss of two infantry soldiers. He referred to the deaths of Nogi's sons, Katsusuke and Yasusuke. "I sincerely sympathize with you in your deep bereavement."

When Kawakami interpreted the words, Nogi responded with a smile on his face. "I am glad that my sons met their deaths as warriors."

The interview lasted two hours. "Of all the people I have ever met," Stoessel reportedly told his staff afterward, "no one has impressed me as much as General Nogi." The sentiment was evidently genuine, his respect for Nogi lifelong.

Stoessel was later court-martialed in Russia and sentenced to death for the crime of "surrendering to the enemy despite having adequate men, ammunition, matériel, and rations remaining." When Nogi heard the news, he contacted Major Tsunoda Koreshige, his former staff officer with the Third Army, who was then stationed in Paris. Would it be possible to start a campaign to have Stoessel's life spared? In response, Tsunoda wrote letters to newspapers in Paris, London, and Berlin, arguing forcefully and in detail that Stoessel had had no choice but capitulation. The campaign may have had some effect, for Stoessel was spared the death penalty.

*   *   *

On to Nosy Be.

Rozhestvensky and his fleet steamed ahead. There was no moon, but in its place an infinity of stars provided comfort to the sailors heading north through southern waters. The crew of each ship watched the lights of the ship ahead and followed in its wake.

Day dawned, and the sun rose in the sky. Along the starboard side stretched the vast Indian Ocean. On the port side, there was still the island of Madagascar, but its coastline had begun to show abrupt curves and projections, a sign that they were nearing the island's northern extremity. The transport ship *Rus* steamed ahead with its usual brisk efficiency, like a guide ship. Having gone back and forth between the fleet and the destination of Nosy Be, its crew knew the route well. Marine charts for those waters were not very precise and gave little guidance on where reefs or shoals might be.

Around two in the afternoon, the *Rus* surprised the flagship *Suvorov* by suddenly hoisting a signal on its mast: "The crew have mutinied." The news was shocking.

"What the devil are they up to?" Rozhestvensky muttered, pulling on his boots. He took a few steps, bent over, and straightened his socks. Finally, when he went out on the bridge and looked through his binoculars, there was the signal, just as the flagman had said. "Send over the *Byedovy*," he ordered, specifying a destroyer. The destroyers played the role of policemen in such situations. Rozhestvensky himself was perhaps better suited by nature to be a public prosecutor than anything else and always presided over his fleet with a prosecutorial style.

He gave the captain of the *Byedovy* an extraordinary command. "Use your powers of discretion as you see fit, and if necessary sink the *Rus*." In other words, "If they give you any trouble, shoot them." A harsh attitude for a commander to take toward his own crew.

The *Byedovy* left the line and caught up with the *Rus* at a speed of 25 knots. With its guns pointed at the *Rus*, it ordered the ship to heave to. Soon enough came the realization that there had been no mutiny or riot after all. A stoker had refused to take the place of a sick comrade, and the officer in charge had had him flogged for insubordination. But the stoker had rebelled and was supported by a large number of his peers. The disturbance scarcely amounted to anything and was quelled before the *Byedovy* ever drew near.

A trivial incident had been blown up in the mind of the captain to the level of a mutiny or riot, the most feared threats to internal control in the navy, causing him to hoist that momentous signal on the spur of the moment. It happened because the *Rus* was a reconnaissance vessel. The captain bought up English and French newspapers, and had read too many articles in them. News of the successive losses in the Far East on land and sea had sown great consternation in Russia, and there were frequent reports of a rash of riots among sailors in the Black Sea Fleet as well as in St. Petersburg.

In any case, the "riot" aboard the *Rus* quickly settled down, and the fleet continued steaming northward.

*   *   *

In fact, another fleet was already at the anchorage of Nosy Be on Madagascar, waiting for Rozhestvensky and his fleet to arrive. That was the fleet led by Rear Admiral Dmitri von Felkerzam, consisting of two battleships, three cruisers, and several destroyers and other boats. They had left Liepaja along with the main force of the Baltic Fleet, but divided at the port of Tangier in Morocco.

"We need to split in two and take separate routes." Rozhestvensky gave Felkerzam his orders. "You go through the Mediterranean and take the Suez Canal to the Indian Ocean, and we'll meet up at Madagascar." The reasons for going separate ways were coal and the problem of draft. The amount of coal a fleet that size consumed was stupendous. Even with a German coal company working full time to supply them, there was barely enough coal to meet the need. Further, not all the ships were able to pass through the Suez Canal as their draft was too deep. Therefore, the best course was to divide the fleet in two and rendezvous later on. The plan worked like a charm.

Felkerzam was a commander with superior powers of leadership, and his crossing went smoothly. Moreover, partly because his fleet passed through a highly developed zone, loading supplies at the various ports went without a hitch, and the crew was able to get plenty of rest ashore. Nor did they have to deal with storms at sea like those encountered by the main force when it went around the tip of Africa by the Cape of Good Hope. Felkerzam's fleet made good time and arrived at northern Madagascar on December 28.

However, France denied them the use of its best port, Diego Suarez, and so they had to make do with the fishing port of Nosy Be. The ships anchored there and waited for the main force to arrive.

The "errand boy" ship *Rus* had rushed back from Nosy Be to let Rozhestvensky know that the other fleet had arrived first and was waiting for them. Knowing that when they got to Nosy Be they could reunite with Felkerzam and his men gave the crew something to look forward to. Objectively speaking, it was a small pleasure, but the voyage offered precious few comforts for the crew, and they were as excited as little boys. Being reunited with specific people wasn't the point. In the closed-off world of the military, the celebration was enough to gladden their hearts.

And so on January 8, the fleet rounded the northern end of Madagascar, by Cape Amber, and entered an archipelago sea—or, if that's going too far, then waters crowded with islands and atolls. The *Buiny*, a destroyer in Felkerzam's fleet, came out to escort them, but the sun had already gone down and navigation was perilous, so Rozhestvensky decided to anchor in the offing and wait for morning light. He showed all the caution of a first-rate mariner.

*   *   *

When Rozhestvensky and his fleet entered Nosy Be, the band was out on deck playing "Little Russian March." Engineer Politovsky, aboard the *Suvorov*, ran from his room out onto the deck.

Apart from the scorching sun, the harbor with its wooded hills was perfectly suited for an anchorage. As a sign that rain was plentiful, thick green forests covered every hill. Not surprisingly, the air was sultry. Nosy Be was known among the local European population as a fearfully unhealthy place, and only a handful of whites lived in the fishing village there. Although blessed with strapping physiques compared to Asians, Europeans were far less adaptable to natural conditions. Nosy Be was well known among them as a den of sickness. The average temperature for the month of July was 23.3 degrees Celsius and higher still for March, at 27.2 degrees. Annual rainfall was 2,671 millimeters. In time, these conditions would cause a large outbreak of illness among the crew, but upon entering the harbor after the long monotony of the voyage up the coast, the men delighted in the complex scenery formed by the mountains, the water, and the islands.

The harbor was as calm as a lake. Anchored on its deep azure water were the ships of Rear Admiral Felkerzam's division, which had already arrived. These included the battleships *Sisoy Veliky* (10,400 tons) and *Navarin* (10,206 tons), and the cruisers *Svetlana* (3,727 tons), *Zhemchug* (3,106 tons), and *Almaz* (3,285 tons). A retinue of destroyers, colliers, transport ships, and commandeered steamers stood by, and a number of steam launches wove busily to and fro among them.

Not only did the fleet that had arrived earlier and the newly arriving one greet each other with music, but their crews poured out on deck and exchanged tireless hurrahs. As soon as the *Suvorov* let down its anchor, a steam launch promptly drew near, and Felkerzam hoisted his huge frame on deck. Rozhestvensky, who had come out to greet him, held out his hand, and the two men embraced. Then they went to the commander's cabin to talk.

Was there any message for him from the Russian Naval Ministry? Rozhestvensky naturally wanted to know. Felkerzam's affable face clouded over, and he shook his head. He had telegraphed the government a number of times, first from a harbor in the Mediterranean and again from Portside in Suez, asking for a letter, but had as yet received nothing.

"Incredible." Rozhestvensky shook his head. Did Petersburg even have a strategic command center?

* * *

Consider the fate, or rather the situation, that the fleet then faced. Astoundingly, the ships were "abandoned" there at the harbor of Nosy Be on Madagascar for two full months.

Port Arthur had fallen, and the fleet once stationed there lay now at the bottom of the sea. The situation had changed utterly from when the Baltic Fleet initially set out. There would have to be new orders.

Despite the expectations of every officer in the fleet, no instructions arrived. "We ought to turn around and head for home." This thought was uppermost in nearly every officer's mind. It was not the dreadful tropical heat that made them think so; rather, almost to a man they were convinced that doing so made sense as naval strategy. They were now completely without support. To use an old descriptive phrase from classical Chinese, they were "adrift 10,000 leagues upon the wide sea."

The strategic raison d'être of the Baltic Fleet had involved joining forces with the Port Arthur Squadron to attack the Japanese fleet. Now the Baltic Fleet was isolated with no recourse. The basis for the original plan had collapsed, and it was time to pack up and go home. Everyone in the fleet knew that they themselves, stuck in a fishing port in the South Seas, represented the entire Russian Navy. If they were wiped out in the Far East, that would put an end to Russian might on the world's seas.

The navy would be annihilated. The great Russian Navy that had demonstrated Russian might around the world since the age of Peter the Great would be no more. There was general agreement that the only way to ensure the preservation of the navy was to return it to Russia, an opinion that Rozhestvensky inwardly shared. But as the commander in chief of an expeditionary force ordered on its way by the fatherland, he was in no position to suggest to the high command back home, "Why don't we call the whole thing off?" He could only silently go on carrying out his original orders.

Russia was torn. Some in the naval command believed the fleet should be called home, and their reasoning was persuasive. But the military bureaucracy in a military state with an antiquated system inevitably cares more about self-protection than about saving the country. Fearing his own destruction if he presented this kind of quitter's proposal, a military man would by instinct argue the point indirectly or behind the scenes. In formal settings, grandiose and bellicose opinions carried the day. "There's no reason to exaggerate the power of the Japanese fleet." That was the prevailing sentiment.

"Back home the command can't rid itself of the notion that Japanese people are apes," Engineer Politovsky wrote to his wife. That pretty well describes the mood in St. Petersburg.

*   *   *

Back when the fleet fired mistakenly on British fishing boats in the North Sea, the incident had threatened to turn into a serious international dispute. On that occasion, Tsar Nicholas II sent the following wire to Rozhestvensky in Vigo Harbor: "Never for a moment have I forgotten about our fleet. Concerning the current diplomatic problem, I have ordered my officials to carry out negotiations, and the matter should be cleared up shortly. The Russian Empire has the deepest faith in you and holds the greatest hopes for your prospects."

If such sentiments were to be believed, even now that the fleet had roved so far from home, surely they had not been forgotten. Rozhestvensky took out the old imperial telegram with its promise, "We have not forgotten you," and showed it to Felkerzam. Although a wire like that was largely ceremonial with no military significance whatsoever, to Rozhestvensky, who had served in court as the emperor's aide-de-camp, it must have represented the tsar's true feelings.

Felkerzam, a man with the look of a simple blacksmith, listened with a small smile but said nothing. He may have been thinking that Rozhestvensky was the sort of admiral who cared more about putting on a show than the real details of his command. Or the slight fever he was running may have made replying too much of an effort. When they left Russia, he had felt almost no symptoms, but it was swiftly becoming apparent that he had lung disease. Later, just as the fleet was approaching its final destination, he would die of pneumonia. A Russian of German descent as his name indicates, Felkerzam was a deeply compassionate leader whose death was a heavy blow to the officers and men of his unit.

Speaking of illness, this trouble-plagued voyage forced Rozhestvensky himself to acknowledge an ailment he was previously unaware of. He called it neuralgia, but later his joints swelled, and he developed a high fever and racking pain. The naval surgeon diagnosed the ailment as arthritis. When it was acting up, he could not eat, and frequently he stayed in his cabin at mealtimes.

Many of the officers and men fell ill too. Some went insane, while others developed a variety of illnesses from the extreme humidity and heat. *Oryol*, the hospital ship, was kept busy.

"The European constitution isn't suited to high heat and humidity," lamented the naval surgeon aboard the *Oryol*. It was an article of faith among contemporary physicians that white people were less able to adapt to an environment than people of color—a theory that would find supporting evidence in the fleet's coming two months of idleness.

*   *   *

The coal problem was one reason for the Baltic Fleet's long layover at Nosy Be. As the top command was well aware, without good British coal, the fleet could not maneuver swiftly. Steps were taken to solve the problem. The Russian government had already entered into a contract with the Hamburg American Line, a German company. There were two key stipulations. One, coal would continue to be supplied for the duration of the voyage to the Far East. Two, the coal supplied would be anthracite.

But anthracite had to be purchased from Great Britain. And the British government, in order to remain faithful to the Anglo-Japanese Alliance and legally hinder the movements of the Russian fleet, had imposed unilateral limits on the amount of anthracite it would sell the German company. Therefore, the hard-pressed Hamburg American Line supplied the Baltic Fleet almost exclusively with German bituminous coal of relatively low power. As a result, the steam output was low, and the fleet was unable to maintain speed.

The Russian government took the above company severely to task and finally resorted to legal action against it. This was the drama that was playing out while the Baltic Fleet was anchored in Nosy Be. Bituminous coal might be good enough to use during the fleet's voyage, but once fighting began the government had no wish to supply Rozhestvensky with coal that gave off great clouds of black smoke. A fleet trailing black plumes of smoke would be all too easy for the enemy to locate. And if poor-quality coal caused the fleet to move more slowly than the enemy, battles that could otherwise have been won were bound to end in defeat.

Rozhestvensky was desperate for good coal, and the Russian government was trying to give it to him. Unfortunately, the British government was blocking their efforts, and all Rozhestvensky had on hand was tarry coal or German coal. This situation alone shows how beneficial the Anglo-Japanese Alliance was for Japan.

The Russian government persevered. Determined to achieve some kind of breakthrough, it ordered the Baltic Fleet to sit tight. But in the end, the coal problem proved intractable.

Another reason for the delay was a new plan from headquarters. They proposed assembling another fleet to increase Rozhestvensky's strength. Having lost the Port Arthur Squadron, they would supply the admiral with power from a different source, and until this new fleet arrived they wanted him to bide his time there in Nosy Be. The fleet they had in mind would be cobbled together from Russia's decrepit old battleships.

*   *   *

Everyone in the Russian Navy down to the last sailor knew there were still Russian warships in the Baltic Sea—warships that Rozhestvensky had deliberately passed over when assembling his fleet because they were decrepit. One such was the *Nicholas I*, an outmoded battleship that weighed only 9,594 tons in an age when battleships weighed over 10,000 tons (the *Suvorov*, for example, was 13,516 tons). All but two of the battleships in Nosy Be were finished in the twentieth century, but the *Nicholas I* was a product of the late nineteenth century.

The cruiser *Vladimir Monomakh* (5,593 tons), another product of the late nineteenth century, was also moored in the Black Sea. It had a top speed of a mere 15 knots. Speed is of the essence for cruisers, and one that could go no faster than 15 knots was not a cruiser in the twentieth-century sense of the term. The cruiser *Oleg* (6,675 tons), for example, which was there in Nosy Be, was completed in the third year of the new century and could attain a speed of 23 knots. If a 15-knot cruiser and a 23-knot cruiser were to team up in fleet maneuvers, the faster ship would have to match its pace to the slower one.

"Floating iron"—that was the derogatory term the sailors later applied to the outmoded warships. Russian naval headquarters came up with the plan of repairing the old warships on the Black Sea and putting together a Third Pacific Squadron to be led by Rear Admiral Nikolai Nebogatov, under Rozhestvensky's command. They sent word of this plan to Rozhestvensky in Nosy Be. His response, understandably enough, was an angry "Hell no!"

Most of the powerful new warships in the Russian Navy had been gathered in the Port Arthur Squadron. Half of them were of foreign make, which in itself was the greatest proof to Russians that they were indeed new and powerful. The *Retvizan*, for example, had been made in the United States, the *Tsesarevich* in France. All of the warships had been newly constructed with state-of-the-art machinery. And all of them had been sent to the bottom of the sea.

"We never had a prayer of winning the battle of the Yellow Sea." Later, Saneyuki would continually marvel at the Japanese Navy's good fortune in winning a battle that had seemed so clearly unwinnable, against a foe with such a powerful new fleet. When Rozhestvensky organized the Baltic Fleet to complement the Port Arthur Squadron, he had taken pains in selecting his warships. Even so, his warships were all in some respects inferior to their counterparts in the Port Arthur Squadron. Now, according to headquarters, ships he had previously discarded as unusable were to be gathered under Nebogatov's command and added to his handpicked fleet. He had every right to be infuriated.

*   *   *

"Those warships aren't just unnecessary, they will lower our ability to fight." In his aggravation, Rozhestvensky momentarily forgot the pain of his arthritis. Immediately, he ordered Chief of Staff Clapier de Colongue to fire off a wire to headquarters. He touched upon three points in his wire.

First came this important declaration: "I have no confidence in my ability to regain mastery of the sea with the fleet I have been given." Translated, this meant, "We are going to lose." Confidence and a sense of superiority over the race of "monkeys" had buoyed Rozhestvensky since setting out from Russia, but these had depended on the viability of the Russian fortress and squadron at Port Arthur. With both of them lost, his expectation of victory was eradicated. As a military man on his way to battle, Rozhestvensky would not have said he was headed for defeat without very serious reasons.

Secondly, he wrote about the Third Pacific Squadron, on its way to rendezvous with his fleet under the command of Rear Admiral Nebogatov:

"A fleet of old, inadequate ships"—ships of Russian make—"even if it is coming as reinforcement, will only be an unwelcome burden." It was true that being saddled with a set of old, mismatched ships of different types and speeds would not increase his fighting power but instead would inevitably drag down the maneuverability of the whole fleet, forcing him to reduce the performance of the superior ships to the level of the old hulks.

Thirdly, Rozhestvensky stated the decision he had made given "our current difficult straits"—meaning the loss of the Port Arthur Squadron. He had decided against a direct frontal attack on Tōgō's fleet. Rather, he would avoid that by rushing straight to Vladivostok, making that harbor a base from which to launch strikes against the enemy's maritime transport. "That is the best and only plan I can follow." He was adamant.

Leaving aside the question of whether the strategy Rozhestvensky laid out was appropriate, one thing is certain: if the old ships tagged along, then "rushing" to Vladivostok was out of the question. If they participated and the fleet wobbled its way into the waters of the Far East, then a direct frontal attack on Tōgō's fleet was inevitable. Rozhestvensky wanted to avoid that and fly instead to the safety of Vladivostok.

But headquarters ignored his suggestion.

"Rear Admiral Nebogatov's Third Pacific Squadron has left Liepaja." When he heard this report, Rozhestvensky asked to be relieved of his command on grounds of illness. The request was rejected.

In any case, he and his fleet lingered for two full months in the port of Nosy Be on Madagascar. This was a stroke of great good luck for Japan.

4

HEIGOUTAI

The front froze at the river Shaho. The military term *tōei* or "winter camp" was coined around this time, but, literally speaking, the front line froze.

The Manchurian plains were dun-colored, a deathly hue made all the more ghastly by the white of the snow. The temperature averaged -20 degrees Celsius; the wind chill felt like -30, and sometimes at night the temperature would drop to -40 degrees or colder.

The two armies dug great long trenches, erected pillars, and roofed them over in order to take shelter from wind, snow, and bullets. The massive armies of both nations effectively burrowed underground.

As we've already described, Kuropatkin, the Russian commander in chief, fought the battle of Shaho less out of pure strategic necessity than out of a bureaucrat's instinct for self-preservation. The court at St. Petersburg had been extremely displeased with his strategic leadership, and finally the decision was made to establish a Second Manchurian Army with General Grippenberg in command. Kuropatkin fought the battle of Shaho to shatter this mood with a strong offensive, but the Japanese Army responded by digging in and fighting back so fiercely that he wavered—and so for the top commander's purely psychological reasons, the battle of Shaho ended in a Russian defeat.

The casualties Kuropatkin incurred at the battle of Shaho were costly. As many as sixty-five thousand noncommissioned officers were lost, thus ruling out the possibility of a follow-up attack.

Waiting for reinforcements—that was the point of Kuropatkin's winter camp at Shaho. Transporting needed men and supplies kept the Trans-Siberian Railway operating busily.

"We sustained some damage," Kuropatkin declared after the October battle of Shaho, "but by the end of November we will revive. More troops will amass on the battle line than before. We'll make our move after that." But by late November only fifteen thousand replacement troops had arrived.

The reason for the huge discrepancy between Kuropatkin's estimate and reality was simple. The Trans-Siberian Railway had to transport not only men but matériel, including ammunition, rations, and clothing. Most of the newly arrived soldiers were not equipped with special winter clothing, which they were told would be sent later. Also, equipment for digging trenches was in extremely short supply, forcing Kuropatkin to file an urgent request for more. The long winter camp dragged on.

*　*　*

Early in December, the volume of railway transport picked up considerably. Just as prospects brightened that another hundred thousand troops would arrive by the end of January, Kuropatkin got some good news. In October, he'd been scheduled for demotion from commander in chief to commander of the First Manchurian Army, but instead he was named supreme commander of the Russian forces in East Asia.

The Manchurian Army was reorganized in the Japanese style, divided into First, Second, and Third Armies under the command of generals Nikolai Linevich, Oskar Grippenberg, and Aleksandr Kaulbars. Of the three, Grippenberg had been in line to become equal in rank to Kuropatkin. When he set out for Manchuria, he fully expected that to happen, only to discover on arriving that he was the same rank as Linevich and that Kuropatkin remained his superior. Furious, he declared he'd been outmaneuvered, as indeed he had.

Back in St. Petersburg, the government was irritated by Kuropatkin's maneuvering. In the end, they decided to stabilize the personnel situation by relieving Far East Viceroy Yevgeny Alexeyev of his command and having Kuropatkin take over as his successor, and that is what happened. "Kuropatkin doesn't try to win victory over Japan, but over the Russian government": the charge rose out of just this sort of behavior on Kuropatkin's part.

General Grippenberg, newly arrived at the winter camp, was not pleased. A Russian of German descent, Grippenberg, seeing Kuropatkin lose battle after battle, was extremely critical: "An officer like him should be back in St. Petersburg, up to his neck in paperwork." When he received his commission, he declared, "Now the true battle begins!" Once in charge, he was determined not to leave one "monkey" alive. He felt such racial superiority that at his farewell party in St. Petersburg he vowed, "I go for the sake of all Europe!" If Caucasians lost to Asians, he felt the defeat should be taken as a grievous insult to all of Europe. He took such pride in his German ancestry that he despised even the Slavs, who made up the bulk of his fatherland. That being the sort of man Grippenberg was, his logic (like most such logic) was based solely on his own personal emotions and aroused no sympathy.

Those who gave Grippenberg a rousing send-off fretted rather about social issues. "If we keep on losing battles the way we have been doing, the Socialist Revolutionary Party will only pick up more strength." They placed high hopes on Grippenberg's fierceness, and Grippenberg naturally had no intention of letting them down.

*   *   *

The troop strength of the Japanese Manchurian Army was only a dozen divisions or so. The Russian Manchurian Army, by contrast, consisted even at this juncture of seventeen whole divisions, and by mobilizing soldiers from European Russia in large numbers they were trying to build it up to twenty-eight. The campaign to mobilize and transport troops, and to assemble them in Manchuria, was active enough to kick up storms in European Russia and Siberia.

During winter camp at Shaho, Kuropatkin did not sit idly by. Taking a serious view of reports that Port Arthur might fall, he centered his strategic thinking on that point. In short, he planned to launch a major operation, defeating the Japanese main force in Manchuria and proceeding with that momentum to ram Nogi's army in Port Arthur from the rear. That way he could rescue the Russians in Port Arthur, from Stoessel on down, and also deliver Nogi's army a serious blow.

If Port Arthur fell, Nogi's army would surge north, and that would mean trouble. It was Kuropatkin's grand idea to prevent that from happening and save Stoessel's army at the same time. His ability as general to come up with an idea of such imposing scale betokens a largeness of spirit.

As early as the beginning of November, he had ordered his chief of operations, Major General Alexei Evert, to draw up detailed plans. But putting the plans into action would take enormous troop strength and firepower. The wounds from the battle of Shaho were still gaping, which was why he had to wait for reinforcements and replenishments to arrive from Russia. They were not coming as speedily over the Trans-Siberian Railway as he had anticipated from his desktop calculations.

The operation would begin in mid-December, he hoped, and he had Lieutenant General Sakharov, his chief of staff, look into it. Sakharov was basically in favor of the grand plan but worried whether fresh troops from European Russia would arrive in time.

"They'll get here all right." Kuropatkin adhered to his plan.

"Sure they will." The newly arrived General Grippenberg snorted in derision at Kuropatkin's chronic perfectionism. He knew you couldn't fight a war by desktop calculations. "Wait for fresh troops to get here from European Russia, and it'll be spring before you know it. In the meantime, Port Arthur will fall. Nogi's army will be free to head north. It's better to act than to sit around and wait. Our troops can beat the Japanese Army right now!" Use what troops they had with intelligence and bravery—that was Grippenberg's idea.

From cavalry reconnaissance and other sources, Grippenberg had learned that the extreme left flank of the Japanese Army was considerably weaker than the rest. By applying strong pressure there and carrying out a frontal attack at the same time, they could execute a pincer movement.

The extreme left flank of the Japanese Army was Akiyama Yoshifuru's cavalry brigade.

The Japanese Army was spread out as far as possible on the other side of the Shaho, in winter camp. Indeed, the extreme left flank of that long camp was undermanned, the "cover" provided by Akiyama's detachment all too flimsy a curtain. If the Russian Army concentrated a large force on that extreme left flank and delivered a crushing blow, the army's left arm would shatter to the bone. And, if they carried out a frontal attack simultaneously, the isolated Japanese troops would not be able to hold the line. Grippenberg's tactical vision was unerring.

But as supreme commander of the Russian forces in East Asia, Kuropatkin had his position to think of. Or rather, like so many bureaucratic individuals, he had a pathological attachment to his position. "I am responsible not only for the enemy in front of us on the Shaho," he reasoned. "Rescuing Stoessel at Port Arthur also falls within my area of responsibility."

Here we see Kuropatkin's temperament coming into play. Rather than claiming victory over the army in front of his nose, he dreamed of creating a brilliant, flawless gem that would encompass his entire "area of responsibility." That was why he planned a great operation that would include a rescue of Port Arthur. Strategy, like art, cannot be separated from the temperament and personality of its creator.

But war is fluid and involves an opponent. In extreme terms, war is made by splitting the weaknesses of each side—which is why perfectionism is something the General Staff Office may think about, but not a commanding officer on the field. The field general's job is to hammer out strategies to suit the reality of changing conditions.

"Abandon Port Arthur." Kuropatkin should have demonstrated bold leadership and done this. For his main field army, the point of the siege at

Port Arthur was to hold the Japanese Army in check. By pinning down the hundred thousand men in Nogi's army for more than two hundred days, the Russian forces there had already served their purpose.

Certainly, if rescue were feasible, then rescue there should be, no question about that. But that would mean months of waiting for an army to arrive from European Russia. (According to Kuropatkin's desktop plan, this could happen in a very short time, but in point of fact, it could not.) Perfectionism took time, and the war would not wait.

In this case, the one with the realistic view of the situation was Grippenberg. The troops spread out on the bank of the Shaho represented the entire Japanese Army, he pointed out. Defeat those troops and the Japanese Army itself would be destroyed, the country of Japan out of the game. Now was the time to strike.

But arguments have a way of turning circular. Kuropatkin had his own view. "Grippenberg is the one who's being unrealistic. He only set foot on the battlefield early in December and knows nothing of the Japanese Army. He's just trying to drag us into using self-serving tactics to promote his own glory."

*　*　*

General Grippenberg's thinking did hold a tinge of self-service. "I'll win a great victory and show Kuropatkin up for the mediocrity he is." That thought was uppermost in his mind.

At General Headquarters in Mukden, the message came through to Kuropatkin as loudly as a drumbeat. But unlike the revolutionary-minded students in St. Petersburg, he had never engaged an opponent directly in a great debate. In the salons of Russia, which accepted and even in a sense surpassed the elegance of French aristocratic salons, such rudeness was not the custom. All the generals did was exchange opinions through their military staffs.

In the end, Kuropatkin yielded to Grippenberg's coercion. "Very well, let's give it a try." But he agreed reluctantly, hoping inwardly that the tactic would fail, as his later actions show clearly. Following the way of thinking common in the superannuated bureaucratic structure of late imperial Russia, he was gripped by fear that the success of Grippenberg's plan might damage his own reputation or lead to his own downfall.

"When do we do it?" Kuropatkin had his staff confer with Grippenberg's to decide when to make the move. Once the decision was made, not even Grippenberg called for immediate action. He too now hungered for troops. Reports from home indicated that the fresh Sixteenth Corps was on its way from European Russia, along with several sharpshooting brigades.

"Wait for them to get here." This was Grippenberg's reply.

Kuropatkin laughed. "Looks like Grippenberg has finally left his desk behind and stepped onto the soil of the battlefield." He meant that the general's thinking had left the drawing board and taken a practical turn.

Kuropatkin proceeded to draw up careful plans. The Sixteenth Corps, due to arrive soon, would be held in strategic reserve and sent to the area west of the railroad (its north–south line) as the operation progressed. In any case, they would have to wait for the fresh troops to arrive, which meant delaying the offensive until late January. He conveyed this information to General Grippenberg, commander of the Second Manchurian Army, and General Kaulbars, commander of the Third Manchurian Army, on December 31.

That Stoessel would surrender to Nogi in Port Arthur the following day, January 1, Kuropatkin had no way of knowing when he drew up his plans. Stoessel, under siege both on land and at sea, was powerless to send him word.

*   *   *

The fall of Port Arthur meant the partial collapse of the plans Kuropatkin and Grippenberg had hatched for a winter offensive. Grippenberg took the surrender as a spur to act, but Kuropatkin, deflated like a balloon losing air, became tentative. "Wouldn't it be better to wait till sufficient reinforcements come?"

This was Kuropatkin's attitude, while Grippenberg took the opposite tack: "We should launch the offensive right now." He meant they shouldn't wait even for the arrival of the Sixteenth Corps, already on board the Trans-Siberian Railway. "While we cool our heels, Nogi's Third Army in Port Arthur will come north and join the Japanese field army. The offensive needs to take place before that."

"That's not a good idea," objected Kuropatkin, but he had no compelling reason to halt plans for the operation, which was already underway. In the end, he had to adopt the stance, an extremely irresolute one for a military man, of "permitting" the Second Army to attack. Never before had the weak character of Russia's top military strategist in battlefield conditions shown so strongly.

"I'd like you to avoid committing yourself too deeply in attacking the Japanese Army's left flank." If they did attack, in short, they were not to cross a certain line. His attitude was less that of a military strategist or commander in chief than that of a government official handing out a business permit.

The line in question was at Heigoutai, the outermost camp on the Japanese Army's left flank. For taking this stance, Kuropatkin would have to be called a fainthearted commander. The Japanese Army was undermanned, stretched out on an east–west axis hardly very deep. While perhaps not as thin as a thread, it was at best a rope stretched out in a straight line, easily broken if the Russians bulldozed through.

The Russian camp was not only spread out wide but was considerably deeper as well, a position of classic strategic depth. Applying Russian habits and rules of field combat, Kuropatkin had been laboring from the first under the erroneous assumption that the enemy layout must be the same. After all this time and after all the battles he had fought against the Japanese, he still could not shake that impression.

Grippenberg had his staff officer register a protest. "Ridiculous. Once the battle is underway, how are we supposed to hold back?"

Kuropatkin was apparently deeply offended. "Then do as you please," he snapped, but then, perhaps deciding that such an attitude was not appropriate in a commander in chief, he came up with a compromise plan. "If the attack succeeds, once the First Army has verified its success, we will make a frontal attack."

*　*　*

The compromise plan was tactically impossible. "Grippenberg, you strike first. If that works, I'll follow suit." The idea was to see how things went before making another decision—a far cry from the golden rule of military strategy that when need arises, the target should be hit with maximum force. As Russia's most brilliant strategist, Kuropatkin must have been privately aware that his approach was flawed, but on this occasion, he didn't have the Japanese Army in his sights. Had he been gunning for the Japanese Army, he would never have adopted such a foolish policy.

"I'll bring about Grippenberg's downfall." Kuropatkin must have had some such thought in mind, for after the operation was finished, he declared it to be "something Grippenberg planned and executed on his own authority," a twist so startling that after it was all over, Grippenberg handed in his resignation and went home in high dudgeon. For a wartime commander to resign his commission and simply walk away is a singular event. Once back in Russia, Grippenberg complained bitterly about Kuropatkin, making world headlines.

Which of them was in the wrong? The question was widely debated in international military circles, but the bigger issue was this: despite being the biggest army in the world, the Russian Army had become a victim of bureaucratization, and order was crumbling.

Kuropatkin was not entirely passive at this point, for he built up the Second Manchurian Army quite a lot. The renowned First Siberian Army Corps, a powerful fighting unit, was moved from the First Manchurian Army to the Second, and Lieutenant General Mishchenko's cavalry detachment, the largest and strongest body of cavalry in the Russian Army, was assigned there temporarily as well. Mishchenko's mammoth detachment consisted of seventy-two and a half companies, four units of hussars, and twenty-two field guns. If need arose, another three infantry regiments could be called into service as well. An attack by a cavalry force that size was bound to crush the puny Japanese cavalry.

Because of the transport of fresh troops via the Trans-Siberian Railway, these movements were large enough to be sensed as far away as Europe. At that time, the center of Japanese intelligence-gathering in Europe was the London embassy. Colonel Akashi Motojirō, who was rushing about Europe on spy missions, sent all the information he gathered to London, where Lieutenant Colonel Utsunomiya Tarō organized it and sent it to Japan. Over and over again, Utsunomiya filed reports to Imperial Headquarters in Tokyo warning that the Russian Army was preparing for a new offensive in Manchuria. Imperial Headquarters relayed the information back to generals Ōyama and Kodama in the field.

* * *

At the Japanese Manchurian Army's General Headquarters, the indifference to the intelligence that came via Tokyo was remarkable.

"The Russian Army launch an offensive? Ridiculous!" That was their unvarying response. Their only justification for rejecting the possibility out of hand was that "in such bitter cold, massive troop movements are out of the question." Staff officer Matsukawa Toshitane took that attitude from the first. Kodama Gentarō had deep faith in Matsukawa and believed his assessment to be correct.

Military tacticians need to exercise extreme caution to prevent their imaginations, which should range free, from becoming tied to a fixed idea. Perhaps everyone in headquarters was worn out from directing strategy so long, or perhaps the tendency to hold intelligence in light regard, a defect that later would become endemic in the Japanese Army, had already begun to appear. In any case, everyone in General Headquarters shared certain fixed ideas to a remarkable degree.

The Manchurian cold so frequently remarked upon by Matsukawa, a native of the northerly prefecture of Miyagi, far surpassed the cold of a Tōhoku winter. Urine froze midstream, and piles of feces froze so hard they could scarcely be broken up with a pickaxe. The ground froze solid. When soldiers tried to dig a new trench, their pickaxes rebounded, barely scratching the surface. Sometimes a hole less than 7 centimeters deep was all there was to show for a day's digging.

Muddy roads froze over, leaving such deep ruts that transporting gun carriages was a tricky business. Horses strained to pull while men pushed the cartwheels from behind.

To begin with, thought Matsukawa, the Russians lacked the Japanese custom of simply dashing ahead for all they were worth in a display of raw courage. When Russian corps pushed ahead, they lost no time in digging trenches, driving in stakes, and putting up wire obstacles, making camp along the way. However strong the Russian soldiers may have been, there was no way they could dig trenches in those frozen conditions. Therefore, he concluded, they were bound to stay put till spring.

Kodama agreed. Not only did he agree, but once that idea took hold in his mind it became immutable and colored everything he saw. If any evidence to the contrary arose, he automatically wrote it off as ridiculous.

One powerful piece of evidence should have been sufficient to shatter that illusion: Napoleon's army had a record of continuous unbroken victories, until, the Russians inflicted a catastrophic defeat on them by drawing the enemy deep into their homeland, using the harsh winter weather to their advantage. Soldiers in the Russian Army excelled at winter operations and were well aware of their prowess. Historically, the Russian Army would launch a major counteroffensive while the enemy struggled haplessly against winter weather conditions.

*   *   *

Russia's crushing wintertime defeat of Napoleon's Grande Armée was not well known to Kodama, and, while Matsukawa Toshitane, his right-hand man, may have known of it, he dismissed the tradition as nothing more than folklore.

For one thing, temperatures as low as -40 degrees Celsius made holding a rifle problematical. Touch the barrel with your bare hand, and your fingers would clap against the steel with a loud sound as if drawn there by electricity, and stick fast. Night sentries had to stomp around constantly or the cold would penetrate their feet through the soles of their boots and freeze their damp socks, causing frostbite. Members of the cavalry too put their feet at risk if they stayed on horseback too long. They had to dismount and walk from time to time in order to improve their circulation.

Winter clothing issued to the Japanese Manchurian Army during this campaign was wholly inadequate. The boots weren't fur-lined, the coats were ordinary winter coats, the hats ordinary hats. Anyone who ventured out of his covered trench felt as if his forehead was freezing and suffered a violent headache.

The Russian troops' winter clothing cost easily three times as much as what the Japanese were wearing. Russian thermal hats, coats, and boots were all lined with fur, and, besides, as a people they were well accustomed to living in ice and snow. As to which army was more disadvantaged by the winter weather, the answer should have been clear any way you looked at it.

Common sense should have dispelled Matsukawa's notion that the Russians wouldn't make any move in midwinter, but possibly, in their first group experience of the bitter Russian winter, he and Kodama had lost some of their ability to think. "We and the enemy are in the same boat," they assumed.

Akiyama Yoshifuru carried out frequent reconnaissance missions, which was one of the cavalry's main tasks. Eventually, he had Naganuma's raiders carry out the hazardous exploit of entering far-off Mongolia and going around behind the enemy to destroy railroads and harass them in other ways while gathering intelligence. As a result, he came into possession of substantial intelligence on enemy movements, all of which he sent to General Headquarters. There was particularly strong intelligence pointing to an imminent Russian offensive, which he duly forwarded to headquarters, only to have Matsukawa Toshitane laugh it off, exclaiming, "There he goes again!" Not once did Matsukawa give the reports serious attention.

The Russians would not attack in the depth of winter; this became an article of faith with Matsukawa. Fatigue was partly to blame for this lapse of judgment, along with pride stemming from an unbroken string of victories. Initially, Matsukawa had hoped, if not to achieve victory over the gigantic Russian Army, then at least to avoid a major defeat. Throughout that time of heightened tension and timidity, he had focused hard on every little detail, but once his army began to rack up successive victories, pride reared its head, thinking grew fuzzy, and he ceased to pay attention to any intelligence that failed to meet his preconceived notions about the enemy.

This was the Japanese Army's time of greatest crisis.

* * *

"Mishchenko's cavalry attack shattered the dreams of the Shaho camp."

This operation by the cavalry, which marked the start of the battle of Heigoutai, is often referred to in those terms in Japanese accounts. The attack is seen as something that "disturbed the dreams of the slumbering Japanese Army at winter camp."

Kuropatkin, at the Russian General Headquarters in Mukden, sought to learn about the state of the Japanese Army before launching an all-out attack.

He wanted to know about the camp disposition, its depth, weaknesses, and supply capacity, and decided the best way to probe was to launch a reconnaissance in force by sending Lieutenant General Mishchenko's cavalry unit into action.

But then Port Arthur fell.

The news was reported to Kuropatkin's headquarters in Mukden on the evening of January 2. Strategy needed to be completely revamped. Headquarters went into an uproar, and deliberations went on until late at night.

The collapse had removed one item from Kuropatkin's agenda: the need to save Port Arthur. But now another serious development had to be dealt with, namely the imminent northward surge of Nogi's army. A new offensive should be launched before Nogi's army arrived, if at all possible. Causing a delay in the army's progress was another possibility. That, as everyone knew, meant blowing up the railway line.

Major General Evert, chief of tactical operations, proposed having Mishchenko undertake this mission, and Kuropatkin, who liked plans that offered assurance of success, replied instantly, "An ideal plan!" His eyes gleamed with pleasure. Sending the cavalry deep to the rear of the Japanese forces might have seemed risky, but Russian history and geography had given the Russians proficiency in independent cavalry operations. Not even Kuropatkin saw this as a very risky undertaking.

As Mishchenko's mission would not only be a reconnaissance in force but would also entail blowing up the railroad and other military facilities, he needed a substantial force. Kuropatkin decided to fortify the great cavalry force of seventy-two and a half companies with an additional four units of hussars and twenty-two field guns. In all, Mishchenko's force was ten thousand men strong. Taking into consideration their greater mobility and firepower, they were easily a match for Japan's standby reserve force of one hundred thousand men.

Mishchenko arrived in snowy Mukden on the afternoon of January 3 and called on Kuropatkin. Evert, chief of tactical operations, explained the plan. Mishchenko bent over the large map spread out on the tabletop and tapped the city of Yingkou. "We will go this far. The Japanese Army's main supply depot is here. We will attack it and burn up all their arms and provisions."

Kuropatkin was delighted and accepted the opinion of this, the boldest leader in the entire Russian Army.

* * *

As Mishchenko had said, Yingkou was a major supply depot of the Japanese Army. Europeans called the city "Niuzhuang," but, in fact, the town of

Niuzhuang was further north, in a separate district. Yingkou lies on the inlet area of the Liao River facing Liaodong Bay, and before Dalian Harbor was opened by the Russians, it flourished as the gateway to all Manchuria. Naturally enough, supplementary rations for the Japanese Army were brought ashore at Dalian Harbor and Yingkou Harbor. There was a supply depot for that purpose in Yingkou.

The Japanese Army's supply center was then in Liaoyang, and Yingkou was one of the relay points. The course that Mishchenko proposed taking to Yingkou was over 200 kilometers long. Had he headed a small and nimble unit of light cavalry, that would have been a different story, but his troops were lugging gun carriages, ammunition, and rations, and they had to stop along the way to fight skirmishes. The operation was quite grand in scale.

Mishchenko had to begin by gathering his troops, which were scattered in various camps. The first assembly point was 20 kilometers southwest of Mukden. When the troops had gathered there, they pushed on to the second assembly point, 50 kilometers southwest of Mukden in Sifangtai, and billeted there.

These movements took several days. As the mixed brigade of cavalry, artillery, and the newly joined infantry proceeded across the frozen expanse, its progress was impossible to conceal. Naturally enough, the procession was noticed by the Akiyama cavalry brigade.

"The enemy definitely appears to be planning a major operation." Each time Akiyama Yoshifuru reported back to headquarters, he persistently added his opinion regarding the warning signs.

"Another cavalry report." Each time, General Headquarters turned a deaf ear. Everyone from Manchuria chief of staff Kodama Gentarō on down was obsessed with one idea: "The Russians won't take action in the winter." Lacking firm supporting evidence, the idea evolved into an article of faith. The Japanese forces were set up for their bloody destiny at Heigoutai.

The long-distance reconnaissance and rear harassment operations Yoshifuru conducted around then were done in a style far more befitting the cavalry than what Mishchenko's corps was doing. On January 9, just as Mishchenko's cavalry corps was setting off, Yoshifuru sent out a reconnoitering party headed by Second Lieutenant Yamauchi Yasuji and also dispatched Lieutenant Colonel Naganuma Hidefumi's raiders to far-off Greater Mongolia. On January 12, he sent a second raiding party led by Major Hasegawa Inukichi out into enemy lines, followed by a scout patrol led by First Lieutenant Tatekawa Yoshitsugu. In this way, he vigorously instigated search operations, but the reports that came in were nearly all suppressed by General Headquarters.

*　*　*

To digress a bit, one day after the battle of Heigoutai, Yoshifuru and Matsukawa Toshitane went out riding together. Matsukawa was known for his outstanding tactical abilities, so much so that when Kodama Gentarō was made chief of staff of the Japanese Manchurian Army, he declared, "As long as I take Matsukawa with me, I'll be all right." Others held that he was an able man but lacking in Kodama's genius.

Where Matsukawa had become a staff officer, Yoshifuru remained a mere troop leader. This was because the Japanese Army recognized the necessity of having him develop and take charge of the cavalry, but that topic does not concern us here. Deep down, Yoshifuru suspected that General Headquarters' tactical incompetence was the main cause of the gruesome fighting at Heigoutai that ended in a virtual defeat for Japan. But all his life, he never said so to anyone. "I lost at Heigoutai. But because I didn't run away, it was taken as a victory in the end." That was his only comment.

As we know, Yoshifuru had sent warning after warning to General Headquarters concerning Mishchenko's attack, which was a prelude to the fighting at Heigoutai. Now, since his data and comments had accurately predicted the Russian movements, he quite naturally wanted to sound off to Matsukawa.

The two men rode along side by side. Behind them rode Naganuma Hidefumi, who clearly remembered the two men's conversation. To the end of his life, whenever the subject of Heigoutai came up, Naganuma would quote what they said.

"That was a bitter battle and then some," Yoshifuru said. "We did well to withstand such desperate fighting if I do say so. On the other hand, I can't help thinking that it was General Headquarters' remissness that got us into that mess in the first place. What do you say?" He pressed Matsukawa in a roundabout way.

Like any tactician, Matsukawa was unwilling to concede any flaw in his tactics. "We were sure our visitors"—by this, he meant the Russian forces—"would come around by the left flank, and we were waiting for them." This was simply untrue. Headquarters had consistently disavowed the possibility of a Russian offensive and certainly never suspected that the Russians would attack the left flank.

Yoshifuru lost his temper. "That is an insult to the men who lost their lives. If you were expecting visitors, you should have prepared a proper reception for them. It is exactly because visitors came when you had nothing prepared that we put on such a sorry show. The enemy. . ." He fell silent for a moment before continuing in uncharacteristically harsh tones. "The enemy was coming in large numbers—that's what I reported any number of times. I sounded the warning. Failure to heed the signs caused that fiasco. Isn't that true, Matsukawa?"

Matsukawa simply rode along in silence, and Yoshifuru let the subject drop.

*   *   *

Another digression. A friend of ours recently traveled to the Caucasus region. Long ago, various tribes mingled in the area between the Black Sea and the Caspian Sea to form a corridor. The Caucasus Mountains, which stretch on an east–west axis, helped preserve the unique spirit and flavor of the people there, who are known for their bravery and conservative ways.

When Russian invasions intensified in the nineteenth century, the region was annexed by the Russian Empire, but the minority peoples there often rebelled at such treatment, and at the time of the Russo-Japanese War they were far from submissive to the Russian regime.

The area is dotted with Cossack villages. "Cossack" was originally a Turkish word meaning "free men." Originally, it referred to serfs and urban poor who, unable to endure the oppression of landowners in fifteenth-century imperial Russia, fled south and banded together, electing a chief and freeing themselves from the shackles of the state. Later, however, due to Russian invasions, Cossacks were forced into the role of farmer-soldiers in the service of the empire.

There are many Cossack groups in the Caucasus and other minorities with similar social forms. Among them is a group granted status in the Union of Soviet Socialist Republics as the "North Ossetian Autonomous Soviet Socialist Republic."

When the Russo-Japanese War was not going well for Russia, almost every able-bodied young man of conscription age among those groups was swept into military service. Part of Mishchenko's great mobile force was the "Don Cossack Fourth Cavalry Division." The conscripts all joined that division and fought on the Manchurian front, riding magnificent horses and armed with rifles on the shoulder and lances in the hand. They were the freshest troops to arrive on the Trans-Siberian Railway.

The Cossacks are called "Don Cossacks," the word *don* meaning "water" in the Ossetian language.

When our friend went to Ordzhonikidze (with a population of over 160,000), the capital of the North Ossetian Autonomous Soviet Socialist Republic, he visited a local museum displaying spoils of war seized from the Japanese Army during the Russo-Japanese War: military swords, bloodstained scraps of the Japanese flag, and so on. Perhaps because the Soviet Union saw the outcome of the Russo-Japanese War as humiliating, there are virtually no museums devoted to it, but the autonomous republic of a minority people does have one.

"Look at this," an influential local man explained with frank cheerfulness as he gave our friend a guided tour of the museum. "Only the Ossetians fought equally against the Japanese, who are a brave race. Here in Ossetia we value these things as proof of our bravery."

Needless to say, the people of North Ossetia do not have friendly feelings toward Russians, who constituted the dominant ethnic group in the Soviet Union. No doubt as a minority people they treasure those war trophies stained with Japanese blood as poignant symbols of ethnic pride.

Ossetians were among those in the Cossack cavalry that Mishchenko led south.

* * *

Mishchenko was on a long ride, headed for Yingkou. "No need to take covert action." He made no attempt to hide or flee from the enemy as he proceeded south. "If you see a Japanese squadron, destroy it." These were the orders he gave the vanguard. He intended to crush the Japanese under his cavalry's hooves.

He divided his forces into four columns on its southbound march. Along the way, he sent a large number of squadrons ahead to destroy the railroad. Altogether they laid explosives in twenty-six locations, of which twelve went off. They also toppled telegraph poles.

As they went along, they frequently came upon groups of Japanese horsemen. These were scouts whom Yoshifuru had sent out. At the sight of a massive cavalry force such as they had never seen in all their lives, the Japanese scouts scattered and fled, evidently scared witless. "From now on, don't let them get away." Following Mishchenko's orders, the Russians took after the Japanese riders they came upon from that time, surrounded them, and killed as many as they could.

One Japanese company camped at Jieguanbao, directly in the path of the great army, and confronted it head on. Out of an abundance of caution, Yoshifuru had sent out Captain Yasuhara Masao's company to the vicinity of Jieguanbao. When Yasuhara realized from his own scouts' reports that the Russian cavalry was in front of them, he set out to destroy it, leaving camp at approximately ten in the morning on January 10 with seventy horsemen. The men's bravery in taking on Mishchenko's vastly superior force was due in part to their lack of clarity regarding the enemy's situation. They never dreamed that so large a force was on its way south.

"There are about 150 enemy cavalry around Xiaomafenpao, 8 kilometers past Jieguanbao." That was the only interim report they had had from their scouts. Yasuhara's bravery lay in taking on 150 Cossack cavalry with 100 cavalry (along the way, they absorbed scouts from other regiments) on inferior mounts.

But when they approached Xiaomafenpao, they found the enemy had increased to five hundred. One officer galloped farther off and spotted Mishchenko's main force in the distance. "It must be the bank of the Hun." That was his first thought on seeing the great cavalry against the horizon.

"That's no riverbank, sir," responded a keen-eyed subordinate. "I believe it is a forest."

The bristling Cossack lances must have looked that way. When the forest began to move, they knew it was the enemy's main force. The officer galloped back to the village to find Captain Yasuhara and his one hundred men in danger of being enveloped by the enemy's five hundred.

Yasuhara was as determined as ever to wipe the enemy out, but if they were to prevail against an enemy of such numbers, no ordinary means would suffice. He fell back to a hollow 200 meters behind Xiaomafenpao and tied the horses there. The entire force assumed infantry combat formation and entered a fire fight.

"Why don't those Japanese cavalrymen run away?" Mishchenko's subordinate, Major General Teleshov, wondered. Those surrounding Yasuhara and his men were units from the Fourth Don Cossack Division and the Caucasian Cossack Brigade, both under Teleshov's command.

*   *   *

In assuming a square formation in the hollow and adopting a firing stance, Yasuhara and his hundred horsemen showed astounding bravery.

The five hundred Cossacks first galloped around and around the hollow, shooting from horseback, but they were overwhelmed by the shooting of Yasuhara's unit and retreated. In the course of the retreat, naval lieutenant Ferdinand Burtin, a French observer, was shot from his horse and perished. Why France sent a naval lieutenant to observe a Russian cavalry battle is unclear.

The Russians fell back and then returned, opening fire on foot just like Japanese troops. Luckily for the Russians, just east of the hollow, there were three private houses, which they seized. They began to fire from the rooftops down on the hollow.

Yasuhara was taken aback. "We'll be wiped out because of those three houses!" The thought made him determined to capture the houses, and he ordered two platoons to charge.

The Transbaikal Cossacks participating in this battle had just arrived in Manchuria the previous October, and this was their first engagement. Surprised by the Japanese attack, they jumped down from the roofs but did not abandon the houses, instead going behind their fences and reopening a fierce fire fight.

Yasuhara himself led the cavalry in an attempt to take the houses but fell with a piercing bullet wound in the gut. His place was taken by platoon leader and next in seniority Iwai, a first lieutenant. A bullet grazed Iwai's neck, but he took command, undeterred. His right arm was then shattered, but he stayed in command of the company. As they finally drew near the houses, a bullet pierced his chest and came out through his back, but even then he didn't fall. After three hours of murderous fighting, they finally occupied the three houses. After sundown, they kept on fighting, using the houses as bunkers.

But Russian troop strength was still increasing. Eventually, the Russians set fire to the houses and subjected them to withering artillery fire. The houses went up in flames, burning to death nearly every Japanese soldier inside. The rest retreated, led by Iwai. Russians who came up after them disposed of wounded, fallen Japanese soldiers by grabbing them by the head and feet and hurling them into the flames with shouts of "Yo heave ho!"

Earlier, when the shooting of the Japanese cavalry never weakened even after two hours of firing, Mishchenko told his troops: "Messing around with a small enemy force like this won't help us achieve our mission. Forget about them and move along."

But that would have meant abandoning the dead and wounded, which they could not bear to do, so reinforcements were dispatched to gather the fallen Russian soldiers. The reinforcements alone consisted of two companies of dragoons (the regular cavalry of the Russian Army) and an artillery platoon. The artillery fired continuously from close range, only 800 meters from the houses where Japanese forces were. Russian losses amounted to eight officers, forty-two soldiers, and fifty-nine horses.

Mishchenko's army billeted nearby that night and in the morning swept on south with the force of a typhoon. Around then, Japan's General Headquarters finally realized that Mishchenko was planning to attack the army's supply depot in Yingkou.

*　*　*

The southward drive and the destructiveness of Mishchenko's raiding party lasted for eight days. Symbolized by horses' hooves, lances, and horse artillery, the raiders swept like a windstorm through the rear of the Japanese Army.

"Enemy mounted force of unknown size headed straight for us!" From all sides, such urgent, screaming wires arrived at the garrison headquarters assigned to guard supplies. Since headquarters' fighting strength was feeble to begin with, all they could do was send General Headquarters emergency wires requesting reinforcements. But General Headquarters, facing off against Kuropatkin's great army, lacked sufficient manpower itself and did no more than dole out small numbers of soldiers on rescue missions as circumstances warranted.

The garrison guarding supplies consisted of transport troops with no combat training armed with heavy Russian hexagonal barrel rifles (captured in fighting). They made a makeshift camp and increased the number of soldiers guarding the railroad. Their orders contained the extreme expression "defend to the death"—a phrase rarely used in military orders of the day. In this fashion, they braced for an attack by the Cossacks, the strongest cavalry in the world.

Mishchenko had assembled three cavalry units for the specific purpose of blowing up the railroad. The first was composed of the Don Cossacks and Caucasian Cossacks, the second of Cossacks and Transbaikal Cossacks, and the third was a regiment of dragoons and a company of Cossack border guards. The men in all three units were valiant soldiers and master horsemen who controlled the movements of their mounts as easily as they did their own limbs. The Cossacks' one fault, if they had a fault, was that their reconnaissance ability was generally inferior to that of the Japanese cavalry.

The difference in reconnaissance ability might have been connected to a difference in the level of national education in the two countries. While Japanese soldiers were all literate, less than a third of the Cossacks could read. Also, and this was true of Akiyama's cavalry brigade as well, city-bred soldiers tended to think more quickly and be more useful at scouting out enemy movements compared to soldiers from farming villages. The Cossacks knew only the Russian rural hinterlands, where there was considerably less need for quick thinking than in Japanese rice-farming villages.

And so, of the three units, the first—the one composed of the Don Cossacks and Caucasian Cossacks, the strongest fighters of the lot—managed to reach the railroad north of Haicheng but never found the all-important railway bridge. In the night, they got lost, wandering around helplessly until the sun came up, when they ignominiously withdrew.

The second unit laid charges on the railway at a point 2 kilometers north of Haicheng, but a Japanese supply train heading south from Liaoyang passed safely by, and somehow the explosives only went off afterward. The third unit also got lost at night and withdrew without ever having found the railway bridge.

Aghast at these reports, Mishchenko lashed the ground with his whip. "Are they all afflicted with night blindness?"

* * *

The story of "Mishchenko's eight days" goes on.

On the night of the eleventh, Mishchenko billeted south of Niuzhuang. His targets of attack were Haicheng, Niuzhuang, and Yingkou. That night, he learned from a report by a Chinese spy about the Japanese Army's general situation. "They have three hundred men in Niuzhuang, four thousand five hundred in Haicheng, and another two thousand in Yingkou. The soldiers are all old standby reservists and military laborers." "Military laborers" meant "transport troops."

That night, Mishchenko stayed in a prosperous farmer's home in the village of Zengjiatun. He gathered all the leaders of every unit on a dirt-floored room of the farmhouse for a conference to discuss the enemy's movements. "Looks like Akiyama isn't coming." He muttered this without raising his face from the map. He knew that Akiyama Yoshifuru was the master of the Japanese cavalry, the only one who could stand up to him. Back when Akiyama had observed the Russian Army's training exercises in Siberia, Mishchenko had invited him to his regiment barracks and entertained him. Several officers who had been present then were also at this conference.

"Akiyama is probably pinned down on the far side of the Shaho." Kharanov, a colonel with a scholarly air, pointed to a spot on the map. The Cossacks knew that the Japanese cavalry was helpless against them, and they even felt a measure of sympathy for the beleaguered enemy troops.

"But there are platoons scattered all along here," said Major General Samsonov.

Beside him, Major General Abramov laughed. "They will become our prey."

The high-ranking officers around Kuropatkin had feared the Japanese Army, but the cavalry officers under Mishchenko had no such leanings. They believed themselves superior to the Japanese cavalry in tradition and ability.

At length, duties were assigned. "Kharanov will lead his composite detachment through the province of Jinan. Then he will cross Qianliushugou and attack Yingkou Station."

Five other columns were formed, each with a different target of attack. Colonel Suvorov's column was to blow up the railway between Dashiqiao and Yingkou. Major General Teleshov's column would provide cover, and Major General Stoyanov's would advance toward Niujiatun and wipe out Japanese troops in the vicinity. Samsonov's column would serve as a commando unit.

Abramov's column Mishchenko himself would hold in reserve. Colonel Sveshnikov's column would serve as transport troops and stay in close contact with the reserves.

All the columns would go into action on the morning of January 12. Some behind the Japanese Army would act as whirlwinds, others as cyclones, while still others rained fire. Together they would run riot and wreak havoc.

* * *

The initial moves of the great mobile force raised to wreak havoc in the Japanese rear were strategically and tactically brilliant. But in every case, implementation exposed flaws in Russians of that era, so that most of the plans ended in failure.

Colonel Suvorov's column, for example, was supposed to set out in advance of the others. The colonel's orders were to leave the encampment (south of Niuzhuang) at two in the afternoon on January 12.

"Don't get the time wrong." Mishchenko stressed the point because a delayed departure by the advance force would throw off the movements of all the other columns. But they left two hours behind schedule. The reason was that the essential explosives were late in arriving.

"I'm not a magician. I'm not talented enough to be able to blow up a railroad without explosives." Suvorov sent a messenger to Colonel Sveshnikov, who was in charge of transport at the rear, to vent this bitter sarcasm out loud.

By the time his column finally drew near the railroad, the sun was starting to set. Just then, luckily or not, smoke appeared on the horizon to the east, in the direction of Dashiqiao. The train was coming.

"Lay the charges immediately!" The colonel ordered a company carrying explosives to advance, but there was not enough time to lay explosives on the rails to overturn the train, which was bearing down upon them. The train consisted of sixteen open cars loaded with Japanese troops en route to Yingkou. It was the Eighth Standby Reserve Infantry Regiment (Osaka), on its way to provide reinforcement against Mishchenko's incursion.

Suvorov decided to assault the train. He split off two companies and ordered them to attack on foot, while the main force galloped parallel to the train. As he gave the order, he himself dashed forward, sword aloft. The Cossacks fired on the train from horseback. "Aim for the locomotive!" If they could kill the engineer, figured Suvorov, that would finish off the train one way or another. But his column lacked firepower, and their rifle attack did little damage.

The Japanese troops began returning fire with a vengeance. Although the freight cars were open, the soldiers inside were at an advantage, being able to use the sides of the cars as shields. One after another, Cossacks racing alongside the train were felled.

Finally, the Japanese Army train raised steam and tore ahead at full speed, so the Cossacks lost the race, and the battle ended inconclusively. This strange contest and skirmish left the Cossack troops in disarray, and it took the colonel a long time to regroup his forces.

While he was so engaged, he received a report that a battalion of Japanese infantry was on the march from Dashiqiao. Managing to avoid clashing with the enemy battalion, he cut phone wires and blew up railroads in five places before retiring. The resulting destruction was negligible, scarcely a hindrance to the Japanese Army.

*　*　*

Colonel Kharanov's column, charged with attacking Yingkou, consisted of the best men from each cavalry regiment, and they made good progress, exactly on schedule. When they arrived at Liushugou, 5 kilometers northwest of Yingkou, they began to hear cannon fire in the distant southwest. Kharanov understood that the encirclement of Yingkou was complete. He knew that the cannon fire was a prearranged signal and that Mishchenko was present in the artillery battery.

As Kharanov proceeded to carry out his assignment, a shocking message arrived from Mishchenko: "No Japanese troops at Yingkou Station." Later, it turned out that Mishchenko was mistaken. The Japanese garrison commander had concealed his men, most of whom were elderly standby reserve or transport troops, so that they could begin firing after they had lured the enemy into close proximity.

Based on his mistaken assumption, Mishchenko ordered Kharanov to storm the site and assured him that he, Mishchenko, would have the artillery cease its bombardment.

Kharanov and his column galloped forward. Along the way, northwest of Yingkou, they came to a swamp that was frozen over. Kharanov had his soldiers dismount there and, leaving behind three companies to look after the horses, marched them toward Yingkou to begin combat. The sun had by then gone down, so they moved by dim starlight.

Just then a fire broke out at Yingkou Station from the earlier shelling. The scenery suddenly grew brighter, which worked to the advantage of the Japanese troops waiting there in storehouses and other defensive positions for the Russians to attack. From a distance of 700 meters, they began to barrage Kharanov's troops with fierce gunfire, routing them almost instantly.

Darkness hindered Kharanov from taking command. He sent out orderlies to verify where his men were, but in the meantime so many fell, wounded or dying, that he had no choice but to summon the bugler. That, ironically, was the first combat order issued by this able cavalry commander in the mobile operation for which his cavalry was well suited: he had the bugler sound a retreat.

The time was twenty minutes to eight in the evening.

In the artillery battery, Mishchenko too debated whether or not to contain the raid. All sorts of intelligence came pouring in: several Japanese battalions were approaching through the city of Dashiqiao, and another Japanese unit had appeared around Niuzhuang, captured a Liao River crossing, and were about to cut off Mishchenko's escape. This last was untrue, but there were plenty of reasons for him to lean toward retreat. At last, he decided to call off the raid and gave the order to withdraw. The enormous expenditure of time and energy had accomplished virtually nothing.

Meanwhile, Akiyama Yoshifuru was carrying out a long-distance initiative similar to Mishchenko's, behind Russian lines.

* * *

Lucky and unlucky coincidences abound on the battlefield, and in strategy also, happenstance plays a big role.

Mishchenko's ten thousand-strong Cossack corps began heading south on January 9, the same day that a raiding party set off from Akiyama Yoshifuru's camp with a similar mission, headed for the Russian rear. Like comets crossing paths, each was unaware of the other's existence.

Known as "Naganuma's raiders," the Japanese cavalry unit was led by Lieutenant Colonel Naganuma Hidefumi, head of the Eighth Cavalry Regiment.

"Naganuma was a mild-mannered, fair-skinned gentleman who looked something like the old master of a merchant family," Yoshifuru liked to say in later years. "Chatting with him in a salon during peacetime, you would never imagine that such a gentleman had ever led so amazing an expedition."

Where Mishchenko had ten thousand men, Naganuma led just 170. His unit acted purely as a cavalry unit, utilizing the strengths of the cavalry without assistance from artillery or infantry. The other major difference between the two raiding parties was evident in the results they each obtained. Mishchenko's Cossack corps was extremely ineffectual. Having failed either to blow up any railway bridges or to destroy Japanese military stockpiles at Haicheng, Niuzhuang, and Yingkou, they corps abandoned its mission after only eight days and headed back north.

Naganuma's raid was far more effective. Leading 170 men, he embarked on a mind-boggling course that was dozens of times longer than Mishchenko's. His foray lasted two months and covered an astounding 1,600 kilometers. Along the way, his raiders attacked enemy logistical depots, fought and defeated Cossack forces, and blew up a railway bridge at the Xinkai River.

Three days after Naganuma's raiders took off, Yoshifuru sent off a second raiding party of approximately the same size, led by Major Hasegawa Inukichi. They covered a course of roughly the same distance as Naganuma's and after over sixty days broke through enemy lines, reaching as far as the second line at Songhua River.

Second Lieutenant Yamauchi and three other officers had set off earlier on a scouting expedition of eighteen days, extending over 1,000 kilometers, followed by First Lieutenant Tatekawa Yoshitsugu and five other cavalrymen, who scouted for twenty-three days, covering 1,200 kilometers.

When Tatekawa returned, he sent Sergeant Toyokichi Shinzaburō to headquarters at Yantai to report. "You have accomplished a superhuman feat!" Ōyama Iwao greeted Toyokichi with deep respect, and Kodama Gentarō flustered the sergeant by bringing out an autograph book and asking him to sign it. Both Ōyama and Kodama had weathered the storms of the Meiji Restoration, but they confessed later that not until this time did they realize what feats of adventure and endurance Japanese people were capable of.

* * *

Yoshifuru was guarding the Japanese Army's left wing. Assigned to a defensive position, his cavalry was underemployed. They should have been used for special assaults and sneak attacks. Japanese Army leaders didn't understand cavalry, Yoshifuru fumed as usual—and he included Kodama in the same clueless category as the rest.

Yoshifuru wanted to send cavalry raiders behind enemy lines to harass the rear guard, create diversions, attack supply lines, and blow up railways and bridges. He repeatedly made his wishes known, but headquarters ignored his requests. Cavalry had little or no place in the thinking of Kodama and his trusted aide, Matsukawa Toshitane. Any thought they did give to their cavalry was full of misgivings—what good could the Japanese cavalry possibly do? The Russian Cossacks were the world's most powerful cavalry. Next to the Russians' superior horsemanship and the greater size of their horses and riders, the Japanese cavalry looked puny. Kodama and Matsukawa assumed that cavalrymen would always be forced to dismount and fire as infantry, hiding in trenches and terrain, just as they had done under Yoshifuru when fighting the Cossacks.

"The cavalry is useless." This line of thinking had existed before the war in the army's inner circles. The army was constitutionally conservative, as shown also in its later reluctance to adopt airplanes and tanks. Faced with this sort of dismissive attitude, Yoshifuru alone urged the necessity of the cavalry and explained how it should be used. "Unfortunately, the usefulness of the cavalry becomes clear only when a brilliant general comes along," he remarked. "Under mediocre leadership, all the cavalry does is periodically get in the way."

The Japanese Army was definitely remiss in its study of cavalry. Major Jacob Meckel himself rose from the infantry and so perhaps had little sense of how the cavalry should be organized. His attitude no doubt contributed to Japan's overall slighting of the cavalry. Perhaps Yoshifuru's being given sole charge of cavalry research while still an army captain signals what a low priority the subject had. He retained sole command over the cavalry thereafter.

When Yoshifuru had been head of the Cavalry School before the war, his teaching of officers stressed the use of cavalry in raids and showed how it should be done and what high strategic value such raids could have, depending on the implementation.

"I was one of General Akiyama's students," said Naganuma after the war, "and all I did was follow exactly what he taught us to do."

When General Headquarters and Second Army headquarters approved the dispatch of Naganuma's raiders, Yoshifuru told Naganuma, "You will encounter great difficulties, but this is a mission worthy of the cavalry so please exert yourself to the fullest. If all goes well, the cavalry may find its true value appreciated at last after being sidelined so long."

The remark shows how undervalued and misunderstood the Japanese cavalry was by army leaders, who lived in fear of the Cossack forces led by Mishchenko and Rennenkampf.

* * *

"I feel constant frustration," Yoshifuru wrote in a letter to a friend. He knew that his men could never participate in a real cavalry battle, one where mounted soldiers from both sides engaged in combat. And if they did take on the Cossacks they would probably lose, as he was painfully aware.

Yoshifuru was not alone in that judgment. The elite military echelon deploying Japanese troops on the plains in sub-zero cold had nearly all studied abroad in the West or been on overseas tours of inspection and were painfully aware of the superiority of Western military forces. Remember, the overriding principle of Japanese leadership in the Russo-Japanese War had been summed up in Kodama Gentarō's statement just before hostilities: "Our chances are barely fifty–fifty. By taking pains with strategy, I'd like to improve the odds to sixty–forty." Rather than seeking victory, try to avoid defeat: this principle governed tactical thinking throughout the Japanese Army.

Accordingly, gambling with troop deployment was kept to a minimum. There was none of the army's later pathological tendency to gamble with its armies for the sheer exhilaration of doing so or for political ends (as in the Siberian Intervention of 1918–1922, the 1939 Nomonhan incident, and the 1944 battle of Imphal).

Having personally formed and trained the cavalry, Yoshifuru yearned to take on the world's best, the Cossacks, in mounted combat. This somewhat childish fantasy was still alive within him, but as battle commander he rigorously suppressed the impulse. As a result, his cavalry had fought the Cossacks by dismounting and becoming foot soldiers, participating in shootouts with them—and was on its way to achieving a victory rate of sixty percent.

Yoshifuru vented his built-up frustration and discontent by sending raiding parties of more than one hundred horsemen far into enemy territory. "Later on," he told Naganuma and his men as they were setting off, "I'll be sending out second and third raiding parties. If circumstances permit, I mean to send the whole brigade." But the army was undermanned, and so General Headquarters had assigned Akiyama's detachment to guard its left flank. Under those circumstances, he could not switch to Mishchenko's tactic of having the whole cavalry move together like a forest.

"I did what Akiyama himself wanted to do," Naganuma said later. "I did it in his place." While carrying out his fearless mission deep in enemy territory, he encountered a Cossack force several times larger than his own. Normally, in such a situation, the outnumbered troops would fight on foot or withdraw, but instead he led his men in an attack. They fought the enemy on horseback and chased them off, thus fulfilling Akiyama's cherished dream.

The day Naganuma's raiders set off, Yoshifuru saw them off on horseback from the top of a small hill. Heavy snow was falling, and the 170 men and horses quickly disappeared from sight. Yoshifuru spurred his horse on, caught up with them, and then saw them off again. He did this several times over.

The raiders' final target was in a far-off place called Yaomen, where they would blow up a large railway bridge that was a major Russian supply artery.

In the beginning, Kodama doubted the plan's chances of success—or, to put it more strongly, he wrote it off as impossible. The Russian front extended south from Mukden, and the bridge lay far to the rear—as far north as 600 kilometers, roughly the distance from Tokyo to Kobe.

The raiders started out from Sumabao, south of Heigoutai, and circled west on their way north. Rather than cross the Hun right away, they proceeded south along its left bank until they came to a place where the river was frozen over and crossed there, emerging on the right bank. That it was the right bank is significant because at precisely the same time, as if by prearrangement, Mishchenko's corps was heading south along that same bank. After making the crossing, Naganuma learned about the enemy's presence from a scout's report.

"It looked as if the whole town was on the move." This description may convey some idea of the enormous size of the Russian troop formation.

Don't let them find us. With this prayer in mind, Naganuma galloped west with his men and then headed north, passing Mishchenko. They went through Dagangzi and continued north. Along the way, to keep the enemy from finding them they remained quiet in the daytime, billeting in private houses and keeping their horses hidden indoors. They rode at night.

Naganuma's raiders were accompanied by a unit known in the Japanese Army as a *batai*, or "mounted unit." They were in essence mounted bandits. Mounted bandits were a unique feature of life in Manchuria, their presence growing out of local security requirements. In the absence of a state in the modern sense, villages had to protect themselves from roving bandits. Mounted bandits thus started out as local vigilante corps, but as their strength grew they broke away, absorbing gangs of thugs and attacking other villages in predatory raids.

Soon after the war began, both Russia and Japan befriended these mounted bandits, controlling them and using them to gather intelligence. In General Headquarters, Colonel Aoki Nobuzumi was put in charge of all mounted bandit units. He had a large number of men well versed in things Chinese who would sometimes dress in Chinese clothing and ride with the bandits.

When Naganuma's raiders set out, they were accompanied by a mounted bandit unit two hundred strong that would engage in reconnaissance. In order to achieve his mission goals, Naganuma avoided all contact with the enemy as he proceeded north. In the event that conflict became unavoidable, his policy was to leave fighting to the mounted bandit unit. For this reason, he had them go first, hiding behind them to conceal the northward movement of the cavalry. The Chinese bandits were contemptuous, scoffing that the Japanese cavalry was scared of the Russians, but Naganuma didn't let that get under his skin.

That policy was one of the foundations of Naganuma's success.

* * *

The northward progress of Naganuma's raiders took one month. The rivers and ground were frozen solid, and sometimes the men rode all day without coming across any sign of human habitation.

Naganuma eased their progress along the way by bribing natives and local authorities and capturing enemy bandit heads, always striving to keep his plans secret. Finally, on February 9, he and his men found themselves a day's ride from their destination of Yaomen. They billeted in the tiny snowbound hamlet of Lalatun. Normally, Naganuma's expression did not reveal his emotions, but that day he said with red-rimmed eyes, "Finally, we are 600 kilometers behind the enemy line. Tomorrow I can die happy."

Having said this, the cautious adventurer did not let up in vigilance or fail to reconnoiter about the way ahead. As he examined enemy activity around the railway bridge in Yaomen, he made some startling discoveries. Naganuma's movements had been detected by Kuropatkin's intelligence network. However, the reports were exaggerated, claiming ten thousand Japanese cavalry were headed north. The advance parties sent out by Yoshifuru—Naganuma's raiders, followed by Hasegawa's raiders, and the two smaller long-distance spy units led by Yamauchi and Tatekawa—appeared as points, lines, then fields, leading to the inflated report of a cavalry ten thousand strong.

Not only that, the movements of Naganuma, Hasegawa, Yamauchi, and Tatekawa had made waves as far away as Europe, taking the Russian War Ministry by surprise and causing urgent messages to be sent to Kuropatkin in Mukden, demanding to know if he had taken adequate measures to deal with the situation. St. Petersburg was informed that "ten thousand Japanese cavalry and another twenty thousand mounted bandit units have invaded Russian territory." Russia habitually overestimated enemy strength. The Japanese military, by contrast, habitually underestimated it.

In any case, Kuropatkin's overreaction to this development was a contributing factor to his defeat in the battle of Mukden. He hastily recalled Mishchenko's great force, which had previously been sent south, and ordered it to leave the Shaho front and take up a position around the Songhua, far in the north. Mishchenko's force had been beefed up from ten thousand to thirty thousand men. And so during the eventual battle of Mukden, the Cossacks, the greatest fighting unit in the Russian Army, were left to drift in the frozen north where no Japanese troops were.

The raiding party thus had significant strategic impact. Yet at the time, Naganuma had no idea that his movements were being reported in St. Petersburg. He was simply surprised that Mishchenko had returned and was once again in the north. That much his sources told him.

Naganuma knew that around the great railway bridge in Yaomen, where he was headed, Cossack infantry and artillery were well entrenched in a position several kilometers deep. As someone who took on adventuresome missions, Naganuma Hidefumi had a sterling quality: he cheerfully changed course, not sticking grimly to his first objective. "It doesn't have to be

Yaomen," he reflected. Since blowing up a rear Russian railway bridge was the goal, any railway bridge would do.

The biggest railway bridge in use by the Russian Army was the one over the Second Songhua River, south of Harbin, but that was too far away. The next biggest was the one at Yaomen, but if taking that was difficult, they could always opt for one further south, over the Xinkai River. Naganuma, who didn't miss a trick, had arranged to have his spies check on the Russian defense there. "It looks possible." With that report in hand, he focused all his resources on a new target—the bridge over the Xinkai River.

The Xinkai flows through the northern sector of the city of Gongzhuling, which was where the Japanese cavalry camped in Manchuria after the war. After the cavalry was replaced by machinery in the 1930s, with horses giving way to armored vehicles, Gongzhuling became a mecca for tanks, along with Sipingjie to the south.

While on the topic, we should mention that Hasegawa Inukichi, who like Naganuma led a cavalry raid across the vast snowy plains in search of railway bridges to blow up, was stationed in Gongzhuling after the war as head of the Eighteenth Cavalry Regiment. On learning that a paymaster on his staff had committed wrongdoing, he took responsibility by committing suicide. This happened in 1906.

As his manner of death shows, Hasegawa was a man of the highest integrity. But in his undercover movements at the head of 170 cavalrymen, he was unlucky. All the bridges he targeted were strongly guarded by Mishchenko's finest troops. Hasegawa tried and failed to blow up the bridge at Zhangjia Bay, north of Changchun (south of Yaomen). He went farther north than Naganuma and blew up an enemy supply depot at Shelidian, then returned to the railway bridge but was routed by a superior Cossack force. Unable to shake his pursuers, he kept his corps on the move until men and horses alike were ready to drop from exhaustion. The mounted bandit units traveling with him became disgruntled at his too-rigid control and began pillaging, forcing him to end the mission. On his way back he summoned all his remaining strength in an attempt to close in on the enemy north of Sipingjie Station and blow up a bridge there, but he came under enemy attack and failed again.

After the war, Hasegawa was awarded high military honors, including the Order of the Golden Kite, Third Class. "I exerted myself to the utmost, but my achievements deserve no commendation," he always maintained. After the war, he was extremely self-deprecating and ended, as mentioned, by taking his own life. He was a Meiji-style warrior to the core.

Naganuma was the more flexible of the two, deciding what action to take based on his observations of a fluid situation. In the end, he succeeded in blowing up the railway bridge over the Xinkai River. It happened at two in the morning on February 12. At the time of the blast, there was skirmishing with the enemy garrison, but Naganuma's raiders endured their greatest assaults after that and retreated.

"Find the Japanese cavalry, and, when you do, wipe them out." This was the order Mishchenko promptly issued to every cavalry unit in his command.

* * *

Naganuma's raiders stayed on the run. On February 13, when they reached a village called Babaotun, an astonishing report came in: "Superior enemy cavalry hot in pursuit."

"This is it," thought Naganuma. In later years, he would learn from Russian records that one of the units Mishchenko had sent after him had already detected his location. How many pursuers there were he couldn't tell at the time, but, in fact, there were some two hundred Cossacks with some horse artillery. They were advancing south from Changchun and were then just 20 kilometers southwest of Babaotun.

Before he decided whether to fight, Naganuma wanted to find out all he could about the enemy position, so that day he and his men remained in Babaotun. The next day, they set off for Xinjichang, for the intelligence report he received had said, "No sign of enemy cavalry."

On Naganuma's tail were three cavalry companies led by Captain Lenitsky and two field pieces, for a combined strength of two hundred cavalrymen. Lenitsky's information exaggerated Naganuma's troop strength. Naganuma possessed neither infantry nor artillery, but as far as Lenitsky knew, he had "four main cavalry companies as well as four companies of infantry, four field guns, and three thousand mounted bandits." In short, even though he had the superior force, Lenitsky considered himself outnumbered. Even so, he bravely attempted to go on the attack and wipe out his opponent. The bushy-bearded, middle-aged Lenitsky was not a member of the aristocracy but was one of the few officers of Cossack origin.

"The enemy appears to be en route to Xinjichang with intent to destroy a railway bridge. We will go there and cut off their escape." Lenitsky explained his plan to his subordinates and spurred them forward. It was around four in the afternoon on February 14 when they arrived at a point 12 kilometers from the village. With his naked eye, Lenitsky was able to make out the Japanese column crossing the silvery fields of snow.

His battle tactics were poor. If he wanted to wipe out the enemy, he should have surrounded them, but instead, without even deploying his troops, he had the artillery placed on a hillside and ordered a barrage. The cannons boomed, and shells fell in front of Naganuma's raiders, exploding with clouds of black smoke that soon broke up in the strong wind.

The sudden bombardment caught Naganuma by surprise and also let him know exactly where the enemy was. He immediately sent his scouts off to reconnoiter and moved his main force behind a nearby hill. When the scouts returned, they reported "roughly a thousand Cossacks, several guns." This too was an overestimation.

Naganuma did not immediately believe those numbers, but even if outnumbered six to one, he decided to take the enemy on head to head. The primary objective of destroying the railway bridge over the Xinkai River having been achieved, there was no further need to retreat.

"I'll try," he resolved.

* * *

They would start fighting after sundown, Naganuma decided. The only way to defeat a numerically superior enemy was to take it on at night. Besides, the enemy was armed with artillery, and aiming it was harder in the dark.

The moon was eleven days old. From evening, it appeared in the eastern sky, an aid to night movements, and the silvery white plains beneath offered no impediment.

Naganuma's spies had pinpointed the enemy's location, and the enemy had scattered itself into an unnecessarily thin line. Clustered together, the Cossacks were a force to be reckoned with, but when they spread out their strength was greatly diminished. One reason was probably that the leadership abilities of lower-grade leaders in small Russian units were far inferior to those of their Japanese counterparts.

After first withdrawing the wounded, the noncombatants, and those leading extra horses, Naganuma hurried with his main force to cut off the enemy's escape route. At a point 2 kilometers north of a village called Zhangjiawazi, they spotted the full enemy detachment.

Naganuma swiftly switched to infantry mode. The troops rushed forward, shooting furiously, but the enemy gradually pulled away, returning fire on horseback. Naganuma ordered his men back in the saddle and had them gallop forward until they were again in firing range.

The troops went in this order: six of Numata Hamanosuke's men formed a vanguard, followed by a column with first the main force, then Nakaya Shigenari's company, and finally Asano's company. As they drew near Zhangjiawazi, the village erupted with withering gunfire.

Naganuma was as calm as if conducting exercises. First, he lined up Asano's company in a row, and had them face the village and open fire. Then he personally took charge of Nakaya's company, formed them into a column, and had them run alongside the enemy's artillery position to cut off their retreat. He was attempting to use the Japanese Army's familiar tactic of encirclement.

"It was around eight at night, with a bright wintry moon in the middle sky." So read Naganuma's later report.

As Asano's company spurred forward, dodging bullets, intending to make a frontal attack on the village, they were utterly surprised to come upon a trench. It had been dug to protect the village and was far too wide for the horses to jump across.

"Trench!" The vanguard shouted out and halted, and at the same time the enemy began to retreat with two artillery pieces pulled by horses. Naganuma and Nakaya, trying to intercept the enemy from the rear, were also blocked by the trench, which seemed to go on for kilometers. The Russian artillery and the sixty Cossacks providing cover began to retreat, following along the trench. Naganuma and Nakaya advanced parallel to them on the other side with their sixty cavalrymen. The two sides came dashing furiously at each other, the Russian horse artillery jouncing over the ground.

After a couple of kilometers, Captain Nakaya discovered a place where the trench happened to narrow. He drew his sword and ordered the entire company to jump across. They fought hand-to-hand with the enemy and after a bitter battle drove them away, managing to capture one gun and one caisson.

The sixty cavalrymen in the Asano company, which led the frontal assault, fought fiercely. Their leader, Asano Rikitarō, came up against the trench in front of the village and was temporarily halted, but eventually he found a place where it could be crossed and so made it to the other side. One after another his men followed after him, but then they encountered an earthen wall surrounding the village. Asano advanced along the wall until he found a place where it was crumbling. He soared over, but his mount staggered as its front legs hit the ground. While he struggled to get the animal back on its feet, out surged the Cossacks, brandishing lances.

The village contained a cavalry detachment two hundred strong led by Captain Lenitsky. The artillery and the sixty horsemen providing cover having retreated in advance, the rest of the troops were gathered there before making their next move. As Asano struggled, a lance pierced his right chest. Ten Cossacks swiftly surrounded him, ready to hurl their lances, and he fell from his horse. He picked himself up and tried to fight with his sword, but his right arm hung useless, forcing him to draw his pistol. With one shot he felled an enemy horse. With his next he "hit the moon," according to Russian records. Probably he shot at the sky from a prone position before breathing his last.

Asano's men came jumping on horseback over the collapsed wall, and one by one they too were surrounded. Horses and men of both sides jostled together in the narrow space. Lances, swords, and sabers flashed, rifle and pistol shots rang out. The soldiers' clothes were drenched with one other's blood—blood that quickly froze.

Traveling with the Asano company was Captain Miyauchi Hidekuma from Naganuma's staff. Miyauchi had been a student at the Army College when the war began, but since he was fluent in Chinese he was sent to Beijing, where he worked as a spy. After that he joined General Headquarters, and when Naganuma's raiders were sent out he was assigned to Naganuma's staff because of his familiarity with the geography of Manchuria.

In the confusion of the battle, Miyauchi couldn't tell that Asano had died, but when he failed to see him anywhere he decided to take over the leadership. He climbed up on the wall and ordered a general retreat. Otherwise, the lances of the two hundred Cossacks were sure to wipe out the sixty Japanese soldiers.

But the Cossacks, having suffered great losses, began to flee by twos and threes without waiting for an order. Barely fifty remained in the village.

Miyauchi assembled the Japanese horsemen and had them dismount, conducting a fire fight while leading their horses. As a result, the remaining fifty Cossacks began to retreat, following their captain's command. The Japanese chased after them so tenaciously that the whole detachment ultimately was routed, men fleeing in a stampede.

In the morning when the Japanese regrouped, their only dead turned out to be Captain Asano. Fifty-nine men were wounded, almost all by lances, which gives some indication of the fierceness of the fighting. Since a small company caused a much larger force to flee, this encounter has to be called an overwhelming victory for the Japanese.

* * *

Later on, Yoshifuru heard about how Kuropatkin, frightened about reports of a huge Japanese cavalry force, had prevented Mishchenko's mobile force from delivering a decisive blow, even though it was the strongest unit in the entire Russian Army, and instead sent Mishchenko to the far-off Second Songhua River with orders to stand guard in the rear. And so by sending out a force of under four hundred horsemen on a long-distance raid, Yoshifuru succeeded in pinning a Cossack force of ten thousand in the north and preventing them from delivering a hammer blow in the battle of Mukden.

"I never dreamed the raids would have that effect," said Yoshifuru after the war. "It could well be that General Kuropatkin's hypersensitivity caused him to err in his use of a hero like Mishchenko."

The raiders' movements had another unexpected effect, influencing peace negotiations. Naganuma's raiders operated far north of the Japanese front, but when they blew up the bridge at Xinkai River, First Lieutenant Tamura Umazō and Private First Class Mochizuki Kōji charged the Russian guardhouse and were killed. The Russians kept pouring in more troops, so in the end Naganuma went off and abandoned the two men's corpses, but afterward the Russians, impressed with the gallantry they had displayed, buried them respectfully and erected a grave marker about 3.5 meters high. Apparently, Mishchenko himself gave the order to build a high marker.

According to contemporary rules of war, the land and transportation lines ceded to a victorious nation were areas occupied by that nation's army. At the end of the battle of Mukden, the Japanese Army had advanced only as far as Changtu Station near Sipingjie. The Russian Army claimed that cessations should be limited to land south of there, but as the facts emerged, ultimately they handed over the railway south of Changchun, in the north. The proof of Japanese occupation was the graves the Russians made for Tamura and Mochizuki.

"Mishchenko built graves for a Japanese officer and enlisted man, but his chivalry cost Russia a railroad." Some in the Russian War Ministry voiced this criticism. Others said in Mishchenko's defense that his greatness lay in his chivalry, and never mind the railroad.

The rules of war, Mishchenko's erecting of enemy graves, the words of his defenders—all in all, when you think about it, war of this era still had a certain chivalry.

* * *

Our story has gotten ahead of itself. To clarify the situation so far, let's remember that Mishchenko's raiding party headed south before the battle of Heigoutai. That operation heralded the battle to come.

Naganuma's raiders set out at almost the same time, heading for the Russian rear, but while the Russians abandoned their mission after eight days, Naganuma and his men plodded on for sixty days. They knew nothing of the ferocious fighting that would take place at Heigoutai; their deployment had nothing whatever to do with that battle.

Mishchenko's force, however, not only would join in the battle but would play a central role in it. To understand the logistics, we must go back in time, back to when Lieutenant General Mishchenko returned from his expedition south. On January 16, he went in person to Kuropatkin's headquarters in Mukden to report on the results of his reconnaissance in force.

"The Japanese Army is nothing to be afraid of." Mishchenko pointed to various maps as he explained. "They appear to be critically understrength."

According to him, the enemy was spread out widely but unevenly. He was right. His analysis of the Japanese position was spot on.

Mukden Road ran north–south through the center of the line, where the camp was particularly dense. This was where Oku's army (the Second Army) and Nozu's army (the Fourth Army) came together. The next densest place was the hilly region to the east where Kuroki's army (the First Army) was encamped.

"Where the line is paper-thin is the left wing. On this map, that would be"—Mishchenko pointed to an extensive stretch of plain between the Hun River and the Liao—"here." He explained that the entire expanse was defended only by a "cavalry screen" with a small infantry unit to support it. In other words, Yoshifuru had drawn a line of cavalry like a curtain.

"They are using their cavalry defensively." To Mishchenko, himself a cavalry commander, the use of cavalry for garrison duty made no sense. What on earth was Japanese General Headquarters thinking? By rights, a cavalry unit should be kept beside the supreme commander so that as he monitored the progress of the fighting, he could watch for an opportune moment and send in cavalry on a massive scale from a direction that would take the enemy by surprise. The sight of cavalrymen shouldering their rifles and staying put like peasants protecting their fields was hard to fathom for Russians, who attached great importance to cavalry mobility.

"It probably has to do with their shortage of manpower," Mishchenko concluded. "I believe that the main focus of our attack should be here, on the left wing."

Basing their deliberations on this report, Kuropatkin and his staff decided, just as Mishchenko had recommended, to hit Akiyama's detachment with massive force.

* * *

As he prepared to launch his attack, Kuropatkin waited anxiously for fresh troops (the Eighth European Army Corps and the First and Fifth Rifle Infantry Brigades) to arrive in Mukden. By the time they all had arrived, it was January 20.

"What fine soldiers!" Kuropatkin commented, watching as, one after another, the reinforcements joined his army's right wing. "Grippenberg is bound to win himself a glorious victory." Mixed in with his praise of the soldiers was sarcasm directed at General Grippenberg, his rival.

Kuropatkin knew that the newcomer Grippenberg mocked him as "General Retreat" behind his back. He was aware that as designer and implementer of the new operation, Grippenberg hoped success would win him kudos at the court in St. Petersburg, perhaps even land him the position of supreme commander of the Russian forces in Manchuria. And he knew that Grippenberg also referred to him as a "topnotch armchair theorist."

Though he was promoted to general after Kuropatkin, Grippenberg had graduated from the Army Academy well before him and was by this time already a grizzled veteran. "A stubborn old coot"—that's how Kuropatkin referred to this rival who'd left behind the warmth of St. Petersburg salons to thrust himself onto a frozen battlefield.

"The old coot has no idea what he's up against in the Japanese Army," Kuropatkin thought. "All he wants to do is pull off a razzle-dazzle stunt for his own glory."

The troops that Kuropatkin spared for Grippenberg's major assault were the First Siberian Army Corps, a division of dragoons, plus the newly arrived Eighth European Army Corps and the First and Fifth Rifle Infantry Brigades, as well as Mishchenko's mobile task force. In all, they outnumbered their intended target, Akiyama Yoshifuru's detachment, six times over.

This is the point when Kuropatkin issued his promise, "You attack first, and, if all goes well, our main force will breach the center of the enemy line." In other words, "If you succeed, we'll join the fray." Coming from the mouth of Russia's most brilliant tactician, this was a highly peculiar statement. He was essentially saying, "I'll sit back and observe whether or not you succeed." He himself was not going to budge.

Needless to say, Kuropatkin should have used his First Manchurian Army to apply pressure on the center of the Japanese line. The pain resulting from a central blow would have prevented the main force from rescuing Akiyama's detachment on the left. The detachment would have collapsed, and, while Grippenberg proceeded to crush the army's left wing and go after General Headquarters in the rear, Kuropatkin could have broken through the center. The Japanese Army would have suffered a devastating defeat.

Fortunately for the Japanese forces, Kuropatkin's silent conflict with his colleague kept him from doing that.

Part 6

Translated by Juliet Winters Carpenter

1

HEIGOUTAI, CONTINUED

In the Russian Army, the Grippenberg operation was being implemented despite the uncooperative attitude of Commander in Chief Kuropatkin. The situation at Japanese Manchuria General Headquarters in Yingtai was even more deplorable.

"Enemy outposts are active, a probable sign of intent to launch a major operation." Vital warnings of this nature, sent by Akiyama Yoshifuru, arrived frequently at Yingtai. As we well know, they were treated dismissively and ignored due to the unshakable, though groundless belief among the top brass that the Russian Army wouldn't launch a winter offensive.

According to the official Japanese history of the war, "the battle at Heigoutai was unforeseen and caught us where we were vulnerable." The claim that the battle was unforeseen does not hold water. A surprise attack may be one thing, but when a major offensive is in the works there are plenty of telltale signs—signs that scouts and battlefield spies are fully capable of ferreting out. Desks at General Headquarters were piled high with such intelligence, including reports filed by Japanese military attachés in Europe that arrived in Yingtai via Tokyo. The offensive was not "unforeseen."

But General Headquarters made light of the threat, solely out of their fixed idea that "the Ruskies wouldn't conduct such a major operation in this freezing cold." This unbelievable rigidity can be blamed on their fatigue, but the thinking at headquarters was so delusional that even when it became clear that the Russian Army had gone on the move, Colonel Matsukawa Toshitane, Kodama's right-hand man, said it was probably a reconnaissance in force, his eyes shut to the changed reality.

Enemy pressure steadily mounted, and when finally it dawned on General Headquarters that this was no reconnaissance in force, pandemonium broke out and reigned for days on end. Orders issued in the morning were reversed at noon. Orders from General Headquarters to the front conflicted with orders given by commanders at the front. Units everywhere hesitated over what course of action to take and grew so fed up with ceaseless running around that they took charge of operations on their own, bringing on widespread chaos.

General Headquarters continued sending out reinforcements piecemeal, a violation of basic strategic principles that invited the risk of losing all. In the end, they were forced to take the emergency measure of withdrawing troops from the center and applying them to the extreme left flank, leaving the center vulnerable and exposed. Had Kuropatkin kept his promise to Grippenberg and struck there, Japan would almost certainly have suffered a devastating defeat. What brought Japan through the battle of Heigoutai was not the leadership of General Headquarters but the valiant fighting of units facing heavy odds—fighting that the top leadership only interfered with.

Let us examine in detail the "unforeseen" hard fighting—for the Japanese side—at Heigoutai. First, we need to clarify the position of Akiyama's detachment. A detachment in the Japanese Army was a mixed force of infantry, artillery, and other units temporarily assigned for independent action. Akiyama Yoshifuru was officially the head of the First Cavalry Brigade, but he also commanded infantry and artillery units. Mishchenko on the Russian side also led an independent combat force temporarily assembled from various branches of the military, so his troops likewise would be known as "Mishchenko's detachment."

Yoshifuru chose the village of Lidarentun for his headquarters. The choice was irregular, as the village was exceedingly close to the enemy front line and, from the perspective of his troops' various camps, off on the extreme right, by Japan's Second Army led by General Oku. Yoshifuru chose that location for ease in communicating with Oku's army, even though it put him within 5 kilometers of the enemy's front line. Just locating his headquarters in such a place took nerves of steel.

Behind the village was the Shaho, flowing southwest, and far in front of it was the Hun River, south of which spread the Russian encampment. Local terrain was harsh. Over time, floods of the Shaho and the Hun, along with shifts in the flow of water, had carved out steep hills and sharply uneven fields.

Akiyama's command included the following:

1. Main detachment (around Lidarentun)
    From the Ninth Infantry Regiment (Ōtsu), a little over one battalion; Third (Nagoya) and Sixth (Kumamoto) Cavalry Regiments, less one company each; from the Thirteenth Artillery Regiment, one company;

the main force of the Eighth Engineer Battalion (Hirosaki); five machine guns.

2. Mitake's detachment (around Hanshantai)

    From the Ninth Infantry Regiment, two companies; Ninth (Kanazawa) and Tenth (Himeji) Cavalry Regiments, less one company each; one platoon from a horse artillery company; also two engineer platoons and one machine gun.

3. Toyobe's detachment (around Sandepu)

    First Cavalry Brigade (Narashino); a battalion from the Second Infantry Standby Reserve Regiment (Sakura); a horse artillery company; a company of engineers; and three machine guns.

4. Taneda's detachment (around Heigoutai)

    Fifth Cavalry Regiment (Hiroshima); Eighth Cavalry Regiment (Hirosaki); a company from the Second Infantry Standby Reserve Regiment; and two machine guns.

What's interesting about this setup is that the only units of cavalry Yoshifuru kept on hand belonged to others. He didn't keep the First Cavalry Brigade, his prized possession, at his side, but rather assigned it to the fortified village of Sandepu (the present-day Shendanbao, which he assumed would lie straight in the enemy's path in case of an attack) under Colonel Toyobe Shinsaku. He figured that all he himself needed was a force to relay orders, that is, division cavalry, and that the fighting cavalry, his First Cavalry Brigade, should stay at Sandepu and keep the Russians from advancing south. Later on, this unusual method of assigning posts would be seen as the heart of his strategy.

*   *   *

Sometime after January 20, Yoshifuru put together reports from his ace cavalry scouts and entertained deep misgivings about the growing enemy activity ahead of him. His judgment that the enemy might come straight at him in a large-scale attack swelled from surmise into conviction. The report he filed with General Headquarters on January 7 setting forth that judgment had been met with silence. Until headquarters woke up, he would have to deal with the situation on his own. He kept his eyes peeled and ordered all the unit leaders in his command to maintain strict guard.

Yoshifuru had every reason for concern, as the enemy front he was responsible for was 40 kilometers long, a huge distance that he was guarding with just over eight thousand men. Though Yoshifuru wouldn't know this until afterward, General Grippenberg was advancing on him with an army of well over one hundred thousand. The movements of a force so large, no matter how well camouflaged, are as apparent to the sharpened instincts of a combat veteran as a change in wind pressure. Around January 20, Yoshifuru was acutely aware that something was in the air.

But General Headquarters was blind—meaning that Yoshifuru and his small defending force would be wiped out. Heroic though it might be to suffer annihilation, unlike many military men Yoshifuru had no tragic leanings in that direction. He didn't argue with General Headquarters or plead for help. Instead, he resolved to go it alone. Knowing the risk of annihilation, he prepared to do everything possible to avoid that fate. No matter how desperate the fighting became, the enemy surge must be halted or the entire Japanese Army would be destroyed.

Yoshifuru used a system of strongpoints. Capitalizing on the strengths of the cavalry would have meant launching a mobile operation—a raid or a surprise attack—but General Headquarters had given him the distinctly non-cavalry job of guarding and defending the army's left flank. The assignment may have been natural in view of the small size of the Japanese cavalry, but guarding and defending a 40-kilometer-long front with so few men was next to impossible. That's why Yoshifuru used fortified strongpoints: the four main ones being Lidarentun, where he had his headquarters; Hanshantai, under Lieutenant Colonel Mitake Otokatsu (head of the Tenth Cavalry Regiment); Sandepu, under Colonel Toyobe Shinsaku (head of the Fourteenth Cavalry Regiment); and Heigoutai, under Colonel Taneda Jōtarō (head of the Fifth Cavalry Regiment). Smaller outposts branched out from each of these. For each one, soldiers dug a firing trench around a small village, set up obstructions, and dug gun ports in a mud wall. By creating walled redoubts, they prepared to fight the enemy's great army.

Even if thirty thousand enemy troops attacked, they would get by. Yoshifuru was confident of that. But to repeat: the army actually coming at them numbered over one hundred thousand.

*   *   *

Earlier, the Second Cavalry Brigade, one of only two cavalry brigades in the Japanese Army, had undergone a change of leadership. Back when the Russians were defeated by withering machine gun fire in the battle of Lake Benxi, the commander had been Prince Kan'in Kotohito. Subsequently, he was transferred to General Headquarters, and Major General Tamura Hisai took his place.

On January 22, fifteen officers from the Second Calvary Brigade set off on patrol, led by Second Lieutenant Katō Hiroshi, and were ambushed around Niaobangniu by three companies of enemy cavalry. Only two officers returned alive. This incident served as a warning to General Headquarters, yet even then they minimized the threat, assuming that a couple of divisions had come south. But a Russian soldier who surrendered to Yoshifuru's detachment around then asserted that General Grippenberg was in command of the operation. If that grizzled general, virtually equal in rank to Kuropatkin, was in charge, then the Russians had descended not in divisions but in corps.

Yoshifuru sent off an urgent memo to General Headquarters—and for the first time, got a response: "We are sending the Eighth Division." They were sending a single division, just over ten thousand men, as reinforcements. But at that point, the Eighth Division was all they had in reserve. Once it was gone, the bottom of the pot would be scraped clean, so to speak, and even if other guests arrived there would be nothing left to serve them.

We have already written about the Eighth Division, which had its headquarters in Hirosaki, a castle town at the northern tip of Japan's main island of Honshu. Its soldiers were from the four northern prefectures of Aomori, Akita, Yamagata, and Iwate. Along with the Sixth, from Kumamoto, the Eighth was held to be one of the strongest divisions in the army. We have also written about the Eighth Division's commander, the veteran lieutenant general Tatsumi Naobumi, who was known for having commanded a Western-style infantry in Kuwana domain at the end of the Tokugawa period and for continuing to fight around the country on behalf of the shogunate even after the shogunate had fallen. In the battle of Hokuetsu, he joined with troops from Nagaoka domain and routed the Satsuma-Chōshū forces time and again. Pro-imperial troops held him in fear. Originally kept in Japan as strategic reserves, Tatsumi and his division had been stationed well back from the front, awaiting further orders, since arriving in Manchuria. At noon on January 25, General Headquarters ordered the Eighth into action—but it was already too late.

An army large enough to blacken the horizon had appeared in front of Akiyama's detachment. The camp at Heigoutai, on the far west, was guarded by a token force consisting of the Second Cavalry Regiment, under the command of Colonel Taneda, plus two hundred infantry draftees, old soldiers all; two machine guns; and no cannons. The Second Siberian Army Corps bore down in full force. Caught in the flames of hell, Taneda and his men put up a desperate fight. In a driving snowstorm with visibility of under 50 meters, Russian shells kept exploding, making the snowfield look as if it were rising toward the skies.

* * *

Japanese people have never been very strong on defensive thinking or technology. With few exceptions, Japanese military history is a history of offensive warfare. The greatest example of successful defensive warfare came in the 1570s, when the temple known as Ishiyama Honganji (where today's Osaka Castle stands) stood up to the forces of Oda Nobunaga over a period of years. The temple maintained its fighting strength to the end, but eventually the diplomatic situation turned unfavorable, forcing it to surrender.

During the Ishiyama War, the defenders lacked engineering expertise and physical power. All they had in the way of physical defenses was a narrow single moat that surrounded the castle. What supported their defense was their religious faith, pure and simple. The same can be said of Christian believers in the Shimabara Rebellion in the 1630s.

Perhaps because Japan isn't a continental nation, the Japanese don't think in terms of physically buttressing their defenses. The sole exception must be Hideyoshi's Osaka Castle. Mindful of how Nobunaga and his forces had struggled to defeat the occupiers of Ishiyama Honganji, Hideyoshi built his castle on the same site, making it into a massive fortress capable of accommodating over one hundred thousand troops. Nothing on such a scale had ever been seen in Japanese history. Yet in the summer campaign of the siege of Osaka, the castle fell to Ieyasu's field army. Why? Probably because, even given adequate defense works, the Japanese national character is ill-suited to the psychological demands of defensive warfare.

In his later years, Maeda Toshiie of Kaga reminisced about the life of his late lord, Nobunaga, praising him by saying that "he always waged war by invading others' territory." The invasion strategy of Oda Nobunaga may be representative of the mindset of most Japanese.

Let us return to our story.

The two armies facing off at the Shaho both adopted a provisional defensive posture by setting up field camps. The strategic flaw in the plan implemented by Japan's General Headquarters was their use of Yoshifuru's cavalry brigade to guard the right flank. To use an analogy from the game of shōgi, it was like using a lance, which lacks the function of a gold or silver general, as guard. Of course, by supplying Yoshifuru with a small amount of infantry, artillery, and military engineers, they did give him functions vaguely like those of a gold or silver general, a rook, or a bishop. But, since the cavalry is basically a lance, using it as the main defense weakened their fighting strength.

Yoshifuru had of course always been privately exasperated by General Headquarters' obtuseness regarding use of the cavalry, and now they had shown they didn't know anything about defense either. Both weaknesses reflect an underlying character trait or mindset of the Japanese.

The idea of cavalry originated among nomadic peoples, while defensive warfare arose in agricultural regions on continents, as seen in ancient fortified defense works in China and Europe. Japan had been an agricultural region since ancient times, but its farming villages had little or no need to mount a defense against foreign invaders. That explains the Japanese people's intrinsic ineptness with cavalry and defensive warfare.

* * *

Before getting on with the battle of Heigoutai, first a short digression on the role of army engineers in the Russo-Japanese War.

The engineers did all sorts of work. They erected field fortifications, made roads and bridges, dug tunnels for sieges, blew up enemy facilities. Forming this branch of the military was difficult, given the state of Japanese technology barely three decades after the Meiji Restoration.

The army first set up an engineering corps by following the example of foreign countries, but it was only for show. In 1877, a talented youth entered the Army Academy. He had been a live-in student in the home of Nozu Michitsura, later the head of the Japanese Fourth Army. "Go into the engineering corps so you can make something of Japanese engineers," Nozu advised him. The youth was Uehara Yūsaku, who was a classmate of Yoshifuru's and went on to become field marshal.

Just as Yoshifuru built a real Japanese cavalry, so Uehara built a real engineering corps. At the beginning of his career, he studied in France, where he was with the Fourth Engineer Regiment at Grenoble, near the Italian border. Back in 1881, in a small country town like Grenoble, anyone dimly aware that a country called Japan existed on the world map would have been a considerable highbrow. When Uehara ate in a restaurant near the station, crowds gathered to stare and ask, "What race are you?" His wearing the French army uniform made him all the more odd to them. When he explained Japan's geographical location, they voiced sympathy. "You were drafted from someplace that far away?" They had no idea what sort of country Japan might be, but assumed it must be a French colony in the Far East.

After his return, Uehara devoted himself to training engineers. Unlike Yoshifuru, who was forced to devote himself exclusively to the cavalry, Uehara was moved around quite a bit within the army, so he did not seriously tackle the issue until he became inspector of engineering, just two years before the outbreak of the Russo-Japanese War. During that interval he transformed Japanese military engineering technology.

Because such a wide variety of reforms was needed, he glossed over one area—the technique of digging horizontal tunnels. "That was a mistake," he said later. "If our engineers had known how to tunnel properly, the attack on Port Arthur would have gone differently, without that appalling loss of life." After the war, he lost no time in putting together a *Tunneling Manual*, and in 1906 he conducted Japan's first maneuvers in tunnel warfare at the Kokura Engineer Corps ground.

That was the level of Japanese military engineering technology.

When the army dug in face to face with the Russians on the banks of the Shaho, the engineers (one battalion per division) were in high demand to build field fortifications. There were never enough of them to go around. Unable to get around to building fortifications in Yoshifuru's camp themselves, the engineers gave pointers to his cavalrymen and infantrymen, who then built their own fortifications during lulls in the fighting. Even so, thanks to the transformation Uehara had wrought in the abilities of Japanese military engineers during the two and a half years before the war, one way or another European-style field fortifications protected Yoshifuru's division from enemy gunfire.

*   *   *

Well before dawn on January 25, Yoshifuru learned that the weight of the Russian Army was bearing down on his detachment.

At three in the morning, scouts at Heilintai on the front line (two platoons of cavalry) ran into a massive night raid by the enemy and had to retreat. When Yoshifuru heard the news over the telephone, he had the feeling that something unimaginable was going to happen. The cavalry often functions like a meteorological station, and he sensed a typhoon coming. He was proven right at around ten that morning, when gunfire and the shriek of exploding shells shook heaven and earth. In the farmhouse he was using as headquarters, plaster rained down every time a shell fell. No matter how many times he brushed off the map on his desk, it was soon covered thickly in dust again.

The Tenth European Army Corps, under Lieutenant General Konstantin Tserpitsky, was the force pounding Akiyama's detachment so hard. Their strategy, as it later became clear, was to bombard Lidarentun on the Japanese right flank so relentlessly that Yoshifuru's strategic instincts would be thrown off. They knew from their Chinese spy network that there was a Japanese military headquarters in Lidarentun.

And so they tried to distract the Japanese Army by bombarding Lidarentun, in order to make their attack on Sandepu easier. At one point, Yoshifuru did wonder if the enemy wasn't making Lidarentun the main focus of its attack. Bombardment was a well-known precursor to an infantry charge, and he braced himself—but time passed, and still there was only the screech of shells, large and small, and no sign of enemy soldiers.

Sometime after ten in the morning, Russian infantry began pouring into the left-hand strongholds of Sandepu and Heigoutai. The attack on Lidarentun had been a feint, Yoshifuru realized. The enemy's real goal was Sandepu or Heigoutai or both. Sharp instincts are a necessary qualification for army leaders from brigade commanders on up, and Yoshifuru possessed these in abundance. Otherwise, he might well have been so flustered by the attack on his headquarters that he persuaded Colonel Toyobe in Sandepu to part with some of his troops to fortify Lidarentun—just as Tserpitsky intended.

Tserpitsky himself was no military genius. Yoshifuru had sent two cavalry companies to Heilintai (near enemy territory) for reconnaissance, and Tserpitsky mistook them for a large force. When he asked his superior officer, General Grippenberg, for permission to occupy Heilintai, the general roared, "I already told you your objective! It's Sandepu!"

*   *   *

This battle went down in Russian history as the "battle of Sandepu," since that village was the main target. The Japanese, who were put on the defensive, call it "the battle near Heigoutai." Since the two villages are geographically correlated, either name will do. But in the beginning, Yoshifuru wasn't able to foresee that the main target of the enemy attack would be Sandepu.

Slightly right of center in Yoshifuru's battle formation was Hanshantai, occupied by Colonel Mitake's unit. All that morning, the pattern of fighting suggested that Russian sights were set there. That's because far more pressure was being brought to bear on the stronghold of Jinshanzhun, jutting north of Hanshantai, near enemy territory. The Russians took Jinshanzhun, and the Japanese cavalry retreated in driving snow. The Russians took Huangdi, another nearby stronghold, at the same time.

"During the Russo-Japanese War, I was always losing," Yoshifuru would often say in his later years, referring to just this sort of situation.

He quickly picked up the phone and ordered Lieutenant Colonel Mitake to recapture the two strongholds. Since he had no chief of staff, he had to do everything himself—all the thinking, all the arranging, all the scolding.

Mitake began to prepare for the job, but he didn't have a big enough force. Yoshifuru then called Colonel Toyobe to the phone and ordered him to assist Mitake. War, they say, is the accumulation of mistakes on both sides. Yoshifuru's biggest mistake at this early stage was his judgment that Jinshanzhun had greater strategic importance than Sandepu. That judgment forced Toyobe to part with a significant portion of his troops; he was put into the position of someone rushing off to extinguish a fire in a neighboring town rather than the one in his own backyard.

Yoshifuru had good reason for what he did. His assumption that the enemy was trying to breach the center of his detachment turned out to be wrong (they were actually breaching his left flank). But had he been right, and a Russian army had come bursting through, they would have been helpless to resist since Mitake's forces in the middle were slightly smaller in number than Toyobe's and had to defend the widest area. Toyobe spared Mitake one infantry standby reserve company, two cavalry companies, and one machine gun. The commander of that provisional unit was Lieutenant Colonel Koike Jun, head of the Thirteenth Cavalry Regiment.

That night in Sandepu, as the fighting in front of Toyobe heated up, it dawned on the colonel that his area was the main target. With no time to notify Yoshifuru, he acted on his own initiative and contacted Lieutenant Colonel Ohara Fumihira, commander of the Thirty-first Infantry Standby Reserve Regiment (Hirosaki), a unit behind under a different command. Toyobe explained the situation and asked for reinforcements, getting Ohara to send two companies. The battle was becoming increasingly difficult, the situation increasingly grave.

* * *

January 26 was a day of intense cold and northern snows falling in the diagonal pattern of a blizzard. The fiercest battle ever fought on the Manchurian plains was in progress, although the combatants, friend and foe alike, frequently lost sight of one another.

At his headquarters in Lidarentun, Akiyama Yoshifuru knew just what the enemy was up to. As he saw it, they were planning to carry out a great encircling operation by capturing Sandepu and Heigoutai, and then pushing south of the Japanese Army's left flank. General Grippenberg, doyen of the Russian Army, was carrying out the most daring operation yet attempted by either side. If he succeeded, the Japanese Army was doomed.

That's how it looked on paper. And, in reality, the operation was unfolding like clockwork. Yoshifuru's premonition, the one he had kept warning General Headquarters about like a steadily ringing alarm bell, had proven sadly accurate.

General Headquarters was thrown into dire confusion. A staff officer would scream something into the telephone at the top of his lungs, and then a different staff officer would send a messenger galloping to the front with orders flatly contradicting what had just been conveyed over the phone. To top things off, Matsukawa Toshitane, who should have supervised, shouted in a frenzied voice, and even Kodama Gentarō, chief of staff of the Japanese Manchurian Army, would be standing in front of a map one minute and rushing to the phone the next, barking at his staff on the way. The room was a madhouse. And on the morning of January 26, the madness was at its peak.

During this time, Ōyama Iwao was nowhere to be seen, having stayed in bed. We know that back when he left Tokyo, he had remarked, "As long as we're winning, I'll leave everything to Kodama. When we start to lose, I'll have to take over to rally the troops." Perhaps now he had started to ask himself, "Is this it? Are we fighting a losing battle?" One has to wonder.

After the emperor appointed him commander in chief, Ōyama went straight to the Naval Ministry and met with Naval Minister Yamamoto Gombei, as we've seen. "When I go over there," he said then, "somehow I'll get everybody"—by this, he meant the various generals—"to get along, so we can wage war peacefully." When he said "peacefully," he made a gesture like a hen enfolding its eggs.

Finally, inside the operations room that had erupted in such panic, Ōyama's bulky figure appeared. He walked over to Kodama's desk, looked around the room, and drawled, "I've been hearing gunfire all morning, Kodama. Where in hell is it coming from?"

Kodama looked up at him, speechless. Some of the younger staff could hardly keep a straight face. Soon from one corner friendly laughter arose, and the tension in the room let up.

"Well, sir," Kodama finally replied, "the enemy is concentrated on our left flank."

"The left flank, is it? Well, well. You've got your hands full then." Ōyama strolled leisurely once around the room before going back to his room. Almost everyone present commented after the war, in a variety of venues, that what impressed them most in the battle of Heigoutai was Ōyama.

* * *

While General Headquarters' sole reserve force, the Eighth Division, was stationed to the rear, biding its time, division headquarters was in Dalanqi, about 20 kilometers behind the front line. Most of the units were billeted west of the Dongqing railroad. The men of the Eighth Division, hardy northerners all, were well disposed to fighting in winter. But until now, the only action they had seen was the end of the battle of Shaho.

During the winter camp, commander Tatsumi Naobumi reportedly said to his aide, "I hear one of the orderlies here is an old man who's one of the last surviving members of the Shinsengumi. Is it true?" He referred to the pro-shogunate group of elite swordsmen who served as a special police force in the late Tokugawa period. The truth of the rumor was never confirmed.

Apart from the French-style training he had received in the shogunate army, Tatsumi had no military education to speak of, but he enjoyed a solid reputation as Japan's outstanding leader on the battlefield and privately prided himself on his abilities. Yet now, despite his experience and ability, he was sidelined. Just as he was beginning to chafe at the inactivity, on the morning of January 24, his orders came in: "Relieve Heigoutai." This was actually a warning order. Formal orders did not arrive until a whole day later, at noon on January 25. The battle situation was grave. He was advised to leave at once with as large a force as he could muster and attack the enemy at Heigoutai and Jiucaihe.

All Tatsumi knew about the enemy's movements was that a single division had appeared in front of Heigoutai. He also knew that the only Japanese troops stationed in Heigoutai were Colonel Taneda's four cavalry companies and one infantry company from Akiyama's detachment, and that they were under heavy attack and in danger of being wiped out. It seemed a matter of time until the enemy had its way at Heigoutai.

Tatsumi ordered the Eighth Standby Reserve Infantry Brigade (Himeji, led by Major General Okami Masami), which was independent of his Eighth Division, to set off in advance. Quickly mustering the rest of the units under his command would be far from easy. A division was composed of various smaller units: brigade, regiment, battalion, and company, in descending order of size. These were scattered in billets over a wide area. Tatsumi called for all units to gather swiftly in Langdongkou, knowing that it would take seven or eight hours for them all to arrive.

Despite Tatsumi's order to leave first, Okami's brigade was in no condition to move toward the target any faster than the division. Some of his regiments had just returned from Sanchahe, and the men were exhausted. Others had been on the march for days when the order came in, causing them to change course midstream and head for Langdongkou. They were extremely exhausted.

Even then, General Headquarters went right on underestimating enemy strength. In their view, since Tatsumi had an extra regiment on top of his Eighth Division, he had plenty of muscle, more than enough to drive away an attacking division of the enemy. But the situation was growing more serious by the second. In consequence, orders from General Headquarters to Tatsumi conflicted with Tatsumi's orders to the advance troops, creating unprecedented confusion.

Tatsumi was a seasoned veteran. "General Headquarters is crazy," he felt. "I've got to act on my own authority." He would manage his troops as he chose, but that meant a night march. Unless they marched all night long, the enemy would advance even farther south, past Heigoutai. Reaching the battlefield with all possible speed was more important than working out a battle plan.

That night the temperature fell to -27 degrees Celsius. Strong winds whipped the falling snow. Factoring in wind chill, it must have felt below -35 degrees. Marching across frozen ground was one thing, but in a snowstorm, freshly fallen snow stuck to the soles of the soldiers' boots and froze. The snow formed a layer of ice that thickened with every step, forcing them to stop every few paces to kick it off. Also their rice balls and the water in their canteens froze solid, so they could neither eat nor drink.

Braving these rigors, this division of Tōhoku soldiers endured a sleepless night march and arrived in Datai by dawn on January 26 with none missing. Despite this considerable feat, they had missed their chance to join the fray.

* * *

Tatsumi's chief of staff was Yuhi Mitsue, a lieutenant colonel of the infantry and a Kōchi man. Along with Matsukawa Toshitane in General Headquarters, he had been in the fifth graduating class of the Army Academy, two years after Yoshifuru. During the battle of Shaho, the Eighth Division's first battlefield experience, Ishikawa-born colonel Hayashi Taiichirō had been chief of staff, but he was transferred away and Yuhi took his place. Yuhi's combat inexperience and his ignorance of Russian habits would compound the horrors of the ensuing battle.

As Tatsumi's division swung into action, the bloodiness of the fighting on the Heigoutai front became apparent. "It would be better to abandon Heigoutai," Yuhi boldly decided. He devised this strange strategy: Tatsumi's Eighth Division would head for Heigoutai on a relief mission, but rather than support the few troops there (Colonel Taneda and his cavalrymen), they would convince them to walk away from the village and retake it later.

"The Russian forces," he reasoned, "want to go around to the left"—that is, west—"of the Japanese forces. For our men to hang on like grim death at Heigoutai to stop them from doing that is pointless. Far better to have Taneda abandon Heigoutai and retreat. Then the Russians will relax and carry on afresh with their maneuver around the left flank. While they are occupied, we can concentrate Tatsumi's division at Tongerbao, 7 kilometers south of Heigoutai, and retake the village of Heigoutai after they leave."

This strategy was flawed by its complexity, like something Zhuge Liang, the storied strategist of China's Three Kingdoms period, might have devised. Furthermore, even if they undertook this complicated operation, there was no telling if the Russian Army would cooperate. Once Colonel Taneda withdrew, would the Russians obligingly vacate Heigoutai and move on?

Yuhi consulted Tatsumi, who said, "If that's what you think, let's do it." It was surprising that a man of Tatsumi's caliber should have acquiesced. Therein lay his mistake. Of course, Tatsumi was another newcomer to Manchurian battlefields who didn't know the habits of the Russian Army. The Russian way was to advance to a certain point, erect defense fortifications, then advance further when the opportunity arose. Russians didn't run around rashly the way the Japanese did. If the Japanese abandoned

Heigoutai, the Russians would in all likelihood strengthen the village fortifications and settle in.

Yuhi phoned General Headquarters, asked to speak to his old classmate Matsukawa Toshitane, and requested permission to implement the strategy.

"Abandon Heigoutai?" Matsukawa was incredulous and protested that it wasn't a good idea. But Yuhi assured him the abandonment would be temporary and explained why, setting out his plan in detail.

"Too tricky," Matsukawa said. But ultimately the area was under the division commander's supervision, and so he agreed. His agreement was based on his underestimation of Russian offensive power. Fundamental errors on the part of General Headquarters led to error after error among the rank and file.

* * *

That is how the plan to temporarily abandon Heigoutai came to be implemented.

To give some indication of how broken the chain of command was, Akiyama Yoshifuru was by rights Taneda's commanding officer, but the order to retreat came directly from General Headquarters at the instigation of the headquarters of Tatsumi's division, his relief force. Yoshifuru, the one responsible for withstanding any Russian offensive in that sector, got no notice at all. Before he knew what had happened, Taneda had retreated, leaving Heigoutai undefended. This happened after sundown on January 25.

Yoshifuru was extremely displeased with Yuhi's provisional abandonment ploy. Impact on the fighting would be ruinous, he thought—but the deed was done. His face betrayed no emotion, nor did he use strong language. As shells rent the air, he said quietly, "This isn't right." After the war, whenever he discussed the tactics at Heigoutai, he always said the same thing: "That wasn't right." When you were under threat from a force so big it amounted to half the entire Russian Army, there was no time to play games. He found unacceptable the spirit of the person who devised the plan in the first place.

The sole task of Colonel Taneda and the rest of the Heigoutai defenders was to obstinately hold their ground. If they defended the village to the last man, then Tatsumi's division, coming in relief, would find it usable and could advance using it as axis.

Yoshifuru had any number of strongpoints in the enemy's path, but the two most important were Heigoutai under Colonel Taneda and Sandepu under Colonel Toyobe. As we've discussed, Western military analysts refer to this engagement not as the battle of Heigoutai, but as the "battle of Sandepu." That's because, although at this very time Sandepu was under more withering attack than Taneda at Heigoutai, Japanese forces there endured to the end and made Sandepu the axis of their push to victory.

Throughout the fighting at Sandepu, Yoshifuru continually ordered Toyobe to "hold on." He had often said of the colonel, "He's more tenacious than I am!" Indeed, in addition to his cavalryman's temperament, Toyobe had the doggedness of a castle garrison commander. Though he had barely a handful of troops at his disposal, he was undaunted. "Unless the enemy comes at us with more than a division, we won't retreat. Even if they do, we can hold them at bay for three days. If we last three days, we'll get through it."

As it turned out, the attacking force was far greater than a single division, yet his men held it at bay without reinforcements.

"I don't know how many times I thought there must not be one Japanese soldier left in Sandepu," Yoshifuru would say later. Keeping the enemy at bay under such grim conditions was truly an admirable feat.

In any case, the battle of Heigoutai began in earnest with the provisional abandonment of the village of Heigoutai.

*   *   *

The twenty thousand men in Tatsumi's division marched in quick time at night through a blizzard without sleep, demonstrating the stamina of Tōhoku men in superlative fashion. Not one soldier fell behind. Their sixty-one-year-old leader Tatsumi went forward with his coat collar turned up and his cap pulled down over his ears, brushing away the ice that formed on his beard with every breath. Now and again, he would dismount and go on foot, for staying on horseback too long interfered with circulation and could cause a man's feet to freeze in his boots.

To the old general, no march in his long military career can have been as painful as this one. Though a fierce engagement lay ahead of him, he remained optimistic, knowing only what he had been told by General Headquarters. At dawn, they arrived in Datai and rested, but most of the soldiers stayed on their feet, unable to sit down in the fresh, deep snow. They needed breakfast, but their rice balls were no use, frozen so solid that only bayonet jabs could break off little chips, and even those were inedible. Finally, some hardtack arrived from the supply center in Langdongkou, and they gnawed on that.

In the meantime, Tatsumi sent a battalion to Guchengzi, where it provided accommodations for Taneda and his troops as they arrived from Heigoutai. After that, he and his men had only to retake Heigoutai, which had been ceded without a fight. His only orders from General Headquarters were to "aid Heigoutai." That was all, although Heigoutai was not the only fortified village in the area to have come under attack. Sandepu and Lidarentun, where Yoshifuru was, were inundated with a tsunami of Russian troops. General Headquarters completely underestimated the seriousness of the situation, assuming that if the enemy was repelled at Heigoutai, enemy troops everywhere else would magically disappear. Neither Tatsumi nor Yuhi Mitsue, his chief of staff, was to blame for that error.

But when the sun was high in the sky, they learned from a scout's report that the enemy was on to Yuhi's little ruse: "The Russian Army is settling in at Heigoutai and starting widespread construction." Actually, it was probably not true that the Russians saw through Yuhi's ruse. They were simply constructing a camp for themselves the way they customarily did. Yuhi's grand strategy had collapsed in grand style.

"Ah," said Tatsumi sourly. "So in order to get back territory that was ours to begin with—territory we voluntarily relinquished—now we have to launch a full-fledged attack." War, he saw, was not something to be left in Yuhi's hands.

Finally, Tatsumi decided on the brigade assignments for the Heigoutai attack. He told Major General Okano's brigade to advance on the right flank and Major General Yoda's brigade to swing around to the left and approach the village from the south. Major General Tabe's brigade he kept on reserve in case of a surprise attack and also as backup for Colonel Toyobe, who was fighting in Sandepu. Assuming Heigoutai was the enemy's only goal, this was a model plan.

*   *   *

But things quickly changed.

When Tatsumi finished making his assignments, he found himself nearly surrounded, a large enemy army coming at him from three directions.

"The enemy situation is nothing like what I was told!" Yuhi exploded at General Headquarters over the phone, almost comical in his apoplexy.

General Headquarters had just heard the news from Akiyama's detachment, and pandemonium ensued. From the Russian perspective, Tatsumi's division came along just as they were about to break through the paper-thin defense of Akiyama's detachment on the left flank of the Japanese Army and descend south. They attacked it with full force. As a result, not only was Tatsumi's division stopped in its tracks, but the various strongholds of Akiyama's detachment were also put at risk.

At Sandepu, for example, where Colonel Toyobe had only two cavalry companies and one reserve infantry company, the Russians were more than a division strong. Not only that, they wielded much greater firepower than contemporary divisions usually did. In guns alone, they were lavishly equipped with over fifty field guns and two 6-inch heavy guns. Toyobe had three machine guns, Yoshifuru's pride, but even though they continuously spat fire, they just attracted concentrated fire from enemy artillery and did little good.

Meanwhile, Tatsumi's division, surrounded on three sides, could neither retake Heigoutai nor help out Sandepu. These conditions lasted all day January 26, with General Headquarters going into a dither and issuing conflicting orders—so many that defending units became all the more confused and losses mounted ever higher, peaking on that day.

That night, General Headquarters decided to commit one more division and dispatched the main force of Nozu's Fourth Army—the Fifth Division (Hiroshima, under Lieutenant General Kigoshi Yasutsuna)—to the scene. As Nozu's army was positioned in the center of the Japanese Army front, removing a division would greatly sap central strength, but there was no help for it. If Kuropatkin was aware of the situation he should have launched a major frontal assault, but he did not.

Kuropatkin was not the only one whose tactics were less than brilliant. Japan's General Headquarters in Manchuria adopted the worst battle strategy of all—sending in too few troops at separate times. The situation on the left flank was so dire that a single extra division was about as effective as a drop of water on a hot stone. Common sense would have dictated a bold commitment, one allowing them to hold losses to a minimum and repel the enemy in short order. But Japanese troop strength was so low that headquarters doled out troops grudgingly and so drove up casualties to no purpose.

* * *

Japanese General Headquarters violated a basic strategic principle by being stingy with their few troops, but that's not all: at bottom, they consistently underestimated enemy strength. Even after having dispatched the entire Fifth Division on top of the Eighth Division, Kodama himself still seemed surprised by the enemy's numbers. After the war, on learning to their shock that the Russians had at this point come at them with fully half their vast force, Kodama's staff marveled that they had been able to hold out so well.

The Russian Army swept toward them in a geometrical plane, but Akiyama's detachment consisted of mere points defending Lidarentun, Hanshantai, Sandepu, and Heigoutai on the left. These strongholds were like rocky reefs swallowed by churning billows when a tsunami roars ashore, their tips poking above water at odd intervals the only sign that they still clung precariously to existence.

Yoshifuru, at his headquarters in Lidarentun, held out against the billows facing him while directing the defense at all the other points. "I don't know how many times I figured Colonel Toyobe and his men at Sandepu were finished," he said after the war. The most effective part of Akiyama's defense strategy was the several machine guns (known then as "machine cannons") he placed at each stronghold.

The Russians were fully equipped with this new weapon; the field army hauled them around in carts drawn by pairs of horses, but at Port Arthur they had been fastened down at each battery, mowing down Japanese soldiers in a constant barrage of bullets.

Early in the siege at Port Arthur, Nogi Maresuke had listened to the sounds of continuous fire coming from Russian batteries and, curious, asked his aide, "What's that pom-pom sound?"

"That's a Maxim, sir," the aide replied. The machine gun was named after its inventor, Sir Hiram Maxim.

"Ah, so *that's* a Maxim gun!"

Though Nogi may have been hearing the distinctive sound for the first time, Yoshifuru had begun campaigning for his cavalry to be equipped with Maxim machine guns ten years earlier, back when he was a lieutenant colonel and head of the Military Riding School. Just before the outbreak of hostilities in the Russo-Japanese War, his two cavalry brigades alone were assigned "machine cannon units." The unwieldy Maxim gun, which harnessed recoil energy, was transported in a horse-drawn cart or else, in the field, set on a tripod. These cavalry machine guns were unusual; the Japanese Army as a whole had none. Yoshifuru used them to try to make up in firepower for his cavalry's main weakness, its inferior numbers. The various Japanese strongpoints were surrounded by Russian forces coming at them in that geometrical plane, but thanks to the cavalry machine guns they managed, barely, to escape destruction.

*   *   *

In any case, Yoshifuru put up fervent resistance. Tactics went out the window. His leadership rested on a single principle, the simple determination not to run away. "What else is there?" he thought.

Yoshifuru sorrowed that his cavalry, by rights an attack force, was now burrowed into a defensive position planned by engineers, mounting a desperate defense for which they were ill-suited. As shells and steel rained on Yoshifuru and his troops, Lieutenant Colonel Tamura Morie of the cavalry rode out alone at Kodama Gentarō's order, galloping from General Headquarters straight through to the front. His mission was to inquire about the situation. Just then the area in front of Yoshifuru's headquarters was infested with enemy soldiers. It seemed as if they might attack in full force at any moment. Headquarters' defensive strength was limited at best, and Yoshifuru himself might well have to join the fray, sword aloft. However, as the sword he carried was a dull-bladed ceremonial sword, he would be unable to engage in any real cut-and-thrust.

When Tamura entered the farmhouse serving Yoshifuru as headquarters, he found him sitting cross-legged on dirty rush mats, hunched over a map as usual. Propped up next to him was his officer's canteen, filled with brandy that he sipped from the cap.

Tamura stood in the entryway and watched Yoshifuru for a while before announcing himself. Yoshifuru slowly looked around. "Tamura, did you get promoted?" Those were his first words. He'd been sure Tamura was still a major.

Tamura brushed aside the question. "Sir, I have come to ask about the situation. What is happening?"

"Just as you see, we are safe." This remark would later become famous. Probably there was nothing else he could have said.

Next to his canteen Yoshifuru had set a loaded pistol. If the enemy came charging in, he was going to "let 'em have it," as he said later. He had no other choice.

"What will you do now, sir?"

"Do? The choice is pretty limited." Yoshifuru looked at Tamura and grinned. All pieces in hand—the reserves—were in play, and Tatsumi's division, on its way to lend aid, had been surrounded and brought to a standstill. Yoshifuru had no recourse but to dig in and hold out to the bitter end.

All the while as they spoke, shells fell and exploded on every side. It seemed a matter of time until headquarters would be blown to smithereens.

"About all I can do is sit here like this." Yoshifuru handed his canteen to Tamura, who was standing, and poured him some brandy. "Drink up," he urged as Tamura hesitated. "It's better than a shot of *shōchū*, believe me."

Soon a message came from Colonel Toyobe in Sandepu. The messenger was a sergeant major, the sunburned face under his visor the color of rust. He said something or other to Yoshifuru's adjutant. Yoshifuru put on his shoes and stood up. His first response was a terse rejection: "That won't do." As he spoke, it struck him as a miracle that Toyobe was still alive and in action.

Toyobe's message was a request for permission to move the horses to the rear. The cavalrymen had dismounted and were fighting a defensive war on foot. Their horses were tied in a trench to the rear, but shelling was so intense that the animals were being slaughtered. As long as they weren't needed, why not remove them from danger? The request made sense.

But Yoshifuru thought differently. His immediate reaction was: "But then they'd be plain infantrymen!"

Yoshifuru had single-handedly created the Japanese cavalry, but the top brass did not grasp the merits of having soldiers who could cover long distances quickly on horseback. There were always those mutterings about how the cavalry was unnecessary. Both Kodama and Matsukawa had used Akiyama's detachment defensively, effectively converting it to infantry.

Even as they spoke, Colonel Toyobe was in Sandepu, fighting off the enemy as infantry. His horses were superfluous. But what if Yoshifuru were to acknowledge their superfluity? What then? More importantly than the high command's obtuseness, wouldn't the cavalrymen's own sense of identity be compromised? That fear was his grounds for opposition.

"Let me tell you something about the cavalry," he drawled. "A cavalryman dies by his horse."

Tamura was perplexed. He was a disciple of Yoshifuru's, but in this case it seemed to him the horses deserved some sympathy. There weren't enough of them to begin with. Why let the ones tied up at the front die in vain?

Toyobe's unit lost over 150 horses, a major loss. But Yoshifuru never relented, insisting to the end that he was right. He never came out and issued the extreme order for the troops to defend their position to the death—but that in effect was what he was saying.

*   *   *

Yoshifuru had a strange sense of humor. When part of the Russian Tenth Corps bore down on him in a blistering attack, the fighting was brutal. Wind and driving snow made it impossible to tell the enemy's numbers. There was comfort in knowing that the brigade he had organized had the greatest firepower of any unit in the Japanese Army. The cavalry guns in which he took such pride spat continual fire, and the machine guns (which Japanese infantry units did not even know how to use) performed the role of "flank defense." In terms of firepower, anyway, the two sides were evenly matched. But the enemy kept throwing in more troops.

Yoshifuru merely sat with his pistol at his side, sipping brandy, while his troops at their various strongholds put up a nearly hopeless fight, like people gamely struggling to hold back a tsunami with a wooden fence. Then Yoshifuru decided to send a few artillerymen to Heilintai, in the northeast, as reinforcements. All he had on hand were two Russian field guns seized in war. He summoned an officer. "Tow those two field guns over to this point in Heilintai." He pointed to the map.

The officer tensed and offered an opinion. Since enemy fire was so superior, two field guns would quickly be silenced. He requested permission to obtain another two and take four in all.

"You'll take what I tell you to take!" Yoshifuru thundered.

At such a time, he had no sense of humor. His intention was not to intimidate subordinates who presented him with their opinions. Rather, there was no time to bother getting and transporting four guns.

In any case, the fighting that day went on some five hours before the enemy finally withdrew. After they were gone, the snow was stained red with the blood of numerous dead horses and men left behind. Yoshifuru ordered an infantry unit to bury the enemy dead, as was his habit after every encounter. He never came right out with awkward expressions of sympathy for the fallen enemy. Oddly for a military man, he could not bear the sight of blood.

But the ground was frozen so hard that they were unable to dig graves, and so instead they packed snow around the bodies to conceal them. All that night a fierce gale blew.

In the morning, Yoshifuru climbed the watchtower to see what the enemy was up to and found that, once again, he could see Russian soldiers. He was genuinely surprised to find them there, but soon realized they were all dead. The previous night's gale had blown off their covering of snow.

"Kiyooka, see there?" Yoshifuru turned and looked back at the captain from headquarters. "Looks like the Russians came charging up while we weren't watching and keeled over all by themselves." The remark made little sense, but Yoshifuru whooped with laughter.

Kiyooka was unable to see the joke. Long after the war was over, he would tell people that Akiyama Yoshifuru was a strange one.

* * *

Meanwhile, small Japanese units were retreating one after another. They were in no condition to hold the enemy at bay. Many of them received such crushing blows that they were all but wiped out.

A particularly grievous case was that of an infantry unit of one thousand men in a village called Niuju. One morning, they discovered that friendly troops in the neighboring stronghold of Wujiazi were gone. The commander at Niuju, a lieutenant colonel named Itō, was outraged. "The damned idiots— how dare they run away without saying anything!" Under the circumstances, surrounded by the enemy and isolated from friendly troops, he could not defend his position either. As small units engaged on the front retreated, men fell back like dominoes to the large stronghold of Tongerbao in the rear.

"The Japanese Army shows signs of collapse up and down the line." It got so bad that Colonel Reis, commander of a detachment from the First Siberian Army Corps, wired this report to Lieutenant General Stakelberg, commander of the corps.

Only Akiyama Yoshifuru's detachment did not yield an inch, with the lone exception of Colonel Taneda's unit, which had abandoned Heigoutai in a tactical retreat. The others held firm because of the strongpoint style of defense Yoshifuru had devised. This approach was at odds with the usual Japanese style of surprise attack, but given the weakness of the Japanese cavalry, it was the only way for them to fight the enemy on equal terms. Reminiscing in later years, Yoshifuru would say that what barely saved the Japanese cavalry from the inrushing sea of Russian soldiers "was, unfortunately, dirt." He meant that the inherent mobility of the cavalry was not what had saved them from certain destruction, but shellproof bunkers. The Japanese cavalry burrowed underground and fought on against the Cossacks and the far superior Russian artillery.

Besides Yoshifuru's First Cavalry Brigade, there was also a Second Cavalry Brigade, the brigade which had soundly defeated the Russians in the battle at Lake Benxi by arming themselves with six machine guns. Just before the battle of Heigoutai, General Headquarters moved the Second Cavalry Brigade to the extreme left flank, beyond where Yoshifuru was. With no time to construct defenses like his, every time they were attacked by a Cossack force twice their size, they were swamped and forced to retreat, again and again. "It appears our cavalry's specialty is retreat!" General Headquarters staff was scathing. But in truth the Russian cavalry was so powerful that the Japanese cavalry could not stand up to it without something to bridge the gap—either firepower or bunkers.

Yoshifuru knew his troops' weakness through and through. He also knew that in war, you have to devise a way to win. That knowledge lay behind the defensive strategy he so sorrowfully employed.

* * *

"Tatsumi's division is at a standstill."

When this news reached Japan's General Headquarters in Manchuria, consternation peaked. The freshest batch of troops in the Manchurian Army, Tatsumi's Eighth Division, had set off to rescue Akiyama's detachment, but now, instead of providing backup support, was itself in danger of being wiped out. For the first time, General Headquarters faced the reality of just how massive the Russian Army on their left flank actually was.

When the Fifth Division, commanded by Lieutenant General Kigoshi Yasutsuna, was quickly dispatched to rescue Tatsumi's division from its plight, this amounted to another case of a piecemeal response. In the dead of night on January 26, Kigoshi and his men set off from their quarters by the river Shili, and after a night's march arrived in Langdonggou at eight-thirty in the morning.

When Tatsumi Naobumi, in a snow-covered farmhouse in Guchengzi, heard that Kigoshi's Fifth Division was coming on a rescue mission, he shouted, "Could there be any greater shame!" It was all his staff could do to restrain him.

Tatsumi was a man of intensely strong will. In his youth, that strength of will was what enabled him to lead a band of several hundred pro-shogunal infantry troops in a round of battles against imperial forces led by Yamagata Aritomo, sometimes vanquishing them, sometimes engaging them in bitter fighting, but always causing them trouble.

"The army commanders are heroes left over from the Restoration," Ōyama Iwao once said to Yamamoto Gombei, meaning they were hard to control. Tatsumi Naobumi was not an army commander, but he was a prime example of the class of men Ōyama was referring to.

Rescue meant shame. From a strategic standpoint, sending in relief is a matter of course, but probably anyone qualified to be a military leader responsible for meeting the extraordinary demands of war would feel insulted at the thought of being rescued.

Yet Tatsumi's division, under siege by the First Siberian Army Corps, was fast approaching the point of annihilation. "Assemble everyone under orders," Tatsumi said.

Although he was from the Kuwana domain in Ise Province, Tatsumi's speech had a distinctly Tōhoku flavor. That's because Kuwana's Matsudaira clan had moved south from Ōshū Shirakawa in 1823, and for the next forty-five years until the Meiji Restoration, they and their descendants continued to use Ōshū speech. By "everyone under orders," he meant "everyone in a battalion or above."

The units in question were fighting under artillery fire so vicious that they couldn't raise their heads, but once the commander's order was made known, all sergeant majors or higher from brigade headquarters, regimental headquarters, and battalion headquarters made their way through the shelling, now crawling on their bellies, now creeping on all fours.

Eventually, officers from each headquarters arrived. Tatsumi's chief of staff had them gather in front of division headquarters and write down the necessary orders and instructions. All the while, blasts of gunfire shook the ground, and snow whipped the fields, often erasing the voice of the chief of staff. The assembled officers scribbled with pencils, frequently looking up to ask him to repeat what he had just said.

Meanwhile, the fighting grew more and more bitter. The enemy poured in as far back as the first aid station in Sansenho, and, of a company of defenders, half were killed or wounded. Finally, the commander too was killed. "We can't hold on without reinforcements!" Urgent requests were sent to division headquarters—but division headquarters didn't have a single soldier to spare and reluctantly ordered them to withdraw. The seventy who had barely escaped with their lives had no choice but to pile the dead and wounded in logistical vehicles and flee. Along the way they were often attacked by Cossacks who would gallop up close and stab Japanese soldiers to death with their lances. The scene was brutal in the extreme. The first aid station fell back as far as Sumapu. For a first aid station to be attacked was extraordinary and gives some indication of the kind of fighting going on.

When the chief of staff had finished speaking, Tatsumi Naobumi got up on a Chinese wooden chest and started in. "This division was left in Japan at the start of the war. We were the last ones to join the fighting. Compared to the rest, we don't have a scratch on us. Now that we've finally had our first encounter with the enemy, what a wretched state of affairs this is! In war, you don't lose if you make up your mind not to. Look at the other divisions. All of them have been through five or six battles, and hardly any have the same commander they started out with. This division from Hirosaki is Japan's finest, so why should we struggle so hard in a skirmish like this? You are sons of Tōhoku! If you want to match the record of other divisions, make up your minds to suffer the same losses in one battle that they do in five or six. That's the attitude to bring to the fight!"

As he spoke, he jumped up and stamped his foot so hard he smashed the lid of the chest he was using as a platform.

This story was passed on in Tatsumi's division for years, and that coupled with Tatsumi's skill at maneuvering troops led to his deification in Japanese war annals. After the war, he fell ill as a result of the hardships he had endured and died in 1907. Before dying, he said, "I should have died at Heigoutai. It's strange that I lived on more than two years after that."

When he delivered that speech, Tatsumi still thought privately that the enemy was stronger than anyone had expected. After the war he examined Russian records and learned that General Grippenberg had surrounded Akiyama's detachment and his own division with roughly ten divisions, and in addition there were two divisions and a half of Mishchenko's mobile force, which the Japanese Army had been supremely afraid of.

The experience always seemed unbelievable to Tatsumi, and he talked about it with frank incredulity. "Never mind me—what was the look on Akiyama's face, I wonder, when he held them off?"

In time, Kigoshi Yasutsuna's Fifth Division arrived, deployed to the right of Tatsumi's division, and attacked the enemy in Liutiaogou and Lijiawo, but the enemy's reinforcements only swelled even more. Their efforts were about as effective as throwing a hot stone in a pond.

* * *

General Headquarters finally saw Grippenberg's intention, which was to breach the Japanese left flank with a massive force, go to their rear, and surround them. Faced with this grave situation, headquarters was forced into making their most dramatic move in the entire war so far: they had to surreptitiously siphon off troops from Kuroki's First Army on the right flank. With no more reserves to fall back on, they had to take their chances and embark on a gamble that could well end in self-destruction.

"There's no help for it." Kodama Gentarō nodded to Matsukawa Toshitane, who came up with the plan.

They decided to withdraw the Second Division of Kuroki's army (Sendai, commanded by Lieutenant General Nishijima Sukeyoshi). But removing an entire division would have been too much, so they took only one brigade and slightly under a regiment, along with an artillery battalion. Nishijima himself led the way.

The Sendai soldiers marched under extremely brutal conditions. After marching all night without sleep through falling snow and sub-zero cold, at seven o'clock on the morning of January 27, they arrived at Dalanqi, in the battlefield vicinity. Horses and men alike were on the verge of collapse.

General Headquarters judged that this might not be enough troops, so they also withdrew the Third Division (Nagoya, commanded by Lieutenant General Ōshima Yoshimasa) of Oku's army and sent it to the left flank, ordering it to go to the aid of Colonel Toyobe in Sandepu. They went right on making the cardinal mistake of committing troops piecemeal. Kodama Gentarō was an outstanding strategist, but his abilities were at their lowest ebb at this time. He started out by underestimating enemy strength. The error was compounded, finally developing into a mistake of this magnitude.

In all, reinforcements for Akiyama's detachment at Sandepu, Hanshantai, and Lidarentun numbered an astonishing four divisions, one standby reserve brigade, and two artillery regiments. They had one purpose.

A force so large naturally needed a single commander. On January 28, Tatsumi's troops were officially named "Tatsumi's provisional army," and thus Tatsumi Naobumi received provisional promotion to army commander.

* * *

The order to form a provisional army came suddenly. An "army" was the largest combat unit in the Japanese Army. As we know, the First Army was commanded by Kuroki Tamemoto, the Second by Oku Yasukata, the Third by Nogi Maresuke, and the Fourth by Nozu Michitsura. There were only the four armies, each one headed by a full general. Further on down the line, divisions were commanded by lieutenant generals, brigades by major generals.

Tatsumi Naobumi, commander of the provisional army, was a lieutenant general. In age, experience, and exploits, he was the equal of any general, but his promotion was delayed either because in the Boshin War he had fought on the side of the rebels or because he was not part of the Satsuma-Chōshū clique. In an awkward development, one of the lieutenant generals in his provisional army had held that rank longer than Tatsumi; this was Ōshima Yoshimasa, commander of the Nagoya division (Third Division), a Chōshū man.

"For me to be taking orders from Tatsumi undermines military order," said Ōshima, and he had a point. Accordingly, he ignored Tatsumi's provisional army and followed only the orders of Oku Yasukata, commander of the Second Army, where he belonged. Naturally, Oku was not fully briefed on conditions in Sandepu and Heigoutai. Even so, in terms of military order, what Ōshima did was not necessarily wrong.

"Has General Headquarters lost its mind?" Ōshima asked. Granted, the circumstances were dire enough to drive anyone out of his mind. But on learning that Ōshima ranted about seniority at a time when the very existence of the army hung in the balance, one General Headquarters staff member said behind Ōshima's back that his behavior was "utterly shameful." The criticism is understandable.

Perhaps the greatest blame lies with General Headquarters, which mishandled the situation. "You say we're under Tatsumi's command," the other division leaders pointed out, "but we can't even set up a phone line to him."

Tatsumi was in Guchengzi, near Heigoutai. He had all he could do to fight the enemy surrounding him on all sides and was in no position to be sending out orders to other divisions. Nor did he have the technical means—a telephone or an orderly—with which to communicate. An army headquarters must be able to gather battlefield information, but Tatsumi's headquarters, geared only to command a division, lacked the necessary equipment. There was no way for them to grasp enemy movements. But it's impossible to move a great army without knowing what the enemy is up to.

"As long as we're ignoring seniority, why not put Akiyama, who is familiar with enemy movements, in charge of the provisional army's headquarters?" Ōshima supposedly suggested—but of course a major general couldn't issue orders to a higher-ranking general.

As a result of these various situations and the general confusion, the division leaders were never under Tatsumi's supervision but remained under direct supervision of their own headquarters. So the name "Tatsumi's provisional army" refers to a phantom that never really existed.

* * *

Meanwhile, from the evening of January 27, the atmosphere in Japanese Manchuria General Headquarters settled down. Kodama Gentarō had briefly exploded but then laughed at himself. "If I go wild what good does that do! General Headquarters gives orders to win the war. No point in raising a big fuss." He went around repeating this with the innocence of a child who had learned something new.

Ōyama mostly stayed in his room reading the paper. "This may be the start of a losing battle." He was only human; surely the thought crossed his mind. From the first, he, like Kodama, thought only of winning the war by a margin of sixty to forty. Any greater victory was impossible. If you stopped and did the calculations, no matter how gallantly the Japanese fought, they would be doing well to come out even against the Russians. It was his and Kodama's goal to stretch the odds to sixty–forty by surpassing the enemy in strategy.

So far, somehow things had gone according to plan. But now, thanks to their strategic error, all hell was breaking loose on the left flank. If the left flank collapsed, the fortunes of the two armies would be reversed, and possibly the Japanese Army would be crushed. In all likelihood, that's what would happen. The time might be at hand for Ōyama to make good on his promise to take over when loss seemed inevitable.

Even so, he stayed away from the strategy room, where the staff was gathered. He wanted the strategy room to function with the smoothness of well-oiled machinery, and, in the present hair-trigger atmosphere, his presence could only clog things up.

He read the newspaper backwards and forwards, and happened to come upon a poem a reader had sent in. It was printed in the *Tokyo Nichinichi Shimbun*, evidently written by the new wife of a young officer at the front. The gist of the poem was that as she sewed his uniform, her tears had fallen on the collar and stained it.

> Forgive me my dear
> these stains upon your collar—
> teardrops shed
> in the burning intensity
> of my longing for you.

Ōyama was so moved that he felt goose bumps. He drew a sheet of paper toward him and wrote an envoi to the poem: "What family is she from? Her thoughts go with her husband in a distant land."

Just then the adjutant, Artillery Major Furukawa Iwatarō, came in. "Take a look at this," said Ōyama, showing him the poem. "Did you ever see anything so touching?"

Ōyama proceeded to rewrite the poem in classical Chinese. He completed two lines and showed them to Furukawa.

> Do not despise the spots upon your collar.
> They mark the tears I shed sewing in the lamplight.

Once he'd shown the poem, Ōyama suddenly grew embarrassed and took it back. "It's better the way it was, as a Japanese tanka. It was written by a beautiful young wife, after all."

Furukawa remained rigidly at attention, so Ōyama asked him what Kodama was doing. Furukawa told him.

"I see." That was all Ōyama said.

For the rest of his life, Furukawa would recount this story about Ōyama in the battle of Heigoutai.

*   *   *

The purpose of this book is not to describe battles but to reflect in a general way on a certain ability or spirit of Japanese people in the era of the newly rising nation. That, in a manner of speaking, is our main theme. But after looking carefully into every detail connected with the battle of Heigoutai, we feel strongly inclined to note all that the youths of Tōhoku did to save the entire Japanese Army from wholesale destruction.

After the war, when stories were told around Hirosaki hearths of the fighting at Heigoutai, survivors were unanimous in their praise for their leader Tatsumi Naobumi. Every memoir ends, "We won because of him," or words to that effect. We learned when researching this section that Tatsumi has long been revered in Hirosaki as a "god of war." But history is in some ways a kind of journalism. Around the hearths of Hirosaki, the name of Tatsumi Naobumi may be held in reverence, but elsewhere in the country he remains virtually unknown.

This may sound strange, but in the words of historian Hayashiya Tatsusaburō, historical figures become famous when they have a popular voice to bolster their reputations. Yoshitsune had the *Gikeiki*, Kusunoki Masashige the *Taiheiki*, Toyotomi Hideyoshi the *Taikōki* to tout their exploits, and so they became household names. Nogi Maresuke at Port Arthur was until a little before the end of the battle a general with an unparalleled losing record, and his unhappy talent for losing pushed Japan itself to the brink of extinction. Yet after the war, he was made a count, and people of Meiji times thrilled to hear narrative ballads telling how, aristocrat though he was, he took pity on a boy peddling fermented soybeans. In that sense, he was as fortunate as Yoshitsune with his *Gikeiki*.

Nogi was lucky, but Tatsumi Naobumi did not have the benefit of basking in the favor of the Chōshū power group. He had been on the wrong side of the civil war and was an isolated figure in the Meiji army.

All of the above is a digression.

On the first day that Tatsumi's division was deployed in the war, the Russians were eight divisions strong. Major General Yoda Kōtarō's brigade was armed only with rifles. They were the focus of concentrated fire from more than fifty Russian cannons and with no place to hide on the flat, frozen wastes, they faced imminent destruction. Russian batteries were laid out with great effectiveness. Sixteen guns on the north, twelve on the south, twelve on the southwest, eight on the northwest, and another eight besides surrounded the hapless brigade. Tightening this "rope of fire," the enemy had its infantry close in on the Japanese.

In Colonel Tsugawa Yasuteru's regiment, Tsugawa was wounded, and Major Tsukamoto took command. Not only did he take command, he himself grabbed a rifle and started firing, blasting away until he was blown apart by a shell. The unit shrank to a quarter of its former size, and the snow was strewn with corpses, a panorama of hell. Tsugawa's right leg was broken, but he picked up his wounded and retreated, using his sword as a cane. When the enemy came after him in hot pursuit, he fought again at Sumapu. For three sleepless days and nights, the men lay in the snow, firing their rifles mechanically. Sometimes one would doze off and lose both legs to a Russian grenade, waking up just long enough to fire a last round before perishing.

* * *

Meanwhile, the brutality of the fighting that Akiyama's detachment experienced was beyond compare. Tatsumi's division had been cut off on its way to provide reinforcement, but Akiyama's detachment was even more cut off. The enemy cordon grew ever deeper, the shelling so intense there were moments when breathing was all but impossible. Now and again the enemy cavalry or infantry would attack, and then there would be close combat, cut and thrust. At such times, the enemy shelling would let up a bit, so the attacks actually afforded some relief.

Since the war began, no battlefield had seen such pounding of ammunition as occurred at Sandepu, the outlying post where Colonel Toyobe was based. It was only to be expected. "One way or another," held General Grippenberg, "we've got to break through Sandepu. If we can open a major hole in their defenses there, pushing south will be easy."

Fortunately for the Japanese Army, Yoshifuru had the brains to see the big picture. He knew that if he allowed the left flank to collapse, the entire

Japanese Army would be lost. And he knew that his only strategic goal was to defend the flank to the last.

The difficulty of putting up a stubborn defense under those conditions becomes clear when you think of the front he was responsible for, stretching 30 kilometers. The proper defense of a 30-kilometer front took six or seven divisions; that was common sense in the art of war. Yoshifuru was doing it with only eight regiments. Common sense said he had a tenth of the manpower he needed.

From Akiyama's point of view, if his men just dug in and held on, eventually Tatsumi's division would come. Until then, they had to go on stubbornly defending their position to the last man. As long as they didn't falter on defense, they could use the new troops as a fulcrum and go on the attack when reinforcements arrived.

"Toyobe is from Niigata, he'll be all right." When the subject of Sandepu came up, this was Yoshifuru's constant rejoinder. Toyobe Shinsaku was born in Niigata Prefecture, and embodied northern stubbornness and tenacity. He had a reputation for being a dolt. Yoshifuru knew that with the fate of the Japanese Army hanging in the balance, Toyobe was the right man for the job of heading the defense at Sandepu, just because he was not quick-witted or clever.

Yoshifuru had spent two months building up the fortifications at Sandepu, but because it was winter they could not dig firing trenches deep enough, and while there were plenty of obstacles to the north and south, there were few in other directions. There was just one row of abatis, and the width of the barbed-wire entanglements was only around 5 meters, so they had no choice but to make use of existing houses and mud walls. To a Russian army engineer, this would have seemed like no kind of fortification at all.

Then, on January 25, shelling from Russian heavy field guns destroyed nearly every house in the village, and the Japanese lost most of their breastworks. On the twenty-sixth, they fought for an hour with a Russian division and drove it back. The Russians left over five hundred bodies sprawled on the snow but afterward pushed their artillery camp forward and unleashed a massive artillery barrage on Sandepu. Altogether they had as many as thirty or forty heavy guns and field guns.

When they ceased bombarding, the Russians attacked again with their infantry, but the three machine guns Yoshifuru had allotted Toyobe were devastatingly effective. Of the 1,220 dead and wounded in the Russian Fourteenth Division alone, almost all were felled by Japanese machine guns.

*   *   *

On the morning of January 28, the various divisions of Tatsumi's provisional army began coordinated activity. With Tatsumi's division in the center, the other divisions advanced together on either side. On the far right, the Eighteenth Infantry Regiment (Toyohashi) of the Third Division (Nagoya) in particular made rapid progress and soon reached one of Akiyama's strongholds, Yabatai, and drove off two enemy regiments surrounding it. That was the beginning of their success. Next the Thirteenth Artillery Regiment entered the stronghold of Hanshantai, one of Yoshifuru's strongholds, and unleashed savage gunfire on enemy troops concentrated in Jinshanzhun and the nearby wasteland.

The main force of the Fifth Division (Hiroshima), which had marched without cease for two days and two nights, swiftly occupied Liutiaogou and Lijiawo, with the cooperation of the Seventeenth Artillery Regiment. One brigade beat off enemy from behind Tatsumi's division and to the left, enabling them to have safe passage.

Also that day, the Second Division (Sendai) put in a somewhat late arrival and chased off enemy troops surrounding Tatsumi's division, making it easy for them to move on. Around eleven in the morning, Tatsumi's division was freed from the enemy's grasp.

"On to Heigoutai!" That was their simple and overriding goal.

But the Russians held Heigoutai firmly in hand. They had fortified every surrounding village, and, as Tatsumi led his division forward, the fighting was desperate in the extreme. Major General Tabe's brigade in the center was pinned down at Sumapu, south of Heigoutai, and Tabe himself was wounded and fell back. After five hours of intense fighting, the situation had not improved. Finally, at twenty after three in the afternoon, a company of two hundred led by Captain Nakamura Kō carried out a bayonet attack, stabbing over a hundred enemy soldiers to death and taking over two hundred prisoners, thus opening a way out of the impasse.

Yet the massive Russian army clustered in Heigoutai remained active, and whenever the Japanese units drew near they came under fierce rifle fire, staining the snow crimson. Tatsumi Naobumi was just the right man for this bitter battle. His reasoning power grew strangely sharp and focused under such conditions, but his spirit went into a frenzy.

At ten at night, he became enraged and made a startling decision: "We will attack tonight with all our force." Immediately, the order went out to all units.

Night attacks with a whole division, even if theoretically feasible, rarely succeed and so are seldom attempted. Tatsumi, however, was a master of the art. In the battle of Hokuetsu (that is, Niigata) during the Boshin War, his surprise attacks by night dealt heavy losses to the imperial troops.

As soon as his mind was made up, he contacted Kigoshi Yasutsuna of the Fifth Division and asked his cooperation. For three days and three nights, Tatsumi's division had been alternately marching and fighting without rest. The toll was high; their numbers had been slashed by a third.

Around two in the morning on January 29, the division (three brigades) rushed through driving snow, and after a fierce fight, some part of the division succeeded in taking a corner of Heigoutai. But the main force was impeded by enemy machine gun fire. Casualties mounted. There were over a thousand dead. Tatsumi galloped to the front and urged his men forward. Finally, at around five-thirty in the morning, he saw the enemy begin to waver and retreat. At half past nine in the morning, Japanese occupation of Heigoutai was complete.

Losses sustained by Tatsumi's division in the battle included 6,248 dead or wounded (of whom 1,555 were killed). The magnitude of the losses suffered by a single division were said to be a world record for that time.

When the morning sun shone again on the snow-covered field, scattered corpses of friend and foe stained the entire expanse blood red. As Tatsumi's division buried the dead, of Russian bodies alone they counted 7,834. There were 2,487 abandoned rifles, 414 prisoners. This was the greatest loss that the Russians had sustained in a single battle since the start of the war.

* * *

The battle of Heigoutai ended early in the morning on January 29 with the retreat of the Russian Army. All told, some 53,800 Japanese combat troops participated, sustaining 9,324 casualties. The Russian side numbered 105,100 and lost 11,743 men.

From the Russian point of view, a great victory had slipped away. It is bizarre for an army so large to carry out such an orderly sequence of movements, routing small Japanese units on every side as it descended south, and then fail to achieve its goal and retreat with ninety percent of its strength intact. Had Grippenberg continued to fight for one more day, he could easily have crushed Tatsumi's division, which had shrunk by half. Had he done so and then brought his army of ten thousand to the Japanese rear, General Headquarters in Yingtai would itself have been forced to scoop up its papers and beat a hasty retreat.

Moreover, Kuropatkin, commander in chief of the Russian Army, had a strong force positioned directly in front of the Japanese Army, and had he used it to strike at the Japanese center and right flank—an elementary tactical move—the Japanese troops would have scattered, spread out thinly as they were to appear greater in numbers, and been torn asunder and ultimately wiped out. The probable outcome was obvious: this battle would have marked the end of the Russo-Japanese War.

Yet strangely enough, on January 28, at a crucial point when over-whelming victory lay within Russia's grasp, Kuropatkin gave General Grippenberg, commander of the Second Army, the order to retreat. His action confounds understanding.

The order went out at eight in the evening. Just fifteen minutes earlier, Kuropatkin had ordered Grippenberg to continue the attack, reversing himself in the space of a mere quarter hour. To explain this turnabout, one that shows a complete lack of will on his part, he claimed the Japanese Army was attacking the Russian center. It was true that with the bulk of the Japanese troops off putting out the fire on the left flank, Ōyama and Kodama conducted a modest diversionary attack on Kuropatkin's center to hide their army's vulnerability. This feint (so small as to scarcely deserve the name) had a remarkable effect on Kuropatkin's sensitive nerves.

"Pull out!" Kuropatkin issued Grippenberg, head of the Second Army's ten thousand, an order that even an amateur in his place would not have issued. Even supposing the Japanese Army had made a central attack on the Russian line, if the Russians had responded in kind, they would surely have broken through the center of the Japanese forces as easily as through paper, forcing the Japanese to recall divisions from the left flank. Akiyama's detachment would then have been decimated, and Grippenberg would have had the momentum to charge Japanese headquarters.

*   *   *

The battle of Heigoutai was initiated by the Russians and followed the Russian lead throughout. Midway through, with victory in their grasp, the Russians retreated.

Heigoutai can hardly be called a Japanese victory. It would be more accurate to say that the desperate struggles of Akiyama Yoshifuru and Tatsumi Naobumi's men overcame the strategic errors and miscalculations of General Headquarters to return things to normal. It was a successful defensive war.

Kuropatkin's strange order left Grippenberg no choice but to stop fighting and, with ninety percent of his force unharmed, retreat.

"I know what he was thinking." Later that night, Grippenberg denounced Kuropatkin to his staff officers. "He was afraid I would succeed! Then his own job would be on the line. He sold a Russian victory to Ōyama for no other reason than that." His bitterness seems justified.

At first, Grippenberg tried to ignore the order, but he was wary of being cut off from the rest of the Russian Army. Had he ignored a direct order, probably Kuropatkin would not have bailed him out if he got into trouble. And so, reluctantly, he gave all the divisions on his long battle line the order to retreat. Late at night on January 28, messengers galloped off in all directions.

On the morning of the twenty-ninth, as he departed north, Grippenberg had his adjutant draft a telegram to St. Petersburg requesting permission to resign. He considered having him write, "The enemy of the Russian Empire is not Japan but Kuropatkin," but in the end thought better of it.

As to why Kuropatkin himself stayed put and had Grippenberg cease fighting, we have Grippenberg's theory—"He did it for self-protection. He was afraid I would distinguish myself"—but that may not be the whole story. Even supposing Kuropatkin did entertain such fears, we don't know what else may have influenced him. One thing is clear. Apparently, Kuropatkin had a two-tier approach in mind: once Grippenberg's Second Army was successful, then he, the leader of the First Army, would go into action. He was a perfectionist who liked to hedge his bets with two-tier approaches, as he had from the outset. This tendency shows most blatantly in the fighting connected with the name "Heigoutai."

In any case, following that operation, Grippenberg returned to Russia, leaving Kuropatkin in charge in fact as well as in name, and embarked upon a successful bureaucratic career. He was definitely satisfied with that outcome. After he returned home, he attacked Kuropatkin in the newspaper and elsewhere, and his comments made world headlines. Kuropatkin was rankled, but he maintained a plan for ultimate success. He would drive the Japanese Army as far north as Harbin, cut off their supply lines, and wipe them out at one blow. Grippenberg's annoying slanders did not deter him in the slightest.

But Kodama Gentarō had already guessed at the plan to stage a showdown in Harbin, and he knew that if that happened, Japan would lose. He was driven by a pressing need to launch a major campaign and win a decisive victory over Kuropatkin.

On the eve of the battle of Heigoutai, he had already mapped out plans for the battle of Mukden.

2

YELLOW FUNNELS

Now let us turn our attention to the Baltic Fleet.

The fleet was still lying at anchor in the fishing harbor of Nosy Be on Madagascar, off the east coast of Africa, where it had been since January 9. Shortly after the ships dropped anchor, word arrived of the fall of Port Arthur a week before—news that would greatly impact the fate of the fleet.

While the Russians launched the offensive at Heigoutai that failed on January 29, the Baltic Fleet continued to swelter at Nosy Be.

Next, the newspapers reported that one of the two Russian generals had angrily resigned and gone back to Russia. The press made the failure of the offensive seem only natural. Members of the fleet also learned from the papers that the whole world was asking the same question: how could Russia be losing? Most editorials, trying to see Russia in context, concluded that the debacle was rooted in autocratic rule and its inevitable concomitant, politicking among subordinate officials. This view became conventional wisdom.

Unlike Japan, Russia had no constitution and no legislature. The tsar maintained sovereign right in a system dating from feudal times, and society had no legal organ of criticism. As we've mentioned, United States President Theodore Roosevelt predicted Japan would win the war based on his conviction that any despotic state was doomed. Despotic governments, he reasoned, granted absolute power to second- or third-rate individuals (tsars), and, when such a person became obsessed with delusions of grandeur, no one could restrain him. The system lacked built-in controls.

Like imperial Japan, which was a constitutional state, Russia did have a cabinet. But unlike Japan's cabinet, Russia's was only an advisory organ to the autocratic tsar, a mere entourage. Every government official in Russia sensed flames at his back, flames that threatened to consume him. The flames were the tsar and his aides. The universal psychology of officialdom in an authoritarian state causes the individual to worry about his own back rather than to try to unite with his fellows in common cause. That's why Kuropatkin strove to undercut his political rival Grippenberg and succeeded, even at the cost of handing the enemy an advantage. Theodore Roosevelt's theory that autocratic states are doomed applies to such battlefield intrigues as well.

But Japanese generals, having no tyrant at their back, didn't need to look over their shoulder and so could focus on crushing the enemy.

Think again of the Baltic Fleet at Nosy Be. Amazingly, it remained at anchor in that unwholesome climate, a hotbed of pestilence, for two long months. The reason can be traced back to the Russian political system.

*   *   *

Still, it's hard to understand why, after sending Rozhestvensky and the Baltic Fleet off to "teach the monkeys a lesson," Nicholas II should have had them sit around at that tiny Madagascar fishing port so long. There was an affiliated reason. As the London *Times* frequently editorialized, the Russian government was "base." The word is vague. Probably the paper meant to say that the Russian government was inefficient, Russian officials indolent and irresponsible.

Around this time, the *Times* calculated Russian war expenditures. Or, perhaps more accurately, the *Times* put its trust in calculations worked out by a French economist named Levy, who pegged the cost of supporting the three hundred thousand-strong Russian Army on the Manchurian plains at between six and seven million pounds per month. The cost of sending the Baltic Fleet to the Far East he estimated to be thirty-two million pounds. The vast expense of maintaining a navy is clear, with half the total devoted to ship maintenance.

The other half was the cost of the voyage, chiefly the necessary coal. Even if coal itself was cheap, on a voyage of 18,000 nautical miles—the longest expedition in history for a fleet so large—the cost of transporting coal and refueling the ships was staggering. Making the arrangements and overseeing them required an enormous expenditure of effort as well. To borrow the words of Fukui Shizuo, the premier authority on naval history, carrying off such a plan required "extraordinary ability." The very decision to embark on a voyage so arduous shows the grandeur of the Slavic spirit.

Back in the age of wind-powered sailing ships, such an expedition would have been far easier, but modern warships needed fuel to run. Sending the fleet halfway around the world necessitated spreading out a map and marking refueling points along the way. Colliers had to be stationed ahead of time at each point. When you consider the precise planning involved, it's clear that Russian organizational ability was excellent, not at all inferior to that of the British and Germans, for whom operational feats were a specialty. And when you factor in that most of the waters the Baltic Fleet steamed through were controlled by Britain, Japan's ally, with resulting harassment, it's plain that the journey was an undertaking whose like the world had never seen.

But in an autocracy, efficient administration is undermined by corruption.

According to the *Times*, many top Russian officials enriched themselves by entering the price of Welsh coal (the finest British coal for navy vessels) in their account books and buying up poor-quality Japanese coal instead. So Japanese coal purchased through German coal companies ended up as black clouds of smoke rising from funnels on Russian warships—which just goes to show the strangeness of international commerce.

* * *

While coaling at every stop along the way was a major operation for the Baltic Fleet, it isn't clear whether the details were handled by Russian brains or left to the talents of the Hamburg American Line. "The Germans are amazingly shrewd," Engineer Politovsky wrote to his wife on January 27. "Every German collier carries not just a captain but a vice captain, German naval officers all." The officers were apparently involved in the actual business of coaling, but Politovsky didn't see it that way. "They are watching us," he wrote. He believed that the German naval officers were observing the state of the Russian fleet as it undertook this grueling voyage, seeking to use the information for the future benefit of their own navy. "Thinking up such a plan and executing it is not something we Russians would ever do."

Politovsky fumed to his wife about the lack of Russian planning. "The Russian Empire does nothing but suffer losses. We have neither a good navy nor a good army. There are no long-range plans or forethought." His own scientific knowledge was far and away beyond that of anyone in the fleet leadership. To this young man trained in scientific thinking, everything his country did seemed wretched. He couldn't help torturing himself with his observations, a factor that must be taken into account when reading a passage like the above.

In any case, it cannot be forgotten that the difficulty of Rozhestvensky's journey lay first and foremost in the provision of coal, a difficulty exacerbated by diplomatic pressure from Britain.

The heavy involvement of the Hamburg American Line in ocean fueling has been noted, along with the fact that Britain had stopped selling the shipping enterprise fine-quality coal. Instead, the fleet burned German coal, among others, which had a rather lower caloric value and produced thick black smoke. We've already told about how this became such a problem that the Russian government took the Hamburg American Line to court over it. The case made little headway, and in the end it was left to the company's Madagascar manager and Rozhestvensky to settle the quarrel directly. That was another reason for the long stay in Nosy Be.

However, the Russian government was being unreasonable in dumping the problem in Rozhestvensky's lap. Such negotiations were the job of the government. The Foreign Ministry or Naval Ministry should have taken care of it. They were being too harsh when they placed such additional work and responsibility on the shoulders of the fleet's commander in chief as he skippered his armada to the Far East.

The coal talks dragged on.

In the meantime, shipboard morale sank, and antiwar feeling spread through the fleet. Incidents of outright disobedience occurred frequently among civilian employees. Though the sailors did not go so far as to stop being obedient military men, news of revolution and riots back home in Russia made the nerves of some right-wing officers hypersensitive to any verbal or other miscues from the men. They became suspicious or adopted a belligerent attitude that only deepened antiwar sentiment among the sailors.

* * *

During this interval, Imperial Headquarters in Tokyo obtained the following scant, yet adequate, information about the Baltic Fleet.

"The main warships are fitted with wireless apparatus."

"They have defensive torpedo nets."

"No submarines."

"A repair ship, a torpedo depot ship, and a hospital ship are with them, and also ships for coal and water supply."

That the fleet had arrived at Madagascar was known; its failure to show any further signs of movement naturally raised questions. Tokyo had expected the fleet to set off right away and head straight for the Malay archipelago, arriving in the Taiwan Strait sometime at the beginning of January. With that in mind, repairs on Tōgō's fleet had been carried out quickly after the fall of Port Arthur. The military harbors of Kure and Sasebo were kept busy around the clock.

Rozhestvensky initially made the same calculations, planning on spending about two weeks at Madagascar. The ships needed to load coal, and anyway it would take about that long to meet up with Felkerzam's detachment, which was coming by way of the Mediterranean Sea. But soon after the Baltic Fleet anchored, word came of the fall of Port Arthur and the sinking of the Port Arthur Squadron.

"Rozhestvensky's Baltic Fleet has lost the ally it was counting on (the Port Arthur Squadron), so it will probably turn tail and go home." The rumor spread around the globe. Afterward, this rumor turned out to have some basis in fact; Rozhestvensky, discouraged about the battle ahead, was seeking instructions from Moscow on his next step. But Imperial Headquarters in Tokyo ignored the possibility of withdrawal, believing this out of the question. As long as the Russian Empire continued hostilities against Japan, they reasoned, it was unlikely that the Russians would relinquish command of the sea.

And indeed news then came that Russia had organized a Third Pacific Squadron. With this gift to Rozhestvensky, the tsar was trying to persuade the admiral to continue on to the Far East. To clarify, the Port Arthur Squadron was also known as the First Pacific Squadron, and similarly the Baltic Fleet was also called the Second Pacific Squadron. The Third Pacific Squadron was formed by selecting seaworthy vessels from the remaining ships in the Russian Navy (apart from the Black Sea Squadron) and putting them under the command of Rear Admiral Nebogatov. All were old and outmoded—"floating iron," the sailors sneered. Along with a battleship, a cruiser, and three coast defense ships, there were a few special service ships.

When Imperial Headquarters heard the news, they felt vindicated. "So the Russians *are* coming." Rozhestvensky, however, remained discouraged. This squadron of obsolete ships would only get in his fleet's way and do nothing to bolster its fighting power.

* * *

"The Port Arthur Squadron was annihilated."

Those who read the shocking news in the paper spread the word quickly, and soon the whole fleet knew. The inevitable question rose in every mind: "Now what happens to us?" Every sailor wondered the same thing.

The only reason the Russian Navy took the drastic step of sending the huge Baltic Fleet to the Far East on such an historic voyage in the first place was, as we have repeatedly seen, because they intended to join it with the Port Arthur Squadron and confront Tōgō's fleet.

To digress a bit, looking back at Russian land battles through history, one is tempted to extract the principle that they launched an offensive only when they had the enemy outnumbered at least two to one, in both men and arms. Perhaps this had something to do with the national character.

Or perhaps not.

As long as the purpose of war is winning, making sure one is poised for victory only makes sense. Napoleon always took that tack, and so did Japan's Oda Nobunaga. Over ninety percent of the effort in undertakings by such great leaders is expended in amassing overwhelming troop strength. To make this happen, the leader must trick the enemy diplomatically to gain time and use his political skills to lure third parties into an alliance. The eventual battle is the mere outcome of all that groundwork.

This approach was commonplace during Japan's era of Warring States but died out later in the Tokugawa period, when, in place of the cold calculation of odds of winning or losing, there arose an unwholesome (for commanders) approach that made much of heroism.

The Tokugawa period, an extended time of peace without parallel in world history, was built on unique principles of law and order established by the shogunate. By means of those principles, the shogunate managed to rob the Japanese people—everyone from lords to commoners—of all spirit of competition. This in turn caused a dulling of the nation's senses regarding military affairs.

As a twisted result, the tales of military exploits that thrilled the Tokugawa populace all had to do with great generals who miraculously halted or defeated a great army with a small band of men. That's why people loved Minamoto no Yoshitsune, the twelfth-century general, and felt a mystical reverence for Kusunoki Masashige, the fourteenth-century samurai. The siege of Osaka, in which Toyotomi Hideyori fought hopelessly and suffered defeat, was reenacted in numerous plays; participants like Sanada Yukimura and Gotō Matabei became national heroes. Tokugawa people were deeply drawn to them because their actions were aimed not at victory, but at heroic beauty. This spirit continued through the Shōwa period.

But the Russian approach to warfare was to refrain from fighting unless poised to win. If for tactical reasons Russian soldiers were nevertheless called upon to fight, rather than becoming drunk on their own heroism, they would suffer a loss of morale or even, on occasion, surrender. Since European civilization had advanced through ceaseless warfare, Europeans understood the essence of war, just as Japanese people did during the era of Warring States.

*   *   *

In the scorching tropical heat, members of the fleet latched onto every scrap of information from the outside world. A rumor that General Kuropatkin was on the march spread quickly. Engineer Politovsky wrote about this in his journal on February 1. But the calm, scientific thinker did not believe the rumor was true. He knew that several times in the past the Russian Army had been reported to be rallying, but the reports had all been false. This time, however, the rumor was true. It was a likely reference to Grippenberg's strike against the left wing of the Japanese Army—the Heigoutai campaign.

Several days later, Politovsky got wind that medals for valor had been awarded to army soldiers in St. Petersburg. "While we're losing like this?" he scoffed and dismissed this rumor too. No matter how corrupt the tsar's court might be, surely this was no time to be passing out medals. And yet maybe the army had some such custom, he thought. While waging war, even a losing war, doing so might well make sense as a way to encourage the troops at the front.

The staff room buzzed with the rumor. Politovsky, though a young engineer of only thirty-two, was included among the senior staff due to his exceptional ability— particularly his knowledge of *Suvorov*-type battleships. Though he had virtually no seagoing experience, thanks to his shipbuilding expertise, he knew the strengths and weaknesses of the Russian Navy inside and out, often better than the deck officers did, and as he assessed the state of the vast Russian military machine, he sensed with every fiber of his being the hopelessly diseased state of the Russian Empire.

When the rumor of army medals was taken up in the staff room, one officer stormed, "He's forgetting the navy!" How could the tsar pass out medals to the land forces and not the navy, he demanded to know. By "navy," he meant the Port Arthur Squadron. By ignoring the valor of officers in that fighting, the tsar had seriously insulted the navy, the officer loudly declaimed.

Listening, Politovsky was thunderstruck. His surprise soon turned to anger. "What did the Port Arthur Squadron ever do?" he felt like exclaiming. Though nearly as strong as the Japanese Navy to begin with, the squadron had gone to the bottom of the sea without inflicting so much as a scratch on the enemy. It not only had a losing record, it had covered itself with unprecedented disgrace, inviting worldwide contempt.

Though he was familiar with Western thought through Western technology, Politovsky was not one of the revolutionaries then infiltrating the ranks of students, military officers, and workers. He loved Russia and the navy. His indignation at corruption ran all the deeper because he loved them both so much. He could hardly stop himself from protesting: "The Port Arthur Squadron was built with the sweat and blood of the Russian people, and where is it now? Did its officers add to the glory of Russia? Its senior officers had a slew of medals pinned to their chests, but did they make any effort or take any action worthy of them?" Inside he was seething.

* * *

The fleet stayed on in the unknown fishing harbor of Nosy Be.

"We've memorized all the stars and their positions here in the southern hemisphere," reported one sailor in a letter home. "That's how bored we are."

This boredom of theirs requires a bit of explanation.

Rozhestvensky never gave the sailors time to be bored; besides endless firing practice, he had them put out to sea for training exercises, and at night patrol duty was rigorously enforced. But the fleet sailors didn't know when they would weigh anchor or whether, when they did weigh anchor, they would be heading on east or going home—though this last bit of wishful thinking was beginning to fade. No one knew the status or direction of his destiny, and so there was a pervasive mood of frustration and weariness. Nothing is so tedious as a daily routine that has lost its sense of purpose.

Rozhestvensky didn't earn from his sailors a hundredth of the goodwill enjoyed by Admiral Makarov, who went down with his fleet at Port Arthur, but he showed his ability as naval commander in the patrol operations he oversaw.

The fleet was bound by the assumption that Japan's cruiser fleet might go on the attack all the way to Madagascar, loaded with torpedo boats or midget submarines—an assumption deemed not fanciful but fully realistic. The Japanese Navy had no midget submarines, then a new weapon, but the Russians didn't believe it. The sinking of every last ship in the Port Arthur Squadron suggested that the Japanese Navy must have some mysterious power, a power that took shape in Russian minds as midget submarines.

To get an early awareness of any danger, every day several cruisers would leave port and circle a prescribed area repeatedly. Destroyers played an active role, too, keeping guard night and day around the harbor entrance, the equivalent of a castle's front gate. At night when the stars came out, every ship in the fleet lowered a protective torpedo net. Lighting lamps was forbidden, and crews stood ready to man the guns and deep-sea lights. In short, at night, every ship remained in a state of combat readiness.

"I don't trust the lot of 'em." This was the attitude Rozhestvensky took. By "the lot of 'em" he meant the entire crew of his fleet—his own men. His lack of trust may have been an astute judgment. The liveliest sailors and noncommissioned officers on active duty in the Russian Navy had all been assigned to the Port Arthur Squadron. Just as Nicholas II aspired to be "tsar of the Pacific," Russia laid great importance on the Far East and maintained a highly proficient naval presence there.

Sailors serving with fleets on the North, Baltic, or Black Seas were second tier, and very few had any experience to speak of. When Rozhestvensky had assembled his fleet, he had gone to great pains to select his crew. He took a large number of older noncommissioned officers and sailors from the reserve list, including some from inland regions who had never before laid eyes on the sea. These he had to whip into shape, hastily fashioning them into an able fighting force.

*   *   *

Around this time, an unlucky prophecy appeared.

The newspaper *Novoye Vremya* ran an essay by naval commander Klado concerning which fleet was likely to emerge victorious, the Russian or the Japanese. Based on his own analysis, Klado concluded that Russian victory was not at all certain and issued a warning to the Russian Navy.

Though Klado's warning proved accurate in the end, his analysis was not necessarily correct. He measured both sides' battle strength by comparing their battleships and armored cruisers, but in such cases, the outcome is heavily influenced by the basis of comparison. On Klado's scale, if Russia was 1, Japan was 1.8. The figures look bleak for Russia, but depending on how the calculations were set up, it could just as easily have come out the other way. Indeed, the opposite conclusion might have been more logical.

"Therefore, it is necessary to form another squadron," Klado wrote, "and send it after the Baltic Fleet." In other words, he recommended scraping together all the old tubs left in the Baltic Sea and giving them to Rozhestvensky—which is exactly what happened. That was the origin of the Third Pacific Squadron (headed by Rear Admiral Nebogatov). Though Rozhestvensky had no wish to join forces with Nebogatov's squadron, in the end they did join forces, giving the Russians a total of over forty ships, with overwhelmingly more artillery than the Japanese.

Japan had only sixteen 12-inch guns on its capital ships—the most important warships in the navy, with the heaviest firepower—while the Russians had twenty-six on theirs. Of 10-inch guns, Japan had one, the Russians seven, and of 9-inch guns Japan had none, the Russians twelve. Japan dominated only with 8-inch guns (applying a lesson learned from the First Sino-Japanese War)—they had thirty to the Russians' eight.

The above comparison of guns on the fleets' capital ships compels the conclusion that the Russians had far superior firepower in 9-inch guns and above. Klado, however, did not say this, which can only mean that he wrote the essay not as a precision study but as a way of intentionally promoting his pessimistic conclusion. Klado was a regular officer in the Russian Navy. Because his essay was filled with such dour prognostications, albeit couched as a warning, some cynically assumed that he must have written it at the navy's instigation. The article was seen as a bureaucratic subterfuge, since, if Russia lost, the Russian Navy would be held responsible. This view may be taking things a bit too far, since Klado was ultimately arrested for what he wrote.

In any case, there is no doubt that when the gist of the article filtered down to sailors in the Baltic Fleet, morale suffered a heavy blow.

* * *

Engineer Politovsky was kept busier than words can convey.

During the anchorage at Nosy Be, ships large and small reported various breakdowns. As ship's surgeon and internist alike, Politovsky had to personally examine each one, diagnose the trouble, and prescribe a remedy. At times, he had to stay on hand to direct the treatment.

One of the main reasons why naval experts around the world had predicted that this epic voyage of Rozhestvensky's would end in failure was the question of how ship repairs (a constant need) would be carried out. In peacetime, they could have just slipped into a harbor with a shipyard or dockyard, and that would have been that; but they were at war, and their enemy, Japan, was allied with Great Britain, the acknowledged ruler of the oceans. Not only would Britain refuse Russia the use of its harbors, but it complained ceaselessly to France and Germany and got them to close theirs as well.

As a result, the fleet could not go into dock even for major repairs but had to do everything at sea. For repairs below the waterline, the repairmen would don diving gear. The greater part of all such work was done under Politovsky's supervision. Smaller ships such as destroyers frequently broke down or suffered damage in collisions. Sending such small vessels on such a long voyage was unreasonable in the first place.

"Destroyers are hell," the sailors said. The destroyers' smaller size meant cramped quarters with severe rolling and pitching. Also, in the tropics, temperatures soared higher in them than in the larger ships. Worst of all, their crews suffered from inferior rations and water. Since smaller ships had no refrigeration, food quickly spoiled. Sailors were frequently served bad meat, to their loud indignation, yet, surprisingly enough, they all managed to endure the privations of the long voyage.

The small ships were also hell for the rest of the fleet, which had to drag them along in order to do battle in the Far East. Their coal-carrying capacity was so small that they had to lay in coal at frequent intervals. Each time, the large ships were forced to wait. On the way to Nosy Be, the entire fleet had halted time and again while the smaller ships took in coal.

On top of this were the constant engine troubles and accidents, all Politovsky's responsibility. This kept him busier than any other officer while the fleet lay in harbor at Nosy Be. The talented young Tashkent native was fully up to the task.

*   *   *

Here let us take a moment to discuss Russian warships.

"Russian technology in the manufacture of ships and ordnance could not of course have been inferior." The aforementioned Fukui Shizuo did a painstaking analysis for the June 1959 issue of Japan's maritime journal *Ships of the World*.

At the time, Japan was manufacturing its smaller warships domestically, including protected cruisers, but ordering its capital ships and battleships in particular from Britain, with only basic instructions. Russia in turn had a large number of ships made in France or the United States, although most were domestic products. The *Rurik*, a large cruiser in the Vladivostok Squadron, demonstrated the excellence of Russian ship design to the world. *Rurik* was an armored cruiser, a type of ship known for its large cruising range; it had a displacement of 10,936 tons, had a speed of 19 knots, and showed impressive fighting power, with four 8-inch guns and sixteen 6-inch guns. It was particularly well suited to commerce destruction and other deep-sea operations. The *Rurik* stimulated the British Navy, causing the world's leading maritime nation to develop the battle cruiser eventually.

"They each had their strengths and weaknesses," Fukui wrote when discussing the quality of Russian and Japanese capital ships. "It is fair to say they were at the same level."

The following discussion draws extensively on Fukui's research; any errors are the author's responsibility. Fukui compared the battleships of the two countries. To borrow his conclusion, "In general, the Japanese battleships excelled as individual warships. They had great displacement, and they were fast. Russian battleships were domestic for the most part, but many of them were made according to French design, and some were of American construction. As a result, they were various in style, function, and armaments."

The Japanese Navy as designed by Yamamoto Gombei adopted the "sister ship" system and moreover operated in sets so that ships of similar power could keep pace with one another. The Russian Navy took no account of such things. Though many of its ships of domestic design were quite original, the Russian Navy put greater effort into introducing superior shipbuilding technology of other countries. In 1898 and 1899, as storm clouds gathered in the Far East, Russia ordered one battleship each from the United States and France—the *Tsesarevich* and the *Retvizan*. The latter proved particularly pleasing, and Russia promptly made four more like it, adding slight improvements. These were the four ships in the *Borodino* class.

In any case, of the seven battleships in Rozhestvensky's possession (one more would be added later), five had just been completed and were newer than Tōgō's four. These five, if formed into a squadron, would arguably have been the strongest naval force in the world.

* * *

Politovsky's account usually contains such pessimism over his own fleet that he sounds like a patient suffering from depression. His entry for February 20, however, is an exception. "I read an article on the damage to the *Tsesarevich*," he wrote. This newspaper article requires some explanation.

The *Tsesarevich*, a battleship of French make, was a representative battleship in the Port Arthur Squadron, and we have described how, on August 10, 1904, during the battle of the Yellow Sea, it was the flagship of the squadron commander, Admiral Vitgeft. He fought valiantly against Tōgō's fleet, and right around sundown it looked as if he might succeed in fleeing to the safety of Vladivostok. Then, at thirty-seven minutes after six in the evening, a "fateful shell" from the *Mikasa* hit the conning tower of the *Tsesarevich*, blowing Vitgeft and his aides to bits. A second shell exploded on the heels of the first, killing the captain, the helmsman, and others. In his death agony, the helmsman threw himself to the left, still gripping the helm, so the burning ship began turning counterclockwise. The ship following behind became disoriented, battle formation was broken, and the squadron fell apart.

The *Tsesarevich* escaped to Jiaozhou Bay, entered the German port of Qingdao in China, and was stripped of its armor in accordance with international law. The German Navy, along with other Western navies, took a strong interest in the pitiful battleship, as well they might. The battle of the Yellow Sea was the first naval battle fought with modernized warships, and every country was eager to examine what damage the *Tsesarevich* had suffered and what structural defects it may have had. They came to an amazing conclusion: "Fifteen 12-inch shells struck the *Tsesarevich*—the heaviest shells there are—and not one pierced its armor."

Politovsky was overjoyed: "How grand our battleship armor is!"

If the *Tsesarevich* had survived more or less intact, then the pride of the Baltic Fleet—the *Suvorov*, *Borodino*, *Alexander III*, *Oryol*, and *Oslyabya*—would be all right, since they had even thicker armor; and, if 12-inch guns, the heaviest in the navy, had proven powerless, then smaller-caliber guns were nothing to worry about. That's what Politovsky thought.

But he didn't understand the reason why the *Tsesarevich* had escaped destruction, and neither did any of the international experts who examined the ship. The explanation lay not in the strength of the Russian armor, but in a defect of Japanese armor-piercing shells: the fuse was too sensitive. As a result, the shell exploded as soon as it touched the hull, dispersing its energy before it could pierce the armor. But the unbelievable incendiary power of Shimose powder had resulted in a large number of casualties, and that was what caused the downfall of the ship.

*   *   *

After the "fateful shell" hit the conning tower of the *Tsesarevich*, shards wiped out the bridge and the chart room. Other shells, a great many, ripped holes in the funnels. But the boiler room was safe, so the battleship's heart kept right on beating, although the holes in its funnels, or breathing apparatus, lowered its speed. When it limped into Qingdao, the ship could manage barely 4 or 5 knots. Still, it was not on its last legs.

Rozhestvensky, who had also read the article in the newspaper, sent for Politovsky. "They say there was only a little leaking."

As Politovsky looked at this detestable man (someone he despised both professionally and personally) full in the face, he realized that he was in a good mood for once. "Yes, sir," Politovsky replied, "there was a hit just below the waterline too, but the armor repelled it."

What about our armor-piercing shells?—was a question Rozhestvensky did not utter, as anyone with an aggressive fighting spirit should have done. Would Russian shells skewer the *Mikasa*? That was the issue.

But Rozhestvensky was satisfied with the armored protection of Russian battleships. This was an extremely important point in executing the Far Eastern strategy he had in mind: "When we enter the waters around Japan, we'll make a run for Vladivostok." Fleeing to the safety of Vladivostok might just be possible, given the ships' strong defenses.

"Very good," Rozhestvensky said, his back turned.

Politovsky saluted and left.

*   *   *

Navies supply their fleets with two kinds of ammunition: armor-piercing shells and regular shells. During the Russo-Japanese War, the former did not live up to their name on either side. Research on armor-piercing shells did not begin in earnest until after the war. They were used with devastating force in the First World War during the 1916 naval battle of Jutland, which was fought between the British Navy's Grand Fleet and the German Navy's High Seas Fleet. Armor-piercing shells exchanged by the two navies were capable of penetrating heavy armor, exploding inside the vessel, and often inducing secondary explosions in the magazine, blowing up and sinking the ship instantaneously.

The Type 91 armor-piercing shells developed by the Japanese Navy later on, in the 1920s, were held to have the most efficient construction of any such shells in the world. They were also known as "diving shells." The projectile was flat-nosed, not pointed, flattened by cutting off the tapered end. The tip was then fitted with a pointed cap (ballistic or wind cap). That was all there was to it, but when one of these struck a steel surface, the cap disintegrated and the body drilled straight through the steel, exploding on the other side. Underwater, the pointed cap would be demolished, leaving the diving shell to hurtle through the water, strike an enemy ship, and bore a hole in it. After the Pacific War, when the United States Navy examined Japanese weapons, this diving shell was what surprised them the most.

But at the time of the Russo-Japanese War, calling navy shells "armor-piercing" was a misnomer; the nose was a mere lump of heavy steel. Regular shells were packed with explosive powder of a force equally devastating as shells of the later era (navy shells were particularly densely packed), but in armor-piercing shells the explosive charge amounted to only three to five percent of the whole.

We've told about how Japanese armor-piercing shells that landed on the *Tsesarevich* had overly sensitive fuses and were unable to penetrate the battleship's armor; instead, they smashed to bits. Though the armor-piercing shells made in Japan and fired from every Japanese battleship from the *Mikasa* on down were all duds, regular shells were not. Packed tightly with Shimose powder—a powder so powerful it was said to "burn steel"—a regular shell could rip into a ship with violent force and reduce it to ruins.

But unable to profit from the battle experience of the Port Arthur Squadron, the Baltic Fleet had no way of knowing that Shimose powder was so powerful. "In the battle of the Yellow Sea," the commanders of the Baltic Fleet consoled themselves, "Tōgō only routed the Port Arthur Squadron and failed to sink a single ship." Indeed, at this time, the defensive strength of battleship plate armor was many times superior to the armor-piercing strength of shells.

*   *   *

The author has a preconceived image of armor-piercing shells, based on the Pacific War, and that seems to be interfering a bit with the narrative— particularly so since the ones used in the Russo-Japanese War were called by the same name. For convenience, let us briefly review the armor-piercing shells used in the Pacific War. We know that the Japanese Navy used a variant of unusual construction known as "Type 91 armor-piercing shell." Besides that, there were some called *tadan*, short for *taisensha dan* or shaped charge, which the army also used. Those were received from Germany in 1941 in exchange for Type 93 torpedoes and diesel engine injection pumps.

In the tadan, the top of the explosive was notched in a V-shape and capped like an artillery shell. In addition to this typical construction, the tadan was distinguished by explosive powder containing a sixteen percent admixture of powdered aluminum. When it struck a steel plate and exploded, an intense burst of heat energy was released, the V-shaped charge instantly melting to form a rod of flame that bore straight through the plate.

Comparable shells in the Russo-Japanese War were armor-piercing in name only, since, as we have seen, neither the Japanese nor the Russians had shells capable of penetrating the armor on each other's battleships. Like Type 91 armor-piercing shells, the earlier shells were capped, but whereas the later versions all had hard caps, during the Russo-Japanese War, the cap could be either hard or soft, with different effects. Whereas later capped projectiles were designed to pierce steel, those of this era were designed to blow up a steel plate with the cap, or else the cap was designed to function like a hoop and hold the projectile in place. In either case, they were based on relatively primitive mechanics.

The Russian Navy was the first navy in the world to use armor-piercing shells. After they were introduced in 1894, other countries hastened to follow suit. Rozhestvensky's fleet was carrying a heavy cargo of them.

Tōgō's fleet had armor-piercing shells too, but more importantly, the fleet had Tōgō, who was more experienced than Rozhestvensky at using the shells in battle and knew that they were not to be trusted. They had little impact on the enemy, and, what was worse, they were prone to explode inside the gun, causing dreadful accidents. On August 10, 1904, during the battle of the Yellow Sea, it was announced that enemy shells had destroyed a 12-inch aft gun on the *Mikasa*, but in fact the gun self-destructed when an armor-piercing shell exploded prematurely. The barrel was left in ribbons, one man died, and a dozen more were wounded. As a result, Tōgō would probably use regular shells in the coming engagement with Rozhestvensky.

* * *

"Japanese shells haven't got the power to penetrate our battleship armor. The *Tsesarevich* showed that to the world."

This was hugely good news for the fleet at Nosy Be. The battleship crews in particular were cheered, but there was a catch: would their own shells penetrate the armor of Tōgō's *Mikasa* and the rest? Nobody thought so. Russians of this era unfortunately put little faith in their own technology.

Objectively speaking, Russian shipbuilding and arms manufacture were at a high level—certainly not at a low level. To the consternation of Russian leaders, however, the populace had unwavering respect for machine-made goods from Western Europe. "Our technology can't possibly be superior." That's what sailors thought, coming as they did from that same populace, and that's what made them apprehensive about their chances of victory.

The truth was, during the siege of Port Arthur, Russian shipwrights were able to mend every ship in the harbor that experienced damage—a considerable feat, even if insufficient to represent Russia's actual technological standard.

Engineer Politovsky, though still a young man, was already an authority on battleships. He was especially well acquainted with the *Suvorov*, the flagship with Rozhestvensky on board, and others of its class. Five years before the war began, he had been named assistant to the chief in charge of the construction of the battleship *Borodino*. Politovsky was surely unequaled in his technical grasp of Russia's modern battleships. He knew the strengths of the design, but he knew its shortcomings as well, and as an engineer he was especially alert to the shortcomings.

As a technician, he frankly doubted whether the navy officers and men would be able to handle the ships skillfully, for a simple reason: there were too many too-new capital ships. "Too new" because, from the standpoint of rapidly progressing shipbuilding and armament manufacture technology, any ship built this year was bound to be a cut above one built the year before. Tōgō's newest battleship, for example, was the *Mikasa*, but Rozhestvensky had several battleships that were newer.

The flagship *Suvorov*, for one, was made a flagship before its rigging was finished. The job was rushed through, and no sooner was the finished ship afloat than it was put in commission and sent on this expedition to the Far East. The timing was so close that undoubtedly there were technical glitches that needed fixing, and no one from the commander on down was used to operating the ships. Not enough time had been devoted to allowing the crew to become proficient.

These flaws were the biggest reason for Politovsky's low spirits.

*　*　*

One other flaw in the new battleships that Politovsky found depressing had to do with stability. In a seagoing vessel, "stability" refers to the ability to revert to an upright position after tilting due to wind or waves. Nothing is as crucial to a ship as its stability.

When a ship tilts after being hit broadside by a wave, its center of gravity must not shift. If the center of gravity stays the same and only the center of buoyancy shifts in the direction of the tilt, the ship can return to its original position. The ship is then said to have "regained its stability."

"Metacentric height" is a technical term often used in Politovsky's field of specialization. When a ship tilts, the center of buoyancy shifts with it. The metacenter is the point at which a vertical line through the center of buoyancy crosses a line through the center of the ship (in its tilted state). The metacentric height is the distance between the center of gravity and the metacenter. Although a ship with high metacentric height has good stability, it doesn't follow that the higher the metacentric height, the better. When the height is excessive, the ship rights itself like a roly-poly toy, regaining stability with sudden movements. A shortened rolling period can cause all sorts of damage to a ship at sea.

Metacentric height generally differs according to the type of warship, but there is no point in going into great detail. Elsewhere in this text, Russian battleships have been described as "top-heavy." In other words, they had a high center of gravity, which naturally made them likelier to capsize. Of course, even with a slightly high initial center of gravity, once a ship had a full load of coal, its waterline would rise, thereby lowering the center of gravity and increasing stability.

To be exact, Russian ships were top-heavy because of their complex superstructure, which, being both large and tall, raised the center of gravity. In a word, the ships were unstable.

In order to lighten the superstructure as much as possible, a ship's bottom is shaped (to use a rough analogy) like the bottom of a laboratory flask. (This is known as tumblehome.) A cross-section of a ship from just above the waterline to the keel will reveal a swelling like that of a woman's hips. This design innovation was developed by the French; French battleships are nearly all designed this way, and the Russians, many of whose ships were made in France, copied this feature in their own shipbuilding. (Japanese ships, being British in style, have no "hips.") And so to anyone accustomed to British-style ships, the shape of Russian French-style battleships is extremely odd.

A cross-section of the hull of one of the new French-style battleships, curved like a woman's hips, may appear extremely stable, but there were serious flaws. To quote again from the research of Lieutenant Fukui Shizuo: "When one of these ships was damaged and tilted, if the tilt was extreme, stability nosedived. . . .The large, high superstructure meant a high center of gravity (detracting from stability). . . . Unarmored sections are extensive. (On the other hand, protection of the waterline was thorough.)"

The *Borodino*-class battleships, bearing these unique features, were fated to have a large superstructure to begin with, and, as more demands were incorporated while they were being built, the superstructure grew even larger. The center of gravity rose; stability fell.

That wasn't all. The scarcity of harbors en route to the Far East meant that the ships had to carry extra-heavy loads including, for instance, repair parts. They had to take with them every conceivable type of equipment and expendable supplies. Tōgō's fleet, located in home waters, had no such need.

When the Baltic Fleet left Liepaja, the displacement of *Alexander III*, for example, was 15,300 tons, considerably greater than its planned displacement of 13,516 tons. On top of that, its center of gravity was high. This was hardly a warship that inspired peace of mind.

Rozhestvensky left Liepaja on October 15 the previous autumn with these new battleships as the main force of his fleet. Just two days before setting off, he received this startling warning from the technology council of the Russian Navy: "Be cautious about the stability of the *Borodino*-class battleships."

These were the very battleships being touted as "the world's newest and strongest"—yet the actual state of affairs was clearly worrying. Indeed, how was a fleet commander setting out on such a far-flung voyage on the orders of the tsar supposed to be confident of victory once he received such a warning so soon before departure? Rozhestvensky was a military man who lived by the principle of doing his duty. But the noncombatant Politovsky, who understood better than anyone the flaws of these new battleships, could hardly be expected to rejoice over his fate in being assigned to accompany the fleet on its epic journey to do battle. It's no surprise that he continued to write letters to his wife expressing hopelessness over the future of the fleet.

The council issued Rozhestvensky a two-part warning. He was to exercise caution when navigating, and to use particular caution during battle. What this meant in practical terms was: "Doing battle in weather when the waves are high will be extremely dangerous. If the battleships suffer damage around the waterline and are flooded, there is danger of them capsizing." To state it even more bluntly, "If shells strike any of these ships around the waterline, they will surely capsize."

That is just what happened.

"Weather today fine but high waves." Written by Akiyama Saneyuki, this line from the telegram sent just before the naval battle reflects his calculation of the odds of victory. He was factoring in his knowledge of what would happen to the new *Borodino*-class battleships in high wave conditions.

*　*　*

When you think about it, the defeat of the Russian Empire was a disaster waiting to happen. The biggest reason—the underlying principle—was the dreadful tsarist regime consisting only of the autocratic tsar and his aides, without any established, healthy organ of criticism. Russia's Far East invasion policy was based on a whim of the tsar and framed by aides who pandered to his whims. They banned their one opponent, Witte, and in the end provoked war with Japan. They had no plan whatsoever for winning.

"Whatsoever": the intensifier is justified since Japan's war preparations were vastly more careful than those of Russia. As a constitutional state, Japan had a popularly elected assembly and a responsible cabinet (though the country was inexperienced in using this cabinet), and, accordingly, the conduct of state affairs was based largely on reason.

The military also showed no sign whatever of the later tendency of the so-called "military clique" to undermine constitutional government by invoking the imperial prerogative of supreme command. True, the emperor had supreme command over Japan's military forces, but only in a purely metaphysical sense; the principle that conduct of military affairs was relegated by the Diet to the army and navy remained intact. In this respect, Japan and Russia were diametrically opposed.

"Russia is moving with unusual swiftness toward invasion of the Far East. It is on a collision course with Japan." This assessment became widespread following the end of the First Sino-Japanese War of 1894–1895. In 1896, the Diet approved a ten-year plan with a budget of 118 million yen (the Second Extended Plan) to increase naval strength vis-à-vis the Russians. Four battleships including the *Mikasa*, six armored cruisers including the *Yakumo*, and six protected cruisers and small protected cruisers—the nucleus of Tōgō's fleet—were made in a highly systematic fashion.

Even after the new warships were ready, sending them straight off to battle the way the Russians did was unreasonable; the crews first needed to acquire the proficiency to handle them. The rationality of the Japanese Navy even allowed for time to build this proficiency, a calculation that factored into the decision regarding when to open hostilities. The difference with Russia, where the risky business of invasion and war turned on an emperor's whim, is startling.

In short, although the Baltic Fleet was able to operate its ships, insufficient time was taken to master their ins and outs—a fatal mistake, as it turned out, that was made merely because the tsar was in a rush. He was in a rush chiefly because aides who had never undertaken any serious comparison of the Japanese and Russian navies assured him that a victory in the Far East would help dispel the revolutionary mood permeating the country. Important political tactics should be decided by taking politics and strategy into account separately, but a despotic tsar and his aides could never be that systematic. They merely counted up tonnage and guns in the two fleets, decided Russia

had the edge, and sent this immature armada off on its far-flung mission to
the Far East.

*   *   *

Though Rozhestvensky's crew may have lacked proficiency with the newly
built ships, in terms of the physical force of individual warships, his fleet
was superior to Tōgō's in many respects. Since most of the Baltic Fleet's
battleships were newer than the *Mikasa*, they incorporated new facilities and
technology—telescopic sights, for one. In Tōgō's fleet, no guns except
those on the *Mikasa* had telescopic sights; gunners did all their aiming with
the naked eye. Every Russian battleship was equipped with the new sights,
and that made a great difference.

In the battle of the Yellow Sea, for example, the battleships *Tsesarevich*
and *Retvizan* fired their 12-inch guns from what was to the Japanese Navy
the absurdly large distance of 18,000 meters, overshooting the *Mikasa* and
Asahi. At the time, the most effective range for solid accuracy was held to
be 6,000 to 4,000 meters. The Japanese were astounded to see the Russians
firing from a distance over three times greater. In contrast, the *Asahi* fired
its first shells only after arriving at a spot 14,000 meters away.

"How can they fire from that distance?" the Japanese sailors marveled
afterward. One explanation lay in the telescopic sights fitted on Russian guns.
Also, guns on the new Russian battleships had a greater angle of elevation
than their Japanese counterparts. Naturally, the shooting range was also
correspondingly greater, and so the Russians were able to commence
shooting from a larger distance.

Russia had a tradition of keen interest in researching and manufacturing
firearms, and indeed the guns on the new Russian battleships were superior
to Japanese guns in many ways. But to make full use of these superior new
guns, they needed superior gun crews. The cream of the Russian Navy had
been concentrated in the Port Arthur Squadron, and many of the men under
Rozhestvensky's command were raw and inexperienced.

Since Rozhestvensky had been aide-de-camp to Tsar Nicholas II, he lacked
Tōgō's battle experience, but he was known as an authority on gunnery.
Partly for that reason, as well as the reasons listed above, he devoted himself
mainly to improving his men's marksmanship during the long holdover in
Nosy Be.

Many of the men assigned to range-finding couldn't handle the range
finders smoothly. "This equipment is too newfangled," they grumbled. The
newly fitted range finders on all the ships were British-made by Barr and
Stroud, and the men struggled with them. Gaining proficiency with the new
battleships included such matters as well.

*   *   *

No one knew when the Baltic Fleet would leave Madagascar.

Problems piled up: disputes with the German coal company, ambiguous instructions from Moscow, the need to link up with Nebogatov's Third Pacific Squadron. Weighing anchor was not an option.

Morale deteriorated. Personnel troubles cropped up constantly, keeping Rozhestvensky as busy as the prosecutor in a high-crime city. Worst of all, seaweed (commonly known as beard) and barnacles attached themselves to, or "fouled," the ships' bottoms. "Being kept at Nosy Be is doing us a lot of harm," wrote Politovsky. The encrustation went right up the sides of some ships.

Nothing could slow a ship down more or cause a greater expenditure of coal than a coating of beard and barnacles. Even merchant ships voyaging from the Indian Ocean to the Far East and back would go into dock once every six months to be cleaned. Politovsky, the ships' surgeon, appealed to the senior staff: "No matter how new a battleship may be, once its hull is coated with algae and shells, there's no way it can reach full speed." But there was nothing they could do.

The only way to scrape off the hulls was to go into dry dock, but Nosy Be had no such facilities. Nor was there any dock available on the way ahead. Rozhestvensky had no choice but to assign divers to clean the ships' hulls underwater, but that was only a temporary, stopgap measure. "Every minus for our fleet is a plus for Tōgō's," thought Politovsky grimly. Did Moscow understand the plight of this immense fleet on which Russia's honor rested? he wondered in dejection.

"Our Russian sailors disdain the Japanese, calling them 'apes.' By reducing the enemy to monkeys they lift themselves up. Such arrogance led to the annihilation of the Port Arthur Squadron. Now we're about to head off to the Far East with fouled bottoms, while they wait for us with clean ships in tip-top repair. . . ." Writing apologetically, "Here I go again, harping on the same tune though it does no good," Politovsky predicted that the ships' foul condition would cost Russia dearly.

In fact, all during the Port Arthur siege, Tōgō had been concerned about the gradual encrusting of the ships' bottoms, which he wanted cleaned off before the Baltic Fleet arrived on the scene. For that he needed time. That was why he hoped to bring about the fall of Port Arthur as soon as possible. Port Arthur's fall gave Tōgō all the time he needed to clean and refit his fleet.

*   *   *

In the meantime, the Japanese did everything possible to check on the movements of the Baltic Fleet. Besides employing spies, they sent ships on long-distance reconnaissance missions to the South Seas. Before the fall of Port Arthur, Tōgō gave such an assignment to a couple of converted cruisers, the *Hong Kong Maru* and the *Nippon Maru*. The pair left Sasebo on December 13 and arrived in Singapore on December 22, proceeding then to the Java Sea, the Sunda Strait, and the Indian Ocean, going past Batavia, the isle of Borneo, and the coast of Cambodia. Though they never did catch sight of the Baltic Fleet, they returned to Sasebo on January 18, having picked up a variety of intelligence.

Next, on December 15, the protected cruiser *Niitaka* (3,366 tons, under Commander Shōji Yoshimoto) left the military harbor of Yokosuka on a similar mission and steamed toward south China. The *Niitaka* went as far south as the Philippine island of Luzon and returned to Sasebo on January 11.

Again in February 1905, a large-scale reconnaissance operation was planned, and the squadron left Sasebo on the twenty-seventh. Known as the "Nanken detachment," it was headed by Vice Admiral Dewa Shigetō and included, in addition to the protected cruisers *Chitose* (4,760 tons) and *Kasagi* (4,900 tons), the *Amerika Maru*, *Yahata Maru*, and *Hikosan Maru*. The squadron patrolled the waters around Hong Kong, Hainan Island, and the Indochina Peninsula. On March 15, it approached the mouth of Britain's Singapore Harbor and exchanged salutes with a British warship that happened to be anchored there. Dewa went ashore and called on the governor general. He obtained a wealth of intelligence from the British before cruising the waters around Borneo and returning to Tokyo on April 1.

Meanwhile, Tōgō and his aides, including Akiyama Saneyuki, had a relatively long sojourn in Tokyo. After destroying the Port Arthur Squadron, Tōgō immediately returned to Tokyo to call at the Imperial Palace and report to Emperor Meiji, as we have seen.

The emperor inquired about his strategy vis-à-vis the Baltic Fleet. "Are you confident of victory?"

Tōgō took his time replying, and when he did, Navy Minister Yamamoto Gombei and Chief of the Navy General Staff Itō Sukeyuki, who were also present, were amazed at his response.

"Should enemy reinforcements arrive," said Tōgō, "I vow that we will destroy them and set Your Majesty's mind at ease." Tōgō rarely committed himself plainly, and his outspokenness on this occasion took the other two men by surprise. Long afterward, they both remembered it, and told how they couldn't help staring at the admiral.

Accompanied by Saneyuki and the rest of his staff, Tōgō left Tokyo on February 6. He went to Kure to inspect the *Mikasa*, whose repairs were by then complete, and stayed a while.

Meanwhile, the Baltic Fleet, with its black hulls and yellow funnels, was sweltering at Nosy Be on Madagascar. Its twelve thousand-odd men and officers were idle and bored to tears, tortured with uncertainty over what lay ahead. Generally speaking, however, Rozhestvensky's leadership had caused no serious trouble, and so the situation was good.

3

GRAND ESPIONAGE

During this time, London was the hub of intelligence not only from Europe but also from around the world. Partly that was because England's geographical situation afforded an excellent overview of the political landscape across the channel in Europe, and also because over the centuries the government had acquired the knack of putting its geographical advantage to good use, making London the convergence point of rich streams of intelligence. British diplomacy at the time was based on that rich information supply.

Also, to be exact, the coolheaded British temper was extremely well suited to the handling of intelligence and the ability to see through such information to the underlying reality. "With the British Foreign Office on your side, you understand the world," said Hayashi Tadasu, the Japanese ambassador to Great Britain, and he was surely right.

Berlin intelligence, for example, tended to be heavily colored by the Germans' subjective views of events, if not deliberately twisted by some German with a bent for scheming. Paris was no longer the diplomatic center stage, and Rome was a diplomatic backwater. The Anglo-Japanese Alliance that Hayashi worked successfully to conclude was not just a tactical diplomatic plus for Japan but gave Japan fair access through its new partner to reams of intelligence. Throughout the war, therefore, despite being off in the Far East, the government in Tokyo enjoyed the unexpected advantage of seldom if ever erring in its assessment of world affairs.

They were likely to learn faster about Russian military matters—how many army divisions were being deployed east, for example, and when—just by having someone in London. Information on the movements of Mishchenko's cavalry detachment, which presaged the battle of Heigoutai, as well as on

Grippenberg's preparations for a massive offensive, had come to light early in London. As mentioned previously, military attaché Utsunomiya Tarō picked up the information and swiftly relayed it to Tokyo. But Japan's military leaders in Manchuria were uncomfortable with intelligence that had circled the globe before arriving via Tokyo at the battlefield, reacting skeptically— "It can't be!"—and disregarding the warnings.

Colonel Matsukawa Toshitane, a staff officer at the Manchurian Army's General Headquarters, had some justification for turning a deaf ear. The only on-ground reports that a major Russian offensive was in the works had come from Yoshifuru's cavalry; the battlefield intelligence unit headed by Fukushima Yasumasa caught no such information in its web. As the warning did not agree with on-ground intelligence, Matsukawa ignored it. At least in this case, international intelligence was superior to battlefield intelligence.

* * *

Let us turn our attention for a while to espionage activities.

Japan set up an intelligence headquarters in London, headed by Utsunomiya Tarō. He kept in touch with other military attachés stationed in Europe and personally perused influential newspapers of Great Britain and other European countries, reading between the lines to detect changes in Russia's political and military situations. He also frequented the British Admiralty and War Office, gaining virtually unlimited access to intelligence there. No one was better informed about European military affairs than he.

Another figure involved in Japan's intelligence gathering was Colonel Akashi Motojirō, the agent provocateur in direct contact with Russia who helped foment revolution there. "Akashi is one of the reasons Japan won the Russo-Japanese War," people said, a sign of how sizeable his accomplishments were.

The two men met in London before the war. "I have a feeling Russia will self-destruct," Utsunomiya remarked to Akashi. "No people on earth are as pitiful as the Russians." He went on to fill Akashi in on what he had learned about Russian history and what was going on in the country.

"It's hard to imagine, but Russia is a place where the land and the people are the personal property of the tsar and nobles. Russian history is the history of their private ownership of the populace. There is no Russian nation in the European sense."

Russia had a peasantry of thirty-five million, of whom twenty million were serfs, a uniquely Russian class. A serf, though a human being, was the absolute property of an aristocratic landowner, and as such could be—and often was—bought and sold as the owner saw fit. The despotic tsarist regime was built on serfdom.

"The Russian serf isn't the same as the Japanese tenant farmer," Utsunomiya pointed out. "Not only can a serf be bought and sold, he can be exiled to Siberia if his landlord takes a dislike to him. And yet," he mused, "they say Russia is Asian." He expressed doubt that similar conditions existed anywhere in Asia. Until several centuries back, Mongols had controlled the land and people of Russia. After the disintegration of their empire (known as the Kipchak Khanate or the Golden Horde), the Mongols were simply replaced by the tsar and his court. Russia was in a class by itself.

"Of course, the notorious serf system was abolished not so very long ago," said Utsunomiya. "But it was abolished on terms that protected the rights and interests of the nobility, leaving twenty million former serfs in more straitened circumstances than ever. The situation is the same today."

*   *   *

Being in London enabled Utsunomiya to take a broad perspective. Akashi was a Russian expert, but it is fair to say that he was enlightened by Utsunomiya before developing his own thinking.

Utsunomiya had probably picked up his observation, "Russia is bound to self-destruct," from British diplomats. "The tsar isn't the people's friend, he is their owner. Seventy or so years ago when Nicholas I visited the British Parliament, had he been truly wise, he would have taken the chance to introduce British-style government in Russia. He merely left with a very unpleasant impression of parliaments. The current tsar feels exactly the same way."

From his long association with Great Britain, Utsunomiya believed constitutionalism to be the highest form of justice on earth. Russia in contrast seemed to him a den of injustice. "The country is a hotbed of discontent," he declared. "What keeps things under a lid is the tsar's unlimited authority and the secret police. How long can they go on oppressing their people this way?"

He continued, "Just as the tsar has ownership over the Russian people, he keeps an iron grip on subject states." By "subject states," Utsunomiya meant Poland and Finland, both of which longed for independence and wanted someday to be free of Russia's iron grip. "The November Uprising in 1830 is an example. The Poles revolted and at one point even established an independent government, but Russia sent in a large force and crushed the Polish revolutionary army, taking Warsaw. Afterward, the tsar refused to recognize Polish self-government and put Poland under his direct control. That's how it stands to this day."

The Poles, though a Slavic people, felt superior to Russians, Utsunomiya explained, since historically they themselves had absorbed advanced culture through Germany and transmitted it to Russia. Though holding Russians in contempt, they lost their country to Russia's superior military power and were brought to their knees, smoldering with discontent. Since then, the Polish independence movement had gone underground.

"Finland's case is even sadder," he said. Finland had been ceded to Russia barely a hundred years before. At first, the tsar granted Finns a Western parliamentary style of government, something not recognized in Russia proper, but then Alexander III, the present tsar's father, decided not to confirm Finland's special status. The present tsar had gone further and suspended Finland's right of self-rule and its constitution. Now he was sending a governor general to impose order, so a Finnish independence movement had flared into life.

"Independence activists in Poland and Finland are joining hands with revolutionary groups inside Russia," concluded Utsunomiya. "The fuse that will ignite revolution in Russia lies there, in the outer block."

*   *   *

Akashi Motojirō is a rather peculiar character whom we met before in passing. He was born in the Fukuoka domain. "Academy students back then were sons of impoverished samurai families, fleeing the provinces," observed Makino Kiyohito, his classmate at the Army Academy. "None of us was fortunate enough to have his tuition sent from home."

In that respect, Akashi was the same as the Akiyama brothers. The student body at the Army Academy, where living expenses and tuition were fully paid, consisted of bright young men seeking a way out of straitened circumstances. Strictly speaking, whether any of them were happy to be joining the military is questionable. Indeed, judging from the entrance examination and selection process, whether all of them were terribly bright is questionable. After the Russo-Japanese War, when Japan's governmental systems were well established, government schools had their pick of the country's brightest and best, but in early Meiji only those few who had ever heard of the academy sat for its examination. The selection process was naturally lenient, and many successful applicants lacked not just academic ability but social skills.

Akashi Motojirō may have been one of them.

He graduated from the Army Academy in December 1883. Checking class ranks for one term, we find that in French he placed first in a class of twenty-seven, and in Chinese studies and arithmetic he achieved a similarly high standing, while in graphics he did poorly. But Akashi's greatest actual talents lay in painting and mechanical drawing; his imagination and fine technique were far from ordinary. The best spy is the one with the best imagination, they say, and perhaps Akashi's talent for graphics is where his imagination showed best. His grades were so poor because the paper was always black from grimy finger marks and snivel. Teachers graded largely on neatness of execution, so it's not surprising that he did so poorly. Despite his poor showing in graphics, he put his heart into it.

For a soldier, he had no athletic ability to speak of. In footraces, he always came in last, and he was a terrible gymnast. He had no clothes sense and was incapable of good grooming. Yoshifuru was like that too, but Akashi was far worse. Starting from the time he was a student until he became an army general, he never changed. His pockets always had holes in them, his uniform was often missing a button or torn, his scabbard was generally rusty. After the Russo-Japanese War, someone like him would have had little chance of entering the Army Academy, and even if he did get in would have struggled to keep up. Akashi got by because of the freewheeling mood of early Meiji.

The reader may recall that after the war, Akashi called on army commander Yamagata Aritomo at his home and became so engrossed in explaining an idea that he wet his pants, continuing to do so without realizing it until the puddle spread across the floor and got the commander's feet wet. Even then, he went right on talking. A personality so strange would be totally unacceptable in an age when order was well established.

* * *

Akashi entered the Army Staff College in January 1887, several years after Yoshifuru. He learned battle tactics from Major Meckel for only a brief time, mostly studying under Meckel's successor, Major Wildenberg. By the time he came along, the faculty was largely Japanese. During his sojourn, all the teachers but Wildenberg were Japanese, and many would later head combat operations for the Manchurian Army during the Russo-Japanese War. Kodama Gentarō taught military science and military formation, while tactics were taught by Iguchi Shōgo (Shizuoka), later General Headquarters chief of staff. Others on the faculty were Ōshima Hisanao (Akita), commanding officer of the Ninth Division; Ōsako Naotoshi (Kagoshima), commanding officer of the Seventh Division; and Kigoshi Yasutsuna (Ishikawa), commanding officer of the Fifth Division.

There were eight in Akashi's class. Utsunomiya Tarō, future coordinator of intelligence operations in Great Britain, was one class below him. After graduation, Akashi's duties were concerned for a while with the troops, and then he reported to the General Staff. He resembled Yoshifuru in maintaining deep ties with his former domain and lived in a row house on the grounds of the Kuroda family's residence, just as if he were a samurai in the Fukuoka feudal domain ruled by the Kuroda clan.

"He was an odd chap. He had a pet cat, and when he came home he'd throw his cap in its general direction. The cat knew the routine and would curl up in the cap and go to sleep. In the morning, he'd shoo the cat away, put the cap back on his head, and set out." This description of the then First Lieutenant Akashi's behavior from someone living in the Kuroda residence at the same time explains why his hat was always covered in cat hair.

After that, Akashi was sent to study in Germany, so the senior officers must have thought highly of him. He had a passion for languages. While he was in Germany he immersed himself in the study of German. In 1901, he was sent to Paris as military attaché, so the army evidently saw something special in his talents. Just as he had done in Berlin, he buried himself in studying the language immediately after he arrived. He concentrated so hard he sometimes literally forgot to eat or sleep.

"Recently I've started brushing my teeth," he wrote in a letter to Japan. "This isn't the old me. I've become quite the civilized gentleman."

In Paris, he went to a party attended by commissioned officers from many countries. "The countenance of a fool" is how he described himself in a poem, and it was true: in such surroundings he was lackluster.

"Do you speak German, sir?" a German officer beside him inquired, addressing him in French.

When Akashi replied that he could barely manage French, the officer promptly ignored him, turned to a Russian officer on his other side, and began discussing top-secret matters in German. Akashi took mental notes on every detail of the conversation.

The following year, in 1902, the army sent Akashi to Russia as military attaché. Clearly, they expected him to engage in espionage. In the capital of St. Petersburg, just as he had done in Germany and France, Akashi no sooner arrived than he shut himself up in a rented room, devoting himself to language acquisition.

Russo-Japanese relations were deteriorating, and a great debate raged over whether to fight or stay out of war. Akashi composed the following poem:

> Cover my ears to others' debate over war with Japan.
> Barring the gate, I just turn myself into a student,
> Look forward at leisure to great success.
> For now I celebrate this, my fortieth spring.

This poem was written on New Year's Day in 1903, the year he turned forty. As he says in the poem, he distanced himself from the swirling debate and did nothing but study Russian. His language tutor was a young university student named Braun. Akashi's progress was rapid, and after seven or eight months he could handle everyday conversation without difficulty.

Akashi's Russian tutor also taught him a great deal about Russia's malcontents. Whatever country he went to, Akashi took care not only to learn the language but to acquire an objective grasp of the country's history.

Earlier, back in London, Utsunomiya had expounded to him on Russian despotism, offering an analysis of the status quo informed by historical context. Akashi listened in silence without interjecting an opinion. The view of Russia Akashi acquired in the short period from his arrival to the outbreak of war was exceptional for a Japanese of his time. He summarized his observations in a lengthy essay entitled "Russian History" and sent it to the General Staff in 1906, after the war was over. Written in fine, succinct prose, the essay shows him to be a master stylist. This was the first brief history of Russia ever penned by a Japanese, and you'd be hard pressed to find a better one even now.

"The territory of the Russian Empire is unique in its vastness, and its history is uniquely strange." The essay opens with this conclusion and goes on to spell out in detail how Russian history differs qualitatively from the histories of Western European countries. Akashi termed pure Russians "original Slavs" and wrote that they did not establish the basis of their independence until the late sixteenth century, or, in terms of Japanese history, the end of the Ashikaga period. The Romanov dynasty was established only 294 years ago, he went on, and its history was one of despotism and conspiracy.

Akashi also summed up the dissident parties in contemporary Russia and wrote about their leaders. Even if he himself did not come out and say so in as many words, anyone reading his essay comes to see that the pillagers of Russian land and oppressors of the Russian people were the tsar and his court, the ultimate source of all political evil in Russia. This was the country's sober reality.

*   *   *

Just before war broke out, Kodama Gentarō in Tokyo cabled secret orders to Akashi in St. Petersburg. While there is no way now to know the details, there is no mistaking the gist: "Incite revolution in Russia." Before hostilities broke out, Akashi had filed exhaustive reports on unrest in Russian society and deep anti-Russian sentiment in outlying states, frequently presenting the opinion that if subversive elements were given financial support, Russia would probably collapse from within or, if not collapse, then at least lose the ability to wage war in the Far East.

At some point, Kodama decided to let Akashi go ahead, and later he had Nagaoka Gaishi send him that one million yen we've already discussed, as revolutionary capital. Kodama's plan of operations depended heavily on strategic factors, including Japan's policy toward the United States (enlisting American sympathy), espionage, and inciting revolution.

As long as the battlefield was to be in Manchuria, Kodama wanted to get China on Japan's side and use battlefield espionage to maximum advantage. To woo China, he went after Yuan Shikai, a man of enormous influence in the Qing dynasty. He knew Yuan Shikai's views on Russia from intelligence reports obtained by the General Staff Office. Yuan was quite friendly to Japan, believing that if Russia won the war, its ambition to annex land in the Far East would be unstoppable. "If the Russian Empire is victorious," he once told a Japanese military attaché, "China will be destroyed. That is why, in the event of war between Russia and Japan, I am prepared to do all I can to assist you."

The man Yuan Shikai most trusted was Aoki Nobuzumi, an artillery colonel from Miyazaki Prefecture. Formerly a classmate of Yoshifuru's at the Army Academy, Aoki was still a colonel at the outbreak of war since he never attended the Army Staff College. He was an expert on China who had been close to Yuan Shikai since 1897. In 1899, when Aoki was military attaché at the Japanese legation in Beijing, Yuan had made a point of asking him to draw up a basic text for the Chinese military forces.

After that, Aoki returned to Japan. Before the war, he commanded an artillery regiment, and he was determined to go to the front as head of an artillery unit once hostilities were underway. One day on the eve of war, Kodama called at Aoki's Tokyo home in Nembutsuzaka, Ichigaya. Kodama wore civilian attire and seated himself on the veranda. "I have no doubt you want to go to war as a soldier, but I have an assignment for you that is a hundred times more important." He sent Aoki to be with Yuan Shikai in Tianjin.

Around the time that Kodama called on Aoki in Ichigaya, he wired Akashi Motojirō in St. Petersburg, directing him to take up a secret assignment.

* * *

Before the war, Akashi accomplished very little.

Since he had been ordered to St. Petersburg just as Japan's relations with Russia were turning ugly, as military attaché, he ought to have acted quickly to forward intelligence on the Russian military situation to Tokyo. That was his duty. Basically, however, he had no talent for spying.

Neither was he a popular figure on the Russian social scene the way Hirose Takeo of the navy had been when he was stationed in St. Petersburg. With the war only a couple of years off, Akashi was unable to make even one friend among Russia's influential aristocrats.

His failure was not for lack of trying. He dreamed of contacting a Russian noblewoman—a spy fancy so rudimentary that it seems childish. With that in mind, he strove to accept every formal invitation to a ball or other social gathering; however, no noblewoman was enough of a free spirit to be attracted to the stumpy, badly dressed, unprepossessing figure he cut.

Kodama Gentarō saw something in Akashi, but Major General Nagaoka Gaishi, who became vice chief of the General Staff at the start of the war, later reminisced: "Akashi's bearing and looks were quite odd. I must say I never thought he'd turn out to be so capable." Nagaoka was known as a pretty poor judge of character, so perhaps this lack of insight should come as no surprise. "One million yen was a huge sum of money back then," he said. "I just sent it to him as an experiment, thinking, let's see what he can do."

Not even Kurino Shin'ichirō, then the minister to Russia, was able to read Akashi. Shortly before the war began, he notified the Foreign Ministry in Tokyo of his desire to set up an able spy. Send me the necessary capital, he meant, but got no reply. On the literal eve of war, Tokyo inquired if he had someone in mind over there, but by then Kurino was in flight from St. Petersburg and finding a spy was the last thing on his mind, so he let it drop. He had no idea that Akashi, who was constantly at his side, would play such an unprecedented role as spy, nor of course did he realize that Akashi had already received secret orders from Kodama.

With the opening of hostilities, the Japanese legation in St. Petersburg was vacated on February 8, 1904. The entire staff headed for Stockholm. Relocating there for the duration of the war was Kurino's idea.

"In Stockholm, information will be plentiful," Kurino assured Akashi, and Akashi too had high expectations. But Kurino was fooling himself, and Akashi's spy instincts weren't great. Sweden, although an independent country, feared Russian aggression as if Russia were a crouching tiger, and Russian authorities kept as close tabs on Stockholm's government organs as on their own. The Russians certainly were not going to tolerate any Japanese spying. All this became clear after the legation staff arrived.

*   *   *

Back in the St. Petersburg legation, when Akashi had first heard reports of the rupture of diplomatic relations between Japan and Russia, he felt suddenly awakened as if he'd "heard a cock crow to announce daybreak." That same day, he expressed his emotions in a poem:

In the city at night I hear a cock crow
Kicking my pillow aside, I stand at my window in moonlight
The dream of leading an army at the Yalu:
One clear sword stroke will slay the leviathan.

On the way to the Swedish capital, some of the civil officials of the legation expressed doubt: "We can never win against a great country like this. Japan acted rashly."

Akashi, however, thought the war was winnable, depending on how they went about it. That's because the more he learned about Russia's internal situation, the more he realized the depth of popular resentment of the corruption and despotism of Russian officialdom. Fan that resentment, he thought, and the tsarist regime would crumble from within. In his grasp of Russian affairs, he was far ahead of the civil officials.

Indeed, he thought there was no other way for Japan to win. But he told no one of his resolution, least of all Minister Kurino, who merely had a vague understanding that Akashi was staying on in Europe to gather Russian intelligence. But Kurino was skeptical of what Akashi could accomplish without an assistant.

To begin with, another military attaché in the legation had served as Akashi's assistant, a lieutenant colonel named Shiota Takeo who was a long-term resident of Russia and spoke the language fluently. Ever since Akashi took up his appointment, Shiota had done the actual spying. When the war started, Shiota said that he hadn't been able to take part in any campaign in the earlier war against Qing China and didn't want to miss his chance again. Since he objected to remaining any longer in Europe, Akashi granted him his wish. Shiota's departure for the battlefield in the Far East would leave Akashi on his own, but he felt confident that he didn't need Shiota's help. Shiota had a better command of Russian but no eye for strategy; all he was really good for was gathering intelligence. For the grand scheme Akashi had in mind, he would be no use.

In the train en route to Stockholm, Akashi kept to himself. He only exchanged a few words with Secretary Akizuki Satsuo, a new friend, remarking, "Whether revolution will come to Russia or not, I don't know. But the trees in the forest are dry as tinder. A lighted match could start a forest fire, that much is certain." Akizuki, a man of sharp wits, guessed that Akashi was mulling over a wild idea.

* * *

Stockholm, the capital of the kingdom of Sweden, had another Japanese legation. At the time, the Japanese minister to Russia served concurrently as minister to Sweden, so for Kurino Shin'ichirō, going there was like going to an annex of his own office.

When the train bearing the diplomatic party pulled into Stockholm Station, a crowd of distinguished-looking men and soldiers filled the platform. Kurino was apprehensive, wondering what it could mean. On learning that the crowd had gathered to welcome them, he and his entourage were astonished.

"The tiny eastern country of Japan has declared war on the Russian Empire." When this was reported, the Swedish people first doubted their ears, then marveled at Japanese courage, and ended by quietly supporting them.

Throughout its history, of course, Sweden had an unending fear of Russian aggression. One hundred years before, Russia had invaded Finland and still occupied the land adjacent to Sweden's northern border. With no way of knowing when the Russians might come storming across that border, Swedish foreign policy was centered on fear. The Swedes were astounded by Japan's declaration of war on Russia, and since they knew from painful experience how formidable the Russians were, they could not help taking a personal interest in what would now become of Japan.

It so happened that the Swedish king Oscar II had just arrived at the station, on the way to his countryside palace. He was, of course, well acquainted with Kurino and summoned him to his royal room in the station. When Kurino came in, the king got up and gripped him firmly by the hand. "I will not say anything about these events for the time being," the king said, continuing to shake his hand. "I will say nothing, but I think you know my heart."

Though moved to be spoken to in this way by a king, Kurino had no idea how to respond. Unable to conceal his emotion, he wept. Then he quickly sent for Akashi in order to present him to the king.

Akashi came in. He was slightly stoop-shouldered, the knees of his trousers were worn, and his features, perhaps because of his combined beard and moustache, gave him the air of a mixed-blood Tatar, like those that could be seen in Russia.

"This is Colonel Akashi." As Kurino presented him, Akashi made a deep bow.

The king hesitated slightly, but finally extended his hand as he had done to Kurino, and Akashi grasped it awkwardly.

Kurino probably presented Akashi to the king in hopes that this might be of some help in Akashi's espionage operations. Akashi received no particular words from the Swedish king, but the royal handshake was so strong that he almost yelped in pain. That gave him a good idea of where the king's sympathies lay.

* * *

The king wasn't the person Akashi really wanted to meet in Stockholm. He was actually hoping to make the acquaintance of Jonas Castrén, head of the Constitutional Party of Finland and chief of the opposition, a man whose name Akashi had heard from his St. Petersburg tutor Braun.

"Last year," Braun had said, referring to the year 1903, "the tsar high-handedly revoked Finland's constitution and took away the constitutional rights of the Finnish people, instead giving unlimited dictatorial power to the Russian governor general." In response, there were subterranean rumblings among the people as the desire arose for national autonomy. At the apex of all the activists stood Castrén, the leader of the underground movement.

"Castrén. . ." Akashi muttered the name to himself over and over, memorizing it, and went to Stockholm with that name as his only asset. He had no elaborate plan of the kind one reads about in spy stories, nor did he have any flair for derring-do.

When he arrived at Stockholm Station, he selected a young interpreter from the legation staff who had come out in force to welcome them. "I'd like you to go on an errand for me." He pulled out a piece of paper with Castrén's name and address, and handed the official a letter containing this basic message: "Colonel Akashi Motojirō of the Japanese Army wants to meet you. Please name a time and place." He didn't bother to choose an appropriate go-between, much less use an alias. It was an approach ill befitting a spy.

"That was all I could do," Akashi commented later on. Rather than stage some elaborate ploy, he chose to make his move suddenly, embracing his purpose and jumping right into the opposition camp. His purpose was to ask this senior Finnish militant to spy for Japan. Castrén would no doubt be dumbfounded.

"I had to ask someone to spy for me, but I had no idea who might be suitable for such a dangerous assignment. There was no way I could know. All I could do was shut my eyes and jump." That was Akashi's position.

He left the station building. Minister Kurino went by carriage, but Akashi, intending to walk to the legation, set out on the sidewalk. By the time he arrived, he figured his reply would be waiting for him. If it contained an invitation to meet right away, he was prepared to go as he was, still in his travel clothes.

This was Akashi's third visit to Stockholm, but as he had never lived there he didn't know his way around. Several times along the way, he stopped a passerby to ask, "Which way is the Japanese legation?"

* * *

There were many Finnish refugees in town. On his way to the legation, Akashi was stopped by an old gentleman whose complexion had the pink tint of a European, but whose face was rather flat with a jutting chin—an apparent legacy from the Ural-Altaic tribesmen who inhabited northern Europe long ago. One glance told Akashi that he was a Finn.

"Are you a Japanese soldier?" the old man asked in Russian, peering into Akashi's face. Four years before, Russia had made Russian the official language of administration in Finland. Akashi was in uniform.

"Yes, I am." He deliberately answered in French. The old man immediately quit speaking Russian and switched over to French. At the same time, his face brightened so much he looked like a different person.

"I read in the paper that Japan declared war against the Russian Empire. As fellow Asians and fellow sufferers under Russian oppression, we pray for your victory in the struggle ahead."

"Thank you. My name is Akashi. Who might you be?"

The old man shook his head sadly. "I'm sorry to say I cannot tell you my name. Stockholm is full of agents of Russia's secret police. All I can say is I am a nameless citizen." And he was gone.

Akashi told himself that the stranger probably was a nameless citizen, just as he said, and therefore believable. He sensed that the Swedes were extremely sympathetic to the Japanese, that they felt a kind of esprit de corps.

The word *kyōro*, "mighty Russia," was then in frequent use in Japan. No comparable expression was used in reference to Great Britain or the United States. Only Russia was described this way, probably because of the Russian Army's image of invincible strength. Added to that was the fact that Russia used its military for naked aggression. Like Poland, Finland was pinned helplessly by the claws and fangs of the Russian bear. Military rebellion was doomed, as Poland's example showed. The only way to escape Russia's clutches was for tsarism to fall.

That an unknown little country in the Far East had dared to take on "mighty Russia" in battle impressed the nation of Finland more deeply than any other nation in the world. Japan was attempting what they had tried and failed to do, so there was intense interest in the outcome of the war. Given this background, Akashi was optimistic that his work would succeed.

* * *

At the Japanese legation, Akashi waited for the interpreter to return.

"Akashi, what are you doing?" Kurino called out as he passed by. Akashi was sitting with a vacant look on his face. Although a fire was crackling away in the stove, he had not removed his coat.

"Um. . .fishing." Akashi said this without a smile.

Kurino let it drop and went away, but later when he heard what Akashi had been waiting for he was appalled. He believed diplomacy meant obtaining the good offices of a mediator (a person or a country). Akashi was attempting to meet a Finnish refugee without benefit of introduction.

"Good as he was, Akashi was bound to fail in Stockholm." In later years, Kurino, a sharp-witted man, made this characteristic assessment. True, Akashi's attempt did fail. Yet it was not a complete failure.

At length, the interpreter returned. "I met the Finnish refugee named Castrén, but. . ." He lowered his voice. ". . .he wouldn't take the letter. Said he didn't know any Japanese officer named Akashi and had no reason to accept a letter from him. Said there must be some mistake. . . ."

So my fish got away—that was all Akashi thought. He didn't lose heart. Anyone who went fishing without checking out his fishing spot or seeking the services of a guide could hardly expect to attract the fish he wanted just by throwing his hook in the water hit-or-miss.

Only Akizuki knew the substance of what Akashi was doing. He came up to him and whispered in his ear: "Don't give up."

"I won't," murmured Akashi. "Finns and Japanese face the same enemy— the supremely cruel tsarist regime. Castrén knows that. When he got my letter, he must have felt some inner agitation."

"Absolutely," said Akizuki, who found these words moving. "And if we lose this war, Korea and we face the same sad fate as Finland and Poland. The Finns understand our position and our hearts better than anyone."

Although Akashi failed to establish contact with Castrén, he did stir up a reaction in a different quarter. It was a bit like trying to catch a sea bream and failing, but then getting an even bigger quarry to take the bait.

* * *

At the legation, Akashi took off his uniform and changed into civilian clothes. For the next two years, he wouldn't wear his uniform again, letting it hang unused in his closet.

"All Akashi left with us was a couple of uniforms, one for winter and one for summer," recalled Akizuki.

After changing, Akashi set out for a small hotel that he intended to make his regular lodging. When he had settled on a room, he wrote distinctly in

the ledger: "Citizenship: the Empire of Japan. Name: Akashi Motojirō."
Definitely not a typical spy, he never took the precaution of using an alias.

His reasoning is unclear. As a spy, he had to accept the high likelihood
of being secretly killed by Russia's political police, one of the most advanced
of such organizations in the world. Akashi understood this completely, yet
he had a soldier's professional instinct to die with glory. Ending up an
anonymous corpse in an obscure corner of Europe must have been an
unbearable prospect to him. His work was in that sense heartbreaking.

"What you did is a major reason we won the war," an army comrade later
said to him in praise.

Akashi instantly bridled. "What great service did I perform? Tell me, in
the voluminous history of the war edited by the General Staff, is there even
one line that mentions my name?"

His comrade was taken aback.

Those twisted feelings of Akashi's suggest that he wanted his body to be
identified by his real name. As long as his body was identifiable, then, no
matter where or how he died, the Japanese legation or consulate would surely
receive notification.

The sky was still light. Having been rebuffed by Castrén, Akashi went
over by his hotel window, planning what he might do next, sat down, and
looked out on the city known as the "Florence of the north." The sky was
overcast, and fresh snow was starting to pile up on the old snow on the street.

Someone knocked at his door. He got up and opened it to find a gentleman
he had never seen before standing there. He saw expensive-looking fur
earmuffs, a rich beard, impressively broad shoulders.

"I run a law office here in town." The caller introduced himself politely
in French.

Akashi thought he had never heard a man's voice of such beauty. The
man's face had various characteristics marking him as Finnish. Akashi
invited him inside and shut the door.

The visitor looked at Akashi, sizing him up. Then, apparently having made
up his mind, he took an envelope from his breast pocket and held it out.
Akashi opened it to find a slip of paper with the following words written in
blue ink: "Castrén's close friend, Konni Zilliacus."

When Akashi realized the identity of the person who had come calling
in this unorthodox way, deep down he was surprised. He knew of the
existence of an underground independence movement called the Finnish
Active Resistance Party. He knew also that it was a far more radical group
than the Constitutional Party led by old militant Jonas Castrén. Its leader
had come to call in person.

Apparently, Zilliacus looked at Akashi and immediately judged him trustworthy. Such insight was a powerful weapon to the leader of an underground movement.

What attracted Zilliacus was the very simplicity of the way Akashi had tried to approach a leader of the Finnish underground like Castrén. A man of such heedless, point-blank style might turn tail and run in case of danger without taking responsibility for his actions, but after looking Akashi in the eye Zilliacus was satisfied on that score.

"A while ago, you sent a messenger to Castrén with a letter. Who told you where to find him?"

Akashi's reply was simple. "A young university student named Braun, in St. Petersburg. He was my Russian tutor, and he also gave me a sense of the state of the revolution."

Just like that, with the ease of a frog swallowing a fly, Zilliacus took Akashi at his word. He had the swift decisiveness of a party leader. "What do you want?" he asked.

"I'm an old acquaintance of the pure Russian Lenin. I know no other fighters but him. Japan, though a weak country, is now giving its all to rise up against Russian imperialism. Please know that all Japanese, even our women and children, are your comrades. I want to get to know the discontented of every persuasion. When I find people I consider trustworthy, I want to support their revolutionary operations."

And so, Akashi went on, he wanted the revolutionaries to hold a major conference so that he could gain a number of comrades at once—a self-seeking request.

But Zilliacus nodded enthusiastically. "The war is already underway," he said. "Whether we seek independence or revolution, now is a golden opportunity." He offered to take Akashi to meet Castrén in the morning, adding, "But this hotel is dangerous. I will take you somewhere else, so be waiting out front tomorrow morning at eleven. A carriage will pull up alongside the hotel entrance. Get in right away. Tomorrow there will be snow."

"Tomorrow there will be snow"—by this, he meant that the hood of the carriage would be pulled down as protection, a good way of avoiding people's eyes.

Akashi's best ally throughout his two years of activism was this man Konni Zilliacus. Had he not won over Zilliacus, he could never have accomplished even half of what he set out to do in Europe.

* * *

The carriage started off. Not only was the hood down, but the small windows were continually pelted by heavy snowflakes. Unable to see the scenery outside, Akashi had no idea where they were or which way they were headed.

At some point, the carriage entered a squalid section of town and stopped before a five-story building. Akashi and Zilliacus went inside and climbed a dim flight of stairs. It took a long time to reach the top.

If Zilliacus, whom he had barely met, turned out to be a member of the Russian police, death might well be waiting at the top of the stairs. But Akashi slowly mounted the stairs, the expression on his face unchanged—what he himself had called "the countenance of a fool." Rather than a quick-witted senior officer of Japan, he kept that look of a Tatar, this time one from a remote mountain village on his first-ever trip to the big city. Akashi's overall bearing reassured Zilliacus that he had not erred in telling the older Castrén, "Akashi is a man we can trust. You should meet him."

Akashi also benefited from a certain view of the Japanese that had gained global currency. People around the world had been stunned when, while fighting in the First Sino-Japanese War and the Boxer Rebellion, the Japanese Army had not engaged in pillaging, an activity endemic to war. The Japanese had been if anything overly scrupulous in adhering to the rules of war, and legends of Japanese samurai that had spread among the educated class made Akashi seem even more trustworthy.

Castrén was an old man who looked at first glance like the genial patriarch of a wealthy family, always smiling and saying little. It was hard to believe that this was the same person whom Russia's political police feared like a wolf or a jackal.

What surprised Akashi even more than Castrén himself was the photograph hanging on the wall of this secret room. Straight ahead was Castrén's own deportation order, signed by Nicholas II. By hanging it up so prominently, he fed and nurtured his hatred of the tsar day by day. The determination this showed reminded Akashi of the Chinese son who "slept on firewood and ate bears' gall bladders" till he had his revenge.

Yet more surprising was a portrait of Japan's Emperor Meiji hanging on another wall.

"We believe that the emperor of Japan will save us," said Castrén. The scene suggested that what drove this old man to carry out such dangerous work was not so much new social thought as, ultimately, his desire for his people's independence.

Zilliacus was the leader of a far more radical group than Castrén, but he paid full courtesy to the grand old man. He thoughtfully arranged for Akashi to meet him, knowing that once Akashi had earned Castrén's trust, he would be spared unnecessary suspicion when encountering other dissidents.

* * *

Akashi talked volubly. He clarified his intent to support revolution and independence, and on that point both men accepted him completely. Akashi's other mission was military investigation. He wanted to know about Russian military affairs and strategy. This was spying, pure and simple. "But I haven't got what it takes to be a spy." He said this with an air of such perplexity that Castrén laughed.

"Me either," he said. "Can't help you there."

"That's why I need somebody to move around for me. Can you introduce me to someone?" Akashi showed his hand, holding nothing back. He admitted the helplessness he felt at having to conduct espionage in Europe on his own.

"But military spying would be detrimental to us." Though Zilliacus would later cooperate, at this point he was reluctant. His nationalist and revolutionary campaigns alone had Russian police spies crowding in so closely that he and his operatives were constantly on the alert, scarcely able to make a move. Taking up military spying under those conditions would give the police an opening and gravely impair their current activities. His thinking was characteristic of the leader of a radical faction.

Though Castrén led a more moderate group than Zilliacus, now he was the more impassioned. "That is so. But if our main intent is to bring down tsarist Russia, then we must use every means at our disposal, miss no opportunity, spare no effort. Colonel, I am happy to cooperate with you."

Then and there he picked up the phone and called Swedish army headquarters. Akashi was amazed. Castrén, a longtime fighter for Finnish independence, had pull even in the Swedish military establishment. Come to think of it, as an independent country, the kingdom of Sweden was under even more intense threat from Russia than Finland, a subject nation, and that pressure was borne directly by Swedish army headquarters.

In every country it had harmed, Russia was intensely hated. This situation, so fortunate for Akashi, was made evident to him by the phone call taking place before his eyes.

Castrén asked to speak to Captain Aminov of the General Staff. He went straight to the point, and the matter was quickly settled.

The phone call soon bore fruit. Captain Aminov consulted with his comrade First Lieutenant Klingerstierna and sent Second Lieutenant Bergen to Russia to spy for Akashi.

A matter of such critical importance was settled an hour after meeting with Castrén. This was a giant step forward. Akashi did not accomplish his mission by his own ability; rather, it would be more correct to say that conditions were already in place for him to accomplish his mission and only awaited his arrival on the scene.

* * *

In short, the foundations for Akashi Motojirō's spy network and his incitement of revolution were laid in Castrén's Stockholm hideout.

Strictly speaking, Akashi never once used inflammatory language that constituted true "incitement." The closest he came was when he said, "Japan does not want to become another Poland or Finland. We have no desire to see Tokyo become Warsaw or Helsinki, with a Russian governor general installed in Tokyo's Imperial Palace."

As a Russian expert, Akashi knew perfectly well what would happen if Russia won the war. The Korean Peninsula would become Russian territory. Japan would certainly become a Russian dependency. To demonstrate its commanding presence, the empire would build an imposing residence in Tokyo for its governor general, just as it had done in Helsinki. And, to realize its long-cherished desire for a harbor in the Pacific, it would undoubtedly build great military installations in Yokosuka and Sasebo. The constitution would be suspended, and the National Diet building would become headquarters for Russia's political police. Ever since the latter days of the Tokugawa period, Russia had had its eye on Tsushima, where it would no doubt build a great fortress to guard the entrance to the Sea of Japan, and a prison for political prisoners with execution grounds where condemned criminals would face a firing squad.

One other magnificent edifice would surely go up in Tokyo. Along with its army, the Russian Empire used its national religion, the Russian Orthodox Church, as a tool of absolutism. Just as there was an enormous cathedral of this heretical (to the Finns) religion in a central square in Helsinki, so the grandest temple in the east would sit right in Hibiya Park.

When Akashi studied Russian, he learned that the name of the eastern city of Vladivostok meant "rule the east." Now it occurred to him that the *vostok* or "eastern outpost" of the Russian Empire might well end up being Tokyo.

So whenever Akashi met with any member of an anti-Russian group, that was all he ever said. People from countries that had already suffered a Russian invasion invariably responded, "Japan mustn't share our fate. If Japan should turn the tables and win, Russia's grip on us would weaken, and we would be able to escape our present bonds." They showed a deep sense of solidarity with Japan.

He said the same thing to pure Russian subversives. They, too, identified with what he said. Many responded sympathetically: "We are ruled by a despotic tsar, and we suffer more than the people in protectorates. We fully understand Japan's fears." Even without making speeches filled with fiery language, Akashi was able to bond with his listeners and establish common interests.

* * *

Akashi had one extraordinary talent. Although he personally was indifferent to money, he had a remarkable gift for keeping track of receipts and disbursements. This was a great asset in his operations.

His meticulousness regarding public funds is evident in the careful expense records he kept as he put to use the million yen he received from Tokyo. He returned to Tokyo with a balance of two hundred seventy thousand yen, every bit of which he handed back to Nagaoka Gaishi, vice chief of the General Staff. "Given the nature of his work, there was no need for him to return any excess, but he gave it all back with receipts and a full account of expenditures." Nagaoka made this comment after Akashi's death.

To be precise, there was a discrepancy of one hundred rubles. This, however, was because on his way home, as he was counting bills in a train lavatory, he carelessly dropped one, and it blew away.

In Stockholm, Akashi consulted with Castrén and Zilliacus over how the money for agents and spies should be paid. With a kind of boyish innocence, he placed full confidence in these two men and asked them about every aspect of the operations. This virtue of his (as it should be seen) enabled the work to proceed smoothly.

"I know just the fellow," Castrén was quick to reply. A comrade of his named Lindberg, one of the top business magnates in Stockholm, could be entrusted with the money, and would handle all transfers and disbursements as proxy.

Because he had faith in the two men, Akashi put his faith in Lindberg and accepted the recommendation.

This was a success. Later when he met Lindberg, the merchant said, "I will act as your proxy without reimbursement. If I am put to death by a Russian firing squad as a result, I don't care. My working on behalf of Japan will weaken the Russian Empire and is in itself an act of utmost patriotism toward Sweden and Finland." Through Akashi, Lindberg became a great Japanophile, and later the Japanese government made him an honorary consul.

Through these contacts, Akashi met more and more underground activists, as well as members of the Russian armed forces who supported revolution. He gave them assignments and funds. Eventually, he also used professional spies as they were more cost-effective, commenting, "Professional spies who had only mercenary motives were far more useful than those who worked out of a sense of moral obligation."

It amazed Akashi that in Europe, human relationships were established by contract. Because of this, he said no one he gave money to ever cheated him.

* * *

As we have seen, Akashi based his operations in Stockholm. But Stockholm was a small town. Also it was infiltrated by Russian police, making it difficult to do much there. Moreover, Swedish news coverage lagged. The papers carried articles that had appeared a day or two earlier in the capitals of Berlin, Paris, and London.

"If I don't get away from here, I'll be trapped like a bird in a cage," Akashi thought as he wrote to Nagaoka Gaishi in Tokyo. He expressed a desire to travel from one European center to another. "But I'm grateful for Stockholm," he wrote. "Here I established the basis of my work and gained leads for the future."

Akashi put so much energy into this project that barely five days after setting foot in Stockholm Station he arranged a secret meeting of Finnish nationalists. Naturally, the meeting was held through the good offices of Castrén and Zilliacus, but as a result Akashi was able to become acquainted with everyone. Castrén and Zilliacus went around and spoke to each patriot individually, introducing them to Akashi and urging them to help him in his work. They each vowed in fervent tones that they would do so, many of them adding, "I know someone in the Russian War Ministry." Akashi worked in concert with each one.

One thing that surprised Akashi at this get-together was the beauty of Madame Zilliacus, an American of sparkling charm known as the queen of Stockholm society. After she held out her right hand to Akashi, she dropped her smile and fixed him with an unsociable stare, looking straight into his eyes as she said, "Your purpose is my purpose too." Akashi never forgot that moment as long as he lived.

"Somewhere in Akashi's vicinity there was always a woman." This rumor, later whispered by members of the armed forces, was doubtless inspired in part by the presence of Madame Zilliacus. Akashi, however, had very little to do with women, according to his one-time assistant Shioda Takeo and secretary Akizuki Satsuo. He never so much as went to a brothel.

Akashi met another surprising person at the secret meeting. One elderly gentleman introduced himself as General Grippenberg's younger brother. A baron in exile, he was a leading figure in the Finnish Constitutional Party.

A number of powerful members of revolutionary parties in Russia attended this meeting, among them Prince Khilkov, the younger brother of Russia's Rail Minister Mikhail Khilkov, who was successful in maintaining the

Trans-Siberian Railway. All of them despised tsarist Russia and told Akashi, "We hope Japan will do away with that devil." The evils and corruption of Russian autocracy had not particularly impressed Akashi in St. Petersburg, but in Stockholm he felt the depth of these with every fiber of his being.

*   *   *

A survey of Akashi's activities during the two years of the war shows that he was constantly favored by good luck. To begin with, his gaining the trust of Zilliacus, an activist with a large circle of connections, greatly speeded up his subsequent work. Gaining Zilliacus as an ally was largely coincidental, but we also must assume that Akashi's eye for strategy played a role.

Finland is a small country. Originally, it was not even a "country" but a region of Sweden; later annexed by Russia, it was still bound in those chains at this time. Finland's small size meant that it had no history of unpleasantness with any European nation and so was able to rouse universal sympathy: "Poor little Finland," people said. Finnish nationalists could travel to any country and win the hearts of everyone they met—even conservatives. The advantage of this is clear if you think of the opposite case: Russian revolutionaries, for example, were regarded with leeriness by Western Europeans, who wondered whether the fall of imperial Russia would result in the birth of an even more enormous Russia. Monarchists were wary too, fearful that the effect of Russians toppling tsarism would endanger other empires and monarchies. But no one needed to be on guard against the residents of tiny Finland.

Also Finns took pride in having a history greatly superior to that of tsarist Russia. Theirs was a more Western culture, and in their adoption of constitutional government, a symbol of national progress, they were second only to Great Britain. All this added to their contempt for the Great Power Russia. Their sense of superiority further fueled their discontent.

Akashi's comrade Konni Zilliacus was the very embodiment of that Finnish spirit. "Zilliacus was a respected leader going back to the time of the Nihilists," Akashi commented in later years. "He was intimate with many prominent dissidents and trusted across all national borders and party lines." Having gained a financial supporter in Akashi through the favorable opportunity provided by the Russo-Japanese War, Zilliacus decided to hold a conference for European and Russian opposition parties in order to settle on an anti-Russian course of action. The conference would be held in Paris, a bastion of freedom. Once the decision was made, he took immediate steps to make it happen.

A man of great energy, Zilliacus left Stockholm that spring, walked all around Europe on a four-month speaking tour, and returned to Stockholm with the conference a near reality. Akashi secretly accompanied him and thus was able to get to know prominent revolutionaries all across Europe.

* * *

Here let us sketch in Akashi's activities over the two years.

He stayed in close contact with every opposition party in Poland. One day, Zilliacus said, "Here in Poland there is someone who is a standing member of the Socialist Party. He has a number of aliases, but for now I'll call him Moto." He apparently took this from Akashi's given name of Motojirō. "Moto is saying he would like to call at the Japanese legation in London. It's necessary for you to meet him if we are to vanquish the devil." By "the devil," he meant imperialist Russia.

This conversation took place just as Akashi was preparing to leave for London. Then, one day in London, a Polish man by the name of "Moto" came calling, just as Zilliacus had said he would. He had a ruddy face and a lanky frame, and a Lincolnesque beard. When Akashi invited him to be seated in the reception room of the legation, Moto declined, walked up close to him, and began speaking in heavily accented French about "the terrible plight of Poland." He went on with such force that Akashi's right ear was soon wet with spittle.

True enough, Poland was indeed in a terrible fix. Of all the Russian dependencies, it was the one country (technically no longer a country but a region) where Russian rule was more tyrannical than in Russia itself.

Moto told how the independence movements of 1846 and 1863 had been stamped out with brutal oppression, speaking as if the events had happened only yesterday. "My father was stabbed and killed"—he gestured to his heart—"by the bayonets of Russians who had just entered Warsaw." He added unexpectedly that now his generation faced death by the bayonets of the Japanese Army.

"The Japanese Army isn't in Warsaw!" Akashi shouted back with equal fervor.

"No, it's in Manchuria!" Moto cried. Polish peasants were being conscripted in great numbers, herded into freight cars like swine, and hauled east on the Trans-Siberian Railway. Then he made a startling claim: "When the war began, fifteen percent of the soldiers bearing arms under General Kuropatkin were Polish, not Russian." The statistic was probably inaccurate, yet it was certainly true that large numbers of Poles were being impressed and sent to the front.

He went on: "The draft has become more pervasive, and now the army is thirty percent Polish. It's idiotic that Poles have to swear their loyalty at the front to satisfy the despicable Russians. And why should Poles have to kill Japanese soldiers against whom they bear no grudge? Innocent young Polish lives are being taken by the bayonets of Japanese, for whom we feel only friendship and love. How can these things be? To the Russians, we Poles are swine, existing only to be killed."

Moto spoke at great length. After prefacing his remarks in this fashion, he rambled on interminably. "What did he come here to tell me?" Akashi wondered, still having no idea. But he had encountered many Germans of this propensity during his stay in Germany, and so he listened patiently, knowing from experience that otherwise the speaker would take offense and never get around to stating his business.

Akashi offered him a cigar. The sight of the expensive-looking cigar made Moto flinch.

"I am strongly sympathetic to the movements for revolution and independence," said Akashi, "but I cannot give up cigars. Though Lenin once warned me that I'd have to if I wanted to get along with workers."

Moto's face brightened. "You're a friend of Lenin's?"

Akashi certainly was entitled to call himself that, but he only said modestly, "I would say I am one who understands him."

The matters that Moto finally brought up were staggering.

"The Japanese Army should pass out antiwar leaflets to the Polish soldiers in the Russian Army and urge them to surrender. To that end, they should also distribute tracts about the revolution. And the Japanese should form their own Polish unit." In other words, they should invite Poles serving in the armies of countries other than Russia to join a new unit. "Send me to Tokyo to do it. No one will suspect if I'm allowed to pass myself off as a special correspondent."

"Form a Polish unit?" Akashi found the idea bizarre. He tried to convey by circumlocution that the Japanese Army was well equipped with soldiers and had no need of foreign assistance, but the point did not get through to Moto, who argued forcefully that the benefit to the Japanese Army would be incalculable.

Feeling that he was in over his head, Akashi consulted Japan's ambassador to Britain, Hayashi Tadasu, and left the matter in his hands. Though Hayashi too was amazed at the idea, he also saw that it could be highly effective to have a unit of Polish troops in the Japanese Army urge Polish soldiers in the Russian Army to surrender. He sent a report to Tokyo discussing all these issues.

But Imperial General Headquarters laughed it off. "No matter how desperate our troop strength might be," some argued, "we don't want to ask foreigners for help. That would leave a dark stain on our history." Japanese people of this era were given to grandstanding, and no leaflets urging surrender were ever even printed. Still, Hayashi's report revealed a major internal ailment of the Russian military.

* * *

As Akashi and Zilliacus traveled around southern Europe, calling for a great coalition of dissidents, they received a letter from Nikolai Chaikovsky, one of the great leaders in the early stage of the Russian Revolution.

"He is a pure Russian and a great revolutionary!" In his excitement, Zilliacus cried out in Finnish. He grasped Akashi's right hand in his enormous mitt and shook it three times.

Akashi knew the name Chaikovsky quite well. The fellow's record as a revolutionary went way back, starting thirty-five years earlier when as a university student in St. Petersburg he had formed a group called the "Circle of Chaikovsky." At first he was part of the so-called Narodnik or "Call to the people" campaign and later on joined hands with Prince Kropotkin and did much to spread the revolution, fleeing eventually to the United States, then London. Like other dissident leaders, he believed that the eruption of war between Russia and Japan meant the time was ripe for revolution. Akashi and the rest did not know where Chaikovsky's letter had originated, but they were greatly encouraged to think that this signal from a senior revolutionary meant they were headed in the right direction.

"The Russo-Japanese War above all will provide the opportunity to destroy tsarism," Chaikovsky wrote in the letter. "The Russian tsar and those in his government are devils who pillage the land and torment the people. Generally speaking, those who fight for our happiness are using the national crisis to agitate the nation. Peculiar as this may seem, given the Russian reality, there is no other way."

He also wrote, "Now is the time for the various factions to bury their differences and come together in one great coalition." The revolutionary spirit, leadership, and influence of this veteran revolutionary were extraordinary, and his approval of Zilliacus' plans sped things along.

Akashi was extremely busy. While supporting this campaign, he was, among other things, also planning to sabotage the Trans-Siberian Railway. He was gathering professional rowdies and sending them to Berlin to learn blast techniques under the tutelage of Lieutenant Colonel Tanaka Kōtarō, a former gunner stationed in the Berlin legation. This bomb squad would later sneak into Russia and blow up train tracks around the country, giving the government the jitters. Apart from this psychological effect, the squad's efforts had little practical effect, however, as the Russians were swift to make repairs.

Looking at Akashi's activities during this period, it is evident that even though he was constantly moving about, his three goals of fanning the revolution, conducting military espionage, and blowing up railway installations were pursued systematically, and each organization that he spawned carried out its activities with vigor. His deep pockets were undoubtedly a source of energy, but we can also assume that he himself was a master at setting up organizations.

No Russian-authored history of the revolution mentions Akashi by name. Yet there is no denying that from the time he entered the scene, the revolution was sharply radicalized, with frequent riots and bombings around the country.

"Akashi is scary." Even his supposed allies in the General Staff Office in Tokyo tended to find Akashi a bit weird. It was his personality. He had the eccentricity of any successful person, planning scrupulously to accomplish his goals, working and reworking his plans and not letting slip any chance to execute them; he moved adroitly and drove himself with nearly manic fervor.

Yet we must not overestimate Akashi's abilities. What really allowed him to accomplish so much was the momentum of the times. Abuses had piled up in Russia until the empire itself was a poisonous beast preying on human society both within and without its borders, a circumstance that worked in Akashi's favor. Victims of the Russian Empire were everywhere, in Russia and out, and people of common sense and decency throughout Western Europe sympathized with them and prayed for the aggressor's early demise.

The mood of the times was captured by Charles Seignobos, the greatest historian of the early twentieth century, in the notable comment he made at the Sorbonne. The French government, being allied with Russia, allowed Russia to float loans to pay its war expenses. Seignobos, however, secretly opposed this policy, partly out of sympathy for the hideous plight of the Russian people, but even more so because in his eyes the Russian Empire was doomed to collapse before long.

"Whatever happens," Seignobos warned his students time and again, "you mustn't respond to Russian appeals to underwrite their expenses. You must tell your fathers the same thing, that they must not respond. The reason is simple: if they do, the family fortune will be lost, and the French economy will be thrown into turmoil." He was saying that anyone who lent money to Russia would lose his shirt and predicting by implication that Russia, the debtor, would one day be defunct.

Akashi's work began with picking up on such currents, then harnessing them and getting them to carry him where he wished to go. In this way, he was able to rack up enormous accomplishments, almost more than seems possible for one man. In that sense, his strategic abilities were far and away superior to those of any Japanese general. "Your accomplishments are worth the equivalent of several army divisions." After the war, one of his superiors told him this, but even that evaluation was too low. His contribution was equivalent to that of the entire Manchurian Army or Admiral Tōgō's entire fleet in the Sea of Japan.

* * *

Akashi traveled around frequently, but any time anti-tsar activists wished to contact him, they could do so readily. All they had to do was speak to the Japanese military attaché in London, Berlin, Paris, or Stockholm, and they could get right through to him. Akashi's communications network was so extensive that during his stay in Europe, his whereabouts were known every single day. That fact alone shows what rare abilities he had.

Once, when he was back in his Stockholm hotel, an acquaintance sent word: "I would like you to meet a certain man of the Caucasus. He is a deserter from the Manchurian front, a second lieutenant in the Russian Army."

Akashi waited, wondering skeptically if such a thing could be true. Himself an army man, he knew what the military was like during combat, and he also knew what tight precautions against desertion the Russian Army was taking, with so many conscripted soldiers from dependencies. Besides, Manchuria was awfully far away. When he spoke about the Far East, Akashi did not use the usual Japanese word *kyokutō* but had taken to using the word *zettō* or "absolute east," the literal end of the earth. Between there and Europe lay vast, sparsely inhabited Siberia, forbidding terrain that was difficult to cross on foot. The deserter would have had to make his way on foot, hitching an occasional sleigh ride. The Trans-Siberian Railway had been pressed into war service, so he could not have used it.

Moreover, he was supposed to be an officer on active duty. For such a person to cut out was something that Akashi, himself an officer on active duty in the Japanese Army, could not fathom. Yet based on what he knew, he thought it possible. The deserter was said to be from the Caucasus, which may have had a large Slavic population but nonetheless enjoyed a separate history from Russia. The Caucasus had been annexed and incorporated into the empire as a result of the Russo-Turkish War of 1877–1878, just a quarter of a century before. The feisty people of the Caucasus always looked on imperialist Russia as the enemy, the entire region simmering with discontent.

The second lieutenant showed up. He had an intelligent face, but fear emanated from every pore. His light-blue eyes looked at Akashi warily, as if he might be off like a shot the moment Akashi spoke.

He was wearing a coat. The room was warm, and there was no need for him to be wearing an outdoor coat, but he stood there grasping the collar of the threadbare garment. To help him relax, Akashi addressed him in Russian. "First take off your coat." Reluctantly, the youth did so, and Akashi saw with amazement that he was naked to the waist. That fact spoke volumes about his harrowing escape to Stockholm from the end of the earth.

Normally unflappable, Akashi caught his breath as he looked at the youth wearing trousers but nothing else. "Siberia must have been tough." He offered him a chair, but the youth made no move to sit down. Fortunately, Akashi had a spare shirt and jacket on hand, and when he handed them over the youth smiled for the first time and put the shirt on. But Akashi was on the small side even for a Japanese, and it wasn't enough to cover him up.

Deciding to go shirtless, the youth next struggled to put on the jacket. He managed to get his arms in the sleeves, but they only went as far as his elbows, and the jacket came just halfway down, leaving the small of his back exposed.

Akashi had an idea. "Why not use the shirt to cover your waist?" The youth nodded, and carried out the suggestion without demurring. He seemed good-natured, with an air of childlike innocence and no shadow of anything else. How on earth had he come to desert the field of battle in the Far East and escape here, an adventure more arduous than any undertaken by Marco Polo or Magellan?

"Unless the Russian tsar, the Russian church, and the Russian Army disappear, we of the Caucasus cannot continue to exist." Eyes wide open, the youth began his tale. At the front, soldiers from the Caucasus were always given the most dangerous assignments, forced to die first. Poles were treated the same way. The Russian Empire was using the blood of minority peoples to protect itself and carry out its ambitions.

"The tsar has ambitions in the Far East, and he has oppressed Japanese people, intending to turn them into slaves just as he did us. To escape that fate, Japanese people stood up to Russia with rifles. For us to fight against our Japanese comrades, who might have shared our same fate, is most distressing. How can God forgive the tsar for forcing us to do something so inhuman?"

"You believe in God?" Akashi asked, and the youth replied in a small voice that he did. This was apparently no Marxist, but a vehement ethnic nationalist.

"Give me an order," the youth begged. Barely twenty, he had had the energy to escape but seemed to have no idea what to do next.

"If you want to join the revolutionary movement, I can introduce you to the right people. For now, I'd like to hear about the state of the Russian Army."

"That's why I came," said the youth. "Hear me out." And he proceeded to tell Akashi all he knew about the Far Eastern front. A low-ranking officer was not of course privy to secrets of the high command, but one thing he said struck Akashi as highly significant: the "disease" of the Russian Army was quite serious.

*   *   *

Akashi used many agents. Some were incredibly talented, others not.

Communications in Stockholm Akashi had entrusted to a Lieutenant Colonel Nagao. "That fellow Kuri is a washout," Nagao confided to him one day. Kuri was a code name; neither Nagao nor Akashi knew his real identity, but that posed no obstacle to their operations.

Once Akashi understood that Europeans bound by a financial contract would never betray him, he ceased worrying on that score. However, he was appalled by agents who used large amounts of money with no results. Kuri was one of those.

The man so nicknamed looked something like an enormous rat, with black hair. When surprised, he had a habit of goggling his eyes, which was why they dubbed him "Kuri," short for *kurikuri*, or "goggle" in Japanese. He himself would sign memos, "From Kuri." His father was a Russian serf. As a boy, he worked in a St. Petersburg factory before becoming a wanderer.

"When I look at Kuri, the good nature of Russian people strikes me as pathetic," Akashi would sometimes say with a sigh. Kuri was so naturally honest that Akashi himself would sometimes wonder how such a person ever came to be a professional spy.

Naturally clean-shaven, Kuri owned a number of fake beards and changed his appearance every time he came. When he came to the hotel, he was always at pains to sneak in unobserved, taking every precaution. His job was to seek information in the Moscow vicinity. Every time he returned from Moscow, he would file a report with Nagao. Never once did he have any astute observations to offer.

Once in Akashi's room, Nagao listened to Kuri make his report and then lambasted its inadequacy. The next thing they knew, the eyes of that man nearing old age filled with tears. "I'm doing the best I can," he said. "The first half of my life I was a wanderer, doing dangerous, life-threatening jobs that barely kept food on the table. Now I'm at an age when my physical strength has started to decline, and I still have to do dangerous work like this to earn my bread because I'm not fit for anything else."

Suddenly, trembling as if he had the chills, he took out of his pocket a pistol and some poison. "But even if the police catch me, I will never betray you. I intend to kill myself either with this revolver or this poison. At least credit me for my sincerity, if not my ability."

This is a Russian vignette that Akashi witnessed with his own eyes.

*   *   *

Here let us reexamine Akashi's view of the Russian Empire.

First, a passage borrowed from Akashi's own writings. His prose is clear and to the point, something like a Western-style essay flavored with Chinese-style expressions. For convenience, the text is rendered here in a modern style:

> Russia has a population of one hundred thirty million, but that one hundred thirty million only expresses numbers, not power. That is because Poland, Finland, the Caucasus, and the Baltic coast are all lands that Russia once invaded, and loyalty to the empire there is weak. Moreover, pure Russians are also fighting among themselves.
>
> The Russian court and cabinet are hotbeds of factional rivalry, which is an inherent characteristic of the Russian people. As one example, take Grand Duke Kirill Vladimirovich, now exiled in Paris. He is a member of the Russian imperial family, cousin to Tsar Nicholas II. While aide-de-camp to the emperor, he was suddenly stripped of his post and banished from Russia. Since even members of the imperial family were subject to such treatment, the seriousness of the Russian propensity for cliquishness should be apparent.

Akashi goes on to cite corruption and bribery among Russian officials as signs of the country's impending downfall. "There is already consensus on this in Europe." His surprise was keen because no such social ills existed among Japanese bureaucrats around the time of the Russo-Japanese War.

When Nicholas II formed the Baltic Fleet, he named Rozhestvensky as its commander, someone who had until then served the court as the emperor's aide-de-camp. Leaving aside the question of whether or not Rozhestvensky was the right man for the job, there is no question but that in the court and the Russian Navy alike he was that rarity, a man of integrity. In the race to form the fleet, he exhibited drive bordering on recklessness. The Russian Navy was said to be a nest of corruption, and in order to procure shells and rations, he had to threaten officials in charge, yell, and practically resort to extortion to get what he needed. That being the state of affairs in the Naval Ministry during wartime, conditions elsewhere can be guessed.

"It is not too much to say that the Russian people living under this corrupt government are as ignorant as horses and sheep, and the Eurasian empire is one desolate pasture." After this declaration, the essay continues: "The Russian tsar makes no attempt to love his people or protect his country. He is a tyrant who loves himself and protects only his court. What those in opposition parties are saying is true."

Akashi was sympathetic to the opposition at this point and lamented its lack of solidarity. Like Russian courtiers and bureaucrats, the opposition formed splinter groups and rival cliques that struggled for power and viewed one other with suspicion. Such behavior has to be described as characteristically Russian.

The essay then examines reasons for this state of affairs, and Akashi makes a keen observation. From olden times, whenever there was unrest in a dependency, the powerful empire would have a different ethnic group subjugate the rebels. When Poland revolted they armed domestic Jews and had them restore order, and when Georgia (the region south of the Caucasus Mountains) revolted they had the Armenians subdue them. As a result, the various peoples became sworn enemies. Akashi points out that this habit carried over into friction between different factions of the opposition.

*   *   *

Akashi hoped that the conference his comrade Zilliacus was planning for various anti-tsarist elements would take place, but at the same time he had his doubts as to whether it was even possible, since the various factions all held such different beliefs and made such different claims.

But Zilliacus possessed two qualities that were great assets for a revolutionary: optimism and tenacity. He went around convincing leaders of the various parties, telling them the conference was necessary "to defeat our common enemy, Russian autocracy"—and nothing else. Many agreed, swayed by his passionate sincerity, but others balked.

One group that balked was the anti-tsarist Bund, consisting entirely of Jewish workers who lived in Poland and the Baltic coastal region. As we have already seen, Russia continually brought severe pressure to bear on Jews, even carrying out pogroms. The Bund was formed in 1897 in the belief that the only way to sever those chains was to bring down the autocratic regime. Its main leader was Arkady Kremer. The party espoused socialism and often collaborated with the Russian Social Democratic Labor Party. Small though it was, the Bund was the first revolutionary organization in Russia to embrace socialism of German origin.

"Zilliacus is the instrument of a Japanese Army officer, so we will not participate." The Bund promptly issued this declaration. They couldn't possibly have had any logical reason to despise Akashi. It's likely that this was actually a pretext, and they were only going along with their sister organization, the Russian Social Democratic Labor Party, which had announced its nonparticipation. Why the latter declined can't be said for certain, but pride may well have been involved; it was beneath the dignity of a major party to send a representative to Paris at the behest of someone as relatively unimportant as Zilliacus. At least that's how Zilliacus saw it.

But the Russian Social Democratic Labor Party had already split in two. In 1903, it divided into the Bolsheviks and the Mensheviks, with Lenin leading the Bolsheviks. He looked favorably on Zilliacus' proposal.

"We won't participate in the conference," Lenin told Zilliacus, "but when the time comes for concrete steps to carry out the revolution, we will make every effort to cooperate." Later, these words were backed by action.

In Poland, the opposition seemed hesitant, afraid that holding such a conference was too risky. The Poles had suffered heavier Russian military oppression than anyone else in history and so were cautious about mounting opposition campaigns, taking a pessimistic view or insisting on elaborate preparation.

* * *

Relations between Russia and Poland bear a slight resemblance to historical relations between Japan and Korea. In ancient times, Japan absorbed continental culture through Korea. Korea was Japan's teacher then, but many years later, Japan, which was first to modernize, would attempt to subjugate Korea. Indeed, not long after the Russo-Japanese War, Japan officially annexed Korea, opening a dreadful chapter in relations between the two countries.

Poland also played the role of transmitting western Germanic culture to Russia in the east. "Everything comes from Poland," Russians said. Moreover, since Poland had become a unified state in the tenth century, it had an older national history than Russia, which didn't get its first native-born ruler until the fifteenth century. Strong ethnic pride based on the creation of a rich culture in Western feudal times was another reason why Poles looked down their noses at Russians.

We've already told about how Poland, having become a Russian subsidiary state, saw young men drafted in large numbers and sent to the Far Eastern front, where they were dying deaths that to their own people were meaningless. Worse, by killing Japanese who might actually help to overthrow tsarism, they were acting against their people's interests. All anti-Russian activists in Poland believed this.

Because of this, Akashi was determined to draw Poles into the conference, but as we have seen, some of the Polish activists were so fearful of Russian oppression that they were starting to make noises about boycotting the conference.

At the beginning of September, Akashi moved from Stockholm to London. Around then, Witold Jodko-Narkiewicz, the leader of the Polish Socialist Party, came to call at the Japanese legation in London accompanied by several senior staff members.

"Some of our people are expressing concern about the upcoming conference," said Jodko. He himself was in favor of it, but some of those under his jurisdiction were refusing to participate on the grounds that "the Japanese spy Akashi is behind it." He was unable to quiet their voices, he said.

Akashi's reply was quick. "The planner and mover of this conference is Zilliacus, from Finland. Zilliacus' sincerity, broad-mindedness, and courage are well known to you. I too have been deeply struck by his willingness to lay his life on the line for the cause and simply want to do anything I can to help. I personally have no direct connection with the conference. It would be highly regrettable if you looked on Zilliacus' sincere activities with suspicion and lost sight of who our common enemy is. However, this cause ultimately is not my concern and so whatever happens is fine with me. Whether your party chooses to participate in the conference or not is strictly up to you and is nothing to me."

These words of Akashi's brightened Jodko's spirits.

*　*　*

Akashi's and Zilliacus' enterprise, the Paris conference, moved slowly uphill toward realization. Along the way there were countless difficulties, but even in later years Akashi seldom touched upon them. He would bring up memories when he was talking about something else, as he did once when the topic of discussion turned to colds: "Colds are funny things. When I was in Europe, one time I was in a forest during a heavy rainstorm. I had to stand there all night waiting for someone, but funnily enough I didn't catch cold. When I was a boy I caught colds all the time, so go figure."

"It's a lucky thing you weren't killed!"

When someone marveled over his good fortune, Akashi would point to his face and say, "It's because of this mug." He maintained that he looked so much like an old farmer that no one ever dreamed he was an important agent of the Japanese Army.

At first, whatever nation's capital he visited, he would stay in a small cheap hotel. He apparently thought that his appearance and bearing made such lodgings the natural choice. But Zilliacus or someone cautioned him that he was being too careless, that he should stay in as large a hotel as possible or he would only make himself more conspicuous. He was such a novice, so unsuited for the life of a spy, that underground professionals had to make a point of telling him such things. Though no spy in history ever carried off a greater mission than Akashi, people who knew him would scratch their heads when they heard about it and say, "Akashi did all that?" No one seemed to think he had it in him.

In the end, we are forced to the conclusion that his success was owing to his nature as a man of action. When he settled on a goal, he worked out a plan and then directed all his energies toward implementing it, to an obsessive degree. That was undoubtedly what made him successful. Moreover, despite his acute focus on his objectives, he always had an absentminded, foolish look on his face, which may also have played a considerable part.

Akashi was a born master of statecraft. Later on, when he was governor general of Taiwan, the consensus of senior statesmen of the day was that he had the makings of a prime minister. Assuming that opinion was on the mark, a man who could have been prime minister had maneuvered to stir up the Russian Revolution. Perhaps it's safe to say that no ordinary spy could have pulled off the enormous task of rocking the Russian Empire to its foundation. In any case, Akashi died of sickness at the young age of fifty-six, so he never got the chance to prove his fitness for the job of prime minister.

*   *   *

The conference was held in a privately owned residence near Rue Hoche in western Paris.

"Napoleon I passed out titles of nobility right and left, but this family of counts was fairly influential at the time." Akashi learned this much from Zilliacus, but no more. Many Russian nobles were active members of revolutionary parties, and they had the necessary connections to rent unobtrusive buildings.

The grand-sounding conference was actually a gathering of some fifty people or so. Each attendee was a party leader, so even if their numbers were small, their influence was great.

"Counting the number of different factions gathered together under one roof, this is the biggest conference in the history of world revolution," Zilliacus said proudly to Akashi. It was indeed unprecedented, and perhaps nothing like it would ever be held again. The parties involved all had such different positions and interests that the likelihood of the conference even happening had seemed dim. Zilliacus had insisted on one thing: "First we overthrow tsarism. The parties come after that. We're all agreed on that point." Stressing only this, he had gone around making his case energetically, and his efforts had borne fruit.

The reason that almost no books on the Russian Revolution make any mention of this historic conference is probably because it happened through the capital and auspices of the Japanese military spy Akashi Motojirō. Zilliacus and other party leaders who attended the conference, however, were unconcerned. "Why, Japan's just the same as us," said a man from the Armenian Socialist Party. By "the same as us," he meant that Japan was a small, weak country about to be invaded by Russia, which put it in the same position as other countries and regions that Russia had invaded. This was exactly right. For that reason, it was decided that Akashi too must participate in an official capacity, though not as a Japanese Army officer. They came up with the provisional name "Party to Maintain Japanese Independence," and had him attend as party head. If Japan lost the war, then the name would be changed to "Japanese Independence Party," and Akashi would have to run around with the other leaders under that party name.

"The Russian Empire is the heaviest burden ever borne by mankind." So said a man from the Polish National League. If imperial Russia were likened to a gigantic beast, the conference attendees might not be beasts strong enough to destroy it, might only be insects who could eat away its skin and blood vessels, but if an innumerable swarm of insects burrowed into its skin and subcutaneous tissue, then the beast, however gigantic, might lose its vital spark.

*   *   *

Akashi stood by the door. Until the conference got underway, people chatted here and there. All of them came up to Akashi and spoke to him, addressing him as "comrade."

The aristocrat Melikov of the Armenian Revolutionary Federation (Droshak Party) wrapped his enormous palm around Akashi's right hand, brought his face close to Akashi's ear and said, apropos of nothing, "I need money." An old acquaintance of Akashi's, he was from an old princely family; his uncle was Count Mikhail Loris-Melikov, an Armenian general.

At this point in Akashi's career, the Georgian-born figure of Ioseb Besarionis dze Jughashvili—who later changed his name to Joseph Stalin—was somewhere around. In the highlands south of Georgia was Armenia, which lost its autonomy in the fourteenth century and by the start of the nineteenth century had mostly become a Russian colony. The people of Armenia have black hair and eyes, though they are of Indo-European extraction, and in some of them the back of the head is flat, as it is in certain Asian peoples. The strangeness of their language and their extremely ethnic version of Christianity (in the sense that it is not Roman Catholic) made them a typical European folk minority.

Despite having lost their country in the fourteenth century, the Armenians never lost their ethnic cohesiveness, thanks to their distinctive language and script, as well as their own indigenous Christianity, the Armenian Gregorian Church. In this, they resembled the Jews, who maintained a cohesiveness based on an unspoken sense of community despite losing their country four thousand years ago.

Having lost their land, most Armenians became merchants scattered mainly through the Near East. Here, too, they resembled the Jews, though on a smaller scale.

Some Armenian political parties were attempting to regain lost land by appealing to the goodwill of the Russian Empire, but they were losing vigor. "As long as tsarism continues, there will be no Armenian independence." This way of thinking was picking up steam, and its advocates were joining hands with Russian activists working inside Russia, out of sight or otherwise, to incite violent revolution. Melikov's uncle, Loris-Melikov, was the ringleader.

"Armenian comrades have passion. We have organization. We can rise at any time to promote riots and destruction. All we lack is capital." Melikov went on speaking urgently into Akashi's ear.

Akashi had already given Melikov three thousand yen, but Melikov said his plan required more capital. "I'll give you all you need," Akashi said. "But spend some of it on meetings, will you?"

* * *

Leaders of all but one of the independence and revolutionary forces in Poland came to the conference. They were all old acquaintances of Akashi's.

The most soft-spoken of the parties was the Polish National League, whose constituent members were conservative farmers and members of the Polish upper crust. Although they held tsarist Russia to be the greatest devil on earth, they were cautious in their approach. "If we fail, the Polish people will be Russian slaves forever." This fear acted as a safety valve on their thoughts and actions. Their fear was well grounded. A monster that is not killed outright will only go on the rampage and produce a vast quantity of victims. The level of Russian brutality toward Poland, and of Polish fear of Russia, can only be understood by putting oneself in Poland's place.

Despite their moderation, the party presented Akashi with this proposal: "We will go distribute flyers urging Poles in Russia's Manchurian Army to surrender." The "moderation" of people suffering oppression is far from ordinary.

In contrast, the Polish Socialist Party advocated violent means, with Polish autonomy the objective. Its membership consisted of factory workers from Warsaw and other industrial areas. This party was on the rise, picking up enough strength to overwhelm the old established Polish People's Party. There was also the Polish Progressive Party, a kind of cross between the other two, and its leadership attended as well.

"It's too bad no one from the Bund came," said Jodko, legal scholar and leader of the Polish Socialist Party. He was referring to the secret party of Jewish workers in Poland, which we've discussed previously.

"More than Poles, the Russians have targeted Jews residing in Poland and killed large numbers of them as bitter enemies. In massacring Jews, they got Polish police or the Polish Army to do their dirty work. Sowing enmity between Poles and Jews is their traditional way, which makes members of the Bund all the more wary. No one hates Russians more than the members of the Bund, but at the same time, no one fears Russians more. That's why they were afraid to show up at this conference and stayed away. It would be a shame to criticize their nonparticipation as a sign they lack revolutionary fervor. The Bund has many railway workers, and it was their cooperation that helped us cross borders to come to Paris. Please understand that, Akashi."

* * *

Many important figures among what Akashi referred to as "pure Russians," those from the Russian homeland, joined the conference. One of them was a woman. Akashi, a poor judge of age where Western women were concerned, had a habit of judging whether a woman was in her thirties or above based on how fat she was—but this one was thin. And yet her face bore many wrinkles. Judging from that, she might be sixty, he thought, but she could just as easily have been forty.

She turned a warmly maternal smile on one and all, sometimes cocking her head and asking solicitously after someone's health, for all the world like a duchess in the salons of St. Petersburg.

"She must be a Russian aristocrat." Akashi surmised this because of the elegance of her slightly classical French. He thought this must be the famous Ekaterina Breshko-Breshkovskaya, but to his knowledge that lady had been deported to Siberia. How might she have escaped? For someone reputed to be the fiercest of revolutionaries, this woman's bearing was exceedingly refined.

As Akashi was pondering this, Zilliacus came up to him, grabbed him by the arm, and led him over to her, then introduced him. As if she'd been waiting for Akashi to come up to her, she spoke first and had a radiant smile on her face. "I regard Japanese highly, as comrades."

The significance of her words struck Akashi. Her background made the words hit home. She was born to an aristocratic family and as long ago as the 1870s had participated in the Narodnik campaign, joining this movement of aristocrats, intellectuals, and students at the early stage of the Russian Revolution. Students in St. Petersburg, Moscow, and Kiev had taken the main lead. When it began to turn cold in 1873, they had spread into farming villages as if possessed, seeking to learn from the peasants and light the fire of revolution in their breasts. The campaign had been a kind of a fad, without any leader, and ended after two years. Some of the students involved had been influenced by Chaikovsky, and Prince Kropotkin, the noted thinker, was among them as well. But the campaign was largely sentimental rather than political in nature, and wanting in strategic analysis and direction. That's because the peasants were ignorant and worshipful of the tsar.

While still a lovely young girl, Breshko-Breshkovskaya had participated in that campaign under Chaikovsky's influence and been deported to Siberia, where she spent her youth and middle age in exile. Her beauty, intelligence, and undying passion for the revolution were legendary among students in St. Petersburg. Some workers even said, "There is a goddess of the revolution in Siberia."

* * *

We have yet to mention what Breshko-Breshkovskaya, the goddess of the revolution, told Akashi. But before coming to that, let's jump ahead in our story and see what finally became of her.

When the revolution broke out in February 1917 and she returned to her birthplace of St. Petersburg, the revolutionary crowd welcomed her with cheers and their highest encomium: "Grandmother of the Russian Revolution." Yet barely two years later she was forced to flee revolutionary Russia and seek refuge first in the United States, then France. She died abroad.

Most revolutions come about by maintaining three things: anger against a corrupt regime, a sense of justice, and passion. Once the revolution gets underway, however, all three are unnecessary or even harmful to the cause. The men of justice and passion who lit the fires of revolution are expelled by the group that grasps the main axis of revolutionary power, then vilified, persecuted, and killed. In histories of the revolution written by those in power, they are obliterated or, like Trotsky in the Russian Revolution, appear only as villains.

As long as people yearn for justice, the impulse to revolt will never disappear. But that impulse, even if it leads to a revolutionary uprising, no longer applies once the revolution has succeeded. After that, all that's needed to consolidate authority is Machiavellianism and some just-for-show justice; genuine justice has a deleterious effect. The reason Breshko-Breshkovskaya, the Grandmother of the Russian Revolution, had to flee the country only two years later has to do with that axiom of revolution. After the Russian Revolution, the world got an object lesson in the way revolution and subsequent consolidation of authority follow separate principles. In Russia's case, the post-revolution drama played out all too brutally, driving home to other countries the incalculable evil influence and grisliness of revolution.

Japan's Meiji Restoration, which predated the Russian Revolution, does not conform to the pattern of other countries' revolutions in the least. There, also revolutionary thinkers of every stripe were involved, but bloodshed was kept to a minimum, and the surprising outcome was that all participants who lost their lives were awarded posthumous court ranks, whatever their affiliation.

The situation in Russia was different in every respect. We have already touched on the realities of power in tsarist Russia. At the time when Akashi encountered Breshko-Breshkovskaya, the revolutionaries were still at the stage when their passion for justice, their determination to see justice done, had romantic currency.

"For the people's sake," she passionately told Akashi, "we fought the devil of tsarism for long decades without achieving our goal. Now through Russia's enemy, Japan, we have been given the opportunity to destroy this devil once and for all. We can only blush at the little we were able to do on our own."

*   *   *

The conference began. Zilliacus presided, moving the proceedings along with a liberal dose of humor. The language of the conference was not uniform, but perhaps because Zilliacus spoke in French, that was the main language. Only the Poles would now and again speak out in German or Russian.

The conference lasted five days. "Our common enemy is the tsar." This theme was repeated often. That's because, when any other factional claims were made, the conference threatened to get out of control. Zilliacus was well aware of this point.

People had warned that the various parties had competing interests and claims, and were so mixed up in imbroglios that any supra-party conference would be impossible. Zilliacus' efforts were largely responsible for its brilliant success. "Our purpose is the downfall of tsarism," was the conclusion. "Whatever party or faction may take power after the fall of tsarism, it can never wreak more damage on Russia than tsarism has already done. We must use this war as a chance to destroy this devil for the sake of Russia and the Russian people. To bring this about, each party must do what it does best. There is no need for a unified front. Each party should proceed in the way it believes possible and effective."

This statement was virtually identical with what Zilliacus himself had planned all along.

Every party had its specialty. "Ours is debate," said Prince Pyotr Dolgorukov, a pure Russian and leader of the radical faction of the Union of Liberation.

Akashi was thankful that the prince had attended the conference. His family had one of the oldest lineages in the Russian aristocracy, and many of them were presently serving in the court of Nicholas II. "To create a true Russia" was his mantra. His party, the Union of Liberation, included university professors, aristocrats, and lawyers; it called for the establishment of a republic and was not given to violence. Party efforts were limited to printed appeals in the bulletin and meetings.

"But we are by no means opposed to violent means and strikes." Pavel Milyukov, a former professor at Moscow University and a party member, got up and made a point of saying this. "In fact, we support them wholeheartedly."

The Union of Liberation was the most moderate. Others, like the Caucasus representatives, said alarming things like, "All we can do is assassinate." Nor was this mere bombast. Backed by a history of action, those words carried weight. Other parties had other strengths: demonstrations for the Polish Socialist Party, inciting strikes for others.

* * *

After the Paris conference, conditions changed. Violent revolutionary campaigns began occurring over a wide area, led by the Polish Socialist Party, which espoused Marxism. In the main cities of Poland, the Polish Socialist Party led a general strike of such violence that the army was called out to restore order. Workers gave battle, refusing to go down without a fight.

The strike spread to Russia. In November and December, demonstrations by students and workers took place frequently in Moscow, Kiev, Odessa, and other cities. The Union of Liberation, which promoted its agenda through the spoken and written word, drew on its base of county and provincial assemblies as well as legal and medical societies to stage anti-government conferences. Even Leninist parties which did not join in the Paris conference became active, inflaming mainly workers.

Japanese newspapers of the day were decidedly lacking in the ability to interpret information regarding such movements. They should have been sensitive to the social unrest spreading through Russia in November and December 1904 but only began to report on it starting January 25, 1905.

"Suddenly, Flames of Revolution Rise in Russian Capital" announced a headline in the January 25 edition of the *Tokyo Asahi Shimbun*, a representative newspaper of the day. The subheading read, "With the war in the Far East not going well, hundreds of thousands of soldiers die in vain."

These headlines show how unsophisticated Japanese reporters were. In the first place, the word "suddenly" definitely did not apply to the Russian Revolution. If Japan was on the same level as European countries, then from the start of the war reporters ought to have been busy reporting on and analyzing Russian politics and society. However, newspaper companies could not yet afford foreign correspondents. Even granting that, reporters failed miserably in doing their homework and learning about the enemy.

That ignorance comes through in headlines suggesting sympathy for the tsar and antipathy to the burgeoning revolution. The editor who came up with those headlines believed the Russian tsar to be essentially the same as the Japanese emperor and saw the revolutionary forces as traitors who were not bothered by the unfavorable tide of war. One senses an underlying fear that the flames of revolution might spread and threaten the Japanese imperial system.

And when it comes to the ignorance of equating Russian tsarism with the Japanese monarchy, we cannot laugh at the editor who came up with these headlines for the article of January 25, 1905. Later on in the Shōwa period and to this very day, that way of thinking has been adopted by certain social scientists and classical left- and right-wing activists.

* * *

In Europe, it was an accepted fact that the Russian autocracy was in and of itself extremely oppressive to the Russian people. This bit of common sense completely failed to register on newspaper reporters in Japan, Russia's enemy in the war.

After the Paris conference, when Zilliacus made approaches to French politicians and journalists and pressed for "attacks on that harsh autocracy," no one he spoke to turned him down—a sign of how general the consensus was. Georges Clemenceau, then a senator, was one who agreed, and Jean Jaurès, a highly respected politician, was another. Anatole France also gave his consent. From the contemporary Japanese standpoint, these men may have been fearsome anti-capitalists, but among French thinkers they were hardly ringleaders of destructive insurgents. Foreigners though they were, they were united in righteous indignation over the tyranny in tsarist Russia, and Japanese newspapermen should have known enough to share their views.

A country's level of journalism reflects its strength and its cultural standard. Japan's military force may have been modernized, but its people were completely lacking in common sense in regard to the international situation. They lagged farther behind than residents of some backward colony.

The newspapers of Russia's enemy running a headline that all but called Russian revolutionaries out-and-out traitors to their country—could anything be more ludicrous? In short, Japanese were waging an ethnic war without knowing the first thing about the country they were fighting.

The same unhappy situation continued after the war. Japanese newspapers never carried one line of dispassionate analysis to answer the question: "Why did Russia lose?" It never occurred to anyone to do so. There's no going back, but if Japanese newspapers had taken stock of the war after it was over and run a series on "Factors Contributing to the Defeat of the Russian Empire," they would have concluded either that Russia deserved to lose, or that the Russian Empire had lost not to Japan but to its own evil regime.

If such dispassionate analysis had been carried out and the people had learned about it, then the myth of the absolute superiority of the Japanese military, a myth growing out of the mystical view of the state that arose after the Russo-Japanese War, would never have spread; or, even if it did, the nation might have had a degree of immunity.

Akashi's work was not a sign of greatness on his part. He simply rode the tide of events or rather was carried along by it, and so accomplished his monumental task.

*   *   *

Not all urban workers in Russia were revolutionaries. However, all of them were angry at the government's incompetence. The inefficiency of the Russian government's organization at this time and the chronic negligence of its functionaries were unbelievable to Western sensibilities.

"The Russian tsar should make his base in the aristocracy, not in the people." This was the opinion of Vyacheslav Plehve, Russian home minister around the start of the Russo-Japanese War and a hard-liner on the question of the Jews. He became famous for saying, as the war was getting underway, "To stem the tide of revolution we need a war. A small war will do fine." By "a small war," he meant war against Japan. That's how little he thought of Japan. Responsible for maintaining public security, he shared with Akashi's "friends" a common desire to use the Russo-Japanese War to accomplish his ends. The only difference was that he planned to use the war to diminish revolutionary fervor, they to fan it.

But the Russian government lacked the ability to conduct a war in an efficient manner. Despite Plehve's important statement and despite Russia's constant goading of Japan in the Far East, little or nothing was being done in the way of preparation for war, which required the cooperation of the cabinet, the army and navy, and the bureaucrats.

Still, just as Plehve had planned or anticipated, at first the war did indeed bring an outburst of patriotism, though consecutive losses soon put a damper on that mood. Workers in St. Petersburg did not blame soldiers at the front for the fecklessness that turned battle after battle into defeat. They knew that the real cause lay in the corruption and incompetence of government machinery—the reality of Russian society that had become common knowledge—and they took out their anger on the government.

"There's no way to save this country except to start a revolution!" This patriotic indignation did lead to revolution in the end. It can be argued that Plehve's plan to rouse patriotism with "a small war" had precisely the desired effect. But because that wave of patriotism was blocked by the immovable wall of Russia's situation, the energy was released in a direction quite different from what Plehve had had in mind.

So fanatical was Plehve in his suppression of revolutionary movements that just five months after the war began he was murdered in the streets of St. Petersburg by a member of the Socialist Revolutionary Party. His killer threw a bomb at him and blew him to pieces.

* * *

Russia began to rock on its foundation.

A revolution consists of fundamental historical change brought about by the complex interweaving of various elements. Looked at from that perspective, the role Akashi played in this one may seem virtually nonexistent. However, his value as catalyst was significant. All he did was hand out money. Organizers used his money to build organizations, activists to launch campaigns. This created a synergy, and by January 1905, Russian social unrest had entered a new and critical stage.

January 6 by the Russian calendar (January 19 by the Gregorian) was the day of the Neva River Festival. The tsar himself was in charge, and on this day Nicholas II left the Winter Palace and appeared on the left bank of the Neva, participating in the grand and solemn Russian Orthodox ritual.

On the opposite bank was an old fort built by Peter the Great in 1703, called the Peter and Paul Fortress. Old guns in the fort participated in the ceremony by firing off a salute. The sound of guns rang out and then, just as the salute was ending, a live shell landed near the Winter Palace and broke four windows. The tsar was unharmed, being away. Naturally, the court took this to be the doing of revolutionary elements, as did the citizens; in fact, it was a simple error. But the trend of the times decreed that even a small anomaly like this would take on great significance and play a major role in adding impetus to the momentum.

Three days later, a demonstration to petition the tsar took place—a demonstration scarcely revolutionary in character, more like a religious ceremony. The government sensed danger and dispatched infantry and Cossack troops, who opened fire on demonstrators and cut them down with sabers. This was the famous incident known as "Bloody Sunday." If not for the previous mishap at the Neva River Festival, the government's nerves would not have been so on edge.

One thousand people were injured on Bloody Sunday, and two hundred killed.

The crowd that gathered that day in front of the Winter Palace was not by any stretch of the imagination a revolutionary mob. They had no red flags, may well have despised them. They were a pious, religious crowd, folks who went to church with their families on Sunday. That particular Sunday, they and their family members had been summoned by Father Georgi Gapon, a priest whom they held in great trust, and urged to petition the tsar. Instead of going to church, they simply gathered in the plaza in front of the Winter Palace.

* * *

Father Gapon is the appealing kind of rabble-rouser who appears in the revolutionary stage of every country's history. Born in a village in the southern Russian province of Poltava, he entered a theological college with the intent of becoming a priest, and while enrolled there was influenced by the thinking of Tolstoy. On graduating, he became a priest, went to St. Petersburg, and, while carrying out missionary activities, became sympathetic to the wretchedness of factory workers' lives. Two years prior to Bloody Sunday, he founded an organization called "Assembly of Factory Workers of St. Petersburg." Funding for the organization is said to have come, oddly enough, from a top-secret government fund through Sergei Zubatov, a captain in the Special Corps of Gendarmes; the truth, however, remains murky.

Gapon was enormously popular with workers. Perhaps no one else was so respected and loved by them in the whole history of the Russian Revolution. The source of his appeal lay probably in his saintly appearance and the stirring appeal of his inflammatory speeches.

After Bloody Sunday, Gapon fled to Europe, where Akashi met with him in London. "A mad monk if you ask me," Akashi later remarked to Utsunomiya Tarō, the London military attaché. Apparently, he didn't take Gapon at face value. Probably any cult figure capable of seducing the masses is in large measure a hypnotist, one possessing power to put even himself in a trance.

After Gapon formed the above-mentioned organization in the spring of 1903, his popularity soared to extraordinary heights. Eighteen months after it was formed, his group had a membership of nine thousand. Members got together frequently, but the meetings were only social in nature, and political topics generally did not come up. The revolutionary consciousness of St. Petersburg workers was virtually nil at this time. They still believed in the tsar and the church, and they trusted priests more than they did revolutionaries. Their sole concern was their poverty.

They came to Gapon with their troubles. He listened and helped resolve their problems, sometimes going to negotiate with an uncomprehending and greedy factory owner. All this bolstered his popularity even more.

Gapon was also a guest member of the Socialist Revolutionary Party. Backed as he was by the triple force of the church, the factories, and this revolutionary group, it's little wonder that on that Sunday when he led the demonstration to petition the emperor, he attracted a crowd in the tens of thousands. Instead of a red flag, he bore images of a saint and the tsar as he walked through the snowy streets. People on all sides sang not workers' songs but hymns. This experiment of Gapon's shows that holy icons, images of the tsar, and hymns were more effective than revolutionary flags in attracting a non-revolutionary crowd of two hundred thousand.

* * *

Witte the enlightened one watched from his window that morning as the demonstration passed by. He viewed Gapon as merely "the leader of a state-sponsored workers' union." By that he meant a trade union created by Home Minister Plehve, who had been assassinated the previous July. Since the idea of such trade unions came from Captain Zubatov, they were identified with him, and Witte also called them "Zubatov unions."

State-sponsored trade unions were formed with the intent of separating the workers from the intelligentsia, but Witte was quick to predict that this wouldn't work: "Whoever drafted the plan must think it's a way to keep workers under police control, but they're dreaming." To paraphrase Witte's meaning, as long as the rain of revolutionary activity kept falling, any receptacle, even one made by the police, was bound to fill with rain. He anticipated that the state-run trade unions would turn revolutionary as a matter of course. "Father Gapon can do nothing to stem that tide." As a leading figure on Russia's political scene, Witte was extremely pessimistic and saw Gapon as a tool of the government.

That a large-scale demonstration would be held that day was public knowledge; word had been widely circulated several days ahead of time. The government had repeatedly deliberated what countermeasures to take. But Witte by then held the purely nominal post of president of the Committee of Ministers and was effectively retired from the political world, so he did not join in the discussions.

Gapon's assembly had prepared a petition to present to the tsar. The contents were public knowledge, and Witte was familiar with them. "Though the language was humble," he wrote, "it was clearly suggestive of revolution." In fact, the petition was not particularly radical, and dyed-in-the-wool revolutionaries, seeing little point in a demonstration that turned for support to the tsar, largely opposed it. That shows how little radicalized Gapon's assembly was.

That morning, Witte looked out from his window at the passing demonstrators, who included a large number of women, children, and spectators. He wrote later about what happened next: "As soon as the parade had gone by, I stepped out on the balcony. Soon I heard the sound of gunfire. Two or three bullets whizzed past my ears, and then came the bombardment."

* * *

The petition drive that propelled people to the Winter Palace was merely a plea to the tsar to reprimand merciless factory owners and unscrupulous officials.

Counter-plans were debated the night before at the residence of the home minister, Prince Pyotr Sviatopolk-Mirsky, with this conclusion: the protest would be quelled by force of arms.

Witte gave the prince's political stance high marks, writing words to this effect: "How a man like Sviatopolk-Mirsky could ever have planned such a foolish measure is beyond me. The explanation lies apparently in the incompetence of General Ivan Fullon, superintendent general of the police, in whom he placed great trust." But whether either of these men was the true architect of this "Bloody Sunday" is now doubtful.

Prince Sviatopolk-Mirsky was a man of even more enlightened thinking than Witte. Witte himself declared him to be "a cultured man of noble and crystalline character, with a soul such as is seldom seen." The prince's only flaws in Witte's eyes were a frail constitution and political inexperience.

Sviatopolk-Mirsky was not power-hungry. After Plehve's assassination, he was named home minister but repeatedly declined the post. He had confidence in the power of the people and believed there was no other hope for Russia's survival. Right-wing newspapers denounced him as a "friend of Poland" or "colluder with Jews," a clear sign of his moderate stance.

One day, he had an audience with the tsarina, the de facto ruler of her husband the tsar, and tried to rid her of her stubbornly fixed preconceptions about the country by telling her how dire a crisis it was in.

The tsarina, however, would have none of it. "Only the intelligentsia is opposed to the tsar," she said firmly. "The people are on his side." The tsarina's assessment of the people was right to some extent, yet to just the same extent she was mistaken.

"It's true that only the intelligentsia is opposed to the tsar," Mirsky observed, "but in any country, it's the intelligentsia that first starts a movement. To serve their tsar, the masses might well kill members of the intelligentsia—but the next day they might turn and storm the palace. That's because the masses act spontaneously."

She didn't listen.

It's hard to believe that Mirsky staged Bloody Sunday entirely on his own judgment and initiative. The decision most likely came from Nicholas II, who possessed "boundless power and a dreadfully impulsive nature" along with a pathological hatred of revolutionary forces.

*   *   *

Gapon's assembly was convinced that if they just went to the plaza, the tsar would meet with them. The Russian people's level of education was appallingly low, and as a result they did not trust their own judgment but constantly sought out a trustworthy religious leader. Once they found such a person, they idolized him. "Surely the tsar will hear us, since Father Gapon says he will." The tsar would do something about rapacious factory owners and indolent bureaucrats. Those were the people's two main requests.

The petition Gapon first drafted included those requests and nothing else. However, individuals from the social democratic camp took the initiative and inserted other demands with revolutionary overtones, which put the court and the government needlessly on guard. The supposedly revolutionary demands were not actually all that radical. They requested freedom of speech, freedom of the press, and the convening of a constitutional convention, things taken for granted in Western society.

As Gapon walked across the snow toward the Winter Palace, he was something of a naïf. Once, he had sympathized with workers. But he disliked revolution and became the tool of the secret police, a shepherd who corralled workers so they would not explode. That shepherd, responding to the pressure of the times, was out in the forefront as leader of the crowd.

As far as Gapon was concerned, all that the tsar needed to do was show himself to the demonstrators in the plaza. That way, he, Gapon, would not lose face, and the crowd's feverish excitement would abate. If the tsar would meet with him, he would respectfully hand over the petition and then kneel in the snow to say a prayer blessing the tsar before dismissing the gathering. That was all he had in mind as he planned the demonstration and stood at its forefront, singing hymns and the national anthem, "God Save the Tsar." He and the assembled masses no doubt sang the imperial Russian anthem from their hearts.

But soldiers from the Imperial Guard were waiting in the plaza. "Entry here is forbidden!" they shouted. Not even Gapon standing at the fore could hear clearly what they said, and the columns of demonstrators kept walking ahead.

Then, from beside Narva Gate next to the plaza, dozens of Cossacks came charging up, sabers drawn.

* * *

In Manchuria, the Cossacks may not have been living up to their prestigious reputation, but against their unarmed brethren they showed absurd strength. Blood sprayed across the snow, staining it red, and the crowd ran in all directions, trying to escape. Those who lagged behind were trampled under horses' hooves.

The infantry's fusillade was evidently triggered by the Cossack attack. The attacks by saber and rifle were absolutely relentless. Each attack was repeated again and again, and in more than one location. The mounted Cossacks would cut down one knot of the crowd, then whirl and pounce on another.

Judging from the method of attack, the incident did not take place on the spur of the moment. As mentioned earlier, it may have been ordered by the emperor or his aides. But Nicholas II was not in the Winter Palace that day; he was resting in his villa, Tsarskoye Selo. Assuming he did give the order, how did he transmit it to the soldiers?

It is hard to know what really happened. A theory has it that Home Minister Mirsky intended to arrest Gapon alone and gave that order to the police chief, his trusted friend General Fullon. A dog lover, Fullon was described as "a man who understands animals' feelings better than human ones." He was said to be a thorough incompetent, but he knew this much: given a demonstration of that size, the feat of rounding up only the leaders was impossible. He supposedly gave Mirsky a flat no. In short, when it came to this demonstration, the police had to fold their arms and take a wait-and-see attitude.

And so it fell to the military.

Security at the Winter Palace was the responsibility of the Imperial Guard. Home Minister Mirsky may have had no recourse but to leave all responsibility in their hands. In other words, all political judgment and measures may have been on hold. If that is so, we can surmise that responsibility for security that day was left entirely in the hands of the military. The emperor or his aides may have expressed some intention or other to palace guards.

Yet another theory has it that the guards had only been ordered not to let the marchers into the plaza in front of the Winter Palace, but when the crowd kept pushing on in, they responded automatically as the trained soldiers they were.

No one knows the truth. No matter how things actually came to pass, news of the incident sent shock waves across the nation: "The tsar had a peaceful crowd killed with sabers and rifle bullets." Of that there was no doubt.

* * *

Gapon was no revolutionary, yet nothing spurred the Russian Revolution as much as the tragedy of Bloody Sunday, which grew out of events he orchestrated. Bloody Sunday was an object lesson, proving to the people that the tsar was not on their side. Through his own actions, the tsar demonstrated the truth of what the intelligentsia had been insisting on all along: "The tsar is a devil."

Modern revolution psychology suggests that as sadistic oppression is increasingly brought to bear, the heat of compression rises until finally there is an explosion. There is accordingly a tendency to provoke authorities into committing acts of a sadistic nature. A pioneering example of this was this incident we now call "Bloody Sunday."

Those in the revolutionary camp could not have manufactured an incident with such great propaganda effect if they had tried. Lenin declared that the incident effectively accomplished in a single day the equivalent of years of revolutionary education.

In that sense, Bloody Sunday was of unparalleled importance to Akashi Motojirō and his country. "A worker dying before my eyes," a foreign correspondent who witnessed the events of Bloody Sunday informed Akashi, "told me with his last breath, 'If there'd been a battalion of Japanese soldiers on our side, I wouldn't have suffered this terrible wound.'"

The incident not only roused the indignation of the Russian people at home, but hardened European hearts toward the Russian government. In

France, the activities of a revolutionary support group called "Société des amis du peuple russe" picked up steam after this incident.

Foreign wire service reports concerning the incident were published in the Japanese papers.

"The disturbance in the Russian capital is becoming more and more like a genuine revolution." So began a January 25 editorial in the *Tokyo Asahi Shimbun*.

> Once blood spilled before the palace, the populace changed overnight, yesterday's obedient subjects of the tsar becoming today's sworn enemies. Violence and mass killings will only increase the depth of the people's resentment, making the rebellion more planned, more structured, and more widespread. Disaffected members of the military who were sent to the front brimming with complaints will be invited to join the revolution and, turning their spears around, attack the government soldiers. . . . Behind the mastermind Gapon there are other, bigger Gapons.

When Akashi heard about the bloodshed he was at his lodgings in Stockholm. Immediately sensing that he himself was in unforeseen danger, he headed for Paris. He also chose Paris because he thought that city would be more convenient than the backwater of Stockholm in keeping abreast of what was happening in Russia.

* * *

All this time, Akashi was busily engaged in the project that would make his name: purchasing weapons for insurrection. The weapons project was not something that Akashi himself planned but grew out of the planning and needs of Zilliacus and other opposition elements. All Akashi had to do was let the tide carry him and his wallet along. His undertakings were all like that. He always responded to others' requests, so in that sense he never overreached himself.

What was a bit difficult was finding a way to purchase and deliver weapons under the noses of the Russian authorities without their catching on. This was where the undertaking half failed.

Be that as it may, the ordnance Akashi bought in Switzerland consisted of twenty-five thousand rifles and four million two hundred thousand cartridges, a massive amount, enough to arm a division. "If we can create partisans with these weapons, Russia will be plunged into indescribable domestic chaos and lose all ability to conduct war in the Far East." Zilliacus was delighted.

Finding a way to transport the weapons was the problem. Carrying them overland from Switzerland required eight freight cars. Then getting them to the Baltic Sea region required a ship. That's why Akashi bought a used steamboat, the SS *John Grafton* (700 tons).

The wholesale purchase of weapons in Switzerland was handled through a Swiss anarchist named Beau who ran a car company and successfully negotiated with the head of the armory in the Swiss Army. To transport the goods, he commissioned Takada and Company, a Japanese trading firm with offices in Europe.

This weapons transport deal was what Akashi worked the hardest on during his time in Europe. It was a half success, because the weapons did not get into the hands of revolutionaries until after the conclusion of the Treaty of Portsmouth, which ended the Russo-Japanese War. Therefore, even though the deal may have been significant in the history of the Russian Revolution, it had no direct bearing on the Russo-Japanese War. For that reason, we will omit the details.

Gapon fled Russia.

After Bloody Sunday, he could no longer remain in the country and turned to revolutionary organizations abroad, seeking protection. Every leader of every revolutionary organization was meeting with Akashi at this time, and Gapon too went to England to meet with him at Zilliacus' introduction. Akashi was staying in London's Charing Cross Hotel, and Gapon went to see him there under a false name. The next day, Akashi realized he was being tailed by a Russian spy and moved to new lodgings. No one knows what he and Gapon talked about during their meeting, but there's no doubt that Gapon knew about Akashi's procurements of weapons.

*   *   *

"When I think of past times," Akashi often said in his later years, "my heart breaks." Many of the brave young men who had carried out anti-Russian activities with him on the European stage died violent deaths or were captured and sent to Siberia, with no way of knowing whether they were dead or alive. The thought of them filled Akashi, a poet at heart, with bitter regret. "I feel as if I did something terribly sinful," he sometimes said. As a soldier, he had wished to conduct field operations and storm castles; the job of sowing civil strife in the enemy country was not gratifying to him.

His comrades in arms, moreover, were not Japanese, but Russians, Finns, and Poles. After the war, when soldiers who'd seen active duty got together at drinking parties to recount their exploits, he always looked uncomfortable. Though he had worked hard to bring about Russia's downfall, he ended up feeling intense love for Russians and maintained a keen interest in the course of the Russian Revolution.

On reading in the paper that someone had killed Gapon in April 1906, he judged that he was "probably killed as a spy by a revolutionary element." Back when he met Gapon in London's Charing Cross Hotel, he had realized that the priest was under a shadow. Just as he surmised, Gapon was killed by his own comrades. "Gapon may have been a humbug," Akashi also said, "but his name will live forever."

After Bloody Sunday, which brought renown to the name Gapon, infuriated workers responded with strikes. The wave of strikes spread, causing serious disruption to Russia's wartime production and transport. Aristocratic homes were frequent targets of bombing, and public order in the capital declined. Unsurprisingly, Home Minister Mirsky was held responsible. The tsar dismissed him from office, letting on to others that it was because "Mirsky is a liberal." When Mirsky assumed his post, the tsar had said passionately that without Mirsky Russia was doomed, yet in the end he abandoned him. That was his way.

"Every unfortunate thing that happened can be traced back to the tsar's character," Mirsky would later tell Witte—one of the unfortunate things being, of course, the Russo-Japanese War. "Today he approves something, tomorrow he prohibits it. With a character like that, he could not possibly stabilize the Russian Empire."

As Mirsky's successor, the tsar appointed General Dmitri Trepov, who was known as a strong-arm politician. Trepov was also made governor general of St. Petersburg and urged to wage a crackdown.

Retaliation was swift. Grand Duke Sergei Aleksandrovich, the tsar's uncle and governor general of Moscow, was killed on a Moscow street when a bomb thrown by a member of the Socialist Revolutionary Party blew him and his carriage to bits.

In any case, after January, Russia's social unrest increased until the country showed every sign of being on the eve of revolution

4

NOGI'S ARMY GOES NORTH

After taking Port Arthur, Nogi's army had to march north.

"You mean you have to fight *again*?" an officer under Stoessel said in surprise to Tsunoda Koreshige, a young member of Nogi's staff.

"Now there's someone from a big country for you," Tsunoda thought. "To them this is like sumo wrestling." Sumo wrestlers appeared in a tournament and could rest afterward. Things were different for the Japanese Army, with its limited troop numbers.

Nogi's army would have to fight again and then some. Troop strength for the decisive battle on the Manchurian plains was at a critical low. Kodama Gentarō had been anxiously waiting for Nogi's army to be free, for no new campaign could succeed without its help. We know that Nogi's army was tied down at Port Arthur. The battle of Liaoyang had taken place, followed by the skirmish at Shaho. Then at Heigoutai the Russians had seized the initiative on the battlefield, putting the Japanese Army on the defensive for the first time. The Japanese held on in the face of a fierce onslaught, some units strategically withdrawing while others were wiped out, the pattern repeating over and over again. Disaster was averted only because the Russian Army failed to pursue its advantage.

General Headquarters was working out strategy for the battle of Mukden. The Japanese Army would bring its full strength to bear, forcing the Russians to engage in a decisive battle; but first they had to wait for Nogi's army to come north.

Tsunoda Koreshige, the aforementioned staff officer, had been ordered by General Nogi to see Stoessel off as far as Dalian on his return to Russia after the battle of Port Arthur. We've already told you about how Stoessel, upon surrendering, had chosen to be repatriated to Russia instead of being sent to Japan as a prisoner of war.

On the evening of January 10, Tsunoda was treated to dinner at Stoessel's residence in Port Arthur and returned to his barracks at twenty minutes after two in the morning. He shivered in his unheated room for over two hours without a wink of sleep.

At five, he got up and returned to Stoessel's residence on horseback. The general was awake and ready to go. The scheduled time for their departure was eight o'clock. "Now there's a soldier for you," thought Tsunoda admiringly, impressed by the general's sense of propriety and his ability to adhere to a strict schedule.

They went to Changlingzi Station by carriage and horseback. General and Madame Stoessel rode in the lead carriage with his chief of staff, Reis. The Stoessels' six adopted children rode in the second carriage. Tsunoda and Lieutenant General Fok rode horseback.

After the little procession passed through the town and came out by the Port Arthur fortifications, still covered with a haze of smoke and reeking of death, Fok suddenly became talkative. Like a guide at a world's fair, he launched into an explanation of the site and the siege.

*   *   *

Lieutenant General Aleksandr Viktorovich Fok was commander of the Fourth East Siberian Rifle Division in Port Arthur. In the estimation of Russian Imperial Army Headquarters in St. Petersburg, Fok, though a general of outstanding tactical ability, was held back on the battlefield by his tendency to take an overly pessimistic view of things and by his coldly critical attitude. As a military man, he was unlikely to dive into the mud and sacrifice himself in the heat of battle.

He was coldly critical of the very Japanese troops that had defeated him. "Your troops were not uniformly brave," he said, raising an arm and pointing at the fort when the procession came to the bottom of Pine Tree Hill. Even though they were standing at a fresh battlefield where much Russian blood had been spilled, he apparently felt no great rush of emotion.

Fok rode alongside Tsunoda. He was a lieutenant general, Tsunoda only a young captain. Though rather outspoken, Tsunoda had been taught that it was proper military etiquette to pay respect to any officer outranking him, even an enemy officer, and so he was deferential to Fok. Fok in turn took the approach of a senior officer teaching a captain a thing or two, treating Tsunoda like a student in his battle tactics class at the Imperial Military College in St. Petersburg. This struck Tsunoda, the victor, as faintly ridiculous. He had a waggish streak—one that kept him from rising very high in the military thereafter—and couldn't help laughing out loud from time to time.

But Fok's point was well taken. "On the evening of November 26," he said, "a unit of your army carried out a surprise attack on Pine Tree Hill."

This was the famous White Sash Troop, a provisional elite assault group consisting of volunteers from the First (Tokyo), the Seventh (Asahikawa), the Ninth (Kanazawa), and the Eleventh (Zentsūji) Divisions. Major General Nakamura Satoru, who had devised the plan of attack, had been chosen to lead the assault.

Nakamura was something of a bluffer and did not enjoy a particularly good reputation as general. While giving instructions to the suicide squad, he declared that any man who left ranks for no reason would be shot.

"All of us volunteered for this suicide mission," one enraged young officer shouted. "This is an insult to us as soldiers!"

The incident was reported in the memoir of a squad member named Hashizume Yonetarō. The memoir also reports that before the squad left, a priest of the Higashi Honganji temple traveling with the army uttered words normally spoken to souls departing on their journey to the next world.

Soon after the assault began, Nakamura was wounded and sent back. After that, commanders were felled one after another until the chain of command was affected and the ranks in disarray. The attack was grisly in the extreme: of 3,000 participants, 1,498 were killed or wounded, and the remainder were forced to retreat.

Fok was critical of this operation.

* * *

According to Private Hashizume's memoir, after the do-or-die attack failed and the sun came up on the morning of November 27, Pine Tree Hill was an appalling shambles, the ground strewn with fallen Japanese soldiers. "A mass of bodies everywhere," wrote Hashizume. Japanese soldiers at the time wore khaki, but those from the Seventh Division of Asahikawa, who had arrived late, still wore black. Mixed in the heaps of khaki-clad corpses, the Asahikawa soldiers were like a sprinkling of black sesame seeds.

General Nogi had staked nearly his last hope on the White Sash Troop, even going to its assembly point at the front to issue instructions, yet the operation ended with failure and the troop's near annihilation.

"We had barely one hundred men manning the fortress here," Fok told Tsunoda. Those few had used machine gun fire to great effect, forcing the Japanese Army to abandon the plan that sent so many to early deaths in vain. Tsunoda was astounded to learn that there had been under a hundred defenders.

"And yet," Fok continued, "it was our mistake to station a garrison so small. Japan caught us napping. Japanese officers were brave. One officer jumped up on one of our field guns with the agility of a monkey and shouted down encouragement at the men following behind him, but they hesitated and never came. That brave officer lost his life in vain to a Russian bayonet. After he was killed, his men scattered and started roaming around an area piled high with bodies, so they were shot and killed. If only they'd been braver, Pine Tree Hill would definitely have fallen on that first assault. After all, our side was caught off guard." This, however, was empty theorizing on Fok's part.

There may have been barely a hundred men in the Russian fort, but they were protected by thick walls of *béton*—concrete—and had artillery of various sizes at their disposal, including a number of machine guns; a single machine gun could and often did kill five thousand exposed troops with ease. Moreover, searchlights swept the ground at night, so they never lost sight of their targets.

The attackers crawling up the hill had no cover. Their attack produced only death amid raking machine gun fire. They were not weak. Trapped in a strategically desperate situation without a gleam of hope, soldiers in any country naturally quail. The attackers' courage was not an issue. The high command was at fault in forcing soldiers into an impossible situation and hoping that their frenzied efforts would somehow carry the day. Fok's assessment—"If only they'd been braver"—was the unrealistic fancy of someone who never actually picked up a rifle.

* * *

The carriage carrying Stoessel and his wife proceeded over the frozen road, swaying violently. Fok and Tsunoda followed the lead carriage on horseback.

"The quality of your soldiers has definitely fallen," commented Fok, who was more of a critic than a general with actual combat experience. "From August through the end of September, no army in the world was a match for your troops. Not a man turned to look back, much less retreat. Then their quality deteriorated, until, by the time of the November 26 surprise attack, some of them refused to follow their commanding officer into battle."

These comments were painfully accurate, and Tsunoda privately had to agree. The quality of soldiers in the Japanese Army was falling overall. Nogi's army in particular had lost a number of brave young men in the early wave of all-out attacks. Those lost troops were replenished with reserves from the homeland, their quality noticeably poorer with each successive arrival. All the replacements were draftees, some quite grizzled, and even the younger ones generally had a wife and family back home. Not only were they lacking in physical strength and training, but mentally their capacity to fight without fear of dying was, naturally, far below that of soldiers in active service.

On top of that, the attrition rate of officers from the Army Academy was heavy. Officers on the reserve list who had previously done one year of volunteer service were called up from civilian life and each put in charge of his own unit. Their abilities were, of course, considerably below those of active duty officers.

In the field grade as well, retired old men were being drafted as battalion commanders. They might have plenty of courage but lacked commensurate strength and having long been away from military life, had lost most of their combat reflexes.

The Japanese Army was not the Japanese Army of the early days. This fact was a headache not only for Nogi's army but for the entire Japanese Manchurian Army now planning an assault around Mukden.

This was what Fok was pointing out, as if to say, "You Japanese can bluster all you like, but I know very well the weakened state of your army."

At some point, he shifted the topic to 203-Meter Hill, known in Russian as Vysokaya Gora—"High Hill": "I knew before the war ever started that it was going to be important." The year before war broke out, he had led an attack force during major maneuvers and captured 203-Meter Hill, enabling him to charge the Port Arthur fortifications. "I said at the time that that hill should be heavily fortified, but others disagreed, and my opinion wasn't listened to. Japan was smart to make that hill the focus of its attack in the end."

*   *   *

They headed for Changlingzi Station, where they would board the train for Dalian.

Ijichi Kōsuke, Nogi's chief of staff, was already standing on the station platform with a crowd of others, waiting to see Stoessel off. Stoessel saluted Ijichi, then extended his long arm and shook hands before boarding the special train.

On the train, the topic of Japanese gunners' abilities came up. "The Japanese artillery have a habit of scattering their fire," said Stoessel. "Especially so at the beginning of the siege, like over there." He pointed to a saddle-shaped elevation outside the window. The train was just approaching Yingchengzi, where fighting had taken place in late July. Echoing Fok, Stoessel said that it was smart of the Japanese to have chosen that hill as a target of attack, but that because they scattered their fire, Russian infantry had been able to hold out for three days.

The discussion focused not on the skills of Japanese gunners per se, but rather on how the Japanese high command used their artillery. Apparently, they had a tendency to disperse firepower too much.

"But by the end, they showed admirable progress," Stoessel said. The concentrated firing toward the end was the doing not of Nogi's staff, nor of Major General Teshima Yōzō, the siege commander, but of Kodama Gentarō from General Headquarters. Tsunoda did not reveal this, and Stoessel of course had no way of knowing.

Fok gave Japanese soldiers scant praise. "The greatest characteristic of Japanese soldiers is their strict adherence to military discipline," he said. "Russian soldiers are different. The worst ones have no idea what military discipline even is. That's the main reason why, even though we have superior strength, the Japanese were able to defeat us at every turn."

He added, "Nowadays, while I wouldn't go so far as to say that individual fighting ability has little value, the importance of group strength, that is, of solidarity, cannot be overstated. Russian soldiers were inferior to the Japanese in that respect. There is no strict order in the Russian Army. Once you have chaos, commands aren't carried out."

That was where Fok laid the blame for Russia's defeat. Finding fault with the rank and file rather than the commanding officers was typical for this general who was so unpopular with his troops. Major General Kondratenko, whom Fok despised, controlled his men well and won their devotion. The men in Kondratenko's division were said to show twice the strength of any other Russian soldiers.

When the party got off at Dalian Station, they walked to the pier and boarded the *Kamakura Maru*. After that, General Nishi Kanjirō, commander of the Liaodong garrison, called at Stoessel's stateroom to bid him farewell.

* * *

General Nogi had already begun transporting troops, preparing to move his army north. Stoessel observed some of the northbound troops when he was leaving Dalian. Stoessel left Port Arthur on January 11, two days before Nogi's army made its triumphal entry into the city.

The following day, January 14, on a hilltop south of Shuishiying, a memorial service was held for the war dead. Nogi stood in the falling snow and read aloud an address that he himself had written. Every soldier present wept. Foreign military observers and special correspondents wiped their eyes, although unable to understand a word. Even the Chinese who gathered to watch shed tears, so it must have been quite a spectacle. Something in Nogi's personal appearance and in the aura of his personality had an extraordinary effect even on foreigners.

That evening after the ceremony, Nogi returned to his headquarters in Liushufang to find a telegram from General Headquarters in Yantai with orders to finish assembling the troops in Liaoyang no later than mid-February.

The following day, January 15, another telegram arrived from General Headquarters relating to personnel changes, and a wholesale restructuring of Nogi's headquarters took place. Virtually every staff member was relocated, a clear indictment of strategy and leadership in the siege of Port Arthur.

Nogi Maresuke retained his command. His chief of staff, Ijichi Kōsuke, was given the sinecure of Port Arthur fort commander. Tsunoda Koreshige, the one who saw Stoessel off, was a mere captain, and perhaps for that reason remained in his post. "The only ones who stayed are General Nogi and me," he crowed and earned a rebuke from Lieutenant Colonel Ōba.

"An exceptionally lively young spark for a Japanese." This was how Ian Hamilton, a military attaché with the British Army, described Tsunoda in his memoir *A Staff Officer's Scrapbook during the Russo-Japanese War.* That liveliness of Tsunoda's led him to be scolded frequently by Nogi and senior staff members, and probably held him back in his later career, which ended at major general.

Tsunoda's father had died fighting in the Satsuma Rebellion. Partly for that reason, Nogi, who had also taken part in the government force to quell the rebellion, scolded Tsunoda but also showed him affection. The Russo-Japanese War had broken out while Tsunoda was studying abroad in France, sending him home in a rush. He returned fluent in the language, able to mimic the speech of a French noblewoman as well as quarrel like a sailor. Because of his genius for French, Tsunoda was responsible for the reception of all foreigners who visited Nogi's army.

* * *

Sir Ian Hamilton, a lieutenant general in the British Army, was the highest-ranking and oldest of all the military attachés and observers on both sides who had gathered from around the world.

One month after the start of the war, Hamilton arrived at his post in Tokyo. After that, he followed Kuroki's army (the First Army) as a military observer and saw the fighting in Manchuria close up. Where most countries appointed army captains or majors as attachés, Great Britain sent one of its most decorated officers, a sign no doubt of goodwill stemming from the Anglo-Japanese Alliance.

Hamilton had participated in the Boer War (1899–1902), which was notorious inside and outside the country as a war of imperialism. He had been chief of staff. "I had my duty as a soldier so I did my best, but that sort of war is no good," he always remarked for the rest of his life.

During the Boer War, Britain nearly succeeded in seizing the land of the Boers, who had moved to South Africa from Holland in the seventeenth century, creating an agrarian society known as the Cape Colony. They called themselves "Afrikaners" and had a strong racial identity as whites; they were also known for their religious piety and solidarity.

In 1814, Britain added the Cape Colony to its map. The Boers took exception to this and migrated en masse, creating two republics: the Transvaal Republic and Orange Free State. Britain then attempted to annex these as well and rashly started a war that no political historian spoke kindly of later. It dragged on far longer than expected, a bitter and bloody clash of arms.

At first, Britain rolled to easy victory. Just four months after the opening of hostilities, they had defeated the main Boer force, and it looked as if the war might be over. Britain naturally held the traditional view of warfare as something resolved by decisive confrontations between two main forces. However, the Boers shattered that concept.

The word "Boers" is Dutch for "farmers." Those farmers grabbed every conceivable weapon on hand and began a guerrilla war. The situation then bogged down in a stalemate. Britain ended up mobilizing a force of four hundred fifty thousand, equivalent to the entire Boer population, and set out to exterminate the Boers by burning their homes and scorching their land. British finances were nearly exhausted before finally a conditional victory was gained.

As army chief of staff, Hamilton came to believe that as far as wars of invasion went, it was all but impossible to defeat people fighting for their nation's survival. When he took up his post in Tokyo and saw all the Japanese soldiers gathered in the capital for mobilization, he thought of the Boers and declared, "The Russian Army is bound to lose." He notified the British War Office of his opinion.

*   *   *

Lieutenant General Ian Hamilton always wore a sympathetic smile in his dealings with people and bore himself less like a soldier than a professor of poetry. He, in fact, wrote poetry, and prose as well. His writings reflected his curiosity on nonmilitary affairs and were richly informative. Man of letters though he was, he remained at the forefront of the British Army till the end of his career as army general. After retiring, he became honorary rector of the University of Edinburgh.

Along with the sixteen other foreign observers attached to Kuroki's army, Hamilton largely saw to his own daily needs. Compared to the Russian Army, the Japanese Army's treatment of its foreign military observers and war correspondents was not good—officers were needlessly secretive, often infuriatingly so. Kuroki's army, however, was an exception.

Although where meals and other material treatment were concerned the Japanese were incomparably less hospitable than the Russians, Kuroki Tamemoto and his chief of staff Major General Fujii Shigeta freely explained new strategies—with some exceptions—and held nothing back. When an operation did not go as planned and losses mounted, they responded frankly to questions.

Hamilton's impression of the pair was therefore favorable. Concerning Kuroki, he wrote, "He looks intelligent, and I would be prepared to hear of his being a scholar or an artist. But I see no trace of the blunt, determined, bulldog expression, which some men of action seem to acquire, or the penetrating look that never lets down its guard for a moment."

The real Kuroki was rather different. He was a typically combative Satsuma warrior and did not as a rule respect others. Even Commander in Chief Ōyama Iwao, a crony from Satsuma days, he always addressed by his nickname, "Yasuke-don." In battle, he was no "scholar or artist" but fought with the stout determination of Satsuma's Jigen school of martial arts, letting his "flesh be cut while severing enemy bone."

Fujii Shigeta, a classmate of Yoshifuru's, was uninhibited from his youth, an openhearted and altogether imprudent fellow who was so overconfident about his own brainpower that he never felt any need to hide anything when called to account and willingly laid his cards on the table. This trait won him favor with Westerners, including Hamilton, who wrote, "Major General Fujii greatly impressed me. He possesses wide knowledge, energy, and exceedingly good humor."

The Kuroki–Fujii duo deserved full honors for dragging the Russo-Japanese War to victory, but after the war the Japanese Army did not accord them even half the accolades they won from foreign military observers. Kuroki had a reputation for arrogance that earned him the dislike of army brass, and he lacked Nogi's stature with the public. Fujii was considered a lightweight and never made general.

Hamilton was exposed to enemy fire along with Kuroki's army, observing both the battle of Liaoyang and the fierce fighting at Shaho, but after the fall of Port Arthur, he and the other foreign military attachés entered the city on January 18 to see the battle outcome for themselves.

Hamilton watched with his own eyes as Nogi's army, after fighting so fiercely at Port Arthur, was then sent off to a new place of assembly in Liaoyang, on its way to fight in the north.

He spent several days living in Nogi's headquarters at Liushufang, where a section of the humble Chinese house had been hurriedly partitioned off. As a general, Hamilton was given a room by himself. To the big-framed Hamilton, it was a virtual animal pen, barely big enough for him to turn around in, but even so he was grateful. That is how appalling conditions had been on the open battlefield up north.

The day after he arrived, Hamilton was introduced to Nogi Maresuke along with the other foreign military attachés. He recorded his impressions of the general. On the day they first met, Hamilton wrote, "He is tall, slender, and gray-bearded, and struck me immediately as bright, sensible, and determined."

Three days later, on January 22, when Hamilton returned from the city of Port Arthur to Liushufang, he found a dinner invitation signed by Nogi in Roman letters.

During dinner, Hamilton was seated to Nogi's right and so had the opportunity to speak with him at length. Their conversation was technical in nature, having to do mainly with defense and offense at Port Arthur. Nogi followed this up with several questions about the Boer War, as courtesy required, his fine sensibilities on such matters giving him an air of urbanity. What impressed Hamilton most of all was the answer Nogi gave to the question: "When during the siege of Port Arthur were you unable to sleep at night?"

"Port Arthur fell on January 2, and that night I couldn't sleep. The sound of gunfire had been so violent that when it ceased I couldn't fall asleep."

This was probably true. When combatants revert to normal life, that must be how their nights go.

Hamilton also wrote, "The more I see of General Nogi, the more he impresses me. I sense nobility of character and a spirit of philosophic heroism that penetrates the mild dignity of his manners and appearance. He is entirely simple, with no trace of pride in victory. If I were a Japanese, I would venerate Nogi."

There was indeed something in Nogi that had a mysterious impact even on foreigners meeting him for the first time. Stanley Washburn, an American journalist who would later have contact with Nogi, all but worshipped the general and wrote a book entitled *Nogi*, the pages of which are filled with highest praise.

Neither Hamilton nor Washburn observed the ongoing siege of Port Arthur, and both men had only vague knowledge of shifts in strategy along the way. Port Arthur did not fall by the force of Nogi's personality, yet in the end his personality had a mysterious quality capable of felling one hundred times as many foes as at Port Arthur. That quality explains why ultimately it was neither Ōyama nor Kuroki nor Kodama but he, Nogi Maresuke, who strongly impressed the world and whose figure became symbolic of the Russo-Japanese War in people's minds.

* * *

"What do you want to do after the war is over?"

"If I should return alive," Nogi said in response to this question, "I intend to go home to Chōshū and retire."

When Hamilton asked Kuroki of the First Army the same question, Kuroki did not say he wanted to go home to Satsuma, but otherwise his answer was similar: "I want to retire from the world, keep out of the way." He added, "If we win the war, society will lionize the military. But society's memory is short. I'm too old to get worked up about ephemeral fame and fuss. I know that wherever you go in the world, soldiers are either made much of or forgotten."

During his stay in Liushufang, Hamilton climbed 203-Meter Hill with the other foreign attachés. They were all given horses to ride. The one Hamilton got was as savage as a tiger, and he had to hang on for dear life. Their guide was Tsunoda Koreshige, the one whom Hamilton had described as "an exceptionally lively young spark for a Japanese."

On the way, Tsunoda declared in French, "I hope there will be a decisive victory soon." The Japanese Army had no money, and every day's delay in securing a decisive victory meant the national coffers were that much closer to scraping bottom, as every commissioned officer knew. While fighting the war, they kept a careful eye on the dwindling wad of bills in the till.

"This is the devil's plowing." So wrote Ian Hamilton with a shudder after climbing the hill. Rocks, concrete fortifications, and all had been smashed into a jumble of stones; shell fragments were cemented with blood or bits of human flesh. The hillside was so completely shell-blasted that not so much as one blade of grass remained. Imagine the ferocity of gunfire that left not one blade of grass standing.

Here and there sandbags remained, made from women's gowns or petticoats of red and purple, the fine cloth in shreds like silent screams. At one point, Captain Vincent cried out, one foot in the air. He had stepped on a man's torn-off arm.

They had to watch where they walked. Here a man's leg was stuck in the earth, there an arm beckoned, seeming to grow out of the ground. Heads rolled about, biting dust. This was no ordinary fresh battlefield: the devil himself, exerting all his powers of imagination, could not have created a ghastlier scene.

* * *

On the evening of January 24, Nogi and his headquarters set out from Liushufang, a place of so many memories, on their way north.

The weather was cloudy. Tops of bare-branched locust trees stabbed the low-hanging clouds like gleaming spires of ice. The north wind was keen, driving the horses along, and the cold was biting. According to the report filed by the noncommissioned officer, the temperature that evening fell to -29 degrees Celsius.

There were no stations in the vicinity of Liushufang. They had to go north all the way to Changlingzi. Along the way, the horses' hooves slipped often on the frozen ruts in the road. The privates assigned to headquarters loaded baggage onto carts and led the cart horses. One of them, Private Tanaka Ryōzō, looked back at the receding Liushufang and said with a tear in his eye, "I suppose I'll never come back again." The noncommissioned officers laughed at him.

For the past five months, Tanaka had done odd jobs around headquarters, living the life of a virtual cave dweller in the village. He was from Fukui Prefecture and had gone to the front with the Nineteenth Regiment from Tsuruga. Luckily, he had been assigned to headquarters, but almost all the officers of his regiment had died in the siege, and only a handful of his fellow enlistees were mixed in with the northbound troops.

Just as Liushufang disappeared from view behind a hill, they came to a small river. It was frozen over, so they didn't need a bridge. The sky darkened. It looked like there might be some snow, but before the snow came, night fell. Nogi and his party plowed on through the dark. They were not a lone force, but their trek north in the black of night had about it the shadow of death, like the lone wanderings of an isolated force.

A train was waiting at Changlingzi Station. There were two third-class cars for Nogi and his aides, and ten covered freight cars for the rest. Neither the third-class VIP cars nor the freight cars were heated. At half past nine, the train started north.

Realizing that they were now leaving Port Arthur for good, young officer Tsunoda pressed his forehead against the train window and stared out into the darkness, unable to hold back tears.

The souls of the dead are pulling at me, trying to stop me from going. This unexpected notion rose in his mind. "You're just tired," he told himself, struggling to cast off the sinister idea.

Nogi sat with his usual erect posture. He too must have felt considerable emotion on leaving the place where he had lost two sons, but from where Tsunoda sat, his profile showed no trace of sadness.

* * *

The train bearing Nogi and his team ran exactly one hour before pulling up at Jinzhou Station. They got off the train, stretched their legs, and had a late supper at supply headquarters, which was heated by a red-hot stove. Everyone felt revived, but while they were eating, water in the engine froze, so they couldn't leave.

"It can't be helped." Nogi spoke without change of expression, not scolding whoever was responsible, but at a time when his main force was gathering near Liaoyang, for only headquarters to be late was a blow. He seemed to be plagued with bad luck.

Nogi had a new chief of staff. With Ijichi—who was never popular with General Headquarters—given the sinecure of Port Arthur fort commander, now Major General Koizumi Masayasu would be devising strategy under Nogi's command. Koizumi was a shadowy figure. Unlike his predecessor, he was not self-centered and although he was a bit indecisive, he listened willingly to others' opinions. When he took his post, Nogi asked him if he was in good health; Ijichi's struggle with chronic illness must have weighed heavily on him.

"Yes, sir," said Koizumi, adding unnecessarily, "although right now I have a touch of a cold." It was true enough that he had caught cold. He shivered in the unheated car all the way from Changlingzi Station to Jinzhou Station.

At three in the morning, the locomotive was finally ice-free, and they could get on their way. Everyone piled back into the freezer-like cars and headed north.

After the night of the twenty-fifth, morning dawned clear. The cold was as severe as ever. Inside the icy cars, water froze so the men could not wash their faces. They had lunch at Telissu Station, dinner at Dashiqiao Station.

Then the train ran along under the stars. Nogi slept, but despite the bitter cold he used no blanket. His aides curled up under blankets and went to sleep.

It happened around two-thirty in the morning.

At some point, the train had stopped. Chief of Staff Koizumi got up to relieve himself, but no one noticed. The train had stopped on a bridge over Huicheng River, south of Anshan Station. Koizumi apparently didn't realize that the train was on a bridge. There was no lavatory in the car, so to relieve himself he had to step outside.

Koizumi stood on the back platform of the train, and then he jumped. There was no bridge girder. He plunged far down into the dry riverbed below.

* * *

If war is a bloody gamble that nations wage, then a general must himself be a gambler in blood, the one who carries out the wager on his nation's behalf.

As such, a general must be a man of innate good luck. Even if technically his staff does the gambling, it has to be the general who brings them luck. Navy Minister Yamamoto Gombei, when choosing the commander of the Combined Fleet, settled on Tōgō Heihachirō, the least known of admirals and a man who had been given the sinecure of commander of the Maizuru Naval Base. When asked by Emperor Meiji to explain his choice, he replied, "Because all his life he's been a lucky man." Yamamoto understood what war, and conductors of war, were all about.

Nogi never had any luck. The first chief of staff he was given had been appallingly unfitted for the job, and now Koizumi Masayasu, who came with the sweeping reshuffle of Nogi's headquarters carried out by General Headquarters, had, without ever firing a bullet or laying eyes on an enemy face, without even arriving at the assembly ground, fallen headlong from the train.

After the train started to move, the occupants of the car realized that Koizumi wasn't there and raised a commotion. They stopped the train, roused the noncommissioned officers and privates, and formed a search party. Eventually, Koizumi was found lying unconscious in the riverbed. He was in grave condition, his chest badly crushed.

They carried him aboard the train and set off. There was a straw mattress on board to lay him on. It had been intended for Nogi's use, but the general could not bear the thought of being the only one to sleep in comfort and did not use it. They laid Koizumi face up on the mattress.

Sometime after six in the morning, the train arrived at Liaoyang Station. The first job Nogi's staff had to do was transport Chief of Staff Koizumi to the field hospital. Next, they had to set up headquarters there in Liaoyang and so set off to do so. Nogi remained at the station.

"The train to Yantai will arrive in an hour," he had been told. He intended to take that train and pay his respects at General Headquarters. Tsunoda, the youngest member of his staff, stayed behind to accompany him.

The train arrived on time. Nogi and Tsunoda got on board and went to Yantai, where they called at General Headquarters.

On that day, the battle of Heigoutai, the next thing to a lost cause, was just getting underway, and headquarters was in an uproar. Some of the staff officers whispered that having Nogi come just at that time was a bad omen. But Ōyama Iwao and Kodama Gentarō were glad to see Nogi and gave him a warm reception.

*   *   *

Nogi's staff set up the new headquarters in Liaoyang, but no troops came. The entire left wing of the Japanese Army was then in crisis, at risk of being wiped out by General Grippenberg's southern advance.

Nogi, while chatting with Ōyama and Kodama at Yantai, was inwardly distraught. The divisions and brigades under his command had left Port Arthur far ahead of him, but due to a shortage of trains they had had to travel largely on foot and were yet to arrive. Under the circumstances, he worried first that his headquarters might be overtaken by the enemy. Secondly, at a time when Yoshifuru's detachment on the left wing ran the risk of extermination amid the ongoing Heigoutai crisis, and General Headquarters needed every soldier they could get, Nogi's army was of no use whatever. Nogi couldn't help feeling small.

"Tsunoda," he whispered, "which division is closest to Liaoyang?"

"The Ninth," Tsunoda whispered back. The Ninth Division (Kanazawa) was commanded by Lieutenant General Ōshima Hisanao. They were still marching.

The march seemed endless. If the Japanese Army had had sufficient rail transport capacity, Nogi's army would have been able to join in the battle of Heigoutai and repelling General Grippenberg wouldn't have been such a struggle. Tsunoda quickly sent a telegram to the commander of the Ninth Division.

The Ninth Division was burdened with a packhorse logistics unit, so not everyone could come quickly. The Seventh Infantry Regiment was singled out to travel by rail, with the permission of General Headquarters.

"Put Ichinohe in charge," said Nogi, tapping Tsunoda on the shoulder as he stood next to the telegraph. Ichinohe was a major general and a brigade commander; the regiments beneath him were commanded by colonels. Nogi appointed Ichinohe Hyōe to the regiment-level task because he knew from the storming of Port Arthur that Ichinohe was a brilliant fighter.

Everything went according to plan. Ichinohe entered Liaoyang at the head of the Seventh Regiment. They were all put provisionally under the command of General Headquarters and rushed off to help save the left flank of the Japanese Army in its critical hour.

The defense of Nogi's headquarters was up in the air. The First Division (Tokyo) managed to arrive in Liaoyang on January 27, ahead of schedule. But only the division command arrived; the infantry troops were not with them.

On that day, Nogi was back in Liaoyang. A field gun regiment then came in, drawing the gun carriages with such vigor that the barrels bounced. Nogi promptly took these and arranged an artillery battery in a field west of Liaoyang Station.

During the battle of Heigoutai, Nogi's army, in addition to the Seventh Regiment, also rushed the Thirty-fifth Regiment to the left flank, but the remainder of the troops were delayed, all of them still on the march. Unavoidable though it may have been, once again Nogi was out of luck.

* * *

Even though Nogi's army may not have arrived in time to fight in the ill-timed battle of Heigoutai, the order from General Headquarters to "gather your troops swiftly in Liaoyang" was carried out with great success.

The operation took less than ten days. This was indeed "lightning swiftness," as one officer boasted. During the march, even on days when blizzards blew, their rate of progress did not lag.

Tsunoda visited one unit after its arrival in Liaoyang in order to check on the men's morale. He stopped several privates and asked them some questions. All used the same expression: "We're having a great time." They explained that in Port Arthur they had spent all their time fighting rock, but from now on they would be fighting other men. Nothing could be easier, they said. Their reaction shows how deeply depressing siege warfare was to the men's spirits, how it filled them with gloom.

The swiftness of the troops' march to Liaoyang reflects their elation at being liberated from the fortress. But at the same time, the nutrition and sanitary conditions of Nogi's army were ideal for the Japanese Army in general at that time, which also contributed to the success of the march. Above all, the fact that the rivers of Manchuria were frozen over gave Nogi's army a big advantage.

The Manchurian winter is bitterly cold, but wintertime was traditionally the time of year when the people of Manchuria would move to other areas in large numbers. The roads were frozen hard so transporting goods was easy, and since every river was frozen they could glide over the ice with no need for bridges or boats.

Nogi's army remained stationary in Liaoyang while waiting for fresh blood—soldiers—to arrive from the mainland. Word had already come regarding the massive reinforcements on their way: the First Division was to be reinforced by 1,510 men; the Seventh Division, 1,300; the Ninth Division, 2,680, each number including commissioned officers. Without these reinforcements, Nogi's army would not attain its original numbers. They would be arriving in Dalian Harbor no later than the end of February and experience their first gunfire in the coming battle of Mukden.

During this time of waiting in Liaoyang, it was arranged for Major General Koizumi Masayasu, the one who had been severely injured in a fall from the train, to be sent home. He was replaced by Major General

Matsunaga Masatoshi from General Headquarters. The acquisition of Matsunaga was good news, giving Nogi something to be glad about for a change.

Matsunaga was from Kumamoto Prefecture. The other fresh major generals were still in their mid-forties, but Matsunaga was already fifty-five and had no official staff training; however, he was known for his skill in combat.

Matsunaga arrived at his post on February 1. Nogi hosted a small welcome party for him at his army headquarters. Everyone present noticed that Matsunaga's face was bright yellow, and they wondered among themselves if something might be wrong with him.

* * *

Soon after arriving to replace Koizumi Masayasu, Matsunaga Masatoshi went on the sick list. The official diagnosis was jaundice. His case was severe, and he was in no condition to serve in open warfare; recovery would be difficult, the army surgeon said. Naturally, he was due to be sent back home.

But Matsunaga pleaded with Nogi: "I beg of you, as one samurai to another, that you be generous. Please let me stay as I am." He would report for duty in bed, he said, and, if headquarters moved forward, he would go along by stretcher. But given Matsunaga's condition, his mental faculties were bound to deteriorate, and he could not possibly withstand the rigors of intense combat. Even so, Nogi said yes.

Nogi had leadership ability, but he totally lacked the makings of a strategist in modern warfare. He needed an able chief of staff. With a chief of staff who was drowsy from fever, the disaster of Port Arthur would be revisited on Nogi's army.

It was certainly benevolent of Nogi to accept Matsunaga's request, and his response to the appeal to his generosity as a samurai was laudable. But at the same time, his acceptance of Matsunaga's terms proves that somewhere inside he lacked the instinctive ability to conduct war so that victory could be obtained with minimal loss.

In the end, it was decided that newly appointed Major Kawai Misao, the vice chief of staff, would take over the duties of chief of staff in Matsunaga's place. Then, once again, misfortune struck.

On February 4, soon after part of the First Division of Nogi's army had arrived in Liaoyang, division commander Lieutenant General Matsumura Kanemoto died of a stroke while marching. Matsumura Kanemoto was from the Kaga domain. At the end of the Tokugawa period, he was one of the few men of Kaga to take arms as a royalist. At the age of fifteen, he left

Kaga and went to Kyoto, participating in the Boshin War at age sixteen and serving as a scout for Saigō Takamori. After the Restoration he became an army captain and was wounded in the Satsuma Rebellion. Like most officers of the rank of lieutenant general and above in the Russo-Japanese War, he had no formal military education, and in that sense his background was similar to Nogi's. His participation in the Satsuma Rebellion, in particular, made him Nogi's comrade in arms. The only reason he was not promoted as quickly as Nogi was because, from the point of view of the Chōshū faction, he was an outsider.

In any case, Matsumura was dead. After that, a lieutenant general named Iida Shunsuke was appointed to command the First Division.

During this interval, the Eleventh Division of Nogi's army was incorporated into the "Army of the Yalu." This new army was organized to undertake a campaign on the far right flank. Its official orders were as follows: "The Army of the Yalu will muster as great a force as possible and advance from Kanchang to Fushun to put pressure on the enemy's left rear." Kawamura Kageaki, a veteran lieutenant general from Satsuma, was promoted to general and simultaneously assigned as commander of this army.

5

CHINHAE BAY

Around the time Nogi's army started marching north toward the Manchurian plains, the Combined Fleet had mostly finished the repair of its ships, and its personnel and every other aspect were in transition toward a new phase— reception of the Baltic Fleet.

On February 6, the reader will recall, Tōgō Heihachirō left Tokyo by train with Saneyuki and his other aides. "Place the entire force of the fleet in the Korea Strait and take action as the occasion arises"—this was the overall plan that had already been accepted. The decision was not made by any one person but was hammered out in meetings by Navy Minister Yamamoto Gombei; Itō Sukeyuki and Ijūin Gorō, chief and vice chief of the Navy General Staff; Yamashita Gentarō, Navy General Staff chief of operations; other members of Imperial General Headquarters; and Tōgō and his staff.

The navy did not adopt a policy of secretiveness regarding the Combined Fleet but would rather generally respond to journalists' request for interviews. After all, the people of Japan had entrusted the navy with a fleet built up as an indemnity against the poverty they had endured for so long. There was a natural, unspoken agreement between the nation and the navy to win the war with that fleet, and the navy was prepared to share any information the nation wanted, apart from privileged strategic secrets.

Saneyuki spent the month of January in Tokyo, and when interviewed at the Naval Ministry by a reporter he did not mince words. "Yes, the Baltic Fleet is still at Madagascar. They're in the Indian Ocean, undecided, wondering if they should go on to Vladivostok or return home to Russia." Saneyuki, of course, knew that Russia was experiencing dire social unrest suggestive of coming revolution. Putting himself in the shoes of the Russian tsar, he thought that rather than send the Baltic Fleet on to the Far East, a more effective plan might well be to return it to the military harbor of Kronstadt to maintain the peace at home.

"In the Indian Ocean, undecided" was undoubtedly where Russia was, mulling over its options. With mounting threats of revolution at home, this was no time to be waging war abroad. If the tsar meant to extend his reign, he needed to abandon the war effort. This opinion was already being voiced abroad as well. Saneyuki interpreted the fleet's delay at Madagascar as a sign of Russia's nationwide hesitation over whether or not to end the war.

Saneyuki also discussed Japan's chances for victory. He explained the enemy's relative strengths (more battleships) and weaknesses (inferior cruisers). He also mentioned that Japan was prepared to counter with repeated rapid attacks.

"Besides, we have submarine torpedo boats too," he said, letting on for propaganda purposes that submarines were lurking in the seas around Japan.

*   *   *

During this time, the Combined Fleet was not altogether at a standstill but was busy with strategic preparations. The main force would enter the Korea Strait. But the Second Squadron would send several of its ships to the Tsugaru Strait to patrol the northern sea, guarding against the chance that the Vladivostok Squadron, supposedly damaged and immobile, should start to engage in commerce raiding.

Meanwhile, any ships carrying wartime supplies to Vladivostok had to be captured. This job was undertaken by the Third Squadron, on watch in the Korea Strait under the command of Vice Admiral Dewa Shigetō. Also a patrol squad had to ferret out news of the Baltic Fleet.

"Admiral Tōgō Sets Out for Undisclosed Location," reported the *Tokyo Asahi Shimbun* on February 6. The unnamed location was where Tōgō would lie in wait for Rozhestvensky: Chinhae Bay, fronting the Korean Strait.

On February 14, the *Mikasa* left Kure Harbor with Tōgō aboard.

During this time, Kure Harbor was extremely active. At Kure Naval Arsenal, besides the repair of warships and other vessels, shipbuilding was ongoing even during the war. At one shipyard, the destroyers *Fubuki*, *Arare*, *Ushio*, and *Nenohi* were being constructed; at another, two large armored cruisers were under construction to make up for the loss of the battleships *Hatsuse* and *Yashima*, destroyed by naval mines.

There were orders to finish the armored cruisers *Tsukuba* and *Ikoma* in two and a half years, an unreasonably short time. Unlike the naval arsenal at Yokosuka, which got its start back in the late Tokugawa period, Kure Naval Arsenal finished its first dock in 1891 and so lagged behind Yokosuka in various capabilities. Commissioning two armored cruisers from the young base was unreasonable, but the job had to be done, and by the time Tōgō set out from Kure Harbor on the *Mikasa*, work on the *Tsukuba* was well underway.

After the *Mikasa* left Kure unaccompanied, Saneyuki stood for a time on the quarterdeck looking out at the color of the water and the shapes of the islands, wondering with a bit of a pang if he would ever be back. But Tōgō, whatever he may have been thinking, maintained his usual composure and said nothing to indicate his frame of mind.

The *Mikasa* went around the island of Eda to show itself to cadets at the Naval Academy before stopping off at Sasebo Harbor. As long as the Baltic Fleet remained at Madagascar, there was no particular hurry, and so the *Mikasa* rested two days at Sasebo.

* * *

Among the company on board the *Mikasa* was a military band. There were bands aboard the flagships of the Second and Third Squadrons too, of course, but as the *Mikasa* was the flagship of the Combined Fleet, its band was especially large.

When fighting began, the musicians would leave their instruments and devote themselves to carrying out duties on the upper or middle deck, mainly transporting wounded and relaying messages from the main gun turret or bridge. Their duties kept them scurrying around the dangerous upper deck and bridge. During the battle of the Yellow Sea on August 10 of the previous year, 1904, a dozen members of the military band were wounded or killed.

Band leader Maruyama Hisajirō, a warrant officer, was apparently not a very skilled musician, but he worried constantly about the musicians upholding their honor as fighters. "When the battle starts," he urged, "don't let the sailors outdo you." Throughout the voyage, he led band members in rescue drills and also drills for orderlies.

There were twenty-seven musicians in all, including Maruyama, and among them was the freshly inducted Kawai Tarō. Born in 1884, he was a senior member of the musical band of the pre-1945 Imperial Navy. During the Russo-Japanese War, he played cornet on the *Mikasa* and now enjoys a vigorous old age in the city of Kure in Hiroshima Prefecture.

"Maruyama was more boatswain than bandmaster, a man of great energy," he recalls.

At sea, the band played twice daily. The battleship flag was raised every morning at eight and lowered at sundown. Each time, the band would perform the national anthem. Afterward, the musicians would join the sailors in running around the decks doing drills.

In the spring of 1971, the author was in the process of writing this manuscript and wanted to meet with Kawai in Kure. He gave his consent but unfortunately the author was sick with a cold on the appointed day. Kageyama Isao of the *Sankei Shimbun* went to visit instead.

Kawai turns eighty-seven this year. "He is slender, of medium height," Kageyama reported. "His conversation is youthful, and he is extremely practical. His hearing is fine, and he seems spry, a man whose wits were sharpened by sea breezes."

Kawai apparently resembles composer Setoguchi Tōkichi, whose face is well known from photographs. In his youth, he was often mistaken for him. He lives with his aged wife, and the bandmaster of the Self-Defense Force band in Kure looks in on him every two or three days to see how he is doing. When Kageyama heard that, he was filled with admiration and wondered if it was a navy tradition.

* * *

While the *Mikasa* continues its voyage, let's discuss naval bands a bit more.

Satsuma, the most progressive domain around the time of the Meiji Restoration, was the first to organize a military band. According to a posthumous account by Nakamura Suketsune, the first leader of the musical band of the Japanese Navy, "In 1869, over thirty Kagoshima youths were dispatched to Yokohama under the leadership of the retainer Kamata Shimpei. They studied military music there under Fenton, the leader of the British naval band."

John William Fenton was the name of a guard at the British legation in Yokohama. He was leader of the military band of the British Army's Tenth Regiment of Foot, which was then stationed in a temple called Myōkōji, in the northern outskirts of Yokohama. By coincidence, Fenton became Japan's first naval band instructor, an event that may well be said to mark the start of the history of Western music in Japan.

The Satsuma domain first became interested in Western music when fighting a British squadron in Kagoshima Bay in July 1863. Tōgō Heihachirō, the admiral now aboard the *Mikasa*, participated in that battle when he was seventeen, alongside his father Kichizaemon and two older brothers. He was dressed in a tight-fitting uniform with a hakama, a wooden helmet decorated with the five-vine family crest, and two swords at his waist. He carried a musket. "Don't lose!" With these words of encouragement from his mother Masuko ringing in his ears, he set out from home and went to his post. The British squadron fired rockets and Spitzer bullets from its ships, and Satsuma retaliated with round shot fired from its coastal artillery batteries.

The exchange ended in a draw, with no clear-cut victory for either side, but frequently during the fighting a military brass band on one of the British warships played music to bolster morale. The Satsuma fighters were impressed by this, and afterward agreed, "That was great." They talked it over and decided that someday, if they had the chance, they would like to have a brass band in Satsuma. That chance came in 1869, when twenty-nine young men were sent to Yokohama.

In 1871, the military band was attached to the Ministry of the Military, and the following year, when the Ministry of the Military was abolished and the Army and Navy Ministries formed, it was divided between the army and navy. At the time of the Russo-Japanese War, a large number of bandsmen were still from Satsuma. Setoguchi Tōkichi, the famous composer of "The Warship March," was born there and became a naval band student in 1882.

"My father's first contact with music came after he joined the navy," says his son, Setoguchi Akira. Around when Setoguchi Tōkichi became instructor of military music, a post equivalent to warrant officer, bandmaster Nakamura Suketsune took him aside.

"Foreign countries have, besides their national anthem, another song that symbolizes their nation, but Japan unfortunately does not. Why don't you compose one?" Nakamura showed Setoguchi lyrics entitled "Warship" written by Toriyama Hiraku, a teacher at the Peeresses' School. Some accounts claim the suggestion came not from Nakamura but from the more experienced band musician Tanaka Hozumi.

In any case, that "Warship" should have been chosen as a national song is highly typical of the Meiji period and in a sense symbolic. The lyrics were first entitled "This Castle." When Setoguchi first saw them, the words had already been set to music; the resulting song was published in volume 6 of *Elementary School Songs*, edited by Izawa Shūji, in 1893. Copyright law was not rigid at the time, and there is no indication that the navy ever contacted lyricist Toriyama.

Setoguchi took up the challenge enthusiastically, and in 1897 he came up with a song he called "Warship." He wasn't happy with it and spent another year revising it. On April 30, 1900, "The Warship March" was performed for the first time at a Japanese Navy fleet review held at Kobe.

"The Warship March" was first performed in the key of C major and was slightly different from its later version. Some declared it too high to sing comfortably, so when the piano score came out in 1910, Setoguchi transposed it to the key of G. The sheet music of the military band aboard the *Mikasa* in our story was written in the key of C.

Although Satsuma retainers remembered that a brass band aboard a British warship played during actual fighting in the Anglo-Satsuma War of

1863, in the Japanese Navy, the band never played during a battle. As we've mentioned, Japanese band members were incorporated into the crew during fighting. Kawai Tarō was to serve as orderly to the 12-inch main gun turret as well as assistant telegraph operator. Other band members would be stationed on the bridge as assistant signalmen or assigned to transporting the wounded. Every one of those posts placed band members where enemy fire would concentrate, so it was anticipated that they would suffer the highest casualty rate.

"Day and night, we drilled alongside the sailors," Kawai recalls. "The musical education we got not only trained our ears but gave us sharp reflexes and good pronunciation, so we came in very handy."

* * *

The *Mikasa* entered Sasebo Harbor. Upon leaving, it would go straight to Chinhae Bay south of Korea. On February 20, the ship left harbor.

"As you know," says Kawai, "Sasebo Harbor is extremely narrow. When the *Mikasa* left, people in the villages lining the banks had a good view. Lots of elementary school kids came out and saw us off, waving small rising-sun flags."

Throughout the fighting in the Sea of Japan, this was the one and only time that this popular song, "The Warship March," was ever performed on the deck of the *Mikasa*. The performance was probably done in response to the flag-waving local children who lined the banks.

"Back then the music was written in the key of C major, so it was awfully high and harder to play, but it may have had more spirit," says Kawai.

Twenty-six men lined up on the quarterdeck, and band instructor Maruyama Hisajirō, wearing his warrant officer's uniform, conducted them. The lyrics, as noted, are from Toriyama Hiraku's poem "This Castle":

Alike in defense and attack,
the floating castle of iron is strong,
protecting the isles of the Rising Sun
from enemies on all sides.
Let any nation that harms Japan
be attacked by the ship of iron.
Coal smoke curls in the sky
like the coils of a mighty dragon.
Cannon fire roars like thunder,
echoing far and wide.
Across ten thousand miles of waves,
shine our nation's light.

A young man named Katō Takeichi (later killed by a bomb) played the flute, and Kawai Tarō played the cornet. Only the oboe part was missing. Of the band members who performed that day, a dozen or more shared the ship's fate when, after the war, there was a gunpowder explosion aboard the *Mikasa*.

"We were young," reminisces Kawai, "and while we played we couldn't keep the tears back."

When they left harbor, the waves were rather high. The *Mikasa* made a beeline for Chinhae Bay.

Along with the Shimose powder in the ship's magazine, the greatest pride of the *Mikasa* was the Meiji Type 36 radiotelegraph equipment located below the aft shelter deck. Right after the war ended, Saneyuki sent a telegram of thanks to the inventor of the equipment, Professor Kimura Shunkichi. Its performance was so outstanding that for years afterward he would say, "In the battle of communications, the Japanese Navy had the field to itself." The navy poured a huge amount of effort and ingenuity into making a practical wireless before the Russo-Japanese War. They could only defeat Russia with superior strategy and fleet maneuvers, and what made that possible on the open sea was excellent wireless equipment.

During the voyage, the wireless apparently was on Saneyuki's mind, as time and again he went below to check on its operation.

* * *

After leaving Sasebo, the *Mikasa* set its course northwest, trailing a white wake of foam. The sea was calm for the time of year, with a bit of haze to the west. The green hills of the Goto Islands on the port side were misted over, as if painted with light brush strokes.

For Saneyuki, this was the very essence of Japan. He had an artist's sensibility and thought that water vapor was what charged Japanese scenery with life. Conveying the impact of such a scene with oils struck him as next to impossible.

After lunch, Saneyuki strolled as far as the forecastle deck. He ducked under the main battery of guns and headed starboard, where he could see Hirado Island. A little white cloud hung over the island, and below it was a thick grove of bamboo. The sight was a reminder of the great fertility of Japan. This too was certainly the result of a climate blessed with abundant water.

With no natural resources to sell abroad, Japan was a simple agrarian country, where people husbanded and ate the rice that grew in the moist soil. By Herculean efforts, they had built themselves a *Mikasa* and put together a Combined Fleet capable of waging major naval battles. To

Saneyuki, it seemed a miracle that his small country had managed to scrape up the necessary funds. Saneyuki wondered to himself whether Japan owed all this also to the moisture in the air.

Speaking of moisture, if the Baltic Fleet should come to Japan when a spring haze hung over the ocean, Tōgō's fleet would be at a considerable disadvantage in the ensuing battle. Firing on the enemy from a distance would be difficult, and some ships might slip from their grasp. If even one or two escaped to Vladivostok, as we know, Japanese maritime shipping would be endangered and their ability to send supplies to Manchuria put at risk. That was why Tōgō was charged with the mission of sinking the entire enemy fleet, down to the last ship.

For that purpose, Saneyuki had prepared the seven-stage strategy that involved launching repeated attacks around the clock. But what if haze rose in the day and fog lay over the sea at night? What then?

Please let them come in May. The thought filled Saneyuki's mind like a prayer. As shown by the old expression *satsukibare*—fine May weather— the month of May had many clear days when visibility was good. A later arrival, after the start of the long rainy season, would spell trouble. If providence was smiling on Japan, the Baltic Fleet would come in mid-May.

The front part of the forecastle deck is also known as the anchor deck. On either side of it was an anchor bed housing an anchor weighing 5,385 kilograms. Saneyuki circled the anchor deck and then walked to the afterdeck, which was made of teakwood. Looking up from there, he saw the towering main mast. Dark-brown smoke skimmed its midsection, streaming aft. The teakwood deck was thicker than strictly necessary, a thickness conveyed through the soles of his shoes each time he took a step. This deck alone showed the extraordinary care that had gone into the making of the ship.

* * *

During the night, the battleship *Mikasa* passed the area west of Tsushima known usually as the "western channel." When morning dawned, the surrounding scenery had undergone a transformation. The yellowish mountain on the port side was on the Korean island of Kŏjedo. The *Mikasa* wove its way between various islands and began to enter Kadŏk Channel.

Here and there in the channel, other ships in the fleet already lay at anchor, and farther in, cut off from the outer sea by Kŏjedo, was the ocean's private salon. This was where Tōgō's fleet had chosen to hide out until the Baltic Fleet arrived, having borrowed the area forcibly from Korea.

A green promontory came into view off the *Mikasa*'s starboard bow. This was a small peninsula called Kosŏng Bando that curved around to embrace Chinhae Bay. The channels in the area had been thoroughly surveyed, and they were sprinkled with lane markers, so there was no fear of running into hidden shoals. Still, the lanes were narrow, with room for barely two ships at a time.

The *Mikasa* steamed into the harbor at a leisurely speed, finally dropping anchor at a place called Sonjinpo. Amazingly, no buildings had gone up on shore for the use of the fleet. There were naturally no facilities for the crew's entertainment. No matter how long the waiting period stretched on, everyone from the commander in chief on down would have to live on the ship. Indeed, there would be no communication whatever with the shore, which was Korean territory.

Here, Tōgō conducted marathon training sessions, until the whole crew was exhausted. "That was the hardest time I ever experienced," the sailors all declared, looking back.

Tōgō's plan for victory was not based on any complicated theorizing. It was sweeping in its simplicity and clarity. He wanted his men to fire as many shells on target as possible in a short amount of time. He prepared them for this by carrying out relentless firing drills.

Japanese were not necessarily skillful gunners. Even in the army, some foreign observers held that the Russians were better shots. Russians traditionally had a strong devotion to artillery, so much so that it seemed rooted in their very nature, though in part that tendency was surely the product of history. Russia had been invaded by Napoleon, who excelled at the disposition of artillery and used guns extensively. That fact certainly had an impact on Russia.

In the navy, too, the Port Arthur Squadron had shown remarkable proficiency. On August 10 of the previous year, Tōgō's fleet had battled them in the Yellow Sea and not exactly covered itself with glory. Tōgō had no desire to repeat that bitter experience. He needed the shooting skills of the Japanese Navy to increase exponentially. He needed to drill his men so rigorously in Chinhae Bay that they would be transformed and rise to the level of genius.

* * *

Contemporary target practice included a method known as sub-caliber firing. A rifle was rigged inside a big gun. The gunner would then operate the big gun, take aim, and fire off rifle shot at the target. There was another technique whereby a small practice gun was piggybacked on a larger one and fired, but at Chinhae Bay, the former technique was mainly used.

The amount of ammunition available annually for such practice was fixed for each battleship. The *Mikasa*, for example, could consume twenty-eight to twenty-nine thousand rounds. In peacetime, they would stretch their allotted amount over the course of a year; even so, thirty to forty percent inevitably went unused. "But at Chinhae Bay, we used up the lot in ten days," recalled Admiral Abo Kiyokazu, chief gunnery officer on the *Mikasa* at the time.

As a result, they soon had to order more ammunition from the mainland. Every day, drills would start at dawn and continue until sundown. Ships moving in Kadŏk Channel and ships at anchor behind the island all spat gunfire without cease, as if the entire fleet suffered from monomania. For the first ten days or so, everyone went nearly mad from the constant noise of gunfire reverberating in the air, but Tōgō's will was firm, and he kept them going.

"We practiced over three months, straight through May," says Kawai, "and eventually we got so good we could fire one hundred rounds without missing. One reason we won such a great victory in the battle of Tsushima was that high rate of accuracy."

"Until May, the men worked so intensively on their gunnery skills that they attained a high level of proficiency," said Abo, "so as chief gunnery officer, I had quite a bit of confidence."

But they also needed to practice identifying their targets. It wouldn't do to shoot the wrong target in the heat of battle. If the chief gunnery officer gave the command to fire on "the ship farthest to the right," for example, or "the ship at the front of the line," confusion could easily arise since the fleets were constantly on the move. For that reason, enemy ships to be targeted were identified not by location but by name. Therefore, the men had to be drilled in the types and names of enemy ships.

But Russian names were devilishly hard for the sailors to muster, so Abo coined humorous nicknames that were easy to remember. The *Alexander III* became "Akiresanta," which means "Stupid Santa"; the *Borodino*, "Borodero" or "Flaws Galore"; the *Oryol*, "Ari-yoru" or "Ant Farm"; and the *Dmitri Donskoi*, "Gomitori Gonsuke" or "Garbage-man Gonsuke."

Every day, Abo would gather the gunners and show them figures of the Russian ships, asking them to identify them by name. When he pointed to the *Izumrud*, he would get the confident reply, "That's the 'Mizu-moru-zo,'" meaning "Leaky Barge."

*　*　*

As he worked to improve gunnery performance in Chinhae Bay, Tōgō used a revolutionary method: "Secure command of the ship's gunfire from the bridge."

This meant that the chief gunnery officer issued a single command for the firing of all shipboard artillery, whether turret guns or sub-caliber guns.

Batteries were synchronized instead of firing independently. For this to happen, the gunnery officer in command had to be up on the bridge where he could have a clear view and judge distances. "Prepare to fire!" he shouted in a megaphone and then stated the range. Every gun would fire at that range simultaneously. No battery was allowed to adjust the range on its own.

How to relay orders was difficult. In actual combat, there was danger that the thunder of gunfire from enemy ships and friendly ships would make the commander's voice hard to hear. Ideally, there would have been a voice tube connecting directly to each casemate, but by the time this system was adopted, there was of course no time left to install new equipment.

Tōgō implemented the new system, but its inventor was Lieutenant Commander Katō Kanji, chief gunnery officer of the *Mikasa* the previous year during the August 10 battle of the Yellow Sea. Katō had thought up the idea long before, and drilled his crew that way when he was chief gunnery officer of the *Asahi*. When he was transferred to the *Mikasa*, he proposed the method to Commander Ijichi Hikojirō, who adopted it with enthusiasm.

When the method was implemented during the battle of the Yellow Sea, the British observer Captain William Pakenham, who was then on board the *Mikasa*, was impressed. He was amazed that the chief gunnery officer was up on the bridge to begin with. Once the battle got underway, the turret guns and secondary batteries began firing shells at the enemy simultaneously as soon as the chief gunnery officer's order went out.

Pakenham quickly notified the Admiralty. By sheer coincidence, at around the same time, Percy Scott, a rear admiral, had come up with the same idea, which he called "director firing" and which was then being put into practice.

After the battle of the Yellow Sea, Katō went ashore to serve as Naval Ministry adjutant, but before that he wrote up the results of his research, which he submitted to Tōgō under the title "Results of an Experiment in Directed Firing in the Battle of the Yellow Sea on August 10, 1904."

Tōgō read through the document and was impressed. He had Saneyuki and his other aides evaluate the idea, and also had the chief gunnery officer on each ship take a look at it before deciding to use that method of directing the artillery battle in the coming engagement with the Baltic Fleet.

But it was vital to train each squad leader to respond to the orders of the chief gunnery officer. And a system of communications was needed whereby the chief gunnery officer's voice could be heard clearly through the roar of guns and cannon fire. Aboard the *Mikasa*, band musicians were employed as orderlies to relay the messages, which is why they were so highly valued.

* * *

The author felt some doubt as to whether Tōgō's fleet actually carried out ex-caliber firing practice and consulted Mayuzumi Haruo, an authority on naval gunnery. "Probably not," Mayuzumi said, "although among the whole Japanese fleet one or two warships may have done so."

The technique of ex-caliber firing was thought up after 1907 or else in the early Taishō period and did not yet exist at the time of the Russo-Japanese War.

But according to the recollection of Kawai Tarō, a band musician on the *Mikasa* at the time, "They would straddle the gun, grab what the Satsuma men called a *peppō*"—Satsuma dialect for *teppō*, a rifle—"aim at the target, and fire. For the target they would set up something 2 meters wide and 1 meter high on a raft, and have a steamboat pull it along." This technique is basically the same approach as the later ex-caliber firing technique, but it was extremely primitive in concept and contrivance, so this may have been what they were up to.

Of course, the method mainly used was that of sub-caliber firing, which involved rigging the rifle in the breech of the gun and firing at the target. This innovation was the invention of Briton Percy Scott mentioned above, and this was what Tōgō's fleet did.

As Kawai remembers it, a steamboat would pull a raft along on a wire rope. The target would be on the raft. It was usually iron plate, about the size of a shoji paper door. A double circle would be painted on it or the outline of an enemy ship.

Before hostilities began, when Hidaka Sōnojō was commander in chief of the Standing Fleet, this fleet got in enough live ammunition practice to blast an island in the Seto Inland Sea to smithereens and make it disappear. The same thing must have taken place in Chinhae Bay, but no one remembers it and there are no written accounts of live ammunition practice. All anyone talks about is sub-caliber firing.

This breaks up our narrative, but although it is generally accepted that director firing was the invention of Katō Kanji, the chief gunnery officer of the *Mikasa* at the time of the battle of the Yellow Sea, others say that the idea and technique had already been researched in the Naval Artillery School by Masaki Yoshimoto (a member of the team that blocked the mouth of Port Arthur Harbor), and still others claim that the technique was not used at the start of the Russo-Japanese War at all, but shortly after the war, and that Nagano Osami used it successfully for the first time when he was chief gunnery officer of a protected cruiser.

Furthermore, there is also the theory that this was not an original creation of the Japanese Navy, that its designer was influenced by the work of Percy Scott of the British Navy. In any case, since it was certainly not the custom for a navy man to use his own name to promote his achievements, there is virtually no way to know for sure.

Still, there can be no doubt that director firing (to be precise, having all guns fire at the same range) was adopted by Tōgō and that he was the first to use it in actual combat.

For strict director firing, of course, he needed to install an apparatus so that orders could be perfectly conveyed. Because that apparatus was lacking, there is also no doubt that in the battle of Tsushima, at no time did the system work as well as it might have.

This has been a long digression.

5

THE INDIAN OCEAN

When Tōgō entered Chinhae Bay to await the coming battle, Rozhestvensky and his great fleet were still enduring the sweltering heat at Nosy Be on the island of Madagascar.

Forty-odd war vessels.

Twelve thousand officers and men.

Ever since arriving at Nosy Be on January 9, their world had shrunk to that desolate island and the sea, with no indication of whether they were to continue on course or withdraw. They were true vagrants, abandoned to exile by their country. Unbelievably, during that whole time, Rozhestvensky never once called a staff meeting. No one from the chief of staff on down had any idea where they were headed.

Only Rozhestvensky knew. Deep down, he probably wished to be recalled. At a time when the Russian Army was losing in Manchuria, all that supported the authority of the Russian Empire at home and around the world was his fleet. If it sank to the bottom of the sea in the Far East, what would become of Russia?

"Russian power comes from its soldiers and bayonets, and that's what other nations fear." Even the enlightened Witte said this about the close connection between Russia and its military might. Could Russia stand to lose the last vestige of that might?

But the Naval Ministry showed no sign of being ready to order Rozhestvensky home. Therefore, his only thoughts were of moving forward. Yet he was faint of heart over the question of whether he could pull off the coming sea battle, which would determine the fate of his country.

"Make it to Vladivostok with a minimum of damage"—this was his policy. In a way, he saw his fleet as a team set to run an obstacle course. Yes, they would face a battle along the way, but he would use his capital ships to fend off attack. In the meantime, he would slip his cruisers adroitly out the back to guard transport ships before heading for Vladivostok. His battleships would head for Vladivostok too, fighting as they went. The destroyers would guard flagships carrying him and his commanding officers. Should any of their ships suffer serious damage, the destroyers would take them on board. This was his plan of operations. Actually, it wasn't a plan so much as a marathon.

Cruisers are designed for speed and agility, to strike blows against the enemy fleet, but Rozhestvensky unaccountably relegated his to the role of nursemaid, setting them to watch over plodding steamships. A destroyer is like a dagger. At the risk of being blown up by enemy shells, the destroyer draws close to a big ship's bosom to dispatch it by torpedo—but Rozhestvensky's destroyers were only assigned the role of battleship nurse, ministering to flagships in particular. This was Rozhestvensky's strategy against Tōgō's fleet.

* * *

During this interval, Rozhestvensky did not let his fleet sit idle. He had them doing constant firing and torpedo practice, though the training was not as extensive as what Tōgō put his men through. Sometimes, Rozhestvensky took the fleet out to sea to practice maneuvers, but every single time he would blow his top: "I haven't got one commander worth a damn!"

A number of the commanders were, in fact, topnotch, but unfortunately the fleet had been quickly thrown together, and they hadn't yet caught on to Rozhestvensky's unique style. From their point of view, the admiral failed to give clear orders, not telling the battleships just what to do, for example, or the protected cruisers what formation to adopt.

In short, Rozhestvensky laid out no strategy or principles of engagement. To put it bluntly, he had no notion of naval strategy. This wasn't a sign of incompetence on his part. At that time, a battle between two fleets anywhere in the world meant warships blasting away at one another every which way. The Japanese Navy was the first to implement the idea of a streamlined battle in which the fleet itself followed strategic principles, every squadron moving with line-dance precision, exploiting its functions and specialties to achieve particular goals within the overarching goals of the fleet.

The designer of the "circle tactics," Yamaya Tanin, was at this juncture commander of the *Kasagi* in Chinhae Bay. When he learned about the strategic genius of Akiyama Saneyuki, his junior by a year or two, he dropped his tactical studies and supported him wholeheartedly. And when the Japanese Navy as a whole entrusted research on strategy to Saneyuki's genius, strategy for a decisive encounter with an enemy fleet came into being for the first time in the world.

In that sense, Rozhestvensky was simply an admiral on a par with other admirals in the world's navies, not above them. Even if he had devised some brilliant strategy, the fleet he commanded was simply the world's biggest, not the best; brand-new battleships apart, it was something of a hodgepodge. Carrying out a brilliant strategy under those conditions might have been difficult.

Still, there was something extremely odd about the plan Rozhestvensky had in mind. To take a hospital ship and a repair ship along to the scene of a battle is not a true warrior's style. Those should have been left behind in Shanghai Harbor or somewhere, but Rozhestvensky took just the opposite tack. He had led his grand armada on its historic odyssey, but now, with the climactic battle looming, he intended to use the entire fleet to protect noncombat steamships. Clearly, he had things backwards. Rozhestvensky was a superior seaman, but if he'd had the true stamp of an admiral, he would have presented his thoughts to his staff and held a captains' meeting to thrash them out. He did not.

In this, he behaved in the manner of one who had found favor with Nicholas II, meaning he was every inch a product of imperialist Russia. He was a little tsar. He knew no other way of exerting authority than despotism. As the tsar of the fleet, he regarded his chief of staff and staff officers as little more than servants.

Like any real tsar, the little tsar Rozhestvensky had no private interest. The word "private interest" here requires some qualification. In the same sense that Chinese rulers of the Qing dynasty identified completely with their country and so had no private interest—even if they were self-seeking—it was quite impossible for any tsar in imperialist Russia to have private interest.

As long as the tsar was a despot, the supreme commander of an expeditionary force with authority delegated by the tsar would naturally become a classic despot in his own right. In that sense, Rozhestvensky was the very model of a little tsar. Compared with the sharp Russian bigwigs in St. Petersburg who engaged in systematic corruption on a daily basis, he was upright, as the tsar was upright.

Just as Nicholas II was always thinking of the welfare of his people in the abstract, Rozhestvensky was full of tender concern for the pay and relaxation of his sailors. Highly commendable as this was, for that very reason, every sailor was conversely an enemy to him and the entire fleet an object of hatred. This apparent contradiction was no contradiction at all, but a perfectly natural outcome. Upright, incompetent, and unfortunately focused only on improving his fleet, he had the character of any well-meaning despot.

When he walked about the ship, he carried a long telescope tucked under his arm in the fashion of those times, and, when he came upon a sailor who was slovenly or shirking his duties, he would leap on the miscreant and beat him with it. This happened no mere half-dozen times or so. Each time, the telescope broke, and the paymaster was hard pressed to replace it.

When Rozhestvensky's noble features appeared on the quarterdeck, sailors quickly alerted one another. The signal spread like wildfire until not only were there no sailors in his vicinity, but no officers either. He could pardon no one. Given the chance, he would probably have screamed that the whole fleet was unpardonable. For all cases of impropriety by fleet personnel, he himself acted as prosecuting attorney and judge.

"Order Number such-and-such," he would write, prescribing what punishment was to be meted out to whom, on what ship, for what charge. Each time, he got so worked up that frequently he broke his pen. Of the vast number of orders he penned on this long haul, far more dealt with disciplinary action than with drills. To Rozhestvensky, justice meant rigid moral discipline, nothing more. He was to that extent a man with a strong sense of justice, but it was a sense of justice brought to bear not against Tōgō's fleet, but his own.

* * *

Chinhae Bay, where Tōgō waited on alert with his fleet, was a little-known place, its name unfamiliar even to most Koreans at the time. Nosy Be, where Rozhestvensky and his fleet were anchored, was equally unknown.

In Tōgō's case, no facilities were built on the grassy shore of Chinhae Bay, nor were sailors allowed ashore for relaxation. Rozhestvensky did permit the latter, following Russian custom, and so the little fishing village of Hell-Ville became an entertainment quarter. "A den of evil," Novikov-Priboy called it. A native man attracting Russians into his house and forcing his wife to prostitute herself—such abnormality became "business as usual."

"Russian-language signs pop up in clusters, like mushrooms after a rain," Politovsky wrote. What the signs were selling he does not say, since he was writing to his wife. Usually such places were houses of prostitution. The men who ran them, hearing that twelve thousand wastrels were idle offshore from Nosy Be, quickly rounded up women from all over. These women were of various nationalities—British, German, French. As they were high-priced, most of their clientele were officers. Native women served petty officers and sailors.

There were several cafés and innumerable bars. Drunken sailors lay in the street where they fell or reeled around in bands. If they came upon an officer just leaving a brothel, they didn't bother to salute. Officers command respect by immaculateness; failing that, they can only cower in fear of underlings' eyes or turn defiant. One defiant warrant officer ordered some sailors to salute him and was soundly thrashed by reckless men who then had to stand a summary court-martial under Rozhestvensky.

Eventually unable to deal with the flood of cases, Rozhestvensky left it to the ships' commanders to mete out appropriate measures in the customary way. Court-martial proceedings were held frequently aboard every ship. Normally, the commander would preside. Rather than thinking of battle tactics or carrying out drills, therefore, commanders were up to their necks in disciplinary action.

"This is what comes of keeping men idle." Rozhestvensky finally decided to round up sailors with nothing better to do and have them practice rowing. For the men, who were actually quite busy, this was bad news. Now during their infrequent time off they were plunked into rowboats and set paddling around warships in circles like whirligigs.

* * *

All sorts of rumors flew, eating into the spirits of the officers and men like a disease, but Rozhestvensky did nothing about it. In the staff officers' room, all agreed: "None of the ships is full to the brim with fighting spirit. We only carry a full load of rumors. How can we go to war encumbered with all these rumors?"

Rozhestvensky alone was capable of sweeping the mountain of rumors into the sea. Getting him to consider doing so was the staff officers' job. But as happens under every despotic ruler, they refrained from expressing their opinions for fear of offending the despot.

The sailors, with the quick sensibility of those under domination, saw what the situation was and began holding their commanding officers in contempt.

"They're all terrified of Rozhestvensky, the whole lot of them. Even if it's for the good of the navy, they won't speak up. So the chief, who's hardheaded to begin with, gets even more hardheaded." The sailors whispered these things among themselves and lost any inclination to rely on their officers, the very ones on whom they should have relied. Morale plummeted. In a sense, the root of all evils lay in Rozhestvensky's autocratic rule.

Rozhestvensky took to his cabin, steadfastly restraining his "righteous" indignation, lonely in his assurance that he and he alone was in the right. At times he would explode, at other times he suffered severe attacks of neuralgia.

What disturbed him most were the officers and men, but he had another enemy as well—the Naval Ministry in St. Petersburg. The way he saw it, the ministry was full of fraudsters, toadies living hand-to-mouth, and hypocrites who had abandoned patriotism and thought only of saving their hides. Not only was the ministry no help in preparing to win the war, but concerning the issue of coal, which required diplomacy on a national scale, their response was a laconic "Handle it on your end." Even this little tsar who believed the Russian tsar to be the source of all good was forced to locate the source of all evil in the fearful corruption, irresponsibility, and inefficiency of the Russian bureaucracy.

The other thing that jangled Rozhestvensky's nerves was a newspaper report that, "on arriving in Vladivostok, Rozhestvensky will trade places with another admiral." It seemed to be hearsay from a source in the Russian Naval Ministry. The other admiral would soon be heading for Vladivostok aboard the Trans-Siberian Railway. If this were true, then the Naval Ministry saw Rozhestvensky as fit only to shepherd the armada as far as its destination.

* * *

Rozhestvensky's partialities and evaluations of his underlings were peculiar.

Engineer Politovsky on the *Suvorov*, a young man of thirty-two, had a touch of melancholy in his eyes but otherwise was a good-looking, athletic youth whose abilities were highly praised by the flagship's chief engineer, Obnorsky. "The day will come," Obnorsky was fond of saying, "when that fellow will be shipbuilder for the whole Russian Navy."

Politovsky was quiet and had a strong sense of responsibility. In the staff officers' room, he always sat by himself on a couch. At Nosy Be, no one was busier than he, as ships were always suffering engine breakdowns, rudder damage, and the like. Whenever trouble arose, Politovsky hopped into a rowboat and set off, personally inspecting the engine or diving into the water to find the problem, then supervising the repair.

This bright and slightly melancholic young man had a keen eye for what was wrong not just in the fleet's machinery but in its leadership and even the preparedness of its crew. As to the probable outcome of the looming clash with Tōgō's fleet, he had no hope. He himself would die in the battle of Tsushima, leaving his memoirs behind, so the views he expressed privately in letters to his wife are devoid of political considerations.

In any case, dispirited though he was about what lay ahead, Politovsky performed his duty with a will. When there was damage aboard the destroyer *Gromky*, he set straight off and found something wrong on the ship's bottom that divers needed to repair. Several divers came from the repair ship *Kamchatka* and set to work. Politovsky directed the operation from the destroyer, getting wet to the skin in spray from the high wind and waves. The divers had it even worse. Waves alternately tore them from the boat and beat them against it, sometimes cracking their headgear. They were rocked about in the water so much that they got seasick, but they gamely persevered.

On the way back, Politovsky was swallowed by waves, arriving at the *Suvorov* thoroughly wet and fatigued. He seized hold of a chain, put his feet against the side, and somehow climbed on deck, where who should he find standing but Rozhestvensky. The admiral gave him not a word of encouragement but only shouted angrily: "What's this! You serve on the staff and only make things worse. You should be ashamed of yourself! The repair of the *Gromky* will take until five o'clock, and here you are back at three!"

It was three in the afternoon when Politovsky crawled up on deck. This was a strange reprimand. "In all this long voyage," he wrote to his wife, "this is the only reward I have had from the admiral. I shall never forget it!"

* * *

Rozhestvensky had a beautifully sculpted face. If God set out to carve in relief the features of an extraordinary man, this, one felt, would be the result. Each individual feature was superb—the clear eyes sparkling with intelligence, the aristocratic nose, the fine mouth showing determination— and together they conveyed a distinctive impression of strength.

Unusually for a Russian admiral, he was not of noble birth, but he had looks befitting the highest level of the nobility. He had graduated from the Naval Academy with top honors, and when he was a lieutenant his abilities earned him the respect of his senior officers. While on active duty, he was assigned largely to shore duty and excelled as an artillery researcher, but he didn't have a spark of originality or inspiration. During his time in the Naval Ministry, he showed competence in administrative work and was good at managing things. He was strict with underlings, forthright with superiors. If he could have lived untouched by war, he would probably have been valued at home and abroad as one of the Russian Navy's finest men, ending his days happily in a villa in some warm climate.

But he was chosen from Russia's many admirals and dragged into a war that needed someone with a reckless spirit of adventure and a great talent for strategic planning. He was chosen because, as the tsar's loyal aide-de-camp, he had long had the tsar's ear concerning the Russian Navy and had offered up his opinions freely. Unfortunately, among those opinions was the idea of a grand sea odyssey by the Baltic Fleet, a notion so outlandish that even a British admiral might have shrunk from undertaking such a voyage.

But Rozhestvensky had spoken only as aide-de-camp, someone who was strictly an outsider to the Naval Ministry, surely never imagining that he himself would be made commander in chief.

As far as the tsar was concerned, he needed a grand plan and a heroic admiral to dramatically reverse the Russian Empire's adverse military situation. Rozhestvensky was very much a hero in the opinions he voiced, but the tsar lacked discernment. If Rozhestvensky hadn't been the aide-de-camp of a despotic tsar, he would have escaped the sad fate of this grueling voyage. Or, to put it another way, he might very well have met a different fate if he hadn't cut such a distinguished figure, one that bore so little connection to the person he really was.

Rozhestvensky had a creed. He believed that all the commanders in his fleet were hopeless idiots. He didn't even trust the abilities of his own staff. Just as others were deluded by his appearance, so he may have been deluded by it himself. There seems no other explanation for his mysterious certainty that everyone but himself was a fool.

*   *   *

And yet Rozhestvensky had a distinct liking for one officer. He approved every action taken by the captain of a certain destroyer, not only praising him openly but telling others, "Follow his example." Even the sailors were aware of this blatant favoritism. All could see that the captain was an obvious bluffer who ran a loose ship; not only that, he drove his sailors mercilessly for no reason, yelled at them and if he found evidence of misconduct, would beat the offender nearly to death on the spot. When the battle came, he put himself shrewdly out of harm's way and was taken captive without ever doing a lick of real fighting.

Another commander, in complete contrast, enjoyed a good reputation with his men, all of whom agreed that they could happily entrust their lives to a leader of such high ability and character. With him, Rozhestvensky took a harsh line, constantly calling him stupid. Even in the midst of fleet maneuvers and torpedo practice, he would heap abuse on the officer, flying signals that mocked and berated him.

Rozhestvensky was cool toward his own staff as well, with one exception: Commander Vladimir Semenov. Strictly speaking, Semenov was not a staff officer but more like a personal aide. Rozhestvensky treated him as a close friend, and when Semenov came into his cabin he would brighten a little.

"How's it going, Vladimir?" he would say, offering him a seat and a cigar. Most surprising of all, given Rozhestvensky's reclusive nature, he would engage him in conversation.

A tubby, middle-aged man whom the sailors called "Walking Sack" behind his back, Semenov had a thoroughly Western-style education and was known as a writer of novels and tales of the sea. He had a rich stock of topics for conversation. The others, with their acute sailors' instincts, detected in him a kind of cunning unbecoming a mariner and disliked him for it.

Semenov himself nursed deep dissatisfaction. He was a survivor of the Port Arthur Squadron. After the squadron's crushing defeat, he had cleverly escaped and returned to Russia, where he was recommissioned to the Baltic Fleet. "I know the smell of Shimose powder," he liked to boast. But despite his high rank, he was never once given a seat at an officers' staff meeting, and his official title, "Coordinator of Marine Affairs," was unheard of and vague.

"I wasn't informed about things that even young officers were in on." As this statement from his war chronicle shows, he was left out of things by the other staff officers, who were not so sociable as to treat this useless appendage as one of them.

Rozhestvensky probably brought Semenov along on the expedition to keep a record of events. His affability toward Semenov may have reflected a desire to be shown in a good light to future generations. In fact, the memoir that Semenov eventually wrote includes passages that sing Rozhestvensky's praises as well as being puffed up with self-justification.

* * *

Around the beginning of March, whispering began on all the ships about how the fleet was soon to leave Nosy Be. Colliers came by frequently, and the ships all took on coal. On March 15, German traders who kept the fleet supplied with rations and other needed items sent a steamer with salt meat, biscuits, tea, and even cheese, all of which was piled on board.

Just before the steamer arrived, Rozhestvensky signaled the fleet to finish loading in twenty-four hours. As soon as the steamer arrived, loading began. Before the operation was over, another signal went up on the *Suvorov*: "By noon tomorrow prepare to raise steam." Every ship burst into activity, and boats and steam pinnaces hummed to and fro in the water. Every single ship took in so much cargo it was bursting at the seams.

Vladimir Kostenko, an engineer on the battleship *Oryol*, served as a kind of physician for the ship and came up with a diagnosis that sent him into despair. The displacement of the *Oryol* was normally 13,516 tons, but due to the overload it had gone over 17,000 tons. This would impact the ship's stability so that, depending on conditions during the voyage, it could turn turtle.

The other warships were in no better shape. Rozhestvensky's policy was to load each craft with all the coal and provisions it could hold. Fighting Tōgō's fleet was not his only duty. He had to get this historically huge armada across the seas so the fight could take place. He had no time to offer sound arguments in rebuttal of Kostenko's criticisms.

Vladimir Kostenko was still twenty-four, younger than Politovsky on the *Suvorov*. Like Politovsky, he had helped build the new, *Suvorov*-class battleships. The two of them had abilities that were indispensable to this adventurous voyage. Engineer Politovsky despaired of the battle ahead because of what he saw as the crudeness of Russian naval strategy and the inefficiency of the fleet. Kostenko felt much the same way. However, Kostenko had come to hold the political conviction that nothing could save Russia but a revolution, and here he differed slightly from Politovsky.

Incidentally, the intelligent young engineer "Vasilyev" who comes up in Novikov-Priboy's book *Tsushima* is Vladimir Kostenko.

*   *   *

On the morning of March 16, the fleet was ready to leave.

Politovsky went ashore to the post office to send a letter to his bride by registered mail. The clerk, a young Frenchman, knew him, having often handled his registered mail before. In sympathy for the clerks who'd devoted themselves to handling the fleet's mail for two months, Politovsky had volunteered to arrange for them to receive Russian medals.

"Will we get our medals okay?" the Frenchman asked. A man of his word, Politovsky had already made the arrangements, so he replied that the medals should arrive by the end of the year. By then, he himself would be dead, but that he had no way of knowing.

"Are you going back to Russia?" asked the clerk.

Unable to say they were headed to the Far East, Politovsky only smiled and shook hands before getting back in the steam pinnace and returning to the *Suvorov*. By eleven o'clock, he was on board.

At noon, while he was eating lunch, the signal flew: "Prepare to weigh anchor." During the prolonged stay, Politovsky had been kept busier than anyone, and fatigue hit him all at once. He was too tired to speak to anyone, let alone feel elated at the imminent departure. At one o'clock, the ships steamed out, and the long, two-month limbo was over. All forty-five ships were setting out, with him on board, to meet their unknown destiny in the waters of the Far East, but even in that moment he felt nothing.

Two French destroyers that had been at anchor in the harbor came along with the Russian fleet. "Bon voyage" read the signals on the masts of the pretty little boats, their hulls painted a dazzling white, as they escorted the fleet out of the harbor. On the quarterdeck of the *Suvorov*, under the burning sun with a light breeze blowing, the band started up a cheerful tune. In gratitude for the goodwill of the French during their layover, they played "La Marseillaise."

Rozhestvensky was on the bridge. Next to him, Captain Ignatzius, the commander of the *Suvorov*, gazed out at the French destroyers with a quiet smile. He had never discussed war tactics with Rozhestvensky, but he felt that God alone could preserve the fleet from what lay ahead. He made a habit of keeping his feelings to himself, however, wearing easy smiles and now and then telling a tasteful joke.

The departure lifted morale. The officers' quarters were lively, and the sailors scurried to and fro with energy.

* * *

The fleet steamed east across the Indian Ocean.

The first adventurers ever to cross this, the world's third largest ocean, were undoubtedly ancient Phoenicians—but their story, while of interest to historians, means nothing to sailors. The figure whose achievement continues to cast splendor on the history of sailing is Vasco da Gama, who reached the shore of India in 1498.

"We've set out on a voyage harder than Vasco da Gama's, haven't we!" This cheerful statement from the junior officers' quarters on the flagship *Suvorov* came out of midshipman Werner von Kursel, a young man with a German name. In the battle ahead, he would play an inspiring role, but no one saw that coming. The officers loved the amiable young fellow like a mascot.

Von Kursel had been educated not at Nikolayevsky Naval Academy but on a merchant ship. He went to sea as a boy, then studied on his own and passed the certification exam to become an officer. He was immediately conscripted.

Vladimir Semenov, a staff officer with nothing to do, was bored, and so whenever he saw young von Kursel he would engage him in some good-natured teasing to pass the time. "He was winsome and always greeted people with a fresh, sweet smile," wrote Semenov. "He liked talking to people."

Von Kursel was probably not so much a chatterbox as he was eager to listen in on adult conversation. He had scant experience of warships and often quizzed the veteran officers. As he had served on globe-trotting merchant ships ever since he was a small boy, he boasted the ability to speak most European languages. Asked which one he was best at, he would answer in dead earnest, "German." His great-grandfather had become a Russian citizen, but the family had continued to speak German at home ever since.

Young von Kursel therefore had good reason to be confident of his German language skills. But he had a loyalty to the Russian Empire second to none and so could honestly say that, to him, German was a foreign language.

Ever since Peter the Great's policy of Westernization, incidentally, German physicians and engineers had been encouraged to acquire Russian citizenship, and so for citizens of German ancestry, life in Russia was good. All Germans tended to be looked on as physicians or engineers, their background affording them respect.

In his merchant ship days, von Kursel had crossed the Indian Ocean many times, usually going from Suez to Colombo, a route that was Main Street on the Indian Ocean for ships from far and wide. But the Baltic Fleet was embarking on a new route, one much farther south. This was because they didn't want to give away their position or any other information to foreign ships along the way, much less run into ships belonging to Britain, Japan's ally: the Indian Ocean was also referred to as a "British lake." Rozhestvensky was leading his fleet on a lonely journey to a distant place where they would encounter no sign of another ship.

*　*　*

The great flagship *Suvorov*, packed with sacks of coal from stem to stern, lumbered heavily across the waves. Fitted uncomfortably in the spaces between stacks were live cattle that formed part of the seamen's diet. There were bulls, cows, and even calves. The cows were there to provide milk, but in the constant rolling and pitching, all udders had gone dry. An endless stream of cattle excrement covered the deck. Every time the cattle made a mess, the sailors and petty officers cleaned it up.

The fleet steamed ahead in line formation, its forty-five ships easily stretching 10 kilometers. Soon it would be joined by Rear Admiral Nebogatov's Third Pacific Squadron. If the expedition of this great armada succeeded, the achievements of the builders of the pyramids and the Great Wall, as well as the expedition of Alexander the Great, would all pale by comparison.

For cruisers and larger ships, the voyage was not so difficult, but for destroyers it was an ordeal. Common sense should have dictated that for small 350-ton destroyers of that time such a voyage was too demanding. But when the time came to fight, the battleships could not perform their function without their pack of hunting-dog destroyers at their side.

Those little boats were a handful. Their crews experienced severe distress too as, continually rocked by swells, they now slid into great valleys and now climbed high mountains, over and over again. From the first, the little boats were a drag on the fleet, as one or another of them (there were nine) was forever running out of fuel and signaling the flagship, "No more coal."

For the Indian Ocean crossing, they decided to alleviate matters by having big ships pull the destroyers along on wire ropes. That way, the destroyers wouldn't have to use their engines, and their little stomachs wouldn't soon grow empty.

The days passed without their running into much bad weather. Sometimes the waves were high, and other times a light rain fell, but the crossing was not difficult. Clear skies alternated smoothly with cloudy. The noon sun was intense, the ships' hulls and guns hot enough to burn anyone who touched them. But the humid heat they had suffered through at Madagascar was blessedly gone, the nights somewhat easier to bear. On clear nights, the starry firmament was a grand sight. Stars as big as gold and silver studs sparkled like cat's-eye gemstones, comforting the twelve thousand men at sea.

Or perhaps "comforted" is the wrong word. They say the Indian Ocean has the power to make those who cross it weary of life. From ancient times, men have thrown themselves into its waters and died for no apparent reason. The same thing happened with this fleet. A sailor on the steamship *Kiev* flung himself overboard. There was a commotion, and his shipmates tried to go back and save him, but Rozhestvensky signaled, "Stop the search" and had them continue on their way. Someone else leaped from the protected cruiser *Zhemchug*.

* * *

The fleet halted periodically on its way. If one ship needed repairs, the whole fleet halted while the damage was tended to, and they also halted to load coal. "Rozhestvensky's miracle," they called this epic voyage, and it was truly deserving of the name. They were traveling to the Far East without a single coaling station along the way.

A warship consumes a prodigious amount of coal. For forty-five ships to travel halfway around the world without regular coaling stations was unthinkable, but the Russians pulled it off. What made the feat possible, as we have touched on before, was the willingness of a German coal company to send out coaling ships at various destinations en route. Details were worked out carefully between the fleet and the coaling company, and the undertaking went off without a hitch.

The greatest inconvenience was having to load coal at sea. Everyone pitched in, even the officers. The intensity of the labor involved was far greater than at harbor.

"To coal ship in this way was utterly exhausting. The lives of galley slaves were probably less arduous than ours." So wrote Novikov-Priboy, a petty officer aboard the *Oryol* whose shoulders, arms, and lungs had felt the strain of coaling ever since the fleet first set out.

The method used was exceedingly primitive. One group of men filled sacks in the colliers' holds. Another group in a rowboat took these in and, when they had a full load, rowed back to the main vessel, where the sacks were hoisted aboard by winch and emptied into bunkers in the hold. As happens with any military operation anywhere in the world, rival contingents from each ship raced against each other.

As this went on, the ships did not drop anchor but simply stopped their engines, drifting with the wind and waves. Once the coal was loaded, steam pinnaces and rowboats had to be hauled back up the ships' sides, an enormously difficult operation in itself.

And in the meantime, rumors flew that cruisers manned by "macaques" had appeared, setting everyone's nerves even more on edge.

7

ON TO MUKDEN

Kuropatkin was in Mukden.

The largest city in Manchuria, Mukden was officially called Fengtianfu. The city flourished under the Qing, but in the previous Ming dynasty, when it was called Shenyang, it served as the base for a frontier garrison. At the time, it wasn't a large city or a dominating presence in southern Manchuria. Nurhaci was a chieftain of Manchuria's Tungusic Aisin Gioro clan, whose descendants founded the Qing dynasty. Late in the Ming dynasty, his forces attacked the city and made it into a capital.

Nurhaci was succeeded by his son Hong Taiji. While the Chongzhen Emperor ruled Ming China, Hong Taiji greatly expanded his powers, building up the capital Shenyang and changing its name. Nurhaci and his descendants were not, of course, of Han ethnicity. They spoke a language akin to Mongol, and they called the city "Mukden," meaning "flourishing capital." Translated into the language of the Han, this became "Shengjing." After founding the Qing dynasty and moving the capital to Beijing, the Manchus went on referring to the old capital as "Mukden," and that is how it continues to be known in the West and in Russia.

Around the time when the city became known as Mukden, some Japanese visitors passed through. In 1644, during the rule of the third Tokugawa shogun Iemitsu, a band of traders, including one Okada Hyōemon, set out by boat from Echizen (today's Fukui Prefecture) to do business in Matsumae, Hokkaido. They ran into a typhoon and were diverted to Manchuria, where they were captured and escorted back to Japan. Along the way they saw the "flourishing capital."

What follows is taken from a transcription of remarks the traders made at an official debriefing upon their return to Japan:

The Tatar capital is about 5 miles in circumference. The place in the middle where the king resides resembles a Japanese castle, but it is not strong like a Japanese castle. There are turrets in every corner. It is generally like a Japanese temple hall, built very large with round pillars. The roof tiles are glazed and shine in five colors. Naturally there are ordinary roof tiles as well. Townhouses are built as in Japan. All of them are roofed with tiles. They are not of very fine appearance. Still, they are large and sturdy. Indoors there are no wooden floors such as we have in Japan. The flooring is flagstone.

Those Japanese castaways in early Qing times did not find the capital terribly imposing, but later, as the Qing dynasty flourished, great construction projects were carried out in the ancestral capital and enormous city walls went up. There were double walls, a square inner wall of brick enclosed in an outer earthen wall with an irregular oval shape. This was how Mukden looked when imperial Russia invaded Manchuria.

*   *   *

The immediate goals of Tsar Nicholas II's planned invasion of the Far East were to take Manchuria and make Korea a dependency. In Masan Bay, a fishing harbor along the southern Korean coast near Chinhae Bay, Russia had been building a military harbor since before the start of the Russo-Japanese War.

In 1896, Russia demanded and won from the Qing government the right to lay track for a Manchurian railroad. Large-scale construction soon began, and then Russia sent a large strategic army to southern Manchuria under the pretext of quelling the Boxer Rebellion. Occupying territory as it went, the army took Mukden by force. While the town was still under occupation, Russia began to build its own urban center there.

They didn't touch the inner or outer towns of the city; instead, their construction veered westward, with Mukden Station as the center. What had been wasteland became crowded with European-style roads and buildings, including offices of the Eastern Railway Corporation, a cathedral, a hospital, and barracks. Meanwhile, Russian sentries stood guard on the city walls. Thus, well before the start of the Russo-Japanese War, Mukden was Russian territory.

Once the war began, General Kuropatkin set up huge field fortifications in the countryside near Mukden to accommodate an army of over three hundred thousand. "The encampment stretched all the way from Mukden to Fushun," remarked someone who went to see it after the war. "It was huge, something they'd been building for a year, nothing they threw up overnight.

What I guess you'd call pillboxes today."

The remarks belong to Kitahara Nobuaki, the father of writer Kitahara Takeo. At the time, Nobuaki was a young army surgeon serving in an artillery battalion of the Imperial Guard under General Kuroki. His remarks appear in the ninety-six-page book *Verbatim Accounts of the Russo-Japanese War* by Uno Chiyo.

The troops Kuropatkin held around Mukden numbered three hundred twenty thousand, the greatest number since the war began. In contrast, the Japanese field army held by Ōyama and Kodama came to no more than two hundred fifty thousand. The Russians had one thousand two hundred cannons, the Japanese nine hundred ninety. The coming battle between these two huge military forces on a 100-kilometer front would be unprecedented, the largest in history.

Until then, the largest battle ever was the 1813 battle of Leipzig, where French forces had numbered only one hundred seventy-one thousand, coalition forces no more than three hundred one thousand five hundred. The coming clash at Mukden would be that much more massive.

Both sides, moreover, planned to take the offensive. "We will not retreat one step north of Mukden," Kuropatkin declared. He intended to force the Japanese into an all-or-nothing confrontation.

*　*　*

We know that for financial reasons, the Japanese government and Imperial Headquarters remained eager to end the war as quickly as possible. This had been their unswerving stance from the first. Cognoscenti the world over agreed that if the fighting went on much longer, Japan would go bankrupt.

Yet, for a country so impoverished, Japan's wartime finances were in surprisingly good shape. The rise in commodity prices that war entails was mild, ranging from two percent to twenty percent—something of a miracle. Compared with Russia, where extremely high prices were a main cause of social unrest, Japan was fortunate indeed.

Japan's wartime national economy differed little from usual thanks mainly to foreign loans, which were easily procured out of international sympathy for the underdog. In the end, the Russo-Japanese War cost Japan one billion nine hundred million yen, of which foreign loans accounted for one billion two hundred million yen. The war was financed almost entirely by borrowed funds.

While Ministry of Finance policy may have helped curb the rise in commodity prices, there was a variety of other reasons too. To begin with there was a tax increase, which the government presented to the Diet with this explanation: "This could fairly be called an unreasonable tax plan, but as the fate of the nation depends on it, we have no alternative." The plan was approved—evidence that the nation viewed the conflict as a patriotic war. People not only took on the burden of domestic bonds but also padded their savings, another sign of a patriotic war, and this also helped to hold prices down.

Still, the war did cause an economic slowdown. Fighting had already gone on for over a year, and, if it were to last another two or three years, Japan faced a financial crunch of potentially fatal proportions.

From the first, there had been a sense of crisis in the government, fed by fear that the war might lead to financial ruin. As a result, the country was run with financial sensibilities honed sharper than at any time before or since. That the same nation would far down the road wage a Pacific War of extreme recklessness, financial and otherwise, seems almost beyond belief.

The dire state of Japanese finances was obvious when, after the battle of Mukden, Imperial Headquarters proposed creating more divisions to make up for the lost troop strength. The army minister was forced to reject the proposal, explaining, "We haven't got nearly enough money."

In any case, Japan was eager to escape its financial woes by gaining a decisive victory and bringing about peace. The country's mood was increasingly jittery. The demand for a decisive battle at Mukden started at the instigation of Imperial Headquarters, while simultaneously the Foreign Ministry was pursuing peace negotiations with United States President Theodore Roosevelt as go-between.

*   *   *

The battle of Mukden was necessary for stringent political reasons. It was also necessary tactically for the Japanese Army, serving as a watershed that would spell victory or defeat. The sooner it took place, the better.

Russia was making a major mobilization effort in Europe with an eye to gaining ultimate victory in Manchuria, and the Fourth European Army Corps was due to join Kuropatkin in the spring. As it was, the Russian general had a great advantage in troop numbers. Once the Fourth European Army Corps pitched in, no matter how desperately the Japanese fought they were surely doomed to be cornered in the Liaodong Peninsula and driven into the sea.

"Before spring": that was the strict time limitation imposed on the Japanese Army. The job needed to get done not just before spring, but before the ice thawed, if possible. But not just "if possible"—timing was crucial. To strike an enemy force of over three hundred thousand with a force numbering just over two hundred thousand required a clever plan, plus speed and agility. It was like a sumo-wrestling match in which one wrestler was so much smaller than the other that his only hope of victory lay in darting swiftly about the ring.

Winter was best for military movements in Manchuria. Rivers froze over and could easily be traversed by men, horses, and carts. In spring, the snow would melt and the roads would get muddy, creating the worst possible travel conditions.

"This year's spring will be early." That was what Kodama Gentarō had heard from the meteorological officer, and indeed, already in February the days were unusually warm. This year's thaw might come all too soon.

After a strategy meeting, Kodama decided to move things up: "We will launch our offensive in Manchuria on February 25." The author of this grand strategy was Matsukawa Toshitane, by now a major general and chief of operations in Manchurian headquarters.

Since just over two hundred thousand men were going up against just over three hundred thousand, the operation would have to be nonstandard. While he worked out his plan, Matsukawa consulted repeatedly with Kodama. When he first explained what he had in mind, Kodama said in surprise, "That's different all right," then fell silent. The general had his quirks, and among his staff it was generally accepted that his silence signaled consent. This time, however, that was not necessarily true.

Kodama was deep in thought, pondering whether there could be some other way. Outlandish schemes were brilliant if they succeeded, but they also ran great risk of failure. Should this plan fail, the loss would be irretrievable.

* * *

"That's different all right." The plan of operations Matsukawa Toshitane came up with, giving the usually decisive Kodama pause for thought, was what's known as a frontal breakthrough.

Kuropatkin's army was positioned in a great east–west line, its wings stretched out far, but the sheer number of troops gave it depth on the north–south axis as well. Especially in the center, around Mukden, Russian defenses were strong.

Matsukawa's idea was to break through that center. From ancient times, the frontal breakthrough has been every strategist's ideal, but successful tries are extremely rare. To attempt a frontal breakthrough with an army so overmatched was to all appearances reckless.

Indeed, against an enemy as bold and lopsidedly large as the Russian Army, launching any strong offensive might have been just as reckless. Yet there was no other way for the Japanese Army to save itself but by executing this truly heroic plan. Going actively on the offensive at such a time—even granting there was no alternative—is in itself praiseworthy, many times more so than the outcome.

But a frontal breakthrough couldn't be carried out immediately. First they had to attack the enemy's left flank. The enemy would then concentrate its forces there in surprise. Next they would attack on the right. Surprised again, the enemy would surely divert more of its forces from the center. The Japanese forces would take advantage of this confusion to thrust their way through the center, which they anticipated would be undermanned at that point.

This was the plan. It resembled jujitsu. But jujitsu is straightforward, relying as it does on dynamic principles; this was closer to a stunt or a conjuring trick. Attack the left, then the right. The enemy responds by lunging now this way, now that. The success of the operation depended on this anticipated response, but who knew whether the enemy would oblige by dancing to their tune?

Such sleight-of-hand might work with smaller armies confined in a narrow geographical space; but, as we have noted, the coming battle would be of a scale the world had never seen before. Even if the enemy felt the urge to dance off to the right or the left, they couldn't do so lightly. Distance and logistical difficulties made shifts in troop strength problematical.

And anyway, the Russian Army habitually constructed semipermanent camps well stocked with ammunition. If the Japanese Army, nakedly exposed, came at the Russian left flank, the Russians could respond comfortably from within their *béton* concrete bunkers. There was no need for them to be startled into shifting their troops.

Matsukawa's plan of operations harbored that danger, that excess reliance on the enemy's anticipated moves, which is what gave Kodama pause. But over the course of repeated campaigns in the past year he had come to know the character of the enemy general. Though brilliant—the Russian Army's trump card—Kuropatkin lacked sturdy nerves and tended to overreact. With him in charge, they just might pull it off.

*   *   *

And so Kodama settled on the Matsukawa plan because he was betting on Kuropatkin's oversensitive nerves—a considerable gamble.

From the following day, he added fervor to his normal morning routine. He would rise before dawn and sit as the sun came over the horizon in an attitude of prayer, palms touching. A man of no religious faith in particular, he could pray only to the rising sun.

"Please help us," he would plead to the sun in a loud voice—a rather ludicrous scene to any impartial observer. It was as if he thought his prayer wouldn't carry all the way to the sun on the far horizon unless he shouted. Any man of weak nerves in his position might well have gone mad, and indeed this campaign was to shorten Kodama's life.

The specifics of the Kodama–Matsukawa plan were these. The Army of the Yalu, the newly formed army about which we shall have more to say later, would be placed on Japan's extreme right where it would shoulder the burden of attacking the enemy's left flank, pushing it further and further to the left, working in concert with Kuroki's army to engage the enemy's reserve troops (in shōgi terms, "pieces in hand") in that direction.

The task of striking on the right was assigned to Nogi's army, newly arrived from Port Arthur. His troops were accordingly stationed on Japan's extreme left. To protect Nogi's own left flank, Yoshifuru's detachment was shifted from the Second Army under General Oku to Nogi's command.

Nogi's role was vital. His army would not just come out attacking from the left but drive forward with great momentum, leaving behind supply carts and all to attack the enemy's right flank, then circling behind to threaten the enemy from the rear and draw out its central reserve, presumed to be stationed northwest of Mukden.

Once General Headquarters discerned that the attacks on either end—by the Army of the Yalu on the right, Nogi's army on the left—had succeeded, it would order the armies of generals Oku and Nozu, poised in the center, to dash forward. Joined by the tiny Manchurian General Reserve Corps, they would carry out the main thrust of the operation, the frontal attack, overturning Russia's main force at one blow.

With Kodama's approval, on February 18, Matsukawa stayed up late at night drafting the following orders:

1. The Army of the Yalu will proceed with as large a force as possible (Author's note: they didn't have anything like a large force) from Jianchang to Fushun and attack the enemy's left rear.
2. The First Army (Kuroki's army) will attack the enemy's left flank.
3. The Fourth Army (Nozu's army) will defend its present position while preparing to attack.
4. The Second Army (Oku's army) will attack the enemy's right flank in the vicinity of Guanlibao.
5. The Third Army (Nogi's army and Akiyama's detachment) will begin by moving into the area south of the line at Qinglongtai, east of the Daliao River and west of the line at Qinglongtai, then advance into the area

between the Hun River and the Daliao River and threaten the enemy's right rear.

*   *   *

The Mukden operation was not a plan hammered out by Kodama and his aides alone; the government and Imperial Headquarters first suggested and then formally approved the plan drafted by the commanders in Manchuria. It represented the combined efforts of the best strategists in the Japanese Army at the time. The idea was to force the enemy into an all-or-nothing confrontation.

Passive thinking played no part in this plan. The infantry was to rush in mercilessly against the enemy while the artillery kept firing till their ammunition ran out and the cavalry risked annihilation to deal their powerful enemy the Cossacks a severe blow. The plan was brimming over with aggressiveness. The Japanese tendency to act as a group is clearly evident in this plan of operations.

At this time, Nogi's headquarters was in Liaoyang.

On February 18, Major General Matsukawa was at General Headquarters in Yantai, busily writing battle orders. The previous day, the Manchurian Army's operational plan had already arrived at Nogi's headquarters. Lieutenant Colonel Kawai Misao was filling in as Nogi's chief of staff. He assembled all the staff officers to discuss the plan's military objectives and details.

"It's full of contradictions," said young Captain Tsunoda Koreshige, rash as ever, as he studied the plan.

We know that Nogi's army was to position itself on the far left and hold the enemy's reserve forces northwest of Mukden in check while menacing their right wing and flank. This called for great maneuverability and manpower. But Nogi's army had been stripped of a major division to form the new Army of the Yalu, and in its place they'd been given a standby reserve brigade full of older conscripts.

"Swing around west of the enemy and draw them in" was the official plan, but Tsunoda pointed out that they lacked the firepower needed to carry out this objective. At least a battalion of heavy artillery would be needed. And with their current troop strength, they couldn't form a reserve corps. They needed one, he argued—you couldn't carry out an army-level operation without reserves. He made a strong case.

"You're right," said Lieutenant Colonel Kawai when Tsunoda was finished. "But it's next to impossible." With troop levels insufficient across the board, Nogi's army alone could not be allotted the luxury of additional troops. Nogi himself would surely decline them. "What will His Excellency say?" murmured Kawai.

Nogi never did take a dismissive attitude toward the army high command but always worked within the conditions they imposed on him. That was one of his virtues. Though he was a classic old soldier, he had none of the brazenness of feudal warriors. He typified rather the highly cultivated samurai of the Tokugawa period.

On the nineteenth, communications officers from each headquarters went to Yantai to receive their orders. On the twentieth, the army commanders were summoned to Yantai headquarters. Kuroki Tamemoto of the First Army, Oku Yasukata of the Second Army, Nogi Maresuke of the Third Army, and Nozu Michitsura of the Fourth Army would all gather at General Headquarters, each with his chief of staff and one more person in attendance. For the first time since the war began, all the army commanders would gather in one room face to face. Anticipating the reunion with old friends gave Nogi a bit of pleasure as he headed for Yantai.

The instructions were to bring along one other person besides the chief of staff, and Kawai, Nogi's acting chief of staff, had selected Captain Tsunoda for the assignment. He was awfully young to attend a war council as advisor to the commander. But with Nogi's chief of staff Major General Matsunaga still unfit for duty, and Lieutenant Colonel Kawai filling in for him, the various tasks at Nogi's headquarters were being handled by younger men, each a rank below his counterpart elsewhere.

"I'm sending Tsunoda with you, is that all right?" Kawai had asked, slightly worried that the smart, brash young officer might say something bold and inappropriate before the array of old generals.

Nogi's gray beard covering the lower half of his face had twitched as he nodded with a slight smile. He was always that way. At Port Arthur, no matter what his chief of staff Ijichi Kōsuke proposed, he had nodded his approval without raising any objection. Young staff officers who disliked Ijichi's dogmatism and hard-and-fast way had rebelled until the atmosphere at Nogi's headquarters became far laxer than elsewhere. Still, Nogi had remained silent. If you searched for someone of that time who was like Nogi in personality and style, you wouldn't find him in either the military or, of course, in politics. The person who most resembled him was perhaps Niijima Jō (who was also known as Joseph Hardy Neesima), the Christian founder of Dōshisha University.

They traveled from Liaoyang to Yantai by railway. Inside the railway car, Captain Tsunoda was his usual talkative self. "Tsunoda," said Nogi, "a soldier shouldn't talk so much." He never admonished his staff, but with Tsunoda he made an exception. The captain was cheerful and easy to scold, and he had great charm.

"Among the taciturn and dour Japanese soldiers, an exceptionally lively young spark." That had been the admiring assessment of Ian Hamilton, the military attaché from the British Army. Tsunoda was indeed so talkative and witty that he must have made all the sourpuss generals seem like idiots. In fact, the two most brilliant of all the staff officers in the entire field army may well have been Kodama Gentarō of the highest army rank and Tsunoda Koreshige of the lowest. But Tsunoda could not survive long in the Japanese Army, which after the war became rapidly bureaucratized in the Russian style. He ended up getting ousted as a major general.

Till his dying day, Nogi loved Tsunoda, and Tsunoda in turn revered the senior commander who bore him such affection, calling him "a saint in a military uniform." One reason Nogi may have felt such affection for Tsunoda is that he was similar in personality to Nogi's second son, who died in battle.

*   *   *

The war council in Yantai was largely ceremonial, in advance of the launching of the new offensive. Nogi arrived first. Just inside the entrance of the Chinese house was a dim corridor. Kodama came out and started to pass the new arrival by when he realized who it was. "Well, if it isn't old man Nogi!" he said warmly. To Kodama, Nogi was not only a fellow Chōshū native but someone who shared his military career, going all the way back to their youth. It was as if they were the only two members of a special class.

Kodama was hatless and not even carrying a sword. "This time you'll have more fun, Nogi," he said comfortingly. By this, he apparently meant that instead of living holed up as at Port Arthur, he would be out taking action, rushing at the enemy. Nogi smiled and said nothing.

"I wrote a poem." Kodama had developed a passion for poetry. Readers will remember that following the capture of 203-Meter Hill under Kodama's command, he had held a poetry gathering in Nogi's headquarters attended by magazine editor Shiga Shigetaka among others. As Nogi's old comrade in arms, Kodama knew better than anyone else what a surpassingly poor soldier his friend was, yet strangely he never looked down on him because of it.

"Take a look when things settle down, will you?" Kodama said. He meant his draft poem. "When things settle down" meant after the fighting at Mukden.

Nogi grunted in assent. Though handsome, his features always made him look on the verge of tears, which added a certain human warmth to his appearance. He smiled at Kodama now with his melancholy face, studying him.

Kodama was busy. It was as if today were festival day at the local shrine, and he was the parishioners' representative, in charge of all the arrangements.

"He's in the back room," Kodama told Nogi before leaving. He meant Commander in Chief Ōyama Iwao.

When Nogi entered the back room, Ōyama was just chasing a little puppy of Chinese breed. About a month before, the puppy had wandered into the headquarters yard, and Ōyama had adopted it. He may have taken after his cousin Saigō Takamori in his liking for dogs, if not to the same degree. When fighting heated up, he would go play with the puppy. The British attaché Hamilton witnessed such scenes.

Ōyama shooed the puppy outdoors, and he and Nogi sat down. "I'm bored out of my mind every day," Ōyama admitted. After that, they talked about local fauna, without ever referring to the looming battle. Then Ōyama took Nogi out to the front steps, and they had their picture taken. Ōyama stood on the top of the stone steps and Nogi, the taller of the two, stood slightly to his left and one step down.

*　*　*

At General Headquarters, noncommissioned officers and soldiers were busy preparing for the commanders' conference, the first such event since the start of the war.

"Their Excellencies came to drink a parting cup," Shinozaki, a droll sergeant major in the cooking crew, said jokingly to a corporal. The corporal took him seriously, picturing the kind of ceremonial farewell gesture familiar from stage dramas. Figuring that the commanders would require earthen cups, using them to gulp down cold sake in one draught before smashing them on the floor, he ran around in all seriousness hunting for earthenware. This gave Shinozaki a jolt. Even the noncommissioned officers and soldiers attached to General Headquarters seemed to grasp that the meeting was a serious one that would decide the fate of the army and nation.

As we said, each of the generals in command of the four armies was accompanied by his chief of staff, a major general, and another staff officer, a major or captain. Even apart from the General Headquarters staff there were thus fifteen or sixteen men in attendance, with another ten or so from General Headquarters. In the middle sat Ōyama Iwao.

The job of explaining the strategy fell to Kodama Gentarō, assisted by Matsukawa Toshitane. The meeting was followed by a simple meal and ended in about an hour. Orders had already been sent to all the armies, so the real significance of the meeting for the army commanders was that they got a chance to gather and see each other face to face; for everyone else, the meeting held importance because they could engage in a question-and-answer session with General Headquarters staff.

After the brief meeting ended, Captain Tsunoda went in search of Matsukawa, who had returned to a large room that could be called the operations room.

"Oh, Tsunoda, it's you." Matsukawa glanced at the captain from behind his desk. There were extra chairs, but he did not invite the captain to sit. He not only held this brash youth in little regard but harbored a dislike for Nogi's headquarters that verged on animosity. The headquarters had a dark history, its conduct of war so lame that the entire army had been put in dire peril. Moreover, everyone at General Headquarters knew that back when Ijichi was chief of staff, relationships among Nogi's aides had been extremely poisonous.

And so Matsukawa couldn't help looking askance at Tsunoda—who did the guy he think he was? Matsukawa was Kodama's most trusted strategist, but he had an intolerant streak and was apt to let his emotions show openly on his face. He may have been a fine strategist, but he was totally unsuited to command.

"It's about the Third Army's plan of operations, sir." Tsunoda then repeated the plan from General Headquarters before concluding, "So in the final analysis, this would be a circling maneuver, would it not?"

"What do you mean, 'final analysis'?" Matsukawa growled. "It's a circling maneuver, period." He was bristling from the start.

Matsukawa Toshitane was the eldest son of Matsukawa Yasusuke, a retainer of the lord of Sendai. He was born in 1859 in the daimyo residence in Tsuchidoi, Sendai, and died in his birthplace in 1928. At Yōkendō, the official domain school of Sendai, Matsukawa was considered a child prodigy. Oka Senjin, Sendai's leading scholar of *kangaku* or sinology, hoped to make the boy into a sinologist like himself. But after the Restoration the Matsukawa family fell on hard times, and in 1880 Matsukawa matriculated at the tuition-free Army Academy. Subsequently, he entered the Army Staff College as a second lieutenant and amazed people by graduating at the top of his class. In those days, it was the custom for the valedictorian to receive a telescope as an imperial gift, and Matsukawa became a member of that select club.

Matsukawa's strategy was always aggressive. However, the content was too elaborate, and that, according to Tsunoda, made it impractical.

Even while inquiring about the role assigned to Nogi's army, Tsunoda obliquely pointed out flaws in Matsukawa's strategic plan. This irritated Matsukawa no end. Back when he taught strategy at the Army Staff College, Tsunoda had been his student.

"You focus on Nogi's army and don't think about anything else," Matsukawa snapped.

In the face of his former teacher's wrath, Tsunoda could not protest. "Yes, sir, of course, sir," he replied. "I intend to focus on Nogi's army and that's all. But our troop strength is totally inadequate for us to do our part.

"It's no different from the other armies."

Tsunoda held firm. "It's inadequate for a circling maneuver. We need a division of reserves, and we need some heavy artillery. Give us a field artillery battalion."

In the course of this dialogue, General Nogi appeared. Having approved the plan Tsunoda had fashioned in response to Matsukawa's, he had come to observe the progress of negotiations. Matsukawa sprang up and offered Nogi a chair. Nogi sat down.

Matsukawa was well aware that the Japanese forces were far outnumbered by the Russians, and that Kuroki's army and the rest all suffered from insufficient troop levels. Nogi's army had been in charge of the Port Arthur siege and had received plenty of troops as a top priority. Ammunition too had been diverted to Nogi's army from the field. It angered Matsukawa to think that Nogi's army had grown accustomed to preferential treatment. He then said something Tsunoda would never forget.

"General Headquarters doesn't expect much from the Third Army." He said this looking steadily at Tsunoda, without a glance at Nogi. Throughout the Port Arthur siege, Matsukawa had been critical of the incompetence of Nogi's headquarters. His pent-up feelings now burst out.

Tsunoda went pale. Nogi peered at a willow tree outside the window, his eyes wide open. His expression was placid, but he must have been greatly shocked inside.

* * *

Matsukawa had by no means shortchanged Nogi's army in allotting troops. Field artillery may have been in short supply, but they had been given Major General Nagata Kame's Second Field Artillery Brigade. They had three divisions of infantry and a brigade of standby reserve infantry. In the Nogi–Tsunoda plan, the brigade would be used as reserves, but it was weak, consisting of doddering old soldiers on standby. Tsunoda sought a crack division to take its place.

"Sheer idiocy!" The request sent Matsukawa nearly into spasms. The reason was simple: General Headquarters had nothing approaching a general reserve force. This is almost unbelievable. Before an operation of such scale, they ought to have had three divisions of reserves. As we have seen, reserve troops in war are like pieces in hand in the game of shōgi. If possible, Nogi and Tsunoda wanted strong pieces like gold or silver generals, plus a rook or bishop. Conducting an operation without such reserves was unthinkable.

On the Russian side, incidentally, Kuropatkin was bothered by this very point. How big were Ōyama's reserves and where were they? It was his job to locate the enemy reserves and anticipate how they would be used. In a game of chess, one player asks the other straight out, "What pieces do you have in hand?" In war, unable to ask directly, the commander sends out a strong cavalry unit behind the enemy to conduct a search. That's what Kuropatkin did.

But no matter how much the Russian cavalry combed the mountains and fields behind the Japanese Army, they never found any trace of reserve forces and in the end reported, "Position unknown." The uncertainty wore on Kuropatkin's nerves to the end. He had to endure the unpleasant feeling that he did not know where Ōyama might trot out his pieces in hand.

But Ōyama had no reserves. He had them in name only—a single brigade of old soldiers on standby reserve. A brigade in name only, more like a bunch of officers' orderlies. Apart from a very few infantry and artillery, there were only guards assigned to General Headquarters. This meant that there were essentially zero reserves. It was like sending the entire army to the front and having them spread their wings wide to make them look bigger, the way an eagle does, only for the eagle to have no body. In that sense this was an unheard-of situation.

But Nogi and Tsunoda insisted that they had to have a division of reserve forces.

Matsukawa knew that the realities of the Japanese Army precluded his granting any such request. It's no wonder that rather than a simple "No," he responded with bitter sarcasm.

* * *

Tsunoda went right on asking for a heavy field artillery battalion.

"Look at General Headquarters," Matsukawa felt like telling him. The only artillery General Headquarters had were several light artillery guns drawn by manpower. But Matsukawa didn't say so. He didn't even let his own side know that headquarters reserves were down to zero.

To keep this quiet, Matsukawa issued an order for the head of the Third Division to lead the General Reserve Corps. A division head was a lieutenant general; with an officer of so high a rank in charge, everyone assumed there must be over ten thousand men in the reserves. Even the army commanders were fooled. Ōyama, Kodama, and Matsukawa kept the truth hidden for fear that word might leak from the high command down to the soldiers and spread from soldiers' mouths to the ears of local people.

Kuropatkin's reserves, meanwhile, were considerable, consisting of the freshly arrived Sixteenth Corps. This discrepancy alone shows just what thin ice the Japanese were skating on as they planned their Mukden campaign.

Tsunoda hung on. Nogi's army would follow orders, drawing near the western perimeter of Mukden and coming up against Russia's semipermanent encampment and the city wall. Destroying those walls would require heavy field artillery.

"If we can't have a battalion, then please," Tsunoda begged, "at least let us have a company, enough to tear down the Chinese enclosure."

But Matsukawa couldn't give what he didn't have. Finally, he had to be forthright. "The Third Army's role in this campaign," he said, "doesn't amount to much. All we want you to do is distract as many of the enemy's reserve troops as you can. If the enemy comes on strong, you don't have to keep going against all odds. Throw up a field encampment around the village of Xinmintun and fend them off from there. It'll be Port Arthur all over again, with the roles reversed. Defend your position and keep the enemy busy, as many of them as you can. That way Oku's army can advance in the central area along the Hun River and open up a new phase."

This was the frontal breakthrough.

"So you see," he finished, "I cannot give the Third Army even one more division or spare a single piece of heavy artillery."

"Understood." Nogi had been silent all this time, but the final word was his.

Calling it a "circling maneuver" put a nice face on it, but, in fact, they would be decoys. It is the fate of decoys to make great sacrifices that yield little or no direct spoils. Such may have been Nogi's personal fate as well.

* * *

Manchurian General Headquarters was ill equipped to launch a campaign in Mukden, being far inferior to the Russians in both manpower and artillery. Yet they did have one advantage, namely a new weapon: the machine gun. These new weapons were sent from the Japanese mainland and added to the line of battle.

We have touched more than once on the machine gun. The Russian Army was the first in the world to adopt it as a regular army weapon. Based on the lessons of the Russo-Japanese War, the French Army introduced it in 1907, the German Army a year later. It is apparent how much more forward-looking the Russians were in their approach to weaponry. Russian machine guns were all foreign-made, and they consisted of two types: the Maxim gun and the Vickers.

The huge effectiveness of machine guns was driven home to Nogi's army during the Port Arthur siege, when the guns killed and wounded innumerable numbers of Japanese soldiers. In the words of Nagaoka Gaishi, soldiers became "moat filler" for the enemy.

The Japanese cavalry alone had been equipped with machine guns, at the suggestion of Akiyama Yoshifuru. You could say this was mainly why his cavalry brigade managed to compete on even terms with the powerful Cossacks and consistently maintain a slight edge. At the time of the battle of Mukden, the Russians had over ten thousand cavalry, Japan only three thousand. The Russian cavalry possessed light field guns but very few machine guns, and this gave the Japanese an advantage.

The Japanese Army awoke to the effectiveness of machine guns. Not only at the Port Arthur siege but also in field operations, only a couple of Russian machine guns had killed or wounded half a brigade, causing the loss of a tactical unit. Imperial Headquarters quickly moved to buy a supply of the new weapon. A shipment going out from Ujina Harbor arrived at the Manchurian front just in time for the fighting at Mukden.

Kuropatkin's army was equipped with fifty-six machine guns, but now the Japanese had 254, so the tables were turned. At this point, the Japanese Army had the most machine guns of any army in the world.

There were six of the new weapons for every regiment. Broken down by army, this translated to fifty-eight for Kuroki's army, fifty-nine for Oku's army, fifty-four for Nogi's army, and thirty-nine for Nozu's army. Not counting the cavalry, which was already fully equipped, General Headquarters liberally supplied its admittedly scanty troops with this powerful new weapon.

* * *

We need to tell more about the presence of the Army of the Yalu on the extreme right flank of the Japanese Manchurian Army.

Kodama Gentarō and Matsukawa Toshitane had vehemently opposed the formation of this new army. With the battle of Mukden just ahead, taking men and arms from the short-handed Manchurian Army to form a brand-new army would obviously be painful. After the army was formed, Matsukawa Toshitane mockingly called it the "goose army," playing upon the characters used to write "Yalu," which mean "goose" and "green."

Moreover, Imperial Headquarters did not include the Army of the Yalu in the Manchurian Army. They placed it under the command not of Ōyama Iwao but of General Hasegawa Yoshimichi, commander of the Korean Garrison Army. Their motives in so doing were hardly out of operational considerations and strongly political. Or you could say this was the first appearance in the Japanese military of the notion of war as a profitable national business.

"When peace accords are signed, we will want to take some portion of Russian territory"—this was the thinking that lay behind the move. The first one to hammer out this line of thinking was Vice Chief of the General Staff Office Nagaoka Gaishi, in the throes of boredom in Tokyo. Once the war began, Ōyama and Kodama had picked up the core of the General Staff Office and moved it to the plains of Manchuria, and so Nagaoka's Tokyo organization had little to do but mind an empty store.

Nagaoka was not as fond of strategy and tactics, which require the ability to make fine calculations, as he was of outrageous political theorizing. "Even if we win this war, when peace comes we won't get any land from Russia under current circumstances." Back when Nogi was fighting desperately at Port Arthur, Nagaoka was already voicing this opinion, causing Chief of the General Staff Yamagata Aritomo and Army Minister Terauchi Masatake to knit their brows. Yamagata was not at all sure whether the war was winnable in the long run, and just then Nogi's bitter struggle in particular was casting an ominous shadow on the Manchurian campaign.

In Nagaoka's view, the area along the railway in southern Manchuria that formed the battleground for the war was land that Russia had as good as stolen from Qing China, while it had Guangdong Province on lease. In other words, the entire battleground legally belonged to China. In contrast, the Primorsky Region—specifically Vladivostok—though once Chinese territory, now belonged outright to Russia. Sakhalin, moreover, was land that Russia had stolen from Japan back when Japan had had little influence, and the Japanese needed to seize it back. If the Japanese occupied the Primorsky Region and Sakhalin, then, when the time came for peace talks, these areas would go to the victor, in accordance with international custom.

Japan needed to prepare an army to carry out the occupation. This was Nagaoka's bombastic talk.

* * *

But the Army of the Yalu could not set straight off for Sakhalin or attack the fortress at Vladivostok.

"Japan doesn't have any troops to spare." Yamagata kept saying this to hold Nagaoka down.

Later, after the battle of Mukden, when Kodama Gentarō returned to Tokyo and heard Nagaoka's plan, he burst out, "That's a stupid thing to say!" The remark became famous. Kodama's words were faithfully transcribed: "Whoever starts a fight has to have the ability to end it. What good would it do for a poor country like Japan to go on with this war any longer?" With this comment, he rejected the idea of attacking Vladivostok.

The above remarks would come at a later date. Back in January 1905, Nagaoka was eagerly absorbed in his dilettantish pastime.

The Russo-Japanese War was a war of national defense, which was precisely why the whole country was solidly behind it. Yet the advantageous situation, from an amateur's perspective, of keeping pressure on the Russian Army on the Manchurian plains (albeit at the cost of using up men and arms) naturally gave rise in a man of Nagaoka's optimistic temperament to a way of thinking that would switch the war from one of fervent defense to something quite different, a national for-profit enterprise. In other words, while rising up to fend off Russian aggression, once in the ring, Japan could look out for its chance and if possible not just snatch back the fruits of Russian aggression but invade Russian territory with the momentum gained. This was how Nagaoka thought. He was, of course, not so much a military man as a swashbuckler. His whole life long, he never could properly estimate national strength or the international environment.

"Nagaoka is a headache." This was the uniform view of Prime Minister Katsura Tarō, Army Minister Terauchi Masatake, and Chief of the General Staff Yamagata Aritomo, who were united in opposition to Nagaoka. The four men were all from Chōshū, Nagaoka included. Indeed, Chōshū origins were the only reason a man of Nagaoka's ability got to be vice chief of the General Staff in the first place. In any case, where national expansion was concerned, a coarsely swashbuckling mood persisted in the Japanese Army in later years, a tradition started, it may be said, by Nagaoka.

Yamagata Aritomo and Itō Hirobumi, both genrō, felt a sense of crisis, fearing that Japan might fall from its tightrope. Nagaoka's plan was the farthest thing from their minds. With ammunition in chronically short supply, they were focused on getting as much ammunition as possible to the battlefield by speeding up its manufacture while at the same time importing more from other countries; that, and bringing the war to a peaceful conclusion through the mediation of a third country. They could think of nothing else.

Still, ignoring Nagaoka's plan was not the most expedient course of action either. For that reason, they formed an army that could be moved for political expediency whenever conditions allowed. That was the Army of the Yalu. Kodama Gentarō naturally wired his opposition to Tokyo over and over again.

* * *

More about the Army of the Yalu.

Out of the blue, Kodama Gentarō received a communication from Army Minister Terauchi in Tokyo ordering him to appoint Kawamura Kageaki, head of the Tenth Division, as commander of the Army of the Yalu. Kawamura till then had been a lieutenant general in Nozu's army but was now promoted to general.

"Tokyo doesn't know a damn thing about war!" Kodama was furious for many reasons, but his criticism of this personnel decision was particularly contemptuous: "They're still choosing personnel in the parlor."

Kawamura was a Satsuma man. His new superior would be Hasegawa Yoshimichi, commander of the Korean Garrison Army (a strategic force removed from combat) and a Chōshū man. At this crucial time when the nation's fate hung in the balance, Tokyo was still obsessed with maintaining a balance between Satsuma and Chōshū. Kodama was infuriated. Though he himself was from Chōshū, this open-minded man had largely transcended the Satsuma–Chōshū divide in his own mind.

"Tokyo is conducting war in the parlor" was Kodama's frequent refrain. If they had that much time on their hands, let them go to Washington and enlist the United States in the role of mediator, he always thought. A man called Kaneko Kentarō was stationed in Washington for that very purpose, and no one wished more intensely for his diplomatic efforts to succeed than Kodama, who knew in his bones that the Mukden campaign would exhaust Japan's fighting power.

But the leaders in Tokyo, to divert themselves, had gone and created the Army of the Yalu. There would be dual command. A fierce debate took place between the on-site commanders and Tokyo, but they had come to no agreement when Kawamura was summoned to Tokyo. On arriving, he received a full explanation from Yamagata Aritomo concerning the point and the purpose of establishing this new unit called the Army of the Yalu, which was so strongly political in nature. But Kawamura had come from the fires of war in Manchuria, and to him the danger of actual combat was far more real. Yamagata's explanation made no sense.

On leaving Tokyo, Kawamura was assigned an Imperial Headquarters staff officer named Igata Tokuzō. Along the way, Kawamura asked him, "Did you understand what His Excellency Yamagata said?" Not even Igata understood.

Kawamura was a man of no education, but back in 1863 when Satsuma fought the British fleet, he had participated as a boy soldier and gone on to be in every major battle that took place in Meiji Japan: the battle of Toba and Fushimi, the Boshin War, the Saga Rebellion, the Satsuma Rebellion, the First Sino-Japanese War. Born in gunpowder, as it were, he liked to say, "A campaign goal should come across in two or three lines of text. If you have to start adding on fancy explanations, it's no good."

Kawamura Kageaki was a somewhat unusual commander. Back when he was head of the Tenth Division in Nozu's army, he would trade in his boots for a pair of straw *waraji* sandals and set out for the front when fighting grew fierce. He had corns on the soles of his feet, and straw sandals were more comfortable for trekking through hill and dale.

Like every division commander, he would hand down orders to each brigade and regiment under his command before fighting began. Afterward, leaving behind the chief of staff and other staff officers, he would set out with his aide-de-camp and a young staff member to watch his units fight with his own eyes.

"This is what I look forward to," he would even say, Satsuma to the core. One day when his chief of staff tried to stop him, Kawamura replied, "Once I've handed out orders, my job is done. After that, the progress of the battle is for the chief of staff and other staff officers to oversee. Even if I stayed in division headquarters, there'd be nothing for me to do. So I go watch my soldiers fighting per my orders, to see firsthand how they do."

Kawamura was no strategist, as he knew better than anyone else. A division commander's job is leadership, and Kawamura's style was to lead not from behind the scenes but by going out to the trenches. Since he arrived wearing straw sandals on his feet, the soldiers felt as close to him as if he were the village head back home.

Kawamura went back to Manchuria, and met with Ōyama and Kodama at General Headquarters in Yantai. "Situation permitting, I will follow the orders of the Manchurian Army," he announced simply. This put him seemingly at odds with Yamagata and Nagaoka, but Yamagata, following Kodama's fierce protest, had afforded him some flexibility.

"The mission of the Army of the Yalu is to protect the northwest borders of Korea. But provided there is no interference with this primary mission, leftward movement toward enemy forces is permitted for the benefit of the Manchurian Army." Participating in the Mukden campaign would thus not be an outright violation of orders.

And so, in accordance with the Kodama–Matsukawa plan, the Army of the Yalu, which was deployed on the right flank of the Japanese Army, sought to confuse Kuropatkin's estimate of the situation by applying pressure on the enemy's left flank.

But could the Army of the Yalu truly be relied on? Matsukawa had his doubts. The core of the new army was the Eleventh Division from Zentsūji in Shikoku, the division that had fought with such valor at Port Arthur under Nogi. However, it also included a poorly equipped standby reserve division consisting of old-soldier conscripts. Though an army had been formed from these elements, how much mobility and combat strength it might display in the difficult hilly terrain to the right of the Japanese Army was open to question.

GLOSSARY

Ashigaru: light foot soldier, lowest rank in the samurai class.

Banzai: This word (lit., "one thousand years") is yelled out with both arms swung upward to express such feelings as joy, congratulations, and encouragement.

Boshin War: (1868–1869) a series of civil war battles around the time of the collapse of the Tokugawa shogunate.

Bushidō: the moral code of the samurai, stressing loyalty, mastery of the martial arts, and death with honor.

Chōshū: present-day Yamaguchi Prefecture; one of the two major domains, together with Satsuma, that led the overthrow of the Tokugawa shogunate (1603–1868).

Genrō: elder statesmen who were "founding fathers" of the modern state of Japan and the chief advisors to the emperor.

Geta: high wooden clogs with a V-shaped cloth thong that passes between the first and second toes.

Go: board game in which two players, Black and White, alternately place black and white stones on a large ruled board to compete for surrounding territory.

Haikai: a form of linked verse from which haiku evolved.

Hakama: formal divided overskirt, worn over a kimono, tied at the waist, and falling almost to the ankles.

Haori: a traditional formal jacket worn over a kimono, with short cord fasteners tied at chest level.

Hatamoto: direct vassals of the Tokugawa shogunate.

Jōruri: a form of narrative chanting accompanied by the three-stringed samisen, commonly associated with the puppet theater.

Kokinshū: classical imperial anthology of waka poetry compiled ca. 905.

Koku: a unit of rice equivalent to about 180 liters (5 bushels); in Tokugawa Japan, land value for taxation purposes was expressed in koku of rice; one koku was generally viewed as enough to feed one person for a year.

Kumi: groups of samurai that made up the organizational structure of the feudal domains.

Man'yōshū: Japan's earliest extant collection of poetry, compiled in the eighth century.

Meiji Restoration: overthrow of the Tokugawa shogunate and restoration of the emperor's direct rule of Japan in 1868.

Minamoto no Yoshitsune: a general (1159–1189) of the Minamoto clan, regarded as one of the most famous samurai fighters in the history of Japan and a tragic hero who was forced to commit suicide by his brother Yoritomo, founder of the Kamakura shogunate.

Oda Nobunaga: warlord (1534–1582) who began Japan's reunification after the hundred years of civil war known as the era of Warring States.

Okachi: low-status samurai (but higher than the ashigaru); light foot soldiers.

Rin: unit of Japanese currency equal to 1/1000 yen (1/10 sen), used from the beginning of the Meiji era until 1953.

Rōnin: masterless samurai.

Ryō: a unit of currency used during the Tokugawa period; the standard gold coin was equivalent to one ryō.

Satsuma: present-day Kagoshima Prefecture; one of the two major domains, together with Chōshū, that led the overthrow of the Tokugawa shogunate (1603–1868).

Satsuma Rebellion: 1877, the last major armed uprising against the new central government, started by disgruntled former Satsuma samurai with Saigō Takamori as their leader.

Sen: unit of Japanese currency equal to 1/100 yen, used from the beginning of the Meiji era until 1953.

Seppuku: ritual suicide by disembowelment, originally reserved for samurai warriors only.

Shinkokinshū: classical imperial anthology of waka poetry compiled ca. 1205.

Shinsengumi: the group of elite swordsmen who served as a special police force in the late Tokugawa period.

Shōgi: Japanese chess, in which a player wins by checkmating the opponent's king; unlike Western chess, players can use captured pieces, and their own pieces can be promoted, sometimes several ranks higher at a time, from pawn to gold, for example.

Tanka: (see waka).

Three hundred feudal lords: this phrase refers to "all feudal lords," for there were roughly three hundred feudal lords (daimyo) across Tokugawa Japan.

Tokiwa Society: educational support organization sponsored by the lord of the former Matsuyama domain to promote the study in Tokyo of talented young men from around Matsuyama.

Tokugawa period: rule of Japan by the Tokugawa shoguns 1603–1868; also called the Edo period, after the name of the capital Edo (now Tokyo).

Toyotomi Hideyoshi: warlord (1537–1598) of humble origin who completed a reunification of sixteenth-century Japan begun by his lord Oda Nobunaga.

Tsubo: a unit of area, roughly 3.3 square meters, corresponding to two tatami mats.

Waka (also tanka): a classical form of poetry dating to the eighth century, with thirty-one syllables in the pattern 5-7-5-7-7.

For Product Safety Concerns and Information please contact our EU
representative GPSR@taylorandfrancis.com
Taylor & Francis Verlag GmbH, Kaufingerstraße 24, 80331 München, Germany